DATE DUE

DEC 13 '95			
MAR 1 9 1989			
APRETURNED99			
AUG 2 3 2006			
GAYLORD			PRINTED IN U.S.A.

HANDBOOK OF MANAGEMENT DEVELOPMENT
Second edition

Handbook of Management Development

Second edition

**edited by
ALAN MUMFORD**

A Gower Handbook

Published by
Gower Publishing Company Limited,
Gower House,
Croft Road,
Aldershot,
Hants GU11 3HR,
England

Gower Publishing Company,
Old Post Road,
Brookfield,
Vermont 05036,
U.S.A.

British Library Cataloguing in Publication Data
Handbook of management development — 2nd ed.
   1. Management
   I. Mumford, Alan
   658.4   HD31

Library of Congress Cataloging-in-Publication Data
Main entry under title:

Handbook of management development.

   Includes index.
   1. Executives — Training of. I. Mumford, Alan.
HF5549.5.T7H295 1986   658.4'07124   85-27051
ISBN 0-566-02563-9

Typeset by Action Typesetting, Gloucester
Printed in Great Britain by
The University Press, Cambridge

Contents

PART III THE PROCESS OF MANAGEMENT DEVELOPMENT

PART V   ISSUES IN MANAGEMENT DEVELOPMENT

Notes on Contributors

Michael D. Abrahams (*Choosing resources*) has been Management Development Manager, Marks and Spencer plc, for the last twelve years and was previously the company's Head of Central Training. He is a Fellow of the IPM and BIM and a Member of the ATM.

David J. L. Ashton (*Handling cultural adversity*). After lecturing in management development programmes, he became Director of Studies, Group Management Centre, B.A.T Industries plc. He is a Member of the ATM and co-author of *Auditing Management Development* (Gower 1980)

Don Binsted (*New ways of learning*) has held various posts in ICI in line and staff management, training and organisational development. In 1974, he founded and became Director of Distance Learning at the Centre for the Study of Management Learning at the University of Lancaster.

Peter Bramley (*Evaluation*) was a trainer for some ten years (in the Army) and also worked for about ten years as a training consultant. For the past four years he has been lecturing in training and development in the Department of Occupational Psychology at Birkbeck College and has set up, within that department, a small research and consultancy group, the Centre for Training and Evaluation Studies.

David Casey (*Team building*). After teaching science for three years, he began carrying out research in industry and became Technical Manager of Berger Paints. Six years later, he switched to management training in Reed International and subsequently to internal consultancy in Reed. In 1972 he went freelance and has built up a client portfolio balanced half in the public sector and half in the private sector. He is co-author (with David Pearce) of *More than Management Development* (Gower, 1977).

Bill Critchley (*Team building*) worked in general management before qualifying as an MBA from Cranfield which led to a career in consultancy. He is currently with Sheppard, Moscow and Associates, where he specialises in helping companies plan and manage strategic change programmes.

John Crosby (*Developing local nationals*). John Crosby is Personnel Director of the British-American Tobacco Company Limited. He joined B.A.T Co. in 1976, initially as the company's Personnel Adviser for its sub-continent and south east asian companies and most recently held the post of Head of Personnel Services. Previous posts have included personnel management appointments with E.M.I. Limited and the Costain Group of Companies and, from 1968–1976, he was a senior management consultant with Hay-MSL Limited. As a consultant he led assignments in many major British companies, as well as overseas in Pakistan, Tanzania and Zambia. He is currently President of the IPM.

Ian Cunningham (*Self-managed learning*) as Director, Metacom-munications Ltd, is engaged in consultancy, research and writing. He is a former head of division at the Anglian Regional Management Centre. Dr Cunningham is a Fellow of the BIM and of the Institute of Training and Development and a Member of the IPM.

Bob Garratt (*The cultural context*) is an international management consultant. He carried out community development work in France and Ulster which led to involvement with the GEC Action Learning Project. Since 1976, he has been establishing western management education practice in China. He is Honorary Secretary of the ATM, and has written numerous articles on management and management education. In 1980, he co-edited (with John Stopford) *Breaking down Barriers*, published by Gower.

Peter Honey (*Styles of learning*) has been a freelance psychologist and management consultant since 1969. He specialises in anything to do with people's behaviour and its consequences. He divides his work into: designing and running courses on interactive skills, team building, creative thinking, problem solving and self-development; consultancy projects on such subjects as customer satisfaction, assessment centre criteria, management training needs, staff attitudes, behaviour in meetings and groups. Peter Honey is a member of the British Psychological Society, the Institute of Management Consultants and the ATM, and a Fellow of the International Management Centre from Buckingham and the Institute of Training and Development.

Alun Jones (*The role of the management trainer*) is Director, Research and Development, of The Industrial Training Services Ltd, an international consultancy in the development of organisations and people. He is a research chemist who was a training manager in the chemical industry before joining ITS twenty-three years ago. Dr Jones is a Fellow of the Institute of Training and Development.

Jean Lawrence (*Action learning—a questioning approach*) is a Managing Partner in the Development Consortium at Manchester Business School, formed in 1982. In this role she works with organisations to develop them and their managers through 'in company' and 'inter-company' work. A visiting staff member at Henley and Oxford, she also works regularly overseas. Jean joined Manchester Business School as a Senior Tutor after extensive industrial experience, including production management at Cadbury Bros. At MBS her topic was project management and she developed skills in providing learning opportunities in small groups, particularly in association with the Tavistock Institute. A founder member of Action Learning Projects International, she has initiated and worked in many forms of action learning programmes since the early one with GEC in 1972. She has been an executive member of the International Foundation for Action Learning since its inception as the Action Learning Trust and is a past Chairman of the ATM.

Charles Margerison (*Managing career choices*) is a Professor of Management at the University of Queensland, Australia. He was previously Professor of Management Development at the Cranfield

School of Management in the UK. Prior to that he worked in manufacturing industry and public organisations. He is a graduate of the University of London School of Economics and did post-graduate work at Liverpool University and Bradford University where he obtained his doctorate. He is currently International Vice-President of IMCB – the International Management Centre from Buckingham and also Editor of the *Journal of Management Development*.

Judi Marshall (*Women managers*) lectures in organisation behaviour at the School of Management, University of Bath. She has researched at UMIST on managerial job stress and, at Oxford Management Centre, on how managers perceive their jobs. Dr Marshall is co-editor (with Cary Cooper) of *Coping with Stress at Work* (Gower, 1981).

John Morris (*The learning spiral*) is Emeritus Professor of Management Development at Manchester Business School and a managing partner of the recently formed Development Consortium. The Development Consortium is an informal association of people working together on management development programmes, with special reference to in-company work. He has had wide experience in industry, commerce and the public sector as a consultant in management selection and development. He was Chairman of the North West Region Job Creation Programme from 1976–1978, and has served as a member of specialist panels of the University Grants Committee and the Council for National Academic Awards.

Alan Mumford (*Effectiveness in management development*) has been Professor of Management Development at the International Management Centre from Buckingham since its inception. In that role he is responsible for developing the Centre's approach to improving management performance through effective learning processes. Professor Mumford's experience in management development has been exceptionally wide. It includes periods with John Laing and Son, IPC Magazines and International Computers Ltd, and a spell as deputy chief training adviser at the Department of Employment. For six years he was Executive Resources Adviser to the Chloride Group. Professor Mumford is a Companion of the Institute of Personnel Management and was its Vice-President (Training and Development) from 1971 to 1973. He has published numerous articles on management development and is the author or co-author of four books.

Bruce Nixon (*Creating in-house programmes*) is Training and Development Manager of the Sun Alliance Insurance Group. After graduating from Oxford University in philosophy, politics and economics, he worked in a department store in Los Angeles. On returning to the UK he started gaining experience of personnel management first at Peek Frean and then Birds Eye. Meanwhile he studied part-time at the Polytechnic of Central London for membership of the IPM. He then worked for over five years for Alcan in Jamaica. On returning to the UK he did management training work in Reed Paper and graduate and executive recruitment with Alcan in the UK before joining Sun Alliance. He is a Fellow of the Institute of Personnel Management and a member of the ATM.

Graham Robinson (*Management development and organisation development*) is Managing Director, Primafact Ltd, a consultancy in organisation research and development. After an initial career in operational research, he worked on organisation development assignments in a number of industries while on the staff of Ashridge Management College. For a number of years he worked in Africa and Holland before joining the UK computer industry in 1973. He was Personnel Director of Sperry Univac Computer Systems in the UK until he returned to consultancy work in 1982.

Don Rose (*Management development in the Thomson Organisation*) is Group Personnel Director for the International Thomson Organisation. He was formerly Personnel Officer, Thomson Regional Newspapers and Personnel Director, Thomson Publications Ltd. He is a Fellow of the IPM, a Member of the Institute of Marketing and a Fellow of the BIM.

Rick Roskin (*Experiential based learning*) is Professor of Organizational Behaviour and Development in the Faculty of Business Administration, Memorial University of Newfoundland, St. John's, Newfoundland, Canada. He has taught in Canada, England and Australia. He is President of Mach One Limited, a management training and software company with clients in Canada and England,

and has consulted with Canadian, British and Australian companies. He is a consulting editor for the American journal, *Group and Organization Studies*, and the British *Journal of Management Development*.

Andrew Stewart (*Diagnosing needs, Performance appraisal*) is Managing Director, Macmillan Stewart Ltd, consulting industrial psychologists. He lectured at Aberdeen and Surrey Universities and was Personnel and Management Development Officer at IBM (UK) and Senior Fellow at the Institute of Manpower Studies. He is co-author (with Valerie Stewart) of *Practical Performance Appraisal*, *Managing the Manager's Growth* and *Managing the Poor Performer*, all published by Gower.

Roger Stuart (*Using others to learn*) is Principal of the British Rail Management Training Centre. He has worked in the roles of manager, trainer, researcher and consultant in both the industrial and the university sectors. He is a Member of the ATM.

John Teire (*Using the outdoors*) has been an independent management training and development consultant for more than ten years, designing and conducting in-company programmes for management, team, and company development. In recent years he has made use of the outdoors as a compliment to other learning by carrying out training and development activities which include company workshops, residential courses and business simulations. He is a Member of the ATM, the Group Relations Training Association and the Business Graduates Association.

Tony Vineall (*Planning management development*) is Deputy Head of Personnel, Unilever. He has held personnel management positions for Unilever in the UK and abroad and his responsibilities now include development of senior managers for all Unilever's operations. He is a Fellow of the IPM, a Council Member of the Industrial Society, and Vice Chairman of Governors, the Centre for International Briefing at Farnham Castle.

Editor's Preface

For some years I have based my work in management development on a definition of it as 'an attempt to improve managerial effectiveness through planned and deliberate learning processes', a definition largely taken from the work of the Training Services Agency in the UK in 1977. I have used that definition first in specifying, and then in placing in sequence, the chapters in this book. I see it as no contradiction from the point of view of the book to state a qualification: not all management development occurs through a planned and deliberate learning process. The capacity of some managers to perform their job more effectively has been brought about by relatively accidental processes, sometimes not even recognised as development or learning experiences either by the manager concerned or by anyone else. Managers themselves tend to call such processes 'learning by experience'. Though the reality of that kind of management development must be acknowledged, the objective of this book is to examine those processes which *are* 'planned and deliberate'.

The way the material in the book is arranged follows the sequence of the definition. The opening chapter by Bob Garratt looks at what could be called the tone for management development in any particular organisation. My own chapter introduces other aspects of the concept of effectiveness in management, using in particular the contributions of Rosemary Stewart and Henry Mintzberg in analysing what managers actually do. I could have added a third author, John Kotter, to create a trinity of powerful writers on this subject. This chapter also forms a bridge to some of the material in Part III dealing with learning processes.

In Part II, the chapters by Tony Vineall and Andrew Stewart respond to the need for 'planned and deliberate' processes. I should also say that they represent an editorial judgement in the sense that another editor might have chosen to include much more on what could without unkindness be called the mechanics of management development. Clearly the relatively small number of chapters I have allocated to this subject may be seen as a reflection of my priorities in management development, and by implication those that I am suggesting to readers. I do not regard these issues as unimportant, but do think that in past years too much attention was paid to the formal and structured aspects of management development systems and not enough to such questions as, 'Management development for what?' and 'How do managers learn most effectively?' The chapter by Charles Margerison offers some innovative ideas on managing careers.

It may again be seen as an expression of a strong editorial view that I have included a substantial section on the learning process. I doubt very much whether the Training Services Agency in 1977 had the same kind of understanding of learning processes as is beginning to be available now. For many years management developers, management trainers and management educators have based their activities either on a single management development process regarded as the only way to develop managers or on a catholic menu through which managers are exposed to a variety of processes. In the latter case there was at least a recognition that some managers learn better from one process than another, but there was no attempt to identify which processes best suited which managers. Part III offers what I believe to be exciting insights into the characteristics of the individual learner by Peter Honey, Roger Stuart and Ian Cunningham. The chapter by John Morris looks at the same kind of issue from a slightly different perspective by discussing learning as an organisational as well as an individually determined process. Readers may also usefully turn back to my own chapter at this point for the comments I make about the learning process. Don Binsted, finally, is concerned not so much with individuals as with the contribution the new technologies are making.

Part IV describes some specific applications within management development. Bruce Nixon gives a fascinating insight into the development of improved answers to management development problems over a period of time. Jean Lawrence, one of the few original workers on Action Learning in the UK not to have written about it, has provided a chapter which is stimulating both in form and in content. The contributions of Rick Roskin and John Teire examine particular forms of management development process. Don Rose presents a company case which re-emphasises the crucial importance of identifying individual development needs rather than working from generalisation.

Organising the text to correspond with the definition with which I started left some significant issues untouched. In Part V therefore I offer Graham Robinson's discussion of the relationship between management development and organisational development, and David Ashton and John Crosby on management development in a multi-cultural organisation. Judi Marshall's chapter takes up the special issues involved in developing women managers. We then revert to more general questions through Alun Jones' review of the role of the management trainer and Peter Bramley on evaluation. Then follows a chapter by David Casey and Bill Critchley which contains a series of challenging comments on the permanently important issue of whether development of particular skills through a particular process may be good management development but not very effective in terms of managerial priorities.

Because the choice of resources depends on the objectives of management development I have left till the end the chapter on this theme by Mike Abrahams, who writes as a consumer rather than a provider.

I did not think it right to force all contributors to adopt one way of recognising that there are both male and female managers. In some chapters, therefore, 'he' is used instead of 'he/she'.

Alan Mumford

Acknowledgements

Thanks are due to:

MCB University Press, for permission to reproduce Chapter 2 ('Effectiveness in management development') and Chapter 8 ('Using others to learn');

McGraw-Hill Book Company (UK) Limited, for permission to use the quotation from *A Business and Its Beliefs* by Thomas J. Watson Junior (published 1963);

The Association of Teachers of Management, for permission to reproduce Chapter 23 ('Team building').

Part I
MANAGEMENT EFFECTIVENESS AND MANAGEMENT DEVELOPMENT

1

The cultural context

Bob Garratt

'When I hear anyone talk of culture, I reach for my revolver'. Such
sentiments are not restricted to Goering. Many of the managers I meet
in the course of my work have similar feelings. Recently, though,
there has been a small but noticeable change in some of the top
managers who rather grudgingly are coming to the realisation that
this area is going to be of increasing importance — whether they like
it or not. This chapter reflects my recent work where I have tried to do
two things. First, to tease out the meaning of the word 'culture' in the
very different contexts of the organisation; the national environment;
and the management of both. Second, to demonstrate that most of
the tools needed to manage the cultural dimensions are already tried
and tested and ready to be applied to the increasing range of cultural
problems.

'Culture' has become a particularly fashionable issue with directors
since it was legitimised through *'In Search of Excellence'*.[1] The
possibility of integrating the three 'hard' areas of business [systems,
strategy, and structure] with the three 'soft' areas [staff, skills, and
style] via shared values, has made possible the discussion of culture
and values at the top level of organisations in a way that has not been
possible for two decades. But culture is in danger of losing its
meaning if those who are so eagerly grasping it use it in profligate and
ambiguous manners. As I write this chapter I notice from today's
issue of the *Financial Times*[2] a range of direct and indirect references

to culture and its effects. Perhaps the most dramatic is Racal reporting some £15 million 'going out the window' through its US operations. Various market conditions are blamed but Sir Ernest Harrison also admitted that the group faced a problem managing their US companies from the UK. 'I do accept that America has got to be run in America', he said.

This statement encompasses in microcosm the problem of beginning to use the word culture in organisational analysis. It is accepted in most multinational businesses that I have viewed that their company culture must, and should, transcend national and all other cultures. Such a notion of culture is implicit in the planning of most executive directors and in their subsequent behaviour. Yet the results regularly refute their assumptions and behaviour. Racal is singled out here only because it is featured in today's paper, not for any more profound reason. It is typical of the problems of many companies when coping with international cultural relations in their businesses. Nor is it a particularly British characteristic. In fact, there is evidence that US and Japanese corporations have considerably greater problems in coping with cross-cultural aspects than North Europeans and Overseas Chinese. [3]

It would be a mistake to think that managing cultures is a problem only for organisations who have to trade across national boundaries. The internal organisational culture is being seen as of increasing importance as companies face up to radical and structural change. Fully understanding the internal conflicts alone is enough for most managers, but few have that luxury nowadays. Increasingly managers, particularly top managers, have to cope simultaneously with both the internal and international aspects. How they cope with this is of great interest to me.

My experiences of working with companies across cultural boundaries has been that the problems are often felt but then hidden. The reasons for this are complex but amongst them is an awareness that to confront them would force a step-change in the board's ability to think about the two cultural dimensions of their work. This, in turn, would force reconsideration of their present allocation of time – and this is often treated as sacrosanct.

Moreover, the obvious subtleties and differences of thinking about cultural dimensions needed would rapidly show up a lack of knowledge and skills in many directors. Such lacunae are difficult to articulate by any individual at board level so progress is rarely made – unless there is group commitment to do so. This is usually not the case and so the issue is hidden again, whilst the already inadequate corporate culture is brought to bear once again on a problem which has regularly proved intractable. Yet the board knows that doing 'more of' or 'less of' the same thing will not change the problem. How can they reframe the cultural issue so that it is resolvable within their organisational resources?

SETTING THE CONTEXT

My experience has been that the very act of saying that it is legitimate to talk of cultural differences at board level, and get people used to so doing, is often sufficient to allow the reframing of the problem so that constructive change can happen. There are often audible sighs of relief around the table when some basic vocabulary and concepts are introduced to help define and explore the area of 'culture'. Often the analogy of 'it felt like a boil being lanced' is used.

I have learned to curb my didactic tendencies on such occasions and to work from the board's existing position on one fundamental issue – difference, and how to value it. Around the table it is usually easy to get agreement that there are physical, social, and psychological differences between those present. It is then not difficult to get agreement that the reason this particular group is charged with giving direction to the organisation is that they represent the synthesis of the various specialised functions needed for the organisation to sustain and develop itself. As such they must subscribe, albeit subconsciously, to the idea that such amalgamation allows for synergy amongst them – that the individual inputs give an output that is quantitatively and qualitatively better than the simple sum of the inputs.

Such statements are usually met with acclamation. This paves the way for me to ask, why do you as a board who obviously value the differences between you, behave in a way that tries to eliminate differences in your operating units and with customers? This question often provokes disorder and some resentment can erupt. But then a dispassionate review of current strategic problems will usually gain support for my plea to develop thinking and procedures in the cultural area. It is at this point that a start can be made on coming to grips with the paradox that the more an organisation tries to impose a unitary micro-culture on its disparate parts, the more the differences become magnified and difficult to manage.

TOWARDS SOME WORKING DEFINITIONS

The word 'culture' is loaded with ambiguity and complexity. In this chapter I will use a single definition:[4]

> an historically transmitted pattern of meanings embodied in symbols, a system of inherited conceptions expressed in symbolic forms by means of which men communicate, perpetuate, and develop their knowledge about and attitudes towards life . . . man is an animal suspended in webs of signification he himself has spun. I take culture to be those webs, and the analysis of it to be therefore not an experimental science in search of law but an interpretive one in search of meaning.

But I do not say that in the boardroom. The cultural divide would be too great.

There is significance in the vocabulary that any operating group uses and the above quotation is so far outside that for business or organisations that it invites hostility and rejection − being made manifest in such comments as 'stupidly academic', 'pseudo-scientific', 'soft' etc. In that form it has no significance for the board. This does not belittle its conceptual value but it does make it indigestible when presented en bloc. So another approach is needed which works out of the existing vocabulary and moves on to a higher plane − towards the second order change which truly develops organisations.

This approach usually starts with getting the board to accept statements such as 'how things are done around here', the 'statement of corporate ethic', the 'working assumptions of our company', 'the ground rules for survival', the 'unwritten laws' and so forth. Exploration of these alone is sufficient, over time, to gain the board's awareness of the 'webs of signification' which they have already spun. An awareness of the organisation's symbols and the ways in which a new entrant becomes moulded and accepted, often through subconscious behaviour and attitude modification, is crucial in opening up the cultural dimensions so that organisations may develop constructively through understanding.

In so doing a veritable maze of dead ends and diversions can be constructed. It is not my intention to do so and I have to contain myself from following those seductive idiosyncracies and differences found in organisations which titillate and captivate but finally have use only in those dinner party conversations where one can add the tag line 'not many people know that'. What concerns me much more in my consultancy role is to get the board to find and focus on those aspects of culture within which they work that effect and determine the effectiveness of their organisation.

TOWARDS A WORKING VOCABULARY

To do this it is necessary to try and give more definition to our use of the word culture. In a small working group 'culture' can be taken to refer to national characteristics, political beliefs, organisational style, individual attitudes, and historical progression. Little wonder that confusion can reign even between those who work together each day.

I have developed my own categorisation of cultures which I use when working with an organisation. This involves three levels of cultural differentiation:

Micro-culture   – which pertains specifically to the organisation and its social position (a sociological notion)

Macro-culture – which pertains to the wider/national context of dramas, rituals and routines [an anthropological notion]

Meta-culture   – which pertains to the transcending of micro- and macro-culture around and within an organisation (an integrative notion).

Micro-culture for me encompasses the social history of specific units or organisations within the corporate whole. How they started, who was involved, and for what reasons are key indicators of micro-cultures. Who holds power now, and what values do they espouse? What is the prevailing party political flavour? Are there strong religious tendencies at board level? Are there particular ethnic characteristics which predominate? These are typical of the types of questions which reflect the micro-cultural aspects I would want mapped and debated. To this can then be added some of the more management orientated micro-cultural analyses. What is the organisational culture? Which stage of the product lifecycle have the various units reached? Which functional specialism is dominant in which parts of the company? In process terms it is usually much easier to begin mapping in the technical areas and work towards the less appreciated aspects rather than vice-versa. The board then starts from what it knows and can ease itself into the 'softer', more difficult areas.

Macro-culture analysis and mapping is a more difficult step to take in the move towards an organisation's understanding and management of culture. Most boards accept that there are sociological aspects to the process of managing even if they would prefer not to express it in that way. They are usually more comfortable with terms like 'managing the human side of enterprise', 'motivating and maintaining morale', or 'proving people matter around here'. However, they do understand that their organisation operates in a wider political and international context which is characteristically much more unpredictable and disruptive to manage. They are unlikely to grace this domain with the terms 'political science' or 'anthropology' but these are the areas with which they are trying to deal. Considering the educational backgrounds most managers have it is hardly surprising that they have difficulty coming to grips with macro-culture.

I have argued elsewhere[5] about the characteristics of boards; of their tendency to keep their eyes and hands on daily operations, rather than policy and strategy, because this is how they have behaved over a long period; and of their rarely being able to retrain to cope with the less tangible world of macro-culture which they are expected to inhabit when they join a board. Ideally there is a strong case to be made for directors being properly inducted and trained in the art of directing − of managing the boundaries between their inherently controllable organisations and the inherently uncontrollable and unpredictable world outside. Because this is rarely done it is hardly surprising that most directors show signs of great stress when asked to attend to such environmental monitoring, analysis, and prediction.

They usually take the comfortable route and return unofficially to their old job whilst keeping the perks of their elevated job title. For the organisation such behaviour is disastrous as the external boundaries are not manned and so it loses touch with the outside world.

In an ideal world directors would add to their range of disciplines political science, anthropology, and design as tools in their directoral kitbag. But as these are not only not offered by the business schools, but actively rebuffed by them, some quick and dirty methods are needed to help transform current problems into useful practice.

Macro-culture is for me about the broader national and inter-national contexts in which the organisation operates. It can be regional but is typically national and, increasingly, international in scope. It encompasses the issues of nationality, religion, politics, language, and combinations of these which boards find often opposed to their organisation's micro-culture — and its assumed primacy when the micro and macro-cultures are in opposition.

It is here that the effective strategic managers are sorted from the chaff. Managers with only a 'binary' thinking style[6] [either something is good, or else it is bad; that it is either right, or it must be wrong] cannot cope with the macro-cultural level of operations. They are comfortable with single cultures once they know how to manage the deviances from them but find the management of the differences and disruptions involved with macro-culture totally unacceptable to their binary style. When the macro-cultural factors are in combination on an n-dimensional matrix, who is to say what is right and wrong? There is no simple choice, no time to get totally accurate information, and each choice made will affect all the others in ways they are not always sure. Moreover, the whole picture is liable to disruption from others apparently way beyond their control. When these others are significantly different from their board's culture and powerbase — northerners against southerners, westerners against easterners but, worst of all, foreigners against us — then trouble will follow. This is the point where the meta-culture can be brought into play for the benefit of organisational effectiveness. Unfortunately, it rarely is.

Meta-culture is for me the synthesis of the organisation's micro-culture and the environment's macro-culture into a workable whole which transcends the cultural aspects of both. It is not a permanent and binding notion, rather a way of understanding and valuing the differences and making the most from them – a design notion which gives both parties common meaning and common objectives for a period of time. To achieve this requires styles of thinking and learning amongst the directors which are far removed from the binary stance. A combination of the ability to value differences, and to use the energies of apparently opposing forces to your own creative ends, has to be the target for the board – the design and management of their meta-culture.

But, again, the skills needed are in short supply in management and management education. The use of opposed forces to achieve creative ends is very much the province of the designer. Valuing differences whilst seeking common ground on which to build is the province of the statesman/diplomat. Neither are commonly found on executive boards, and yet the future of business through the exchange of learning, know-how, and technology would seem to involve more and more the crossing of national cultural boundaries in a sympathetic manner to those boundaries.

It would seem that major reconsideration need be given to the selection processes for a board. If what I am finding is transferable, then it will be necessary to select those who can tolerate ambiguity, cope with uncertainty, think creatively, determine policy, manage cultural boundaries, implement strategy, and delegate effectively. As many of these are 'right brain'[7] functions, outside the usual managerial areas of logic and certainty, careful selection must be made on the potential for such skills and not as a reward for previous good performance in 'left brain' functions. It seems a normal process for boards to reward long-term left-brainers to join them. That they are usually incapable of them coping with the right-brain functions necessary for their new role is rarely addressed. The consequences in organisational effectiveness are often profound. In many of the less effective organisations I think that we are seeing the consequences of twenty or thirty years of 'brainless' thinking by their boards and top managers. This seems to be particularly so when the organisations have been run entirely by engineers or accountants.

What thinking is needed about the future of business which incorporates concepts of culture and draws additional energy from it?

FUTURE BUSINESS SURVIVAL

For me the future of world trade is increasingly to be found in the soft technologies. It is no mere chance that high-tech industries are increasingly interested in codifying and protecting the Intellectual Property Rights [IPRs] of their organisation. Their copyrights, patents, and know-how, will form the software 'products' for their future trade. Nor is it mere chance that such software rests in the heads and hearts of the people in the organisation. Such folk are much less controllable than manufacturing machines and have a habit of walking out when they are dissatisfied with the micro-culture of an organisation. The skills of retaining and managing such people are much less developed than manufacturing management at the moment. Yet they will have to be developed if the organisation is to survive and grow in the twenty-first century. How can this be done?

Codification and Dissemination

It may seem paradoxical but I shall argue that, at the time when boards are becoming more pragmatic in their thinking, they should apply some academic rigour. The two dimensions are complementary and if the organisation is to develop policy and implement strategy in a useful manner, then it must have systems which allow for the simultaneous codification and dissemination of the operational learning of their organisations. This requires the skilled management of the three levels of culture in their organisation.

Both aspects usually cause problems with boards who are often wedded to the notion that their sales are directly related to the artefacts sold. As software and systems start to predominate over hardware sales, especially on international markets, this will be less so. Now the know-how, the learning locked up in the organisation, becomes the important generator of added value − here lies a crucial problem. When the emphasis has been placed on the finished product being the epitome of the organisation's learning, the process by which this happens is rarely valued by the organisation. Hence it is usually not possible to look at the design and manufacturing decisions which created the product in any rigorous manner − a lot is held in the heads of those who participated. It is even less likely that one can look at alternative design ideas to see what of commercial use was rejected

11

but can still be profitably held by the organisation. It is here that the true value of an organisation lays – in the Intellectual Property Rights. Yet organisations are rejecting or devaluing their IPRs every day.

What seems to be needed is for the board to confirm its role as the focus of the codification process so that as people go about their daily 'operational' work there are rigorous organisational systems which pick up the potential IPRs, whether verbal, know-how, or fully codified, and evaluate them. When properly running such a system would look very much like the original drawings by Williamson for the Quad amplifier – a series of multiple feedback loops which constantly monitor and refine the signal. I think it significant that some Japanese corporations have used Williamson, as one of three English management gurus, for organisational design. It is crucial to note that the process of codifying in an organisation presupposes the skill of delegation by the board of their day-to-day operations. This means letting go twenty or thirty years of learned responses – and of retraining. I have yet to meet a board which has rigorously set out to regularly develop both itself and its individual members.

Once the rigour of codification at operational levels is properly in hand then the board can concentrate on its proper roles – the formulation of policy and the implementation of strategy. Here the important psychological notion, and reinforcing behaviour, of 'brain on, hands off' comes to the fore. Most boards do not operate as the direction-giver of their business. They tend to be deeply involved in the immediacy of daily operations at the expense of time to think and plan. Hence they can never assume their true function – as the brain of the firm.[8]

Getting a board to focus on dissemination of their IPRs in relation to the formulation of policy and its subsequent implementation through strategy will be a key determinant of an organisation's ability to survive in future. By dissemination I refer to the way in which a product or service is transferred from the organisation to its customers. The simplistic, previous notions of a basic cash nexus are now usually inadequate. This is especially true of those organisations which must cross national boundaries. They know only too well of the rise of economic nationalism, religious fundamentalism, political discrimination, and their consequent manifestations of tariff barriers, difficult barter deals, curious 'agent's commissions', third party trading etc. Yet many continue to think and behave as if straight sales from the organisation to the customer of artefacts is the only way to behave.

It is here in the dissemination of the IPRs that the board's grasp of cultural analysis — both its own and the customer's — is crucial. If this can be done rigorously then there is every chance of creating the necessary meta-culture through which continuing successful business can be done. If not, expect trouble in the medium to long-term on what may seem immediately successful sales — the expectations and aspirations of the client are unlikely to have been fully understood so the deal may well sour as the underlying conflicts become manifest.

The crucial strategic activity for a board is to monitor the macro-culture, codify their micro-culture, and design with their customers an appropriate meta-culture which allows constructive business to be done, at least for a period of time.

NECESSARY ROLES

When John Stopford and I started looking into these issues in 1978, we produced a list of the different types of manager who seemed to be operating at the macro-cultural level:[9]

Ambassadors	— senior general staff on peripatetic missions outside the organisation
Diplomatic technicians	— senior functional specialists on visits or short-term secondments
Expatriate residents	— medium to long-term stay career-builders living abroad
Home country nationals	— indigenous local managers of multinational organisations
Third country nationals	— managers in international organis-ations who are neither from the head-quarters country nor the local home country
Home country hosts	— managers of any organisation who receive foreign clients, and guests, and ease them into the local social and business environment.

The list was not exhaustive, nor exclusive as managers can hold various combinations of these roles, but it was an attempt to cope with defining the strategic boundary managers and the operational boundary managers. The board are, in my definition, the strategic boundary managers – monitoring the external environment, analysing, and predicting, disruptions from that environment; and lubricating the critical boundaries so that there is a sporting chance in being able to design at least part of the future rather than simply having to continually react to it. This is the *brain on* part of the business. The operational boundary managers are the senior functional managers, and heads of operational units, who have to co-operate in the daily co-ordination of agreed plans and deviations from them. This is the *hands on* part of the business.

A critical area of organisational confusion seems to arise in the area of marketing and sales. Using my notions above it should be relatively simple to both define and determine the boundaries between marketing [policy] and sales [operational] with strategy being the two-way implementation process. However, few businesses behave in this way and sales, especially of international projects, are often made on a random and supposedly culture-free basis. The work of Max Boisot [10] shows that this is not so. He has shown how the culturally determined needs of the foreign client are rarely understood in the macro-cultural context by the producer organisation. The micro-culture of their organisation is looking to maximise its internal return and tends to discount macro-cultural considerations as outside their remit. Most boards do not have any notion of designing and operating a temporary meta-culture for a project, it is not seen as part of their remit either, and so the project goes sour. Boisot has suggested that the amount of time needed to design a project from the cultural viewpoint is relatively large. As this cannot usually be done during the tender process it is crucial to do it as soon as the contract is won. I would add that, in cases where high-calibre ambassadors are operating in a meta-culture mode, then there is less need to win business via competitive tendering – the specific needs are already understood in their context and the organisation can work as a joint venture partner even in the early phases of project definition. In this mode it is often not necessary to go through a full tender at all.

My work continues but it is clear to me that proper definition of the policy, strategy, and operational levels of the business, and reinforcing behaviour by the board, is crucial to allow the management of culture within and around organisations. Unless this is done it is not possible truly to direct a business. In a world that is increasingly dependent on international trade, but with growing national cultural barriers being erected, such a lack of direction will spell the death of that business.

All of this causes great stress in many management development specialists. They often lack access to either directors, and their development, or to 'culture' in any of the three senses mentioned. For those management developers who see their role as essentially passive – the mere instrument of top managers who have pre-determined the decisions in these areas – there is little chance that they will be able to operate effectively in such fields. Most top managers are not sensitive to the dimensions of culture in their business – yet. Most management developers are not held in sufficiently high esteem by their top managers to be seen to be of use in this area – yet. Passive developers are unlikely ever to cross this credibility gap.

Active management developers can at least gain respect for their contribution to the development of their business. But this is insufficient to have an effect on the process of developing the three levels of culture in their organisation. Management developers can be useful subcontractors to the wider organisational development processes, but they are not crucial to it. Even organisational development folk as presently operating cannot be expected to deal with all three levels of culture. They can be expected to cope with micro-cultural issues – with the development of appropriate organisational climate and structures. Very few are competent to cope with macro-cultural issues. They tend to be locked into reinforcing the organisation's existing micro-culture, often at the expense of the macro-culture. Any changes in this area will have to overcome the problems of resistance to changes in the roles of organisational developers – a fine paradox when one looks at the espoused values of such folk. Opening up developers to both levels of culture is a contemporary challenge. To the best of my knowledge, there are no agencies or institutions involved in the development of skilled practitioners in multi-cultural development.

Development, therefore, is likely to be slow in this area. If we then add on meta-culture as a third dimension, and one in which even less developmental work has been done, we are likely to see little noticeable progress in the near future. It will only be when top managers perceive the need for multi-cultural management that matters will change. When they do, their demand will meet with little supply. Those who risk gearing up to supply this demand may well need to position themselves in a way that is much closer to a combined consultant and project manager at a strategic level in a business before they can face the new issues of organisational transformation.

A CASE STUDY

I have a delightful client, a fast-growing and socially aware electronics company, who asked if I would look at the directing team of a recent US acquisition they had made. In the few months since their bid had been accepted things had not gone as fast nor as well as they had anticipated. What could be done?

I do not like to tackle cultural issues head-on. This is usually unacceptable because most people do not speak the language of culture. So I try and work from where they are – from where it hurts – and then work the top team back to a broader, second order, view from which true change can be made. In this particular case I ensured agreement that I would have access to all the people involved on both sides of the Atlantic with no preconditions.

I needed to get detailed and personal evidence both of the technical problems that were being faced and of individual's gut reactions to them. I worked on the assumption that the emotional temperature of the unit is at least as important as the technical difficulties. To do this I used a modified version of an organisational climate survey originally designed by Roger Harrison which looked at the dimensions of responsibility, standards, conformity, rewards, organisational clarity, warmth and support, and leadership. One hour interviews with each participant during which they mapped their view of the existing, and also ideal, positions on each dimension gave very rich data on the emotional temperature of the organisation stated in terms of their daily work.

Such data provided the basis of debate amongst each national group as to whether the combined scores, and anonymous quotes, provided a true picture of their organisation now, and how it might be improved. The process of debate enabled the areas of friction to be pinpointed in a way that said it was legitimate to talk about micro and macro-cultural issues when they impinged on policy, strategy, and operational matters.

As these issues arose it was possible to give some intellectual frameworks with which a vocabulary could be developed to discuss these unfamiliar areas. On the macro-culture front we used Geert Hofstede's national culture maps[11] and looked at the differences between UK and US nationals in terms of their social history. This led to much more open discussion of some of the technical problems of trying to cope with the 'Brits' and their curious ways of doing business. Specifically, it became obvious that the UK's power came from being a sales-driven organisation whilst the US had come out of an engineering and production-driven history. These power sources had not yet found a meta-culture through which they could operate.

Talk of power led to deeper consideration of the issue of power within, and between, the organisations. Using Charles Handy's definition of organisational micro-cultures[12] we decided that the US was firmly rooted in a 'role' [bureaucratic] culture whilst the UK came from a mixture of 'people' and 'power' culture. The differences were marked once defined but had not been consciously realised or acted upon. Hence quite deep frustration had grown on both sides as each puzzled away at why on earth the others would say and do those things when 'they knew we did things this way'.

Understanding this led to a deeper level — worries over the political stances of each top team. The UK were publicly characterised as strong supporters of the Social Democratic Party and were recognised as liberal and enlightened employers. The US were strong supporters of President Reagan and finally admitted to a deep distrust of 'limey pinkos'. Yet the US found the UK individuals both charming and highly skilful. The problem was that their behaviour was not always helpful in a US context. One example given was on the handling of holiday [vacations]. The UK top team wanted to reward the US managers for making huge efforts to upgrade their organisation since the takeover. They decided that the best way to do this was to raise the annual holiday allowance from three to six weeks. This made them feel good and so they were shocked when it led to a negative reaction in the US. This was strongly felt by the US managers to be a way of rewarding the lazy! Consternation was felt on both sides. The US had not wanted to raise the issue but their line of argument was that in a US macro-culture 'good' people do not take their full holiday allowance anyway. Therefore to double that allowance would merely be a direct invitation for 'lazy' employees to take advantage of the company. No amount of attempting to transfer the UK micro-culture to the US, nor insistence that the UK one was the only one to be used, would be sufficient to solve this. A working appreciation of the US macro-culture and a joint venture in developing an appropriate meta-culture are needed before we get anything near the business synergy which was hoped for through the takeover.

We are now starting to work on longer-term organisational development projects in both organisations which respect their macro-cultures yet allow the strategic and operational boundaries to be managed in such a way that we develop a meta-culture strong enough to cope with a further dimension — the projected establishment of a Far East business.

A MORE MANAGEABLE FUTURE?

It is usually with relatively minor incidents that unhelpful organisational stereotypes become part of folk history, and the organisational behaviours become much more difficult to manage. I have had many similar experiences, one with the European Space Agency where after the analytical phase the start of the healing process was to get the 'Brits' to shake hands with the French and the Germans at least once a day. And these examples are when we are at least notionally in control of our micro-cultures. When this sort of problem is transferred to the much less controllable macro-culture and to potential, or actual clients, who are not fully sure of us and are hypersensitive to our words and behaviours, then the study of culture and directors' roles becomes crucial.

The good news is that all the tools already exist. We know enough about analysing organisational and national cultures to be able to draw our benchmarks from which we measure organisational change. We know how to develop teamworking at all levels. We know how to develop intelligence systems which allow us to monitor environmental change, and increasingly we are becoming skilful at managing that change. The bad news is that few organisations have the intellectual frameworks within which to deploy them. Hopefully the stringency of world trade should force us into using more thought and wasting fewer valuable resources – human or material. The next great challenge is to develop organisations which truly learn and that is where the junction of directors and culture is crucial.

REFERENCES

(1) Peters, T. and Waterman, R., *In Search of Excellence*, Harper & Row, 1982.
(2) *Financial Times*, 29 January, 1985.
(3) March, R. M., 'Manpower and Control Issues', (eds) Garratt, R. and Stopford, J., *Breaking Down Barriers*, Gower, 1980.
(4) Geertz, C., *Interpretation of Cultures*, Basic Books Inc, New York, 1973.
(5) See for example: Garratt, R., 'The Power of Action Learning', in Pedler, M. (ed.) *Action Learning in Practice,* Gower, 1983.
(6) See for example: Mant, A., *The Leaders We Deserve*, Martin Robertson, 1983.
(7) See for example: Wonder, J., *Whole Brain Thinking*, Morrow, 1984.
(8) See for example: Beer, S., *The Brain of the Firm*, The Allen Lane Press, 1972.
(9) Garratt, R. and Stopford, J., (eds) *Breaking Down Barriers*, Gower, 1980.
(10) See for example: Boisot, M., 'The Shaping of Technological Strategy: European Chemical Firms in South East Asia', *International Management Review,* Autumn, 1983.
(11) Hofstede, G., *Culture's Consequences*, Sage, 1980.
(12) Handy, C., 'So you want to change your organisation? Then first identify its culture', *Management Education and Development*, Vol. 7, Part 2, August, 1976.

2

Effectiveness in management development*

Alan Mumford

For someone like myself who has been involved in management development for more than 20 years it is possible to be alternately optimistic and pessimistic about the progress that has been made during that time. Perhaps the most crucial development, at least in the United Kindom and probably in the United States, was a growing recognition that the purpose of management was to achieve results rather than to administer bureaucratic processes. The early impact of Peter Drucker, followed in the 1960s by the Management By Objectives wave, caused a recognition, at least at the conceptual level, that the improvement of management performance centred on the definition of results to be achieved; this became expressed as the idea that what mattered was outputs rather than inputs.

This revised outlook was by no means fully incorporated in managerial work. The flood of MBO work reached full tide and then receded. The flood left behind however some useful sediment. Not only do more managers, than would have been the case 20 years ago, talk about objectives, standards and criteria of performance, but in the particular field of management development, performance appraisal processes have in many organisations adopted objective setting as a crucial first feature in the process of appraisal. There have

---

*This chapter is based on a lecture delivered at the 1984 World Congress on Management Development.

been other significant developments in our understanding of what effective managers do to which I shall refer later in this chapter. However, it seems to me that these partial although important recognitions of what defines effectiveness in management have not been drawn together to create effective management development processes.

THE THREEFOLD NATURE OF EFFECTIVENESS IN MANAGEMENT DEVELOPMENT

Effectiveness in management development will arrive only when we manage to understand and then implement action on three different aspects of effectiveness (see Figure 2.1):

1 Varying definitions of effective managerial behaviour.
2 A developmental process which emphasises activities in which managers are required to be effective, rather than emphasising the knowledge necessary for action.
3 The identification of a learning process which is effective for the individual or group rather than being economical and convenient for tutors or trainers.

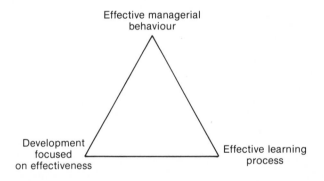

Figure 2.1 Effectiveness triangle in management development

EFFECTIVE MANAGERIAL BEHAVIOUR

The MBO approach mentioned earlier has been one of the major causes of a shift in attention to what managers actually do rather than to abstract and generalised statements of what they ought to do. The other major impact stems from the work of Carlson[1], Rosemary Stewart[2] and Mintzberg[3]. Peter Drucker[4] provided in two sentences a crucial bridge between the two kinds of discovery. 'Efficiency is concerned with doing things right. Effectiveness is doing the right things.' What might be called the classical view of the nature of management can be summarised as:

(a) forecast/plan
(b) organise
(c) motivate
(d) co-ordinate
(e) control.

The work of Carlson, Stewart and Mintzberg showed that the ways in which these concepts have been created, and the attempt to apply them as a structure for developing managers was misconceived, unrealistic and unhelpful. However the most useful though most devastating aspect of their work is not their demolition of one list of vital managerial tasks and the replacement of that list by another one, but by their common discovery that any generalised statement about managerial activities was likely to be at least partially and possibly substantially incorrect for any particular manager or group of managers. They found substantial variations in required managerial behaviour. In much the same way as organisational theorists such as Lawrence and Lorsch[5] were conducting the research to show that effective organisation structures were contingent upon a large number of factors rather than on some single ideal view of an organisation, the managerial activities in which any individual had to be effective was seen to depend on the specific kind of job and on his interpretation and others' interpretation of his role and responsibilities within it.

These discoveries have not, for a variety of reasons, had the crucial impact on our management development process that they ought to have done. There has been insufficient acceptance of the implication of these discoveries, i.e. that work to help a manager be more effective depends more on recognising and dealing with the specifics of his or her job than on helping him or her through generalisations about what managers need to know. Although there may have been some improvement in the capacity of organisations to analyse management training requirements, it does seem that, probably for a majority, needs analysis is relatively superficial and leads to the facile adoption of training courses whose content differs remarkably little from one organisation to another. Even where the professional management development adviser knows what he ought to do there can be considerable obstacles in terms of actually engaging line managers in the analytical process. The definition and interpretation of what is meant by effective behaviour takes time and energy which managers on the whole would rather give to some other activity. This is most obviously but not uniquely true for a demanding process such as repertory grid.

I believe that one of the causes of relative ineffectiveness in this area within organisations has been an over-emphasis on developing managers for the future instead of working on issues of current requirements. This argument almost certainly applies with even greater strength to training and education institutions which offer taught experiences outside the organisation. It is even clearer that for such institutions the identification of the nature of effectiveness in management has been scarcely affected by the work described above. It is understandable, although not acceptable, that they should see themselves as having to operate on generalised views of management processes because they were offering 'open' programmes, and not dealing with individual companies. Since, however, all the main institutions now offer 'in-house' programmes we might have hoped to see a substantial shift towards effectiveness. It seems more likely that what we have seen is a relatively cosmetic shift to the design of specific material for particular companies rather than a basic shift in the nature of the programme. The primary teaching institutions seem to show exactly that, i.e. they are more in the business of conveying generalised knowledge than they are in the business of helping managers to define and improve their own effectiveness criteria.

As we shall see again later the significance of the particular kind of contribution made by the major business schools is that inevitably and properly the contribution they make for the tiny number of managers, with whom they deal, is extended through the use of their concepts by trainers, tutors and educators in less creative and research based teaching organisations.

The thrust of my argument takes me to the view that too much of our management development work derives from an inadequate assessment of effective managerial behaviour, and that that assessment is too often based on a view which deals with what is efficient rather than what is effective.

DEVELOPMENT PROCESSES EMPHASISING EFFECTIVENESS

One of the problems in management development has certainly been that we have detached it from the reality of managerial processes. As I have just illustrated I think we have detached it from the reality of managerial behaviour. We have also detached it from the reality of the perceptions and understanding of managers themselves. With rare exceptions (see the contingency theory mentioned earlier) managers are not concerned about the knowledge possessed by boss, colleagues or subordinates. Their characteristic expression about a manager's effectiveness is whether he or she can get things done. The fact that they are not aware of and tend to be impatient about the knowledge and skills required to enable a manager to get things done is not of course in itself an argument for not providing these elements. It is a practical and psychological argument (insofar as these two are different) for starting from the reality of where managers are rather than imposing on them our views about what they need. Since effectiveness is defined clearly by the results actually secured and not by the knowledge someone possesses it would seem sensible to concentrate in our management development processes on helping managers to learn from actions undertaken rather than providing them with conceptual statements of what managers ought to do or even with analytical experiences of what other managers have done or might have done. Instead of giving emphasis to the provision of knowledge and asking managers to interpret and use that knowledge in subsequent action, it would be both more appropriate and more likely to be successful if we gave prime attention to issues of action and secondary attention to issues of the required knowledge. Knowledge and the capacity to analyse and produce solutions to problems are necessary but insufficient contributors to effective action. In the same way primary attention to managerial skills may be misplaced although not inappropriate. By this I mean that the first stage of attention should be on a desired managerial result rather than the skills required for managerial activities.

The description so far may sound like another plea for action learning. In the sense that I am proposing prime attention to working on real management problems there is certainly a common basic philosophy. In the sense that I am not talking exclusively about the use of defined projects, or the creation of a group of managers discussing projects, I am in fact advancing a rather wider proposition. I am arguing that by taking issues of effectiveness as the prime focus of a development activity we are engaging managers in a process with which they would be more familiar and more sympathetic than if we engaged them in a process (the acquisition of knowledge and skill) with which they are less familiar and sympathetic. I will quote briefly four illustrations of this shift of emphasis.

Case 1

The final stages of a two-week management development programme were geared to the participants reviewing the corporate strategy of the group for which they worked. The intention of the sessions, which included a presentation to the chief executive, was that participants should be more familiar with the reasons for the corporate strategy instead of just criticising it from their level in the business. In later programmes we made a significant change since it seemed to us less relevant that participants should know the corporate strategy than that they should be encouraged to take action on strategic issues affecting their own business. They were instead asked to make proposals on a significant business problem currently affecting most of them. One example was that they were asked to work on the nature of and possible reactions to competition from Japanese manufacturers. While they could not do anything about corporate strategy, except perhaps understand it better, they could do something in their own companies about the Japanese 'threat'.

Case 2

A company which had revised its sales objectives and organisation structure had some concern that the managers involved might not have the skills necessary to achieve the changed objectives. As a result of analysis with them it became clear that, although probably a number of them were lacking in some skills, the more crucial problem was that, although apparently committed to the revised objectives, they had not fully set up the action necessary to implement them. The prime effectiveness concern was not therefore the skills of sales management, but the identification of specific actions to implement the broad objectives agreed.

Case 3

A company which had changed the composition and structure of its marketing function found that a number of those involved would be unable to produce what was required because they were not fully equipped with marketing skills. In the course of discussion with them the emphasis was shifted from the acquisition of skills to the implementation of skills. An in-house marketing programme was devised which, in addition to giving managers the necessary tools, took them through to the identification of specific marketing projects which needed to be undertaken. The programme was designed to meet both general marketing skill requirements in the organisation, the specific requirements of the projects which had to be undertaken, and the completion of real work to meet the needs of the business.

Case 4

MBA programmes normally provide participants with a better understanding of the various functional areas of management such as marketing, finance and production. The expectation is that managers, who have acquired this knowledge, may be able to manage these functions better, or may through a better understanding have a better relationship with other departments. In our MBA programme we start at the other end of the process by requiring our associates to analyse the nature of relationships between their own function and others in the business, and to make proposals for improvement. While we believe that it may be important for most managers to 'understand finance better', we see it as at least as important that they should be helped to take specific actions relevant to their needs in dealing with other functions.

In all of these situations we avoid simplistic generalisations such as 'managers learn by doing' or 'all managers should learn through doing a project'. There are some signs that such generalisations are being employed as readily in supposedly sophisticated management development processes as were the older generalisations about management. Learning processes focused on effectiveness must always deal with the reality of the manager's job, and always involve him in action on it. However a manager will not learn enough simply by taking action; it is clear from the literature on action learning that this is not sufficiently understood. The emphasis on projects and action is wholly dominant, to the exclusion of any serious discussion of the learning process.

Of course the greatest reality of all is what a manager is doing day by day in his normal managerial work. All too little has been done in management development to make effective use of the day by day experiences; most attention, as indeed I have just illustrated, has been given to off the job processes. I have written elsewhere at length about the possibilities of learning from normal work activities[6]. I have no doubt that this is the vital area in which we could improve our productivity. I will not repeat here the illustrations I gave in my book; our need is to be able to help managers to learn from their real time experience in attending meetings, conducting negotiations, using management control information and so on.

If we tackle issues of effectiveness in these various ways, we will come much closer to resolving the essential paradox of management development. That paradox is that managers claim to learn from experience. Characteristically they talk about the jobs they have done, the bosses they have worked for, rather than about the courses they have attended. Management development schemes have apparently tried to resolve one part of this paradox by encouraging movement between jobs. More often, however, management development processes have continued to emphasise formal off the job training and education. Not only have they offered a prescription which does not meet the managers' realities just described, but the processes themselves, i.e. courses, have given no help to managers in re-interpreting and making better use of their on the job development opportunities.

EFFECTIVE LEARNING PROCESSES

If we manage to work successfully on the issues of managerial effectiveness in the ways I have now described, we will have created for ourselves the opportunity to set up a virtuous learning circle (see Figure 2.2). It is clear that for many managers involvement in formal management development processes particularly off the job has

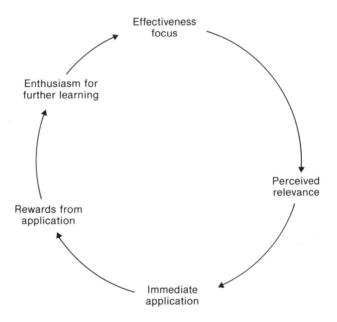

Figure 2.2 The virtuous learning circle

created a vicious learning sequence (see Figure 2.3). Modern motivational theory tells us that behaviour which is not rewarded is not willingly engaged upon again. Clearly some managers have had useful management training or educational experiences and return to similar experiences subsequently. However the reaction of a majority of managers can scarcely be said to equate to a belief in the probable usefulness of the exercise, although they may have reasons of status, company culture or fear of something worse which may cause them to participate at some level of willingness. Nor is it simply a question of the ways in which many managers experience the unreality of off the job processes. The continued absence of evaluation processes as a

Generalised knowledge/skills

Transfer to own situation

Difficulty in application

Absence of rewards for
learned processes

Full Stop

Figure 2.3 The vicious learning sequence

necessary accompaniment to off the job activities ought to be seen as more of a surprise and criticism than it often is. This is more particularly true in my mind given the attention that many pro- grammes pay to aspects of knowledge or skill, the acquisition of which can certainly be tested. Ironically the emphasis I have given to effectiveness issues certainly makes the evaluation process more difficult and probably makes it less absolutely necessary. If you design a process actually to engage people in action you reduce the requirement to test the extent to which they have applied that which they have learned.

Indeed the whole shift of emphasis to action based learning helps us to remove one of the major traditional problems of management education and training. It is a logical oddity that having created a situation of unreality, i.e. a structured off the job learning experience, and then having done in many cases very little about directing attention to those issues of real personal concern to managers, tutors and trainers have then complained about and written learned articles about the problems of transfer of learning. If we create unreality and do not deal with issues of effectiveness we ought not to be surprised that managers have problems in transferring what they are supposed to have learned back into their real job situation. Nor should we be surprised that the boss and colleagues to whom they return from the off the job experience give no welcome to the kind of learning which the manager brings with him. Concentration on those issues which are practically relevant to the manager and his colleagues in the real life situation certainly reduces the transfer problem both because of the perceived reality of what the manager is engaged in and secondly because there need literally be no transfer in the sense that he can be involved in projects and real time problems drawn from his own work which do not then have to be translated. Where learning activities are not primarily and directly based on the manager's own work, we should tackle the transfer problem on our programmes instead of leaving it to the manager to resolve on his own on his return to work. This means less time on teaching, and more time on how the manager will implement what he has learned.

However, emphasis on effectiveness and reality will not, as some writers seem to assume, in themselves completely overcome the need for careful choice of effective learning processes. Management development has been far too subject to 'flavour of the month' approaches each of them claiming to be uniquely appropriate to developing managers. Over the years we have been told that T groups, grid training, coaching, self-development, action learning, were, successively, the answer to our management development problems. In my view the adoption of any single technique, as the predominant answer to our management development problems, is lazy and incompetent. Nor is the answer in a further proliferation of management development processes. In his most helpful book[7] Huczynski identifies around 300 management development techniques. While in no way wishing to inhibit future creativity, it is my view that productivity in management development will derive from the appropriate use of methods already relatively well-known and tried rather than the identification of new processes. I take this view because the application of management development methods is at the moment so clearly both inefficient and ineffective. We have failed to fit our processes to the needs of the learner. Just as we have not satisfactorily dealt with the reality of how a manager manages, we have not dealt with the reality of how a manager learns. Just as we have swept aside the common perception of managers that they learn through on the job processes, a matter of common experience apparently too simple for researchers to cope with, so we have ignored the reality that different managers actually learn differently from the same process. It is an extraordinary fact that educators, trainers and developers know very well that if Brown and Jones both have the same need to improve an aspect of their managerial performance, and both are taken through the same learning experience, Brown learns and Jones does not. It seems that most tutors having stumbled across this truth painfully, when an individual reacts badly to a learning process, then pick themselves up and hurry on as if nothing had happened. In designing courses the best that may occur subsequently is that the designers offer a catholic menu of activities, hoping that everybody will get something out of the course. Thus the supposedly well designed course will include role-plays, films, case studies, lectures, an afternoon in the resource centre; if you are bored by one there is always tomorrow.

It is an extraordinary commentary on management education in both the United Kingdom and the United States that only in the last dozen years has there been attention at any level of significance to differences in the ways in which people learn. The field was for a long time dominated by fundamentally sterile debates about the virtues of case studies, of business games, of experiential exercises. I take again the absence of action on the part of the major traditional business schools because of their perceived dominance in the rest of the management development world. I cannot think of any important university level contribution in this field apart from the original innovative work by Kolb[8], and the work done in this country by the Centre For The Study of Management Learning. CSML have made a considerable contribution in the literature on issues of the general design of different kinds of learning event, and the significance of the interaction between the tutor and the learner. Although much of their written work is understandably directed at the tutor I believe they would share with me the view that one of the problems is that the tutor has been given too great a prominence in the learning process. Their efforts quite rightly are geared to helping the tutor be more effective by assessing the learning situation in which he is involved.

No doubt because I started from a different kind of environment my own concern has been with the learner rather than with the tutor. I should not repeat here the arguments and evidence produced by Peter Honey and myself on ways in which it is possible to identify the nature and consequences of an individual's likely preferences on learning. This information is set out in other books for the management developer[9] and for the learner[10]. Since the arguments are deployed in full there, I need only say here that the crucial contribution of choosing a learning process appropriate to the style of the individual is going to be the major cause of increased productivity in management development. Whether it is choosing a course, or choosing to place somebody on secondment, or selecting someone for a working party, the ability to make use of that experience is going to determine how productive it is.

Honey and I have also argued that knowledge of the learning preferences of managers, actually arriving on a learning experience, can be used to provide a more specific experience. We think it is irresponsible simply to throw a ragbag of activities at a group on the general assumption that their learning styles will be different. Our general proposition is, of course, that the experience should actually be designed as a learning experience not as a teaching experience. This undoubtedly increases the difficulties for the designers and operators of learning events, and perhaps it is the prospect of such difficulties which has deterred training and education institutions from actually thinking seriously about the learning process. Nor would understanding by designers and providers of development experiences, while helpful, go sufficiently far. It is surely another prospective leap forward in management development that we should share with managers our improved understanding of learning and cause them to recognise and improve their own learning processes. That is to say that we should incorporate our improved understanding not merely in the design of a more effective event, but that we should treat learning as an overt part of the programme. Instead of being an implied and unstudied part of most management development activities, learning should be drawn to the forefront as an explicit activity. Nor should this be confined to an interesting session at the beginning of a programme and perhaps some review of personal development growth at the end of it; we must provide time and resource to help managers consider their learning processes during the programme.

I have carefully used the word programme rather than course because I see this as being applicable just as much in the situation in which an advisor is counselling someone's development on the job as it would be with a tutor running an off the job experience. The reason for this extended attention to the learning process is not merely a matter of logic, of the extraordinary fact that many programmes which claim to help managers to learn never actually address that issue, but also that it is essential as one of the ways in which we will manage to draw together on the job and off the job development experiences. If in our off the job experiences we give sufficient time and attention to engage a manager in understanding his own learning we can also help him to see how to apply this knowledge so that he continues to learn from similar or equivalent learning experiences when he is back on the job. Just as dealing with issues of effectiveness will help reduce substantially the problems of transfer of learning, so by giving substantial attention to the learning process itself we can reduce the notorious problem of managers seeing experiences as a series of one-off events with no connection with each other in learning terms.

The phrase continuous learning is now becoming popular. It will be no more than a promotional phrase if we do not provide the learning processes necessary to secure it. It seems clear that some of the people writing about continuous learning are really only talking about a series of training events and not in fact about continuous learning at all.

SUCCESSFUL MANAGEMENT DEVELOPMENT

I have tried to draw together in this chapter three different aspects of effectiveness which I see as principal contributors to effectiveness in management development. There are a number of other issues, many of them not course centred, which affect whether management development will be successful in an organisation. Charles Margerison[11] offers a very substantial review of causes of success and failure in management development with which I am in substantial agreement. I want to pick out only two additional factors. Neither will come as a particular surprise given the nature of my earlier comments. Firstly it seems to me that too many management development schemes are dominated by issues about the so-called system and too little influenced by the needs, requirements and potential for growth of individuals. We will not have effective management development as long as we encourage systems which are in fact geared to process individuals rather than to develop them. I am surely not alone in shuddering when I hear a personnel director or management development advisor say 'All our managers have been through . . .' It has become all too obvious that some management development schemes measure results by the number of people who have 'been through' rather than by achieved results in development.

Nor will it be a surprise to see that I feel we need a better lead from our 'centres of excellence' on the processes of management development. Given that it is of their nature to offer open programmes inevitably concentrating on generalisable issues, we could perhaps hope that they will increasingly concern themselves also with the issues of how generalisations can be applied in practice.

If I offer more criticisms than praise of the business schools in this chapter, it is because I am not evaluating the full range of their work. In case, however, my comments should be seen as not merely unbalanced in that sense, but also partial because I belong to a new business school, I should perhaps say that some, although not all, of my criticisms are shared elsewhere. The nature of that criticism has remained remarkably similar over the last decade and more. J. S. Livingston[12] told us in 1971 that formal management education 'tends to distort managerial growth because it over-develops an individual's analytical ability, but leaves his ability to take action and to get things done under-developed'. This kind of criticism has surfaced again recently in the United States through Peters and Waterman *In Search of Excellence*[13] and Behrman and Levin[14].

In this country the BIM report in 1971[15] and Nancy Foy's report in 1978[16] both suggested important shifts in the provision made by the business schools in the UK. It is also significant to note that Professor Jim Ball, then Principal of the London Business School, while able to claim success in his own terms in other aspects of management education, said that they were 'a long way from fulfilling a commitment in any formal sense to enable people to handle their own learning'. Finally it is significant that, according to Freedman and Stumpf[17], the relationship which I have sought to establish in this chapter between effectiveness in management and effectiveness in management development is clearly not present even amongst management researchers. Those who have studied the criteria for managerial effectiveness have not seen management education as a determinant of managerial performance.

I return to my mixed views of optimism and pessimism about the past of management development; I think we can be optimistic about the future if we manage the triangle of effectiveness well. If we do not even change the emphasis in the individual areas I do not believe management development will be more than a peripheral process pursued by a minority of devotees.

REFERENCES

(1)   Carlson, S., *Executive Behaviour*, 1951.

(2)   Stewart, R., *Contrasts in Management*, McGraw-Hill, 1976.

(3)   Mintzberg, H., *The Nature of Managerial Work*, Prentice-Hall, 1980.

(4)   Drucker, P., *Management Tasks, Responsibilities, Practices*, Harper & Row, 1974.

(5)   Lawrence, P. R. and Lorsch, J. W., *Organisation & Environment*, Harvard, 1967.

(6)   Mumford, A., *Making Experience Pay*, McGraw-Hill, 1980.

(7)   Huczynski, A., *Encyclopedia of Management Development Methods*, Gower, 1983.

(8)   Kolb, D., *Theories of Group Process*, Cooper, C. L. (ed.), Wiley, 1975.

(9)   Honey, P. and Mumford, A., *Manual of Learning Styles*, 1982.

(10) Honey, P. and Mumford, A., *Using Your Learning Styles*, 1983.

(11) Margerison, C., 'How to Avoid Failure and Gain Success in Management Development', *Journal of Management Development*, Vol. 1, No. 3, 1982.

(12) Livingston, J. S., 'The Myth of the Well-Educated Manager', *Harvard Business Review*, January 1971.

(13) Peters, T. J. and Waterman, R. H., *In Search of Excellence,* Harper & Row, 1983.

(14) Behrman, J. N. and Levin, R. I., *Harvard Business Review*, January 1984.

(15) *Business School Programmes*, BIM, 1971.

(16) Foy, N., *The Missing Links*, Foundation for Management Education, 1978.

(17) Freedman, R. D., Cooper, C. L. and Stumpf, S. A., *Management Education*, Wiley, 1982.

Part II
PLANNING FOR MANAGEMENT DEVELOPMENT

3

Planning management development

Tony Vineall

The literature of management development planning has grown a great deal in recent years and with a more practical and less academically statistical slant. What this chapter aims to do is to answer the question which anyone who is believed to have some practical experience in the subject gets asked several times a year — How do we begin? The question usually comes from a senior executive who has been given the task of 'doing something about management development', usually in a medium or large-sized group which operates in more than one country and in more than one product or service area. The group will often have been through several phases of management development. There has often been a period in the past of excessive and overstructured activity from which little remains other than a lot of forms collecting dust. Most commonly there is an active recruitment programme and some, not very long-term, succession planning for the very top jobs; and not much in between. The group wants to do something systematic to get a grip on its longer-term management resource situation. What follows charts a path to do just that — it will involve quite a lot of work, especially in the early stages, and serious commitment coming down from the top; but experience shows that the balance of what it can contribute over its demands in terms of inputs is such that it can rapidly become accepted as a valuable institution and be seen as just as indispensable as the basic financial accounting procedures or annual operating plans.

THE BASIC DISCIPLINES

Like all planning, much depends on the quality of the basic data. Certain preliminary activities have, therefore, to be carried out to provide the data on which all management development planning is based. Examples of these are as follows.

A systematic grading of jobs based on their content

Job classification based on content is usually first introduced primarily for determining salary scales. It is, however, equally important to management development, providing a ready common language to describe and group jobs according to content. Where management development is to be planned on an international group basis, the grading system should ideally be one which applies throughout the group. Where this does not exist, a series of broad seniority bands may have to be introduced for management development purposes and local grades converted to them. One way or another there must be a clear and common perception of the relative levels of jobs before planning can begin — and titles rarely suffice for this purpose.

A system of performance appraisal

Performance appraisal has also usually been devised initially for other purposes — to provide a basis for differentiating rewards; or for counselling the individual; or, less happily, to build up a case for remedial action or termination.

Appraisal systems should, however, also serve to ensure that there is a regular recording of achievement on the job which forms, especially over time, an indispensable foundation for management development. Management development is not just about performance, but if predictions about the future are not firmly rooted in what the manager has actually delivered, the whole exercise will fall into disrepute.

Potential assessment

Performance appraisal is, however, only a beginning. More specifically relevant to management development planning is the assessment of potential – the judgement of how far the manager may be promotable in the future. Such judgement has to be related to performance, but goes further, and is, of its nature, more speculative and more judgemental than performance appraisal. The relationship between performance and potential is not a simple one – the best performers are not necessarily those of high potential. Accordingly, the process of potential assessment has to be more complex; whereas performance appraisal focuses on what the manager achieved, potential assessment is equally interested in how he achieved it; and it must involve more people, such as the boss's boss or the head of the appraisee's function, and also the individual himself.

Most organisations include a brief assessment of potential as something of a footnote to the annual appraisal exercise and this is useful – although the form in which it is communicated to the individual needs care. It is also, however, desirable to organise more extensive potential assessment exercises at key stages of development. A few companies set up assessment centres, or use external ones; more commonly companies make some in-house arrangement to set aside time on specific occasions to think through, in a structured way, with the help of all those who are in a position to contribute, the likely future pattern of an individual's progress.

A system of development lists

The results of such potential assessment then need focusing and firming up into a form which can guide action and provide a useful input to planning. This is best done with a framework of development lists. Jobs are divided into three or four main levels, each therefore with a salary breakpoint about 50 per cent above the level below, and each of these main levels thus incorporating probably three or four normal salary grades. A development list will then be drawn up of those individuals in any one main level who are judged to have the potential to reach the next higher level within five years. Thus, if the main levels were termed junior management, middle management, senior management and top executive, the first list would be those likely to be promotable from junior management to middle management within five years; the second list those promotable within five years from middle management to senior management and so on.

Such a system of development lists contributes to management development planning in several ways. First, it focuses and sharpens judgement about potential with specific questions – judgement of potential can otherwise be sloppy, with too many people being vaguely 'promotable within a few years' without commitment to how much or even how soon. Secondly, they provide the raw material for basic planning comparisons of promotable resources and known and likely future needs. Thirdly, they highlight training and development needs; challenging and testing opportunities, which are often in short supply, can then be directed to those on lists. Finally, the system provides a useful language in which different parts of a large complex organisation can communicate about the sort of people they want for a certain job.

People change and develop and sometimes disappoint, and it is vital that names are deleted from lists as well as added to them. Therefore it may be desirable not to tell individuals when they are put on such lists lest the need to tell them that their names are being removed becomes a deterrent to actually deleting them.

These activities have been described here as 'basic disciplines'. They are to management development what the basic accounting records are to financial management. They do not themselves constitute or guarantee good management planning; but without them what follows will probably be in vain. It is now possible to consider the regular, usually annual, management development planning cycle.

MANAGEMENT RESOURCE PLANNING MEETINGS AT COMPANY OR UNIT LEVEL

Appraisals of performance have been completed, judgements of potential have been made, what happens next?

What happens next is the most central feature of a system of management development planning – a review at unit level (typically the operating company) which provides the focus for the appraisals and potential assessments and sets priorities and plans which will guide the individual appointments, attachments, training courses, etc., which will move the organisation and those who manage it forward in the coming year. This is the crucial point at which, in respect of that particular unit, the organisation 'gets its act together' in respect of management development − it is amazing how frequently the need for a well prepared meeting of this kind is not appreciated.

The first thing to establish is who should attend and that will depend on the structure of authority and responsibility in the particular business. For a subsidiary company the review is essentially between the chief executive and his boss − probably the director to whom he reports at group level. Indeed, together with the annual operating budget, this review is a key control for these two. Each will have his personnel executive with him and where there is some other arm of the business closely involved with management development it should be represented also. The criterion is that anyone whose authority is needed to effect a major personnel change should be there.

This unit/company review should address the key areas of management development and ensure that they have a full picture of the management resources of the unit in the context of likely future needs. Accordingly, they will consider:

1 major business plans and any likely organisational and establishment changes. This link with operational planning is fundamental and should be clear and overt. For this reason, management development reviews can usefully be timed to follow long-term planning meetings. This will enable management development planning to accommodate the likelihood of a move into a new product area or an important technological change in the industry or plans to acquire subsidiaries in another country − or, indeed, a strategic withdrawal from a certain market segment.

2 an individual review at the senior levels in the unit − the level has to be defined according to the individual unit but as a guideline would, in an operating company, clearly cover the board members and the level immediately below them. This review should be based for each individual on a sheet recording quite simply:

(a) the basic personal details (age, service, qualifications, grade, pay, etc.)

(b) a brief summary of his performance appraisal

(c) a statement of the individual's potential.

As the system becomes more sophisticated a statement of how the individual feels about his own career is a useful addition.

Those conducting the review must first establish that they really understand and agree with what is being said about the manager: then they should determine what to plan for the next stage of his development. This might take the form of a recommendation that he should be considered for certain kinds of job move – to widen his experience; to fill a gap in his knowledge; to test him in a more demanding post; to extend his base by operating in another product area or country. Or it could recommend a training course. In other cases it may conclude that he is ideally placed for the time being and that the most important priority is that he should *not* be moved but should remain long enough both to contribute in and benefit from the job he is doing. Specific moves can be agreed in this way but that is not the main aim – what is basic is to establish agreement on the priority for the coming year.

3 a review, on the same lines, of those who have been included on the development lists because of their potential. It will also normally be at this review that individuals will be added to these lists. In the case of such people it is particularly important to identify gaps in their experience and to plan moves which will enable them to develop and further prove their abilities.

4 identification of possible successors for vacancies which are likely to arise at senior levels – because of retirements, or because the incumbents are likely to move, or because of organisational changes or, where numbers are large enough, where past experience suggests that there may well be some losses to posts outside the organisation. Such lists of possible successors are, of course, tentative; but like so much in this field, they begin to point the way to possible problem areas. The same few successors may keep appearing against several vacancies or in some areas all the candidates may look less than

ideal. The reviewers will then want to reconsider the agreed plans for some of the successors in order to speed up or replan this development.

Succession will not always − particularly at the most senior levels − be provided within the individual company and this succession planning at unit level is only one part of a wider exercise − the personnel executives involved must ensure that the particular succession planning is related to the wider group situation.

5   at this stage it should be possible to take an overall view of the company's situation. No one can produce a checklist of what should be discussed. In one unit it will be the lack of any managers of development potential in the engineering function; in another it may be the unfortunate coming together in time of a series of top level retirements and promotions, and how to arrange them successfully; elsewhere it may be the fact that none of the financial managers seem to stay in their jobs for more than 18 months. The review paperwork will have provided the basic data to show up these issues, but there is a skill in spotting them. If this skill − essentially though not exclusively a contribution of the personnel specialist − is lacking, no acceptable amount of forms and checklists will compensate. A system of management development planning needs a lot of managing.

6   *Action notes* The meeting should be summarised quickly in clear action notes. The temptation will be to record everything that was said; succinctness with an emphasis on action will not only make it more likely that the notes are not immediately filed but may actually result in people moving.

REVIEW OF RESOURCES AT HIGHER LEVELS

Even at the level of the individual company or unit the review will inevitably and rightly consider issues of balance of resources and needs − but planning will not always be viewed within the group context and imbalances in particular units are, to an extent, to be expected. It is therefore important that a further review is conducted at a higher level − probably for all group resources in a particular

A. REVIEW OF MANAGEMENT STRENGTHS, AGES, RESOURCES, ETC.

	Senior Exec.	Dev. List III	Senior Mgt.	Dev. List II	Upper Middle Mgt.	Dev. List I	Junior Mgt.	Total Mgt.
Under 35								
36—50								
51—55								
56—60								
61+								
Total								

Establishment forecast in 3/5 years

Leavers (other than retirement) last 5 years
Resigned
Dismissed
Redundant
Died

B. RECRUITMENT OF TRAINEES

Year	No. Recruited	Number In					
		Jun. Mgt.	Dev. List I	Upper Middle Mgt.	Dev. List II	Sen. Mgt.	Left the Coy
1975							
1976							
1977							
1978							
1979							
1980							
1981							
1982							
1983							
1984							

Plans

1985

1986

1987

Figure 3.1

46

country. Thereafter, a similar exercise needs to be carried out for the total group. These reviews may well address themselves to the individual details of the highest levels of management and to succession at that level. It will certainly give priority attention to a more 'aggregated' approach to management development planning; to reviewing the promotable management resources in the light of likely needs as determined by the age structure of the existing management, business plans to change the management establishment in the future, and best estimates of patterns of leaving. The kind of basic information appropriate to this exercise is set out in Figure 3.1. This should certainly be prepared in total for all functions and the same exercise can be carried out for specific functions.

On that single sheet can be found the signposts to most of the chief management development problems which will crop up over the next few years. From an informed review of the data will come the lead to provisional conclusions such as that:

1 there is a hump in the age distribution of senior executives and that those with potential to replace them (List III) are too few and, apparently, rather young;
2 the age distribution at the top (or at some other level) is such that, in combination with planned establishment reductions, there is going to be a shortage of promotion opportunities over the next five years, followed by a further five years of intense demand for replacements. How will the succession candidates be stimulated meanwhile? Or will they leave? Maybe someone should talk to them about it!

Once such problems have been identified, discussion must move to specifics and individuals. The review will have done the essential task of management development planning and drawn attention to a problem which, if nothing were done, is likely to creep up on the business.

Most large organisations regularly recruit graduates either straight from university or within a few years of graduating. The review just described will form the basis for deciding what the level of recruitment needs to be for the next few years. Such trainees are typically recruited with the intention that they should progress fairly rapidly through the ranks of junior management in their first 5/10 years in the business. Accordingly, it is useful to have the information in section B in Figure 3.1, which highlights the success in retaining and developing the recruits and gives a picture of how careers are actually experienced by those who join.

These overall reviews at higher levels will form the basis of plans for the coming period.

PLANNING OF INDIVIDUAL CAREERS

Some further comment is needed on what planning means in terms of the careers of individuals – something which is often misunderstood. Clearly, management development planning does not prescribe in detail the future advance of an individual's career. The development lists focus on how far an individual looks capable of progressing in five years, and it is also reasonable to forecast the kind of job, e.g. a specialist rather than a generalist, someone who will be in a line job rather than an adviser. It is right for the individual to know this information, although it needs to be communicated within clear indications of its limitations, in particular that any such forecast is dependent on continued performance in the job and, equally importantly, on the availability of appropriate jobs in the future.

The organisation also needs to think through typical career paths in the main functional areas, not to ensure that everyone's career slavishly follows the model, but to plan that the careers of most individuals will meet most of the requirements. This will ensure that those who progress to reach the most senior positions, particularly in general management, have passed through a range of the most appropriate experiences. The detail of such a model has to be worked out in every individual organisation, but a typical checklist could well be:

1 To cover the full range of responsibilities in his basic function. Thus, it could be appropriate to plan that engineers have experience not only on development and design but also the management of ongoing engineering departments, including maintenance, etc. Similarly, it might be decided that accountants should have experience of both financial management and management accounting; that personnel managers have experience of both industrial relations and also management development and pay.

2   To have operated in more than one environment, preferably at a reasonably early stage in a career. This means working either in a different market or a different country.
3   To actually have been 'in charge' with responsibility for 'hands on' management of a distinct part of the business. Few will have experience as general managers in an early part of their career, but it is important to ensure that careers do not continue permanently in headquarter organisations and that those of potential operate away from the company's base, perhaps running the accounts department or the engineering function at a distant site. Like riding a bicycle, this is something which has to be learnt in practice and preferably when young.

It will never be possible to ensure that all careers meet all the criteria but a regular analysis and the availability of the model as an objective can significantly raise the number of careers which meet most of the criteria. Without such a model the tendency could easily be to use people's experience in further jobs which only develop and further test the same capacities. There is a huge difference between *ten years' experience* and *the same years' experience ten times over*.

CONCLUSIONS

These are the elements in a management development planning system. It is a system in the sense that it is a series of regular tasks which highlight the shape of the present situation and point to potential problem areas. But how useful it is will depend on the use made of it – it will give no automatic answers. More than most planning systems, it will be a continuously rolling exercise, always a best updated forecast, always open ended, usually a bit untidy.

Three points are worth making in conclusion. The first is to re-state the importance of the middle levels which are the most elusive in the process of getting a grip on the development of managers. It is very difficult – but vital – to plan and influence careers between the 'bottom up' activities of recruitment and early training and the 'top down' plans for top level succession. One very experienced consultant who advised medium sized companies in this field once put it more caustically when he said he usually found that management development consisted of 'an interest in young men and a sort of mafia surrounding the chairman'. It is usually because they are concerned to get more order – or less disorder – into that middle ground that groups want to institute management development planning and it is by progress in that difficult area that it will in the end be judged.

The second point underlines a theme running through this paper – that the regular systems are valuable to point to a specific trend or problem. Accordingly, there will be frequent occasions when it is right to follow this up by setting up ad hoc exercises. A senior working group to study the high turnover of engineers or to look at the gap between well trained accountants and their ability to move on to financial director jobs between which there are many discontinuities in the skill requirements. Such exercises can, as well as coming up with a good answer, put the right political clout behind such programmes. The need to set up such ad hoc exercises is not a weakness of the regular system. The fact that the need for them is perceived is, in fact, the system's strength. It is also important that such one-off exercises do not get incorporated into the regular procedures involving continuing work long after it has ceased to be necessary.

The final point is the most important of all. It has been stressed that the planning systems must be seen as a support for, and only useful insofar as they support and contribute to, good decisions about actual people and their careers. This is a two-way relationship. The systems must usefully guide the individual appointments; in addition, the appointments must be seen to forward the overall objectives of the plan. There is also an even more important interaction and mutually supportive relationship with the organisational culture – those shared attitudes and values in respect of people and their development which exist in the organisation. The systems will be frustrated if the culture does not incorporate a belief that it is right – for the business – to regard longer term career development as important; and on occasions to make short term operational level sacrifices to that end. This will only come about if the systems make it reasonable to assume that such sacrifices are not in vain and, above all, that the systems bring benefits in terms of the availability of well developed people as well as demands for the release of others. It is such a culture which marks the company which has really integrated its management development planning into the running of the business.

FURTHER READING

The Institute of Personnel Management publish pamphlets on many of the individual activities in the field.

For a further and deeper treatment reference could usefully be made to:

Human Resource Planning, James W. Walker, McGraw-Hill, 1980.
The Manpower Planning Handbook, M. Bennison and J. Casson, (Institute of Manpower Studies), McGraw-Hill, 1984.

4

Diagnosing needs

Andrew Stewart

Managers often try to solve assessment or development problems by adopting new techniques. If those new techniques are seen not to be successful, the techniques are blamed as being ineffective. The fault more probably lies with an inadequate or non-existent diagnosis of the needs which the technique was trying to meet. If the problem is not properly defined, a solution is likely to be elusive.

This chapter is primarily concerned with the training and development needs of individuals and groups, but there is another set of needs which should be established before specific training and development needs are addressed. These needs have to do with the commercial or functional effectiveness of the organisation, and may be seen to exist at three levels.

At the strategic level the question is whether there are shortfalls in the performance of the organisation, now or in the future, which can properly be traced to ineffective performance on the part of some managers or employees. In addition, new developments in the market or customer base may create a demand for different ways of doing things which implies no criticism of current performance, but which will lead to difficulties if no change in approach occurs.

At the manpower planning level the question is whether the stocks and flows of people through and around the organisation are appropriate both to current needs and future trends. More importantly, perhaps, is the quality of individual concealed in the statistics such that the operation will be enhanced rather than held back for lack of talent?

At the individual level it is advisable to check whether there are people who are under-performing compared to expectation, and if so, why. They might have reached their level of incompetence, or they might simply be in the wrong job, or they might be perfectly capable of performing better with some developmental help.

These three levels of question are primarily concerned with the way in which the business of the organisation is being conducted, whether this be in the commercial style of private enterprise or in the service orientated style of the health service, local or national government. If it can be shown that the performance of individuals or groups is impacting the attainment of the organisation's declared objectives, then it may be worth while to probe training and development needs in some depth to establish what kinds of intervention are going to yield the best pay-off. This chapter is primarily concerned to present a range of techniques for probing those needs.

TYPES OF TECHNIQUE

Training needs analysis techniques can be classified in two distinct ways. There is a distinction between group techniques and individual techniques; and there is another distinction between deficiency and ideal based techniques.

Group techniques are particularly useful at a macro level, for strategic planning and for deciding training priorities. Individual techniques are designed to make accessible the training needs of single persons. Deficiency based techniques are aimed at discovering short-falls in current performance in order to design remedial action. Ideal based techniques are designed to achieve statements of what, in the best of all possible worlds, people should be doing, and then set out to help people to get closer to that ideal. The trainer needs to know about both the ideal and reality, but the order in which this is achieved may be determined by the diagnostic techniques used. Most of the techniques presented in this chapter can be used in either group or individual mode; only some of them can be used in ideal mode, but most of them can help to uncover deficiencies.

CRITICAL INCIDENT

In this technique, the interviewer selects a group of managers who are representative of the target population and asks them to talk about the most difficult problem they have had to deal with in the last period of time. This period can vary from around one week to not more than six months. Memory for detail will fade seriously after this time. Six weeks is often chosen as a period of time which will be meaningful to most people, and the starting question might be: 'Can you tell me about the incident in the last six weeks which has caused you the most difficulty?' Follow up questions might include:

when?	one-off problem or regular?
why?	your problem or someone else's?
who with?	what caused it?
at what cost?	will it happen again?
how was it solved?	any long term effects?

After a number of interviews have been conducted, it then becomes necessary to classify the information. Some categories which have emerged from the data include:

alone/other people involved
technical/financial/managerial
type of product/service involved
if other people involved, insiders/customers/suppliers/others
if other people involved, senior/peer/junior/other
producing new ideas/servicing old ideas
new problem/old problem

Although it is more difficult, it provides a more accurate reflection of the data if the interview content is allowed to dictate the categories into which it is sorted. In some other systems the interviewer comes with a prepared list of categories into which the data will be fitted. This seems to suggest that the content is already known, in which case it might be hard to justify the research.

Critical incident technique is fairly rough and ready, but will give fast information about priorities. For example, a service engineering organisation was putting about eighty per cent of its training effort into technical product training and twenty per cent into interpersonal skills. A critical incident survey showed that less than fifteen per cent of the problems were generated by the equipment, and that all the rest required customer handling skills. A rapid shift of priorities could then be seen to be justified, together with congratulations to the technical trainers who had clearly been doing a good job.

Critical incident interviews do carry an implied commitment to those interviewed that something is about to be done about their problems. If no tangible results appear within a relatively short time those interviewed may well feel let down. Some form of feedback and action should therefore be made apparent at the earliest opportunity.

SELF-REPORT QUESTIONNAIRES

In self-report questionnaires managers are asked fairly straight-forwardly what training they think they need. The manner of putting the question varies from providing a list of courses to tick to providing a list of skills to tick. Sometimes the managers are simply given a blank sheet of paper. The problems with this approach are that the managers may not know their own training needs, may not know enough about the training courses on offer, and may regard the questionnaire as just another piece of paper to be filled in and leave it in their in-tray or fill it in negligently.

Self-report questionnaires are more useful on the technical and financial sides than on interpersonal relationships. A good questionnaire begins by providing some background information and asks the respondents to refer to their year's objectives or to think of their most recent critical incident. Then it asks respondents to tick relevant courses or to tick the skills and knowledge they feel they lack. Some typical answers include:

management training	statistics
management of people	survey methodology
encouraging creativity	finance
joint problem solving	negotiating skills
problem definition	interviewing
management by objectives	technical updating
experimental design	influencing company policy

These answers are not condensed, except in the area of technical updating. They are a good example of the lack of detail which most self-report questionnaires yield. The technique is very frequently used, but cannot seriously be recommended.

STRUCTURED INTERVIEWS

In a structured interview the trainer visits a number of managers with a standard list of prepared questions which it is hoped will throw light on their training needs. Clearly the questions will vary from company to company and from situation to situation, but once the list is prepared it should remain constant across all interviews, otherwise any differences that appear between interviewees may be due to the questions they have been asked rather than to any real differences. An example of one set of questions follows:

1 What sorts of things in your job give you most satisfaction?
2 What changes would be needed to make your job more effective? Who could make these changes?
3 What sorts of activities take up a lot of your time? Does this please you?
4 How far are you responsible for planning the way you use your time?
5 What proportion of your activities do you have no choice about?
6 Which aspects of your work interest you the most? Which the least?
7 Where is the work you do initiated?
8 Do you often come under pressure for quick results? Where does the pressure come from? How do you react?
9 How are your standards of performance set? By whom?
10 How do you get feedback on the results of your work?
11 How, and by whom, does the work you are doing get stopped?
12 How much public presentation of your work and your department's do you have to do?
13 Do you find yourself working very much in committees?
14 How much do you have to do with the data processing department?
15 Do you have much to do with unions or staff associations?
16 Do you find the job different from what you were expecting?

17 Has any job you have been involved with failed to reach completion because of lack of technical knowledge or skill on someone's part?

18 Have you any skills you feel are being inadequately used?

19 Where do you see your career going over the next year? Five years?

20 What training have you had? Do you remember any training as particularly useful, or useless? Why?

21 What training do you think you need, either that you know is already available or that you would like to see introduced?

22 What kind of person would you advise the organisation to recruit to replace you if you were to move on? What technical knowledge should they bring with them? What training and experience would you want them to be given in the first three months? What advice would you give them? What sort of mistakes do you think they would make at first?

Some questions will be more fruitful than others. Questions 9 and 10, for example, did not work with some technical/professional managers since they had not considered that setting standards of performance and organising feedback systems was a useful activity. For them, the technical job set its own, unique, non-negotiable standards of performance. In the case of a company legal department it was held to be unethical and an invasion of privacy to even attempt such a thing, since it implied that their legal qualifications were in some unequal one with another and did not represent the ultimate statement of legal competence! Questions 18 and 22 usually unleash a great deal of information, regardless of occupation.

The results should ideally be analysed independently by two or more people. In this way any classification which emerges has the added reliability of having been arrived at by two or more separate individuals, and is less likely to be influenced unduly by one strong set of values. Generalisation should wait until all the data have been sifted.

Structured interviews are usually better than self-report questionnaires for anything other than the most straightforward needs diagnosis, but they do take time. Only some of the questions will pay off, and it may be difficult to achieve standardised administration between two interviewers, or from the same interviewer on different days. Critical incident may yield more information faster, but carries a greater implied commitment to action.

DIARY METHOD

In this method those involved are asked to keep diaries which record their activities under a variety of headings. This record is then analysed to deduce the demands being made on the individual and the skills needed to do the job. This form of analysis moves away from the identification of deficiencies towards the description of actual performance and the deduction of ideal performance. This feature can help to obtain people's commitment to the work involved in making the record.

Diaries can be general — attempting to cover a whole range of potential needs — or highly specific when one or two needs are to be examined in depth. For example, a supervisor in a garment factory was asked to keep a diary to assist in the introduction of new procedures under the Health and Safety at Work Act. She was asked to place a tick in the appropriate space each time she had to deal with one of the following:

Workshop tidiness
    materials obstructing free passage
    made-up goods obstructing free passage
    dangerous goods stacked at unsafe heights
    personal belongings lying around
Machine maintenance
    machines being serviced with power on
    untrained people attempting to service machines
    unsafe parts not being properly disposed of
    machines left uncleaned
    operatives transferring machines without permission
    machines not being switched off during breaks
Personal
    long hair in danger of being caught
    smoking in prohibited areas
    liquid refreshment being passed around at work stations

shoes making foot controls difficult to operate
pregnant operatives lifting heavy weights

The supervisors ticked each item and used a code to show whether they had taken action themselves, told someone else to take action, or taken no action. They were not asked to state how long each incident had lasted or who else was involved.

Much fuller diaries have been sought in order to obtain a broad picture of the activities carried out by managers. In the example below, managers were asked to record the length of time spent in each activity, who else was involved, and the degree to which the activity was planned.

Activity: talking on the phone, with one other face to face, with more than one other face to face, and was the contact scheduled? Touring (inspecting the work place). Mail handling. Other paperwork. Lecturing. Travelling. Operational work.

Contact: alone, with boss, with secretary, with subordinates, with colleagues (i.e. peers reporting to the same boss), with peers (i.e. people of similar level not reporting to the same boss), other senior, other junior, external (specify), new contacts.

Interruptions: in own office, other (specify).

Nature of activity: crisis (drop everything to sort out), choice (need not have done that day), deadline (done for a definite time goal), new work (different from anything done before), recurrent tasks, urgent work, unexpected work.

In addition, mail in and mail out was analysed, and the whole was supported by a detailed questionnaire. Results were classified into choices, constraints, demands, and skills required.

In designing a diary the following sequence has proved useful:

1 Conduct a pilot investigation to determine the greatest areas of interest and whether they are general or specific to one or two skill areas.
2 Since the diary is intended to demonstrate the demands being made on the individual, some definition of the specific demands to be investigated should be made. Examples might include duration of activity, contact with others, amount of discretion in choosing the activities, need for information about the results of the activities.
3 Each of the desired categories is broken into codes − one for

type of activity, one for contacts, and so on. If the length of time spent in each activity is important, then an appropriate breakdown should be offered. It is important to make the job of completing the diary as easy as possible by using ticks or some other simple code rather than seeking substantive written information.

4   A questionnaire containing the diary is then assembled, together with a statement of its purpose and instructions on how to fill it in. This is first piloted on one or two friendly individuals, and then sent to a small but representative sample of those from whom the final responses are sought. At this stage, irrelevant questions can be removed and those that have been found difficult to answer can be modified. The method of analysis should be tried out at this stage as well.

5   The full set of questionnaires is sent out, the returns analysed, and a report prepared on the demands made on respondents, broken down into sub-groups if this is useful. Full discussion of these demands is then followed by decisions about the needs revealed and the early stages of planning to meet them.

Diary method can offer a complete and well-aimed account of the key areas of individuals' work and the support they need to do it. It can bring to light the dull, day-to-day training needs that few bother to look for, and it can provide an informative contrast between what really happens and the job description. It does, however, take time to set up and run, and some statistical skill to analyse. Respondents may resent the time taken to complete it, particularly if there is no space to record the time taken filling it in. There is also a slight danger of asking questions because they look nice rather than because they will yield useful information about how the job is being done. Despite the labour, diary method can be one of the richer sources of information about training and development needs in the organisation.

PERFORMANCE QUESTIONNAIRE

This technique is useful particularly at the interface between individual training needs analysis and organisation development. Having identified the level of individual whose training or development needs are to be investigated a questionnaire is designed which contains a series of bipolar statements describing, for example, managerial behaviour, with a five point scale between the poles. Some items from a group of senior managers in an international bank included:

Prefers to work in the field	....	Prefers to work in the office
Is better at relationship skills	....	Is better as a technician
Reacts	....	Anticipates
Prefers action	....	Prefers evaluation
Prefers the client to set priorities	....	Prefers the bank to set priorities
Would rather explain a situation	....	Would rather improve a situation
Knows when to cut losses	....	Does not know when to cut losses
More concerned with short-term (less than 2 years ahead)	....	More concerned with long-term (2 years or more ahead)

The questionnaire is distributed to managers of the position under consideration, and if possible to current occupants of the position and those of their colleagues who have a close working relationship with them. Each is asked to think of the most effective holder of the given job they know, or have working directly for them, and to describe him or her on the questionnaire anonymously. Both good and bad points should be allowed to emerge. When the completed questionnaires have been returned a second set is sent out. These are exactly the same as the first set, but the instructions now ask the respondents to think of the least effective holder of the given job they know. Anonymity is understandably even more important on this occasion. A simple statistical analysis of the comparisons between the two sets of returns will reveal which items discriminate between perceived effective and perceived ineffective performers. Other analyses will yield a list of items solely associated with effective behaviour, and a list of items solely associated with ineffective behaviour. The analysis involves no more than counting the number of times each response option is used for each question. There will be no particular pattern which emerges from some questions, and they may be discarded. In other cases there may be a clear pattern. For example, take the item:

Reacts .... Anticipates

Suppose that fifty people have responded to both the first (effective) and the second (ineffective) administration of the questionnaire. The results might look as follows:

(1st administration) Reacts   0 0 5 15 30 Anticipates
(2nd administration) Reacts 20 25 0 5 0 Anticipates

The results are now weighted to reflect the extremity of view expressed. Thus the frequencies in the outside two columns are multiplied by 3; the frequencies in the next two columns are multiplied by 2; the centre column remains unaltered. The results now look as follows:

(1st administration) Reacts   0 0 5 30 90 Anticipates
(2nd administration) Reacts 60 50 0 10 0 Anticipates

The difference between the results of the first (effective) administration and the second (ineffective) administration are clear. The maximum frequency for the first set appears at the extreme righthand side; for the second set at the extreme lefthand side. There is a clear picture of effectiveness in that virtually all votes went for anticipation; there is a clear picture of ineffectiveness in that the great majority of votes went for reaction. An unclear result is obtained when the votes are spread fairly evenly across all five options. (A more detailed account of this procedure will be found in Stewart & Stewart, 1981).[1] The analysis of results thus yields the material from which a pen picture can be constructed, both of the effective and the ineffective holder of the position. In this way both information about behaviour for development and behaviour to be avoided or trained out can be obtained.

The items which make up the performance questionnaire can be brainstormed or produced by selective interviewing, but the best method seems to be to conduct a short series of repertory grid interviews, which will yield results already in bipolar format. This method is discussed later in this chapter. The performance questionnaire has the advantages that the information has been generated directly by those who are likely to be involved in any action for change that may follow, and concerns real people and real events. It therefore provides a good basis for asking whether the characteristics revealed should be perpetuated or changed. It also tends to generate information of a kind which is directly observable and amenable to change rather than personality statements which make for difficulty in observation and may not be possible or proper to try to change. The main drawbacks are that it requires that there be at least thirty, and preferably fifty, respondents for the statistics to be reliable, and it is therefore unlikely to be of use to very small organisations or at the top layer of any organisation, unless great care is taken not to try to generalise the results beyond the immediate group surveyed. Further, if the questionnaire is not couched in terms which are in the language and culture of the people responding, and if they are not asked to respond about real people, the result will be a poor response rate and resort to 'ideal' types. This in turn leads to unrealistic or inappropriate statements of needs.

CONTENT ANALYSIS

This technique presents the analyst with an unusual opportunity to conduct a diagnosis of training or development needs which does not impinge directly on those being investigated. This non-reactive research depends on obtaining access to written records of various kinds, and going through them systematically to extract training needs. It is possible to look for skills being exhibited, for deficiencies being shown, for demands being made, or for all three. It can be done on a group basis or for an individual. Since historical data are being used, no one in the field is being disturbed, nor will the information be faked for the occasion.

Sources of information for content analysis can include performance appraisal records, internal memoranda, letters to outside people (customers, suppliers, competitors), complaints, training literature, sales proposals, indeed almost any written material can prove a valuable source of information.

For example, despite the existence of an in-house written communication course, it was clear that the reports being produced by one particular research organisation were failing to meet their twin objectives of communicating the research and maintaining a high profile in the market place. It was agreed to undertake a content analysis of a range of reports recently produced. It was also, unusually, possible to gain access to previous drafts of the final reports, so that not only could the finished version be seen, but the contributions of the various reviewers along the way could also be reviewed and training needs extracted. The following were found, with a note of the frequency of occurrence after each:

Strategic errors

facts not distinguished from opinion	7
benefits not clearly stated	5
context missing (and needed)	4
purpose of report unclear	4
political implications of work missed	4
lack of awareness of readers' special needs	4
making statements that could easily be taken out of context and misused	3
claiming too much in the title	1

Grammar and syntax

'data', 'criteria', and 'media' used with a singular verb	21
subject not agreeing with verb	17
spelling mistakes	15
inappropriate use of bracket commas	14
misplaced apostrophe in possessive cases	14
misplaced qualifying clause	7
confusion between its and it's	5
use of jargon abbreviations without explanation	4
use of quotation marks to show emphasis only	2

Presentation errors

unreadable handwriting	5
tables too dense	5
terms not defined clearly	4
results given without mentioning sample size	3
paper, to be read verbatim, clearly too long for allocated time	2
different typestyles used on final document	2

Editing and management errors

paper too late for publication deadline	5

editor offers clarification; author responds with
    'I know what I meant'.   5

editor puts check mark instead of specifying what
    is not clear   4

editor, having asked for report, forgets why it
    was wanted   3

Two courses were set up as a result of this analysis. One replaced the existing report writing course, which clearly either made assumptions about basic competencies which were not justified in practice, or failed to meet its objective to teach them. The second course was specifically aimed at editing skills. This was partly because they were clearly needed, and partly because senior managers were flattered to be invited on to an editing course whereas they would be insulted by the implication that they needed help with writing skills. It is also worth mentioning that correspondence files were reviewed, revealing the fact that over fifty per cent of replies to external letters began with some variation on 'I am sorry for the delay in replying to your letter . . .' The improvement in style produced a dramatic change in the management of customer relations.

It may require some imagination to trace the places where information truly relevant to the diagnosis of training and development needs may be found, but because it is non-reactive, can be checked, uses historic and usually unfaked data, and can be fitted into odd time corners, content analysis is an attractive technique. New trainers can also be inducted into their jobs by offering them some content analysis in order to help them find their way round the organisation and some of its problems. However, care needs to be taken about breaching confidentiality, so that personal records should be used with considerable discretion, if at all. The day-to-day paperwork of the organisation will generate enough information for most needs.

BEHAVIOUR ANALYSIS

Behaviour analysis is a special case of content analysis in which people's actions and statements are categorised in a running analysis performed by themselves or the trainer. The behaviour of each individual, either alone or in a group, is monitored under a series of simple headings, and a checkmark made every time one of the listed behaviours occurs. The exact headings will vary with the area of need under investigation, but for a course in general interactive skills the following might be appropriate: proposing, supporting, building, disagreeing/criticising, seeking information, giving information. The trainer looks for the overall contribution level of each person (too high? too low?) and the relative importance of the various kinds of behaviour. Building behaviour is usually important in developing a cohesive team, so people low on this behaviour might need help to increase it. People with a high level of proposing and giving information might need help in learning to listen.

Using different categories of behaviour, some ratios can yield useful information. The ratio of caught proposals to escaped proposals (those that get some attention even if only rejection, and those that get none) can be useful when helping someone to get their ideas accepted. The ratio of bringing in to shutting out behaviour can be useful for developing teamwork skills. It is frequently observed, incidentally, that those who profess most vehemently the virtues of participative management are those who most seriously exhibit shutting out behaviour. The ratio of defending/attacking behaviour to admitting difficulty can demonstrate a person's way of coping with challenge. For help with committees and other groups operating to an acknowledged formal structure, the ratio of backtracking to jumping the gun behaviour can be useful in helping control and to distinguish between (a) going over old ground or (b) against leaping ahead to matters that are not yet ready to be dealt with. Feedback of the ratios, together with charting of changes in the ratios as the training progresses can provide both an elegant diagnosis and a direct measure of change in the one package.

A full account of the use of behaviour analysis in training will be found in Rackham and Morgan (1977).[2] To make the most effective use of behaviour analysis, simple category systems should be used with very few assumptions about what right and wrong behaviour look like. Value judgements occurring too early will impede flexibility of style and accuracy of self-analysis. More than one person should be observing, and the results should be checked against one another frequently. Feedback should be given early and often, as soon as the observations can be shown to be reliable. It should then be possible to depart in a controlled manner from the original training programme to address new needs as they emerge.

TESTS AND QUIZZES

One simple way of assessing training needs is to ask people questions and discover how many right answers they give. In technical areas this is a useful and neglected approach to analysing training and development needs.

For example, as part of the diagnosis of training needs of personnel managers, questions could be asked along the following lines:

1 How many warnings must an unsatisfactory performer be given before dismissal?
2 How long must a woman have worked for an employer before she is entitled to maternity leave?
3 Give two examples of conditions of employment that might be construed as indirect discrimination against women.
4 Joe has been on the hourly paid staff for five years and four months. How much notice is he entitled to should we wish to dismiss him?
5 Consider the following list of our suppliers. Tick those that operate a closed shop agreement. Name the main unions recognised by each of them.
6 On average, how long must a newly recruited salesman stay with the company before the cost of recruiting and training him or her is recovered?
7 An executive aged 55 dies while in our employment. His salary was £16,500 plus £1,500 profit sharing last year. What is the payment due to his widow?

It is not difficult to see how this kind of exercise can serve as a diagnosis of training needs, especially if it is self-scored and used from time to time as a progress check, perhaps involving a parallel form version at the end of whatever remedial work takes place.

In order for this approach to work the quiz constructor requires a clear idea of the ground the training needs analysis must cover and of the objectives of any course to which it is linked. The more open the question the more difficult it will be to score. Interactive skills are less amenable to this approach, since questions which pose a hypothetical situation and then ask 'what would you do?' tend to receive answers of the kind that the respondent thinks are required rather than necessarily a genuine response. To make matters more complicated, the respondent may not know that he is doing this. Where factual information is concerned, therefore, the quiz can perform a valuable role; where interactive skills or matters of opinion are involved it is less effective and may be misleading.

PSYCHOLOGICAL TESTS

There is a mythology about psychological tests which it might be useful to dispel. A test is no more than a conversation, frozen into a standard form so that as near as possible the identical conversation is held with everyone who enters the situation. In this way any differences which are detected between individuals are likely to be genuine differences and are not caused by differences in treatment. That is all. The rest is merely technology to try to ensure that the things work.

Tests are designed to provide answers to three levels of question. The more interesting the answer, the more difficult it is to provide. At the lowest level, tests provide answers to the question 'Has this person actually done/learnt what he claims to have done/learnt?' These are the achievement tests.

At the next level, tests provide an answer to the question 'Could this person do the thing we want him to if we gave him the task and trained him?' He has not done it yet, and has no relevant track record. These are ability and aptitude tests. Finally, there are tests which try to answer the question 'If we gave him this to do, would he choose to do it?' These are personality and attitude tests. They yield the most interesting answers, and are the most difficult to construct, administer and interpret.

Achievement tests will indicate at once whether there is a training need. Ability and aptitude tests will give an indication of whether the person has the brains or inclination to learn what has to be learnt. Personality and attitude tests (or, more properly, questionnaires, since there are no hard and fast right answers) may help to decide what likelihood there is that any training, development or appointment to a position may be successful.

Achievement tests are simple to score in that the person either produces a performance (typing speed, colour vision acuity, etc.) of the kind claimed, or they do not. Ability tests are fairly straight-forward in that a person achieves a score which can be compared with that achieved by other people, and conclusions can be drawn about the probability of his ability to do the job. Perhaps for reasons of self-flattery, the level of ability judged necessary to perform many jobs is over-estimated. Personality questionnaires represent a quite different order of difficulty in interpreting. A questionnaire will permit some form of classification of an individual into a particular personality type. This enables the interpreter to say that some occupations will be more congenial than others, or that there may be a preference to tackle situations in one way rather than in another. But there are no absolutely right or wrong answers. There are simply new pieces of technical information upon which an individual or a manager has to make some judgements.

Tests and questionnaires are very high profile techniques and are easy to challenge. It is both technically proper and tactically wise to ensure that the instruments used are properly validated for the kind of people upon whom it is intended that they are to be used. Such tests should have fairly bulky manuals containing a wide range of statistical information about both reliability and validity over a number of different groups of people. Instruments which cannot offer this information, and whose proponents are making no systematic effort to produce such information, should be avoided. The best indicator of all is how easy it is to obtain access to the instrument. If it is freely available for a fee or licence, then it may not meet the necessary standard. If, on the other hand, the supplier insists that the potential user shows evidence of being qualified to use such an instrument, then it may be worth considering.

REPERTORY GRID

Most kinds of interview carry with them the danger that the results will be contaminated in some way by the views of the interviewer. The repertory grid approach is designed to go some way towards preventing this. A grid interview begins with the selection of the topics for discussion, called elements. These are concepts, items, people or behaviours representative of the area of interest. Examples of element lists might include:

1 accidents to discover the training needs of a safety officer;
2 brand names of competing products or services to discover the training needs of a marketing manager, or indeed some of the marketing needs of the organisation;
3 names of managers occupying the level potential for which replacements are ultimately to be sought lower down the organisation;
4 job activities undertaken by those managers.

Eight or nine elements is usually enough, although it is possible to use the technique with as few as three elements.

The interviewer checks that the interviewee is reasonably familiar with the elements on the list. Then the elements are taken, three at a time, and the interviewee is asked: 'Can you tell me some ways in which any two of these elements seem like each other to you, but different from the third?' If managers' names have been used, the interviewee might say that two of them are usually to be found in the field while the third is normally in his office. Another two might be thought to be approachable while the third was difficult to get to know. Yet another two might be described as fast workers while the third is thorough. Each of these bipolar distinctions is called a construct. It is the constructs which yield the information that is sought in a needs diagnosis.

By constant repetition of the process, long lists of constructs can be obtained. The interviewee is then asked to go back over his or her list and to indicate which end of each construct is their preferred choice for effectiveness as a manager, or as an attractive feature of a product or service, or as having importance for a safety officer to deal with. At the end of such discussions with a number of interviewees, the interviewer will have accumulated lists of constructs with value judgements indicated by most of them. It is then possible to group the results in such a way as to produce a pen-picture of the kind generated by other techniques. It is also possible to translate the bipolar constructs quite directly into bipolar items for a performance questionnaire. Note that the interviewer contributes no content at all, but merely guides the process along set lines.

This technique can be used to accumulate data from a range of people, or it can be used to interview a very few exhaustively. Only construct elicitation has been described; to go on to a full grid requires some more steps in the logic, and may not always be a cost effective approach for diagnostic purposes. Construct elicitation will often suffice. A fuller discussion of repertory grid and its uses in business will be found in Stewart & Stewart (1981). [3]

CONCLUSION

A number of techniques for diagnosing training and development needs have been presented in this chapter. They have in common that they are intended to provide a statement of what people could do better, expressed in measurable terms. The depth to which it is thought worth while to probe, the type of need to be investigated, and the breadth of coverage intended all influence the choice of diagnostic technique. The better the diagnosis, the easier it is to design the subsequent evaluation of the training or development, since the measures will already have been suggested. It has been indicated that desired behaviours and performance should be considered first, then translated into training needs afterwards. Care should be taken not to present needs that are beyond reasonable efforts to accomplish. Prospective trainees should participate in the diagnosis and not have the results suddenly thrust upon them.

Finally, attention might well be given to something strangely seldom addressed when training needs are being considered – the preferred learning style of the individual about to be trained or developed. Honey & Mumford (1982)[4] have developed a simple instrument to enable an individual to detect his or her preferred learning style: activist, reflector, theorist or pragmatist. Most people have elements of all four in their approach, but one or two are likely to predominate, and it is possible for training or development to be designed to take account of the learner's preferred style of acquiring information or skill. It seems unwise to spend a great deal of time and effort in diagnosing training or development needs if no effort is put in to making the subsequent experience 'user friendly'.

REFERENCES

(1) Stewart, A. and Stewart, V., *Tomorrow's Managers Today*, Institute of Personnel Management, 1981.
(2) Rackham, N. and Morgan, T., *Behaviour Analysis in Training*, McGraw-Hill, 1977.
(3) Stewart, V. and Stewart. A., *Business Applications of Repertory Grid*, McGraw-Hill, 1981.
(4) Honey, P. and Mumford, A., *Manual of Learning Styles*, Honey, 1982.

FURTHER READING

Guion, R. M., *Personnel Testing*, McGraw-Hill, 1981.
Miller, K. M., *Psychological Tests in Personnel Assessment*, Gower, 1975.
Stewart, R., *Choices for the Manager*, McGraw-Hill, 1982.
Stewart, V. and Stewart, A., *Managing the Manager's Growth*, Gower, 1978.

5

Performance appraisal

Andrew Stewart

A great deal has been written about performance appraisal. A great deal more has been said. It is odd that, despite all this attention, so few organisations say that they are satisfied with their particular way of conducting appraisals of employee performance. It is all the more strange since the task is, in principle, very straightforward. Two people, one the manager and one the managed, sit down together perhaps once during the year, in order to find answers to the following four questions:

What did we set out to achieve during the year?
Have we achieved it?
What are we going to do next?
How will we know if we have done it?

Anything more elaborate than the above could be said to be complicating a simple matter more than it merits and to the confusion of all concerned. This chapter presents some of the approaches that have been adopted to trying to obtain satisfactory answers to those four questions.

First, some of the more usual varieties of appraisal system will be described, together with a discussion of the performance criteria associated with them. Some comments will be offered about system design, and this will be followed by an account of some of the ways in which organisations try to train their managers to use their systems. Ways in which systems can be monitored and controlled will be presented, and then two further issues will be explored which often cause difficulty: assessing potential, and problem performers. Some future trends will also be discussed. Finally, there will be a simple checklist to help managers to ensure that all the necessary steps towards a successful performance appraisal interview have been carried out.

VARIETIES OF SYSTEM

People do not learn unless they are given feedback on the results of their actions. For learning to take place, feedback must be both regular and frequent, should register both successes and failures, and should follow soon after the relevant actions. In the daily rush of getting things done, much of this can be forgotten or not put into effect. Performance appraisal schemes give people the chance to learn how they are doing, to correct their mistakes and to acquire new skills. Since manager and appraisee are together reviewing past performance and planning to meet the needs of the future, it should follow that some of the necessary conditions for the successful management of change are also being met. A performance appraisal scheme can also offer the opportunity to consider and agree longer range targets for achievement, thus making positive growth more likely for the organisation, and avoiding the trap of doing nothing more than daily firefighting. Finally, since employees are expensive, it makes sense to try to encourage their best efforts. A performance appraisal interview can be one of the most motivating events in an employee's year. Badly handled, it can be a disaster.

There are usually four parties to an appraisal: the appraisee, the appraiser, the central planning and personnel departments, and external bodies such as training boards, trade unions and bodies set up in the interests of equal opportunity legislation. The interests of the first two parties should dominate. If the main focus is either planning or defence, then the chief objective of the exercise may be lost.

Appraisal systems may be used for three main purposes: remedial, maintenance and development. A system should have a mix of all three. Systems become out of balance if any one purpose predominates. If the remedial purpose is foremost, then the appraisal interview may become a disciplinary interview, and the form a charge sheet. If maintenance is the main objective, then the process can become a short, skimped, unthoughtful ritual. If there is too much emphasis on development, then the focus falls on the next job rather than the one presently in hand, and the interview may be construed as a promise of future progress.

Above all, the appraisal interview is a time for listening. The appraisee probably has a good idea of how his performance appears to him, and this is unlikely to be badly at variance with his manager's view. Indeed, there is some evidence that an appraisee is likely to be harder on himself than his manager intends to be.

Many variations in appraisal systems have been tried in order to support the basic purpose of looking backwards in order to look forward. The chief ones appear to be:

1 Eligibility: all staff, or managers and salaried staff only
2 Appraiser: immediate line manager, technical specialist, personnel specialist, 'grandfather' or grandmother (manager's manager)
3 Employee access: employee sees all the form, some of the form, or none of the form
4 Self-appraisal or preparation for counselling form used, or not used
5 Past performance only, or past and present performance measured
6 Measurement against: performance targets or objectives, rating scales of performance, rating scales of personality, or no measurement criteria specified
7 Rating scales: present or absent, together with variation in the number of divisions on the scale
8 Opportunity to set targets for future performance, or not
9 Discussion of training and development needs: for present job, for next job, or for longer term
10 Potential rated: on a one-dimensional scale, a multi-dimensional scale, or no formal rating of potential

11 Discussion of salary: forbidden, mandatory, or optional
12 Frequency and regularity of appraisal interviews
13 Disputes: resolved by appeal to grandfather, or personnel, or no procedure
14 Who may see the appraisal forms, and for what purpose
15 Use of forms for central planning purposes
16 Use of forms for day-to-day management and coaching purposes.

Each of these variations is held to be helpful by different practitioners, depending on the circumstances in which they are working. It is not possible to offer a single best method, merely a selection from which a choice may be made. The area which seems to cause the most anxiety, however, is the link with salary.

If salary is seen as compensation for work done, then perhaps the link with performance is more tenuous. If salary is used as an incentive, to reward outstanding work and to encourage rising standards, then some form of link seems inevitable. If salary review and performance appraisal occur at the same time, there may be a tendency to drift the rating unjustifiably upwards in order to be able to offer a satisfactory increase. One way to prevent this is to have both performance and salary rated on the same scale and in the same way, but to have the events occur six months apart. In this way all concerned understand the system, but managers have the freedom to vary the salary rating if the employee's performance has either improved or worsened since the performance review.

PERFORMANCE CRITERIA

In order to be satisfactory, both to those directly involved and to the law, the criteria for a performance appraisal system should be genuinely related to success or failure in the job, and should be as far as possible amenable to objective, not subjective, judgement. In addition, it is helpful if they are easy for the manager to administer, appear fair and relevant to the employee, and strike a fair balance between sensitivity to the needs of the present job and applicability to the company as a whole.

Most appraisal systems offer some guidance to appraising managers on the way they should measure performance. There are two major kinds of measure: personality measures and performance measures.

Personality measures have largely fallen into disuse. They are difficult to apply reliably, depend too much on the quality of personal relationships rather than employee performance, and if the employee is judged deficient on a personality measure there may be little incentive or ability to change. Their use is now generally discouraged.

Performance measures have replaced personality measures in most cases. They have two main forms. There are rating scales which are generally printed on the form and held to apply to all employees. There are objectives, which are an individual performance measure, agreed between manager and employee. Rating scales allow the measurement of change in one employee over time. They also allow comparisons between employees. They are therefore necessary if the appraisal records are to be used for any kind of central manpower audit, leading to the planning of salaries, careers or succession. They have the disadvantage that not all scales may be equally applicable to all employees, and that managers may not share similar standards in the use of the scales. Objectives give greater freedom to both manager and employee in deciding how performance will be measured. They may also have a greater motivational effect by demanding that standards be discussed and understood by manager and employee, whereas rating scales can be imposed without the opportunity for understanding. The disadvantage of objectives is that no common yardstick may exist between different appraisers and appraisees. It may be possible and desirable to have both rating scales and objectives in one system.

Personality measures might include such items as drive, loyalty or integrity. Performance measures might include accuracy, clarity, analytical ability. Objectives might include 'sell x widgets by y date to z customers'. Clearly these measures are offered in increasing order of precision. Some systems have aimed at the maximum precision at the expense of measuring what is important but not easily quantifiable. Under these circumstances, a qualitative measure, the meaning of which is clear to both parties to the interview, is probably preferable to a quantitative measure which assesses with great accuracy something which is not important.

The derivation of performance criteria demands research. A specification for the universally effective employee does not seem likely to be a realistic target. Each organisation should evolve its own performance measures, and should monitor them continuously to ensure their relevance. The needs of organisations and individuals change. If the performance criteria do not change as well, preferably a little ahead of the need, then the appraisal system will serve no useful purpose, and may even do damage by insisting on performance measures which no longer relate to the work in hand. A variety of methods for establishing performance criteria will be found in the chapter on diagnosing needs.

SYSTEM DESIGN

Each of the four main parties to an appraisal has different but overlapping purposes, all of which have implications for system design.

The appraisee will wish to make a contribution to the appraisal process, which implies a face-to-face interview. If acceptance of the appraiser's evaluation is to be indicated, or at least evidence that the appraisee has seen the comments is required, then the appraisee may need to sign the form at the end of the interview. If there is to be an opportunity for long-term guidance, then the system will need to provide for planning or objective setting for the future, together with discussion of ambitions, training needs, and abilities not yet evidenced in the work currently being done. If appraisal is to be used for self-development, then goals will need to be agreed during the interview, some variety of preparation for counselling form might be helpful, written objectives should be retained by both manager and appraisee, and there should be further mini-appraisals during the year.

The appraiser will want the employee to work to agreed goals, which implies the setting and recording of objectives and personal goals. These goals may need co-ordinating with those of other employees, which will require control over the timing of appraisals from the top of the organisation downwards, with the minimum time lag possible between appraisals at top and bottom, and fairly close co-ordination and control of appraisals from the centre. Coaching the employee will require the setting of specific performance targets, as much as possible suggested by the employee, including both targets and measures, and both parties will need to keep records and use them for frequent and regular reviews. To encourage the appraiser to listen to the employee, a preparation for counselling form should be strongly encouraged, and the appraiser may wish to record the employee's comments separately, possibly for later integration. In order to make the early detection of problems more likely, general, open-ended questions should be used concerning aspirations, unused skills, constraints on performance and other self rating techniques. The preparation for counselling form can be a vital aid here, as can the need for the grandfather to sign-off the appraisal form before the interview takes place. In this way it is also possible to achieve some measure of equity between employees. The management information system can also be used to detect broken trends or unusual patterns if rating scales are being used. If the training of subordinates is to be controlled, then there needs to be a record of both training needs and the extent to which they are being met. If money is being used as compensation, then a salary increase may be communicated at the appraisal interview, since pay and performance are not directly linked. If money is being used as an incentive, then it is suggested that the salary review should be a separate but related exercise.

Central planning and control may have a wide range of purposes, but some of the most common are mentioned here. A manpower skills audit will require that there are some common performance criteria across all employees, and that there be central collation of measures on these criteria. For manpower planning purposes the form may need to record not only the employee's performance as measured on required characteristics, but also information about age, job history, mobility, family circumstances. Succession planning also requires that some form of assessment of employee potential takes place, as objectively as possible, and that information about employee aspirations, judged suitability, and current performance is co-ordinated. Salary planning may require that the manager gives an overall performance rating across all characteristics, and central collation will be necessary, either with or without intervention to produce conformity to agreed norms. A record of training needs will be needed if overall decisions about training priorities are to be taken on an informed basis. Equity between employees can be monitored by defining and communicating the scope of the scheme to all concerned, by grandfather signing-off appraisal ratings, by central monitoring of both quality and promptness of appraisals, and by a formal system for handling unsatisfactory performers. Problem and grievance detection and handling becomes easier if the employee signs-off the completed form, if the employee is invited to comment on the form, if grandfather or central personnel have the power to intervene in critical situations, and if there is a formally defined and agreed procedure for improving the performance of those judged to be unsatisfactory, followed by a declared system for asking them to leave the organisation. Finally, downward transmission of organisation objectives can be achieved by centrally co-ordinated cascading of appraisals, so that no manager is put into the position of having to agree objectives with a subordinate in the absence of their own agreed objectives.

Outside parties can also have interests which impinge on the appraisal system. Industry training boards may lay down requirements for schemes, compliance with which offers levy exemption. Local, industry or national codes of good practice can usually be adhered to by ensuring that the performance criteria are relevant to the job, that no group of employees is given special treatment, and that appropriate guidance is offered on the use of appraisals with poor performers. Pay restraint has been a feature of many political programmes in the recent past. In this case, the system needs to ensure that both immediate parties to the appraisal understand clearly the restrictions on the manager's discretion, and increased use needs to be made of the remaining motivational characteristics of appraisal. Finally, privacy or right of access legislation may require that forms be designed so that the employee can see the whole form, adequate safeguards are in place against misleading interpretation – such as employee sign-off and comment space, a formal grievance procedure is in place, and there is a clear policy about who has access to appraisal data and for what purposes, together with location and duration of storage of records. This is now a particularly sensitive area where any part of the records are stored in a computer.

Rather than approaching this set of problems in terms of the various purposes of the parties involved, it is very common to spend much time and effort designing the paperwork. Given the strong arguments sometimes put forward for a blank piece of paper being the ideal appraisal form, some of this enthusiasm may be misplaced. Assuming, however, that the purposes have been thoroughly investigated, certain specifics then need clarification. If individual objectives are to form the core of the process, then a common form is simply a blank piece of paper divided down the middle, with objectives on the left hand side and standards of performance on the right. It is important to offer some guidance so that managers do not try to set too many objectives, try to set objectives to cover the whole job, or only set as objectives those things that can be measured quantitatively.

If narrative summaries are to be used, then the form will contain a list of key words, such as accuracy, speed, cash control, or timing, and the manager will be asked to write a two-line summary of the employee's performance on each of these characteristics. This method has the advantage that it does apply common yardsticks across large groups of people, but does not demand undue precision. Differences may occur in the way in which individual managers interpret and judge these characteristics, however.

Rating scales require that the appraisee is rated on each characteristic, using a scale with a number of divisions. While useful, rating scales carry some issues which need resolution. There is no point in offering more than five divisions on the scale. Scales with seven, nine, or even thirteen points have been seen. Managers tend to use them as if they were slightly vague five point scales. There is often dispute about whether there should be an odd or even number of points on the scale. It is possible to avoid this discussion entirely in the following way. Label the points on the scale, avoiding the use of the word average, so that the first four are concerned with above the line performance and only the fifth records below the line work. For example:

Exceeds in all respects
Exceeds in most respects
Exceeds in some respects
Meets basic requirements
Fails to meet basic requirements

In this way, ratings are being made against the requirements of the job and not against colleagues, and the scale can be described either as a five point scale, or as a four point scale with an extra box for the unsatisfactory performer. It can also be helpful to offer a separate 'not applicable' box. Any overall rating should follow the separate rating scales, preferably at a distance. It might also be useful to consider a separate column to record immediate past performance. This emphasises the fact that the appraisal is supposed to be a review of the entire previous year, and allows any recent changes in performance to be noted without unduly affecting the rest of the year's evaluation.

Perhaps the most important consideration in system design is to ensure that the system responds to the developing needs of all those using it, and to avoid the situation in which an entrenched system dictates inappropriate behaviour by those upon whom it is inflicted.

TRAINING

Appraisal training falls into three parts. They need to be kept distinct and to be carried out in the sequence shown, otherwise confusion and ineffective implementation are almost certain. The first stage involves obtaining managers' commitment. The second stage trains them in the formal systems and procedures. The third stage trains them in the necessary interview and interpersonal skills.

Commitment is best obtained by holding a series of meetings at which all those who will be affected by the system have an opportunity to hear what is being proposed and to discuss it. It may be helpful to lobby one or two key managers in advance; there should be a clear statement about the purposes of the appraisal system, there should be a readiness to negotiate about system design, but it is better to avoid being side-tracked into form design. This should follow as simply as possible from the agreement of purposes. It may also help to de-emphasise the judgemental role of the appraiser and to stress the benefits that employees will gain from being appraised – in other words, help them discover what they will be able to do as a result of appraisal which would otherwise have been difficult or unlikely. If no such benefits are apparent, the value of the system as proposed must be questioned.

Training in the systems and procedures should only occur after commitment has been obtained, otherwise much time will be consumed trying to answer the question 'why' when the training is designed to answer the question 'what'. This stage of the training should include the history of the appraisal system and the organisational problems it is supposed to solve, what actually happens in the interview, how the form is filled in, when, and by whom, who receives the form, what happens to the information, and whose responsibility it is to see that actions recommended on the form are actually carried out. Special emphasis should be given to ensuring that managers understand the grievance and poor performer procedures. Practice in handling and completing forms should be offered, together with the opportunity to criticise and spot mistakes in forms already completed. This stage of the training would respond well to some form of programmed instruction, either in text form or on a computer.

Training in skills depends on successful completion of the previous two stages. Otherwise disruption is highly likely. Three training techniques may be worth considering.

Role play is used automatically by many trainers. It can have many drawbacks, including the passivity of most of the audience and the fact that participants can always opt out by stating, correctly, that it is not real life. Poorly chosen role plays can compound these difficulties. Role play can be useful, however, particularly where attitude change is important. Trainees can be asked to play the part of someone whose attitude they need to understand, such as someone passed over for promotion. They can also be useful in unfreezing people by trying on a completely new appraisal personality.

Real life counselling involves one participant counselling another about a genuine work or personal problem, while the remaining participants observe. This certainly lacks the artificiality of role plays, but can get a little sharp. For this reason, perhaps, it is generally a better vehicle for learning counselling skills than the normal role play.

Live appraisal of real tasks involves the following sequence:

1 a participant performs an appraisable activity while the remainder of the small group observe;
2 all prepare to appraise the volunteer, who prepares to be appraised;
3 one person then appraises while the rest observe;
4 all prepare to appraise the appraisal, while the appraiser prepares to be appraised;
5 one person then appraises the appraisal, while the rest observe.

This module can be repeated as often as necessary, and concludes with a general review. The exact nature of the kick-off task is relatively unimportant, so long as there is enough to appraise. Subsequent appraisals quickly become surprisingly real, and the whole approach can be highly successful at making apparent issues of objectives, standards and measurement. Rich feedback is essential, and should be as accurate as possible, backed perhaps by video recording the entire episode. Objective matters should predominate, such as the balance of talking at various points of the interview, the amount of time devoted to extremes of performance versus the amount of time used to talk about the regular performance, the use of open and closed questions, and the amount of positive versus negative feedback offered.

An interesting variant is to offer training in being appraised. This has worked particularly well where managers have been reluctant to appraise or to be trained. The prospect of their subordinates being better equipped than they are has sometimes led to both appraiser and appraisee being better equipped to fulfil their roles.

The most common issues arising in the skills training stage include:

1 knowing one's own biases;
2 being prepared to discuss both good and poor performance in a straightforward manner;
3 using open, closed or reflective questions;
4 handling conflict;
5 listening and summarising skills.

The most common pitfalls encountered in appraisal, which therefore require to be looked at in training include:

1 the halo effect;
2 avoiding extremes of rating;
3 talking too much;
4 failing to support opinions with evidence;
5 inadequate briefing of the appraisee;
6 pre-judging performance;
7 not allowing adequate time for the interview;
8 choosing the right environment;
9 basing assessments on feelings rather than facts;
10 over-stating weaknesses or strengths;
11 failing to take account of special circumstances;

12   basing judgements on too short a time span;
13   making false assumptions.

Understandably, looking at that list, skills training can be a fairly intense experience which has benefits well beyond the immediate task of the appraisal interview.

MONITORING AND CONTROL

All appraisal systems need constant monitoring, and from time to time they need alteration of some kind. In the early implementation of a system the designer should look out for two main kinds of misunderstanding.

Misunderstanding of terms may occur, particularly such common ones as objective, job description, man specification, training needs, development needs, counselling, personality, performance and behaviour. These may well be familiar to trainers and management developers, but many line managers have no real idea of what is meant by them, or may have developed some eccentric definitions.

Misunderstanding the system will be shown by forms going to the wrong place or being filled in late, inadequate coverage of certain employees or groups, peculiar use of rating scales, or partial completion of the forms.

Later on, as part of a more general research programme, some other types of monitoring may seem possible and appropriate. Appraisal action may be checked by following up the actions recommended on the appraisal forms to see if anything has actually happened as a result. The types of objectives set can also be reviewed as part of this process. Appraisal predictions, particularly of potential, can be checked to see if they are actually proved to be correct in practice. Employee attitudes can be checked, either with a purpose-designed survey or as part of a larger attitude survey. Examples of some items that have proved significant indicators of effective interviews in the past include:

I had a clear idea of his/her career path
He/she and I had the same idea about the direction of his/her career

My manager agreed with my rating
My rating came as no surprise to him/her
She/he accepted my rating of her/him
My manager agreed with my rating of her/him
She/he fitted in with the rest of the work group
We wanted the same outcome from the interview
I could visualise him/her as my manager some day

Whether the interview was conducted in the office or outside, and whether the manager had selected the employee for the job initially or not, were not significantly related to the effectiveness of the interview.

As any survey of employee options will increase their expectations, there should be a policy about feedback of results, a method of feeding back locally useful results fast, and a commitment by top management to action should the results indicate a need for change.

IDENTIFYING POTENTIAL

Performance appraisal is designed to look backwards in order to look forwards. The best predictions of potential, using performance appraisal as the basis, are made when the next job is not greatly different from the previous one. The greater the proportion of new demands, the less likely that track record alone will suffice. Performance appraisal seems to be essential but insufficient as predictor of future performance.

Objections to the use of performance appraisal records for the prediction of potential include the following. Single-scale measures of potential, such as most systems still use, are too simple to permit a full statement of what the employee may be able to do. Although supported with words, it is the number that goes into the manpower planning system. In addition, a statement of the kind 'ready for next move in x months/years', if seen by the employee, can be construed as a promise. Managers' confidence in their ability to make ratings of potential is usually very low, and they are very rarely trained in using the potential assessment part of the form. Thus they receive the least support at precisely the point where they feel they most need it. Managers find it difficult to assess potential for positions much above their own or in parts of the organisation with which they are not familiar. Promotion solely on the basis of past performance almost inevitably leads to promotion to the person's level of incompetence. Discontinuities in the system will occur, where past performance is a particularly poor indicator of success in the next job, for example, the first move from a non-management to a management position.

Poor performers who are in the wrong job are difficult for the system to detect. For them, appraising potential on the basis of past performance is doubly unfair. Finally, in the absence of experience, the appraisee has no basis for judging whether the post under consideration would appeal to them. The more people know about the job for which they are being considered, the more likely it is that they will succeed in it.

There are many alternatives and additions available to performance appraisal as a means of identifying potential. These include assessment centres, psychological tests, assignments, secondments, peer and self assessment and action learning programmes. Ideally, ratings of potential should involve the use of more than one criterion or trait, more than one assessor, and more than one technique. In this way a more reliable judgement may be reached.

If the performance appraisal system is to play a useful part in the prediction of potential, then it should ensure that appraisal is on the basis of performance, not personality. The performance criteria should be related to success in the job for which potential is being assessed. Appraising managers should be trained to use this part of the form and to extract appropriate information during the interview and at other times. Promises of specific jobs should neither be made nor implied. Preparation for counselling forms should be used. Ratings of potential should be checked as a matter of course rather than as part of the grievance procedure. There should not be sudden and major discontinuities in the requirements for jobs in adjacent grades. Finally, there should be a buyer's market for important staff.

Unsupported by other techniques performance appraisal can be seriously misleading as a predictor of potential. The information which it yields is a vital component of any decision reached by whatever other methods may be used.

PROBLEM PERFORMERS

People perform unsatisfactorily for a wide variety of reasons. The first task is to discover which particular combination of reasons applies in the specific case. The problem may lie in a number of factors:

Intelligence – too little, too much, specific defects of judgement or memory

Emotional stability – over-excitable, anxious, depressed, jealous, sexual problems, neurosis, psychosis, alcoholism, drug addiction

Motivation to work – low motivation, low work standards, lack of organisation, frustration, conflict

Family situation – domestic crises, separation from family, social isolation from peer group, money worries

Physical characteristics – illness, handicap, strength, age, endurance, build

Work groups – fragmented, over-cohesive, inappropriate leadership, wrong mix of personalities

The organisation – inappropriate standards, poor communication, too little investment and management support, span of control too large, responsibility without authority

External influences – employment legislation, consumer pressure, safety legislation, changing social values, economic forces, changes in location

The appraisal system can be used as part of the process for dismissing people who do not perform satisfactorily. Alternatively, and preferably, it can be used to manage those people so that their performance improves. This can be achieved in a number of ways.

Counselling – self appraisal, preparation for counselling, some form of job climate questionnaire, vocational guidance, mid-career guidance, medical help, financial counselling

Training and development – as a reward and encouragement, not punishment, set up with precise, measurable objectives, careful monitoring and close follow-up

Changing the job – physical layout, timing, induction, responsibility without authority, no feedback on performance, late or distorted feedback on performance, too many figurehead duties, little or no control over the job content, insufficient warning of changes, shared management of subordinates

Termination – which does not have to be rushed or graceless, can take proper account of financial arrangements, time off to look for a new job, vocational guidance, interview training and exit interview.

Note particularly that there is an option to change jobs within the organisation. Several appraisal schemes specifically exclude this possibility. The options there are either to improve performance in present post to an acceptable standard, or to dismiss. This runs the serious risk of sending away someone who could do a perfectly satisfactory job if they were in the right place. While the logic of not wanting managers to shuffle poor performers around the system instead of addressing uncomfortable issues cannot be denied, it seems potentially wasteful to make a rigid rule that prohibits trying an employee in a different role.

There are particular groups who perform badly simply because they are unhappy or bewildered in some way. These people might include new graduates who are experiencing a mismatch of abilities and assigned task with inadequate induction. Older employees might be feeling that they have reached their ceiling or be experiencing difficulty with the slower learning patterns that can come with older age groups. People without clear career paths would appreciate information and options. People with a sad history in the organisation need help to discover whether the problem is real and not merely a reputation which is following them around without justification. The performance appraisal system should be able to generate information, objectives and controls to assist with most of these situations, making the unhappy necessity to dismiss for poor performance rarer, but more sure-footed when it does occur.

FUTURE TRENDS

The only certain thing about today's business environment is that it is changing rapidly and somewhat unpredictably. It follows that no performance appraisal system should expect to be the same in five years time as it is now. There is therefore a need for continuous monitoring and control of the relevance of the system to the organisation's shifting requirements. Some of the primary influences on change as it affects performance appraisal include increasing public scrutiny of performance criteria, coupled with open record systems. It does, after all, seem perverse to deny access to information about someone when that someone is the person who might benefit most from knowing it — quite aside from the ethical issue about whether there is any right to deny access to information about an individual to that individual. Self appraisal is a growing component of many systems, and is a logical outgrowth of the open record. The increase of on-the-job training and self-development, wherein people take responsibility for their own learning, increases the inevitability of self appraisal, and matrix management makes the older, hierarchical approach to performance appraisal almost unworkable. Pressure towards professional and technical career paths to parallel the more traditional managerial career progression also puts pressure on performance appraisal systems. Managers have to be better informed about the technology they are managing, or have to hand over some of the responsibility for appraising performance to those who do not manage but do perform a technical/professional function. Special efforts need to be made to counsel those who are experiencing mid-career change, possibly coupled with personal life crisis. The phenomenon of middle managers who feel that their worth is in question, reinforced maybe by redundancy, is more common. Many more people are now questioning whether they are pursuing the right path, and would welcome informed advice about alternatives. There are pressures to bureaucratise. While it is true that some of these pressures can legitimately be traced to the door of government at various levels, more come directly from within the organisation. The first reaction to difficult trading conditions is often to tighten controls and to administer more effectively what is already there, rather than to go all out to discover new ways to do things or new things to do. Under these circumstances, negative feedback and talk of where people are failing becomes the norm, and the appraisal system becomes the vehicle for stifling initiative and motivation rather than a stimulus to new directions and originality. There is a feeling that smaller business units may be helpful. Some organisations have become too large to manage, and breaking up the monolith into more viable pieces needs to be accompanied by local control and adaptation of the appraisal scheme. It might be necessary for the large unit to put things on to a computer, but a manual system may be perfectly adequate for the smaller organisation. The move to smaller units offers an encouraging chance to simplify over elaborate systems. Finally, there is a greater inclination to treat people as valuable investments, not merely as units in a card index or computer file. The return to an organisation on investment in good recruitment, selection, induction, appraisal and assessment of potential practices is now more rarely questioned. Performance appraisal systems are being seen as less concerned with discipline, control and record-keeping, and more orientated towards development, self-development and growth. This seems to me to be a useful trend.

APPENDIX: PERFORMANCE REVIEW SEQUENCE

The following is offered as a rough guide to the sequence of events which a manager might wish to initiate in order to be fairly sure that nothing of importance in the performance appraisal process has been overlooked.

1 Agree a time and date for the review well in advance
2 Arrange for the location to be private and free from interruptions
3 Set aside at least an hour and a half, and possibly two and a half hours
4 Bring all relevant results and information concerning the appraisee's performance in his/her area of responsibility
5 Ask the appraisee to review his/her performance in the work situation point by point
6 Ask the appraisee about any problems which might affect performance
7 Ask the appraisee about the implications of any problems or events, and their effect on the individual, the team and the work
8 Ask the appraisee what needs to be done by either of them to help improve performance
9 The appraisee should ask about anything which he/she feels is affecting his/her performance
10 Agree the key result areas
11 The appraisee should set/agree standards of performance for the next review period
12 The manager should set/agree standards of performance for the next review period

13   Agree future action
14   Close with a firm date for the next interim review

FURTHER READING

Boyatzis, R. E., *The Competent Manager*, Wiley, 1982.

Gill, D., Ungerson, B. and Thakur, M., *Performance Appraisal in Perspective*, Institute of Personnel Management, 1973.

Handy, C. A., *Understanding Organisations*, Penguin, 1977.

Margerison, C., 'Turning the annual appraisal system upside down', *Industrial Training International*, February, 1976.

Stewart, V. and Stewart A., *Practical Performance Appraisal*, Gower, 1977.

Stewart, V. and Stewart A., *Managing the Poor Performer*, Gower, 1982.

Stewart, V., *Change: the challenge for management*, McGraw-Hill, 1983.

Williams, M. R., *Performance Appraisal in Management*, Heinemann, 1971.

6

Managing career choices

Charles Margerison

The importance of a career today is accepted, just as acquiring a trade was originally recognised in the days when craftsmanship was the basis for securing lifetime employment in a prestigious role. The concept of a career now goes well beyond the original legal, medical, educational and religious professional careers which were the major professional roles prior to the emergence of the modern industrial and commercial organisations.

Today when there are a vast number of people in universities and colleges acquiring qualifications in everything from accounting through to zoology, there is a tremendous pressure for the development of a wider base for career mobility. The chief focus for this pressure is the work situation and in particular the medium and large industrial and commercial organisations, together with public service organisations.

People who have acquired qualifications and skills in a particular area want to go on and use these and acquire roles in an organisation. However, there are simultaneously the organisational problems of co-ordination and management. This brings to the fore different aspects of career work than the original technical specialisation in which a person qualifies. Therefore in developing a career many people have to look at the extent to which they pursue particular roles which concentrate more on administrative and managerial roles rather than their original specialisation.

The concept of the managerial career in contrast to the craft and technical career has become established only over the last twenty to thirty years. The predominance of the managerial role in terms of the status and rewards associated with it has however overshadowed the other equally important career roles in industrial and commercial organisations.

This chapter concentrates on career roles related to organisational levels and performance criteria. Van Maanen and Schein have argued that we should indeed examine 'the person within the total life space and throughout his lifetime' (Van Maanen and Schein, 1977[1]). It is important to identify the different career roles people can play in the modern organisation and the transitions that need to be made for success at the different levels.

A number of approaches have been taken in the literature to the study of careers and career development. Several theories exist which explain careers in terms of life cycle stages (Miller and Form, 1951[2]; Erikson, 1963[3]; Levinson, 1978[4]; Schein, 1978[5]). Schein (1978) has 'identified' three distinct models: biosocial life cycles, family-procreation cycles and work-career cycles. Within this last group the focus of attention becomes the stages through which managers move as they pursue an organisational career (Super *et al.*, 1957[6]; Hall and Nougaim, 1968[7]; Schein, 1971[8]. In a different approach Holland (1973)[9] distinguished six major orientations to work. Margerison (1980)[10] showed that British chief executives ranked themselves in priority order as enterprising, social, conventional, investigative, artistic and realistic in that order on Holland's scale.

In looking at managerial career prospects, however, we need to examine the key role factors that should be used to assess career progress at both the technical and managerial levels.

As the traditions of long service, loyalty and the gradual evolution to a senior executive position in western industrial organisations have declined, an increasing emphasis has been placed on performance review and appraisal. The essential aim of performance appraisal has been to assess people on their merit and ensure that promotions and pay reviews are related to a review of performance against agreed criteria. Alongside this has emerged the assessment centre method (Bray, 1966[11]; Byham, 1970[12]) for identifying in particular those with executive potential. These trends reflect the increasing competitiveness of organisational life.

In contrast to these developments are a number of organisationally orientated problems which have a direct bearing on the development of careers. Van Maanen (1977)[13] identifies areas of concern such as the changing values relating to work life and leisure, alienation from work, reduced organisational effectiveness and lack of understanding of adult identity and development.

Too often the study of careers concentrates exclusively on the managerial or executive role. However for an organisation to function adequately it needs to have policies and practices reflecting the different roles and different expectations people have. Therefore this chapter provides a model for comparing career roles at different levels and functions.

MANAGERIAL CAREERS AND ORGANISATIONAL ROLES

There are many individual roles in organisations, which enable people to develop their career paths. Careers according to Hall (1976)[14] are 'the individually perceived sequence of behaviours associated with work related experiences and activities over the span of the person's life'. However these experiences and activities take place through recognised professional bodies and in employing organisations based on particular roles. The significance of roles at the general level of the organisation has been well documented (Katz and Kahn, 1978[15]). In the career context Louis (1980)[16] has developed a typology of career transitions, comprising two main categories – inter-role and intra-role transitions.

Concern has been raised at the extent to which modern organisations force people to leave their technical specialisation role in order to get promotion within the organisation and the reasons for this (Jennings, 1971[17]; Beckhard, 1977[18]; Van Maanen, 1977[13]; Vardi, 1980[19]; Veiga, 1983[20]).

While financial rewards and higher status may result, they are often achieved at the expense not only of a person's original career interest, but also of individual and organisational performance (Peter and Hull, 1969[21]; Jacques, 1976[22]).

A key aspect of this process is the relationship of technical to managerial work. While each person has a personal career line there is an overall trend which can be seen in Figure 6.1.

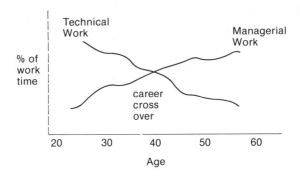

Figure 6.1 Career choice model

When a person starts in the workforce it is usually in jobs at levels that are primarily technical. Gradually, the person who is successful is asked to take on more responsibility. This usually involves supervising the work of other people and therefore involvement in the process of management is initiated. More time is spent at the next level in allocating and delegating work, reviewing that work, sitting on committees, ordering resources, budgeting and the various other tasks associated with management. There is for many therefore a definite role transition from a technical job to a managerial job in terms of the time spent, although clearly the technical background knowledge and experience is usually essential to do the managerial task. Nevertheless as the role of senior managers has only been examined in depth recently (Mintzberg, 1975[23]; Lau and Pavett, 1980[24]; Kotter, 1982[25]), the task of explaining the personal processes of such role transitions is not fully developed.

Driver (1979)[26] postulated that individuals have one of four basic approaches to their organisational careers and personal development – transitory, steady state, linear or spiral. Driver has drawn on Schein's 'career anchor' scheme of career motivation (Schein, 1978[5]) to develop further an active-passive subtype within each main career concept type.

What seems to be missing from previous research are the critical factors that govern a person's career prospect. Is it possible to reduce the complexity associated with career assessment to two central factors? I believe that in any career decision the two underlying factors must be competence and achieved capacity to manage. If we extend this to identify the factors underlying promotion through various roles to a senior managerial position then we should relate achievement specifically to the capacity to manage factor (Jacques, 1976[22]; Stamp, 1981[27]), and competence to a person's experience and expertise.

The capacity to manage others involves not only the desire but the ability to exercise influence in a managerial role. There are many people who would desire to reach a senior organisational level and have lots of people reporting to them. However many do not have the interpersonal skills and ability to tolerate ambiguity while at the same time giving direction for action and achieving results through people.

It would appear that the capacity to manage others is a very difficult concept to measure. However most people know what it means. There are few people who voluntarily indicate when they have reached what they believe to be their preferred level. It is always the temptation to take on more than we can do if only because the incentives, such as the rewards, the status and the fringe benefits that tend to go with managerial roles are attractive. However, as Jacques (1976)[22] has indicated, there are individual differences in capacity and this relates to management as much as it does to any other aspect of life.

Likewise the achievement factor can be applied to the managerial role capacity just as much as it can be applied to a sporting role such as a golfer or tennis player. Figure 6.2 outlines the factor of managerial capacity contrasted with the competence (experience/ expertise) factor. This produces four specific roles which have been named the specialist, the adviser, the supervisor and the executive.

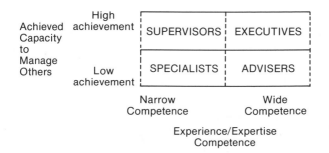

Figure 6.2 Types of role within organisations

The specialist

The specialist is a vital part of any organisation. Specialists usually have very narrow experience in a particular area such as a research chemist working on one product or an engineer on one machine. In so far as they have penetrated their particular discipline or function to a considerable degree they do it within narrow boundaries.

Very often they have low inclination to manage others. Their key interest is in pursuing that which they know best. They often like to do their work in their own way and with the minimum of interference. Very often they will not wish to have the responsibilities of administration or of managing others.

Such people are very important in research and development, in planning jobs and in other technical work requiring concentrated endeavour assessing specific issues in depth. While such work must be done and must be done well, it is unlikely that people with such an orientation are likely to make successful managers. They have neither the interest in doing so nor the experience. While they may be highly achievement orientated in their discipline, their achievement level in terms of management is low.

However, where a specialist shows an interest in managing others his experience and work allocation will need to change in order that he gains opportunities as an adviser, a superviser and an executive.

The adviser

The adviser usually also has a low concern for managing others. However in contrast to the specialist who acts within a narrow field, the adviser operates on a very wide basis of experience and knowledge. The very nature of their job involves them in working with a variety of clients in different parts of the business. The accounting or finance person will usually, for example, have a wide understanding of the systems applying to production and sales and be able to make a substantial contribution to the personnel department in terms of wage costs. Through their own discipline they therefore pick up a very wide understanding of the overall business. This stands in contrast for example to the specialist chemist whose area of expertise does not facilitate the crossing of organisational boundaries.

The adviser, therefore, may have wide experience but little interest in managing subordinates. While their achievement orientation in terms of managing is usually low they may have high personal needs for achievement within their discipline or function. However, if a person who is in an adviser role shows interest in the managerial role then it is important he or she gain a leadership position in a supervisory role and if successful then in an executive role to test their abilities and achievement.

The supervisor

The supervisor is a generic term to cover those people who have a high capacity to manage others but only within narrow functions and disciplines. They enjoy taking on integrating and administering tasks but do so within specific and limited areas of knowledge and experience. These are usually confined to their traditional area of technical training. They have not usually gone beyond that knowledge and training to acquire the language and skills of the other functions. An example could be the foreman in charge of the engineering maintenance area. However it could also apply to an accountant who reaches a high level in the organisation but still only has experience of managing people in the financial area.

However where a person shows an interest and ability in managing it is important to assess their performance by widening their range of experience and developing their competence. This can only come through real experience on different jobs.

The executive

The executive is the person who understands the three roles that we have mentioned and brings about an overall approach to what has become known as general management. They have a high capacity for gaining achievement through managing others.

They have acquired wide experience and expertise through various job changes and self-development activities. Their competence is therefore widely based so they can assess organisational issues on a broad front.

Executives develop a wide picture of the organisation through gaining personal experience in managing different functions and tasks. They initially have team leadership experience in a specific area, but then move to manage a cross-functional team of people from different backgrounds. From then they often move into a role whereby they manage a part of the organisation where they have profit and loss responsibility. Beyond this they can, in large organisations, move to corporate roles involving the strategic management of many profit and loss units or divisions.

The executive role therefore demands widespread competence and understanding of the legal, financial, marketing, operational and personnel aspects of organisations combined with a high achieved capacity for managing others.

IDENTIFYING PEOPLE'S CONTRIBUTION PROSPECTS

In addition to the four main career roles identified it is also important to identify how well a person works in a given role. It is rare for a person to take on a role and immediately perform to a high level. Normally there is a learning period during which adjustments are made. In choosing a person for a role we are always taking a risk that they will not learn and adapt quickly enough to perform the duties as required.

How do we assess therefore whether a person can make the transition from one role to another? Organisations use a variety of means from interviews, psychological tests, temporary postings, special project assignments and other means. However, one of the key tests is how well a person is performing in their present role. This may or may not have any bearing however on a person's output, for example, if moving from a specialist role to an executive role, or from a supervisory role to an advisory role.

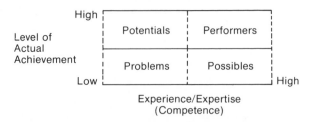

Figure 6.3 Perceived career prospects model

Given the significance of the factors of achievement and competence that have already been identified it is useful to outline a simple model for assessing a person's career situation within any role.

Figure 6.3 shows a model designed to indicate the perceived outcome of several role influences on an individual, regardless of the level in the organisation at which he or she is located. It is based on two criteria: the level of achievement that a person exhibits in a particular role and the experience/expertise (competence) that a person possesses. It is these two factors that are central to effective individual action. The model therefore produces four ways of viewing a person at a particular point in his or her career, namely as a performer, potential, possible or problem. Let us examine each of these terms.

Performers

Those people who have a high need for achievement and produce results based on a wide background of experience and expertise within particular roles.

Potentials

Those people who have shown a high need and level of achievement but so far do not have the range of experience or expertise to do a wide range of work in their professional area.

Possibles

Those people by contrast who have been exposed to a wide range of experience and have expertise but have yet to show commensurate levels of achievement in a particular role.

Problems

Those people who within particular roles have shown little achievement and have a low level of expertise/experience.

Thus in any organisational position or level at which a person finds themself, the sum total of the role influences to which he or she is subjected may take on any one of the four dimensions.

Role	Role Assessment			
	Problem	Possible	Potential	Performer
Specialist				
Adviser				
Supervisor				
Executive				

Figure 6.4 Assessing role performance model

MERGING CAREER PROSPECTS AND ROLES

Although the described roles provide a general framework for the analysis of organisation positions and the skills associated with those positions they indicate only half of the total picture. People can have a high desire to manage others and wide experience but they may not have the interpersonal skills or political awareness to carry out their managerial role as an executive. Thus it is essential that the concepts developed from Figure 6.3 be integrated with the roles developed in Figure 6.2.

A person can be a performer in an executive position but could be a problem in terms of his or her contribution to another role such as a specialist. This might be because the person has not occupied the role of specialist for 20-30 years, during which time the type of work in the area in which they originally qualified has radically altered. This could place the executive performer in the position of a problem specialist if they had to revert to that role. Likewise someone in a specialist role can be a performer in that role but would be a potential in one of the other roles, such as an adviser, through lack of experience/expertise in that role.

Thus in assessing people's careers we need to examine their strengths in relation to particular roles. As shown in Figure 6.4, for every role we need to assess a person's work.

This approach differs from that of Driver (1977) in that it applies regardless of the type of organisation concerned or the level at which the individual operates within that organisation. Thus a trainee chemist in a bureaucratic organisation may be a performer in that role but have difficulty in being a performer in a supervisory or executive role. A general manager in a multinational public company may be perceived as a problem in that role despite the fact that in his career he has successfully been a performer at the specialist, adviser and supervisor roles.

Figure 6.4 therefore provides a basis for making assessments within particular roles and a guide for manpower planning. People who wish to progress in their careers are normally expected to show performance in specialist roles before becoming advisers. Equally there is usually an expectation that an executive will show prior performance as a supervisor and perhaps as a specialist and an adviser before an executive appointment. However, it is possible that people who can excel in an executive role may not be performers as specialists or advisers. Therefore it is important to discriminate when making career promotions. Equally there are dangers in appointing supervisors and executives from people who succeeded as specialists or advisers. The oft quoted example of the best salesman being promoted and becoming a poor manager can be replicated many times with chemists, engineers, computer specialists, teachers, accountants and others.

This is why it is important to identify the capacity to manage amongst those people who are to be promoted into supervisory and executive positions. The work of Ghiselli (1971)[28] is instructive here as is the work of Jacques (1976)[22] and Stamp (1981)[27] on managerial capacity. Essentially those people who will become performers at supervisory and executive levels must have the desire and determination to influence others as well as the competence of experience and expertise.

Margerison (1980) asked chief executives what were the primary influences that had helped them develop as a manager and they cited the following seven items in order of importance:

1 The ability to work with a wide variety of people
2 Early overall responsibility for important tasks
3 A need to achieve results
4 Leadership experience early in career
5 Wide experience in many functions prior to age 35
6 An ability to do deals and negotiate
7 Willingness to take risks.

The chief executives therefore recognised the capacity to manage depended heavily on the ability to work with and influence others combined with wide experience and expertise plus high achievement. However the important point emerging from this research is that the executives stressed the importance of early leadership and wide responsibility at an early age, building on their personal need for achievement.

Many specialists and advisers have high achievement but either do not wish or are unable to influence people appropriately in the managerial role. It is increasingly recognised that career paths must be charted for such people so they obtain the status, prestige and rewards that go with senior positions of a non-executive or supervisory level nature.

A number of important organisations have now established such specialist/advisory career paths. This is akin to what happens already in hospitals where a specialist surgeon does not need to become chief administrator to gain similar rewards or status, or in a university where a professor can be a specialist or adviser and a senior member of the organisation. There is a danger that in business organisations we lose people who perform as specialists and advisers because they feel that career progress will cease if they do not become executives.

CAREER PATHS AND POSITIONS

Some implications

Clearly, a person's interpersonal/political skills and their leadership style have a lot to do with their overall success as a manager. However, from this work, far more attention needs to be paid to the person's individual desire to manage and capacity to achieve in that role as a basic measure of potential. Few organisations when selecting new managers from outside put sufficient emphasis on these issues. Equally, alongside this there needs to be the recognition of experience being related to outputs rather than just a series of involvements with different kinds of work.

It is possible to conclude a number of strategically important issues which organisations need to address if they are to obtain the people who are best equipped to contribute to the organisation in the future. It is important to have a policy which enables the lessons of the present research to be put into practice. This would certainly include many of the following points:

1   People should be tested through experience in various roles and enabled to gravitate to that which is their strongest role.

2   The reward structure of the organisation should provide status as well as financial comparability to those who excel in specialist and advisory roles as well as supervisory and executive roles.

3   The organisation should enable people to assess themselves as specialists, advisers, supervisors and executives through direct experience, through projects, task forces and other limited term activities.

4   The organisation should be sufficiently decentralised to enable people identified as executives at a young age to have a profit and loss responsibility to test their capacity to manage.

5   Opportunities should be provided for people who have been identified as supervisors and executives prior to the age of 30 to have an early chance to take on leadership positions where they will have the various inter-personal issues to manage.

6   The organisation structure should facilitate the movement of people to meaningful jobs in different parts of the business where competence at a wide level can be tested through experience.

7   The organisation should establish a career development structure that is taken as a serious part of managing at all levels, so that appraisal and counselling form an integral part of management practice.

8   The organisation should recognise people's strengths and enable them to work in roles where they can perform best without having to change for salary or status reasons.

9   A consequence would be that specialist and advisory roles are given equally high status as supervisory and executive roles.

10 The assessment of people for supervisory and executive positions should assess their capacity to manage others rather than just technical performance in a previous role.

REFERENCES

(1)   Van Maanen, J. and Schein, E. H., 'Improving the Quality of Work Life: Career Development', in Hackman J. R. and Suttle,

L. (eds), *Improving Life at Work: Behavioural Science Perspectives*, Washington, D.C., Department of Labor Monograph Series 2, 1975.

(2) Miller, D .C. & Form, W. H., *Industrial Sociology*, New York, Harper & Row, 1951.

(3) Erikson, E. H., *Childhood and Society*, (2nd Ed), New York, W. W. Norton & Co., 1963.

(4) Levinson, D. J., *The Seasons of a Man's Life*, New York, Knopf, 1978.

(5) Schein, E., *Career Dynamics: Matching Individual and Organizational Needs*, Addison-Wesley, 1978.

(6) Super, D., Crites, J., Hummel, R., Moser, H., Overstreet, P. and Warnath, C., *Vocational Development: A Framework for Research*, New York, Teachers College Press, 1957.

(7) Hall, D. T. and Nougaim, K., 'An Examination of Maslow's Need Hierarchy in an Organizational Setting', *Organizational Behaviour and Human Performance,* no. 3, 1968 pp. 12-35.

(8) Schein, E. H., 'The Individual, the Organization and the Career: A conceptual scheme'. *Journal of Applied Behavioural Science*, vol. 7, 1971, pp. 401-26.

(9) Holland, J. L., *Making Vocational Choices: A Theory of Careers*, Prentice Hall, 1973.

(10) Margerison, C. J., 'How Chief Executives Succeed', *Journal of European Industrial Training*, vol. 4, no. 5, 1980.

(11) Bray, D. W. and Grant, D. L., 'The Assessment Centre in the Measurement of Potential for Business Management', *Psychological Monographs*, 1966.

(12) Byham, W. C., 'Assessment Centres for Spotting Future Managers', *Harvard Business Review*, vol. 48, July-August, 1970.

(13) Van Maanen, J., 'Summary: Towards a Theory of the Career', in J. Van Maanen (ed.), *Organizational Careers: Some New Perspectives*, New York, John Wiley & Sons, 1977, pp. 161-79.

(14) Hall, D. T., *Careers in Organizations*, Santa Monica, California, Goodyear Publishing, 1976.

(15) Katz, D. and Kahn, R. L., *The Social Psychology of Organizations* (2nd Ed.), New York, McGraw-Hill, 1978.

(16) Louis, M., 'Surprise and Sense Making: What Newcomers Experience in Entering Unfamiliar Organizational Settings',

Administrative Science Quarterly, vol. 25 no. 2, 1980.

(17) Jennings, E. E., *The Mobile Manager,* New York, McGraw-Hill, 1971.

(18) Beckhard, R., 'Managerial Careers in Transition: Dilemmas and Directions,' in Van Maanen, J. (ed.), *Organizational Careers: Some New Perspectives*, London, John Wiley, 1977.

(19) Vardi, Y., 'Organizational Career Mobility: An Integrative Model', *Academy of Management Review*, vol. 5 no. 3, 1980, pp. 341-55.

(20) Veigh, J. F., 'Mobility Influences During Managerial Career Stages', *Academy of Management Journal*, vol. 26, no. 1, 1983, pp. 64-85.

(21) Peter, L. J. and Hull, R., *The Peter Principle*, London, Souvenir Press, 1969.

(22) Jacques, E., *A General Theory of Bureaucracy*, London, Heinemann, 1976.

(23) Mintzberg, H., 'The Manager's Job: Folklore and Fact', *Harvard Business Review,* vol. 53, no. 4, 1975, pp. 49-61.

(24) Lau, A. W. and Pavett, C. M., 'The Nature of Managerial Work: A Comparison of Public and Private Sector Managers', *Group and Organizational Studies*, vol. 5, 1980, pp. 453-66.

(25) Kotter, J. P., *The General Managers*, New York, Free Press, 1982.

(26) Driver, in *Career Concepts in New Dimensions in Human Resource Management*, ed. R. Katz, Prentice Hall, 1979.

(27) Stamp, G., 'Levels and Types of Managerial Capability', *Journal of Management Studies*, vol. 18, no. 3, 1981.

(28) Ghiselli, E., *Explorations in Managerial Talent*, Santa Monica, California, Goodyear Publishing, 1971.

Part III
THE PROCESS OF
MANAGEMENT DEVELOPMENT

7

Styles of learning

Peter Honey

I always remember reading a piece written over 25 years ago by Chris Argyris where he predicted, amongst other things, a move

> *from* management development programmes that teach managers how they ought to think and behave
> *to* programmes with the objective of helping managers to learn from experience.

He argued that it was necessary because 'no one can develop anyone else except himself. The door to development is locked from the inside.' He went on to say 'Emphasizing the *processes* of how to learn, how to diagnose administrative situations, how to learn from experience – these are timeless wisdoms.' His conclusion was that we needed less emphasis on developing *learned* managers and more on developing *learning* managers.

When I first read Argyris's words I agreed with them wholeheartedly, but I did not fully understand how to put them into practice. What exactly were the processes of learning from experience? How could management development be designed to give managers practice in these 'timeless wisdoms?' Was it just a question of exposing managers to different experiences and hoping they would learn from their successes and mistakes? Or did the mechanics of learning need to be understood and designed into management development as a deliberate strategy?

I confess I did not know the answers to any of these questions. Then I came across Kolb and Fry's 'Learning Style Inventory' together with their description of the stages involved in the business of learning from experience. This was the spur for many years of work in conjunction with Alan Mumford which has resulted in our publication *The Manual of Learning Styles* together with its sister booklet *Using Your Learning Styles*. (Honey and Mumford, 1982 and 1983)[1,2]. In these publications we describe the full range of uses of learning styles information in the design of programmes, boss/subordinate relationships and selection of structured learning activities.

In this chapter I intend to concentrate on the use of learning styles by individuals for themselves. I shall:

1 examine the process of learning from experience and the short cuts that managers characteristically take to truncate the process;
2 describe four different learning syle preferences and show how they affect the sort of activities managers learn from;
3 show how it is possible to develop an underdeveloped learning style and thus become an all-round learner from experience.

THE PROCESS OF LEARNING FROM EXPERIENCE

Alan Mumford and I have developed a simplified version of Kolb's model (Kolb 1984)[3] which looks like Figure 7.1.

It is rare to find managers who consciously discipline themselves to do all four stages as shown in Figure 7.1. Depending on their learning style preferences (this will be discussed later) managers are likely to take a number of liberties with this process. Some of the better known ones are as follows:

1 Indulging at stage 1 i.e. rushing around have lots of experiences and keeping frantically busy but never bothering to review, conclude or plan. Such managers equate having lots of experiences with learning and conveniently assume that if they have experienced something they have automatically learned from it.
2 Limiting stage 1 by repeating familiar experiences over and over

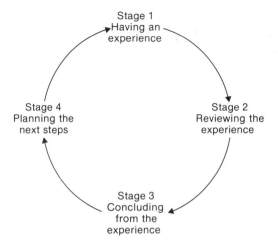

Figure 7.1

again and never going out on a limb and trying something new or different.

3   Avoiding stage 1 by being a 'voyeur' and learning from other people's experiences rather than their own. This reduces the risks of making mistakes or making fools of themselves.

4   Avoiding stage 2 by having a stock of conclusions and forcing experiences to fit the conclusions rather than the other way round. This is closely akin to the wellknown process of jumping to conclusions. The attraction is that it avoids the uncertainty of reviewing an experience and the hard work of reaching conclusions.

5   Limiting stages 2 and 3 by collecting readymade ploys and techniques of the 'how to do it' variety. This avoids the hard work of discovering and creating practical ways of doing things via reviewing and concluding experiences.

Of course all these short cuts are entirely understandable and all have their attractions but they, and others like them, all tend to erode the amount that can be learned from experience.

DIFFERENT LEARNING STYLE PREFERENCES

Kolb and Fry's Learning Style Inventory suggested that people develop preferences for different learning styles in just the same way that they develop any other sort of style — management, leadership, negotiating etc. Naturally I did the inventory to discover my own learning style and started to include it on training courses I ran as a way of predicting who would respond in what sort of way and so anticipating learning difficulties. Unfortunately, whilst I bought the theory, I found some problems with the inventory itself (the predictions were not as accurate as I wished and the face-validity was poor). Accordingly, together with Alan Mumford I started to develop a questionnaire that would do a better job.

After three years of intensive experimentation the result was an 80 item questionnaire that takes ten minutes or so to complete and identifies whether someone is predominantly:

Activist — what's new? I'm game for anything
Reflector — I'd like time to think about this
Theorist — How does this relate to that?
Pragmatist — How can I apply this in practice?

The learning styles tie in with the four stages of learning from experience as follows:

A preference for the activist style equips you for stage 1
A preference for the reflector style equips you for stage 2
A preference for the theorist style equips you for stage 3
A preference for the pragmatist style equips you for stage 4

All-round learners, or integrated learners as they are sometimes referred to, are clearly best equipped to manage all four stages. However most people develop learning style preferences that assist with some of these stages and hinder others.

These style preferences very significantly affect the sort of activities that people learn best from. For example we have found that activists learn best from activities where:

1 There are new experiences/problems/opportunities from which to learn
2 They can engross themselves in short 'here and now' activities such as business games, competitive tasks, role playing exercises
3 They have a lot of the limelight/high visibility

4   They are thrown in at the deep end with a task they think is difficult

Reflectors, on the other hand, learn best from activities where:

1   They are encouraged to watch/think/chew over activities
2   They are allowed to think before acting, to assimilate before commenting
3   They have the opportunity to review what has happened, what they have learned
4   They can reach a decision in their own time without pressure and tight deadlines

Theorists learn best from activities where:

1   They have time to explore methodically the associations and inter-relationships between ideas, events and situations
2   They are in structured situations with clear purposes
3   They have the chance to question and probe the basic methodology, assumptions or logic behind something
4   They are intellectually stretched

Pragmatists learn best from activities where:

1   There is an obvious link between the subject matter and a problem or opportunity on the job
2   They are shown techniques for doing things with obvious practical advantages currently applicable to their own job
3   They have the chance to try out and practise techniques with coaching/feedback from a credible expert
4   They can concentrate on practical issues

The dovetailing between learning styles and learning activities has led us to postulate some key questions that people can use to assess the appropriateness of different learning opportunities:

Key questions for activists

Shall I learn something new, i.e. that I did not know/could not do before?
Will there be a wide variety of different activities? (I do not want to sit and listen for more than an hour at a stretch!)

Will it be OK to have a go/let my hair down/make mistakes/have fun?

Shall I encounter some tough problems and challenges?

Will there be other like-minded people to mix with?

Key questions for reflectors

Shall I be given adequate time to consider, assimilate and prepare?

Will there be opportunites/facilities to assemble relevant information?

Will there be opportunities to listen to other people's points of view – preferably a wide cross section of people with a variety of views?

Shall I be under pressure to be slapdash or to extemporise?

Key questions for theorists

Will there be lots of opportunities to question?

Do the objectives and programme of events indicate a clear structure and purpose?

Shall I encounter complex ideas and concepts that are likely to stretch me?

Are the approaches to be used and concepts to be explored 'respectable', i.e. sound and valid?

Shall I be with people of similar calibre to myself?

Key questions for pragmatists

Will there be ample opportunities to practise and experiment?

Will there be lots of practical tips and techniques?

Shall we be addressing real problems and will it result in action plans to tackle some of my current problems?

Shall we be exposed to experts who know how to/can do it themselves?

BECOMING AN ALL-ROUND LEARNER FROM EXPERIENCE

A knowledge of learning styles can either be used to help dovetail learning activities to suit learning styles or be used as a starting point for self-development. The latter option is the one I want to explore now.

The advantages of having a broader range of learning skills are that you become a more effective learner from life's events and, if you are a trainer as I am, you are more likely to be able to help a greater range of trainees by being a more effective trainer. I want to illustrate how I personally have made use of a knowledge of my own learning style preferences to become a more effective trainer. I do this not in any boastful way but as a means of trying to encourage readers to develop their own learning skills and thus become better at helping other people to learn.

THE PROBLEM

I have been an active trainer since 1965 but it is only recently that the implications of my own learning styles really dawned on me. My own preferences are for the activist and pragmatist styles. This means that my strengths and weaknesses tend to be as follows:

As an activist my strengths are that I am:
    flexible and relatively open minded
    happy to have a go
    happy to be exposed to new situations
    optimistic about anything new and therefore unlikely to resist
       change

As a pragmatist my strengths are that I am:
    keen to test things out in practice
    practical and realistic
    businesslike and down to earth
    keen on specific techniques

That's the good news! On the other hand my preference for the activist and pragmatist styles means that I have some important weaknesses.

As an activist my weaknesses are that I am:
    likely to take the immediately obvious action without con-
       sidering alternatives
    likely to take unnecessary risks

likely to do too much myself and hog the limelight
likely to get bored with implementation and consolidation

As a pragmatist my weaknesses are that I am:
likely to reject anything without an obvious application
not very interested in theory or basic principles
likely to seize on the first expedient solution to a problem
impatient with disorganised people who 'waffle'

Clearly these strengths and weaknesses affect my performance as a trainer. For example I am likely to design training courses that are packed with lots of activities and to sell people short on theory and basic principles. I am likely to warm to trainees who display activist tendencies and to have difficulties with trainees who hold back and are more cautious and less assertive. Also, paradoxically, the more I try to jolly along trainees who have reflector/theorist preferences the more likely they are to take fright and withdraw still further.

THE CHOICES

Once I knew my own learning style preferences (the Learning Styles Questionnaire together with its score key come as a package with *The Manual of Learning Styles*) and realised their implications for me as a trainer I had two choices. Either I could specialise and only train fellow activists and pragmatists or I could set out to develop my underdeveloped reflector and theorist styles so that I was better equipped to help a broader range of trainees.

The idea of specialising has some practical difficulties and having seriously toyed with the idea I dropped it in favour of self development. The practical difficulties are not by any means insurmountable — indeed on an in-company basis where there may be a team of trainers with various styles there is much to be said for more thoroughly matching trainer and trainee styles. It would require a system where trainee's learning styles are identified *before* they attend a training programme so that they could be catered for either by allocating them to courses designed to suit their styles or to trainers with compatible styles.

THE SOLUTION

I decided to set about consciously strengthening my reflector and theorist styles so that, through an extended repertoire, I would be in a better position to adopt styles suitable for all types of trainees. More specifically, I set myself the goal of strengthening my reflector style by becoming:

more thoughtful, thorough and methodical
better at listening to others and assimilating information
more careful not to jump to conclusions

In order to strengthen my theorist style I set about becoming:

more rational, objective and disciplined
better at logical (vertical) thinking
better at asking probing questions

MY SELF-DEVELOPMENT PROGRAMME

Here are some of the things I did in order to strengthen my reflector and theorist styles.

1   Each month I sat in the public gallery at the Town Hall observing our local district councillors during their meetings (for an activist this is ideal because you are not allowed to speak − only to observe). I kept a careful record of what was said and later did an analysis of the arguments used, and the processes that led up to a decision.

2   It so happened that a general election was called soon after I had embarked on my self-development plan: I bought myself copies of the Manifestos for the three main parties and did a painstaking analysis of the policies each was advocating. Having done this I designed a self-scoring questionnaire to help people decide which policies they agreed/did not agree with.

3   I put myself on a Rational Emotive Therapy course. RET is a rigorous form of therapy that surfaces and challenges your irrational beliefs and as such is an excellent vehicle for developing the theorist style in particular.

4   I read articles in the 'quality' newspapers and did a thorough analysis of the arguments they were using, and tried to identify

and write down the fundamental assumptions they were based on. I compiled a list of probing questions that I wished to put to the authors.

5   I forced myself to compile lists for and against a particular piece of action. I tried this on domestic decisions not just work ones and it nearly drove my wife mad! Never mind, it helped me to think of alternative courses of action rather than revelling in instant (activist) on-the-spot decisions.

6   I deliberately increased my serious reading. To give myself an incentive I volunteered to write reviews of books. This is an excellent way of forcing yourself to read the book in question carefully enough and analyse its good and bad points.

7   I took a list of criteria to be used as the basis for designing an assessment programme for middle managers and broke each down into a number of specific behavioural indicators. Previously, the criteria had been global and vague (leadership, flexibility, decision making etc). I spent a concentrated day pinpointing six key behaviours for each criterion.

8   Finally, and perhaps most helpful of all, three times a week I make an entry in my learning log. The procedure I have devised is as follows:

   (a) start by thinking back over an experience and selecting a part of it (a 15 minute period or so) that was significant or important for you.

   (b) write a detailed account of what happened during that period. Do not at this stage put any effort into deciding what you learned – just concentrate on describing what actually happened.

   (c) then, list the conclusions you have reached as a result of the experience. These are, in effect, your learning points. Do not limit the number and do not worry about the practicality or quality of the points.

   (d) finally, decide which learning points you want to implement in the future and work out an action plan which covers: what you are going to do and when you are going to do it. Spell out your action plan as precisely as possible so that you are clear what you have to do and that it is realistic.

I have been so impressed with the worthwhileness of keeping a log like this that I have introduced it as a twice-a-day feature on most of the training programmes I run. Activists need some cajoling: reflectors, theorists and pragmatists take to it more easily.

IDEAS FOR STRENGTHENING THE ACTIVIST AND PRAGMATIST STYLES

Of course none of my personal examples will help those who want to develop their activist and/or pragmatist styles. Here then, taken from *The Manual of Learning Styles*, are some 'thought starters' for people in that position.

Self-development activities to develop the activist style:

1   Do something new, i.e. something that you have never done before, at least once a week. Hitch a lift to work, visit a part of your organisation that you have neglected, go jogging at lunch time, wear something outrageous to work one day, read an unfamiliar newspaper with views that are diametrically opposed to yours, change the layout of furniture in your office, etc.

2   Practise initiating conversations (especially 'small talk') with strangers. Select people at random from your internal telephone directory and go and talk to them. At large gatherings, conferences or parties, force yourself to initiate and sustain conversations with everyone present. In your spare time go door-to-door canvassing for a cause of your choice.

3   Deliberately fragment your day by chopping and changing activities each half hour. Make the switch as diverse as possible. For example, if you have had half an hour of cerebral activity, switch to doing something utterly routine and mechanical. If you have been sitting down, stand up. If you have been talking, keep quiet, and so on.

4   Force yourself into the limelight. Volunteer whenever possible to chair meetings or give presentations. When you attend a meeting set yourself the challenge of making a substantial contribution within ten minutes of the start of the meeting. Get on a soapbox and make a speech at Speakers' Corner.

5   Practise thinking aloud and on your feet. Set yourself a

problem and bounce ideas off a colleague (see if between you you can generate 50 ideas in ten minutes). Get some colleagues/friends to join in a game where you give each other topics and have to give an impromptu speech lasting at least five minutes.

Self-development activities to develop the pragmatist style:

1   Collect techniques, i.e. practical ways of doing things. The techniques can be about anything potentially useful to you. They might be analytical techniques such as critical path analysis or cost benefit analysis. They might be interpersonal techniques such as transactional analysis, or assertiveness or presentation techniques. They might be time saving techniques or statistical techniques, or techniques to improve your memory, or techniques to cope with stress and reduce your blood pressure!

2   In meetings and discussions of any kind (progress meetings, problem solving meetings, planning meetings, appraisal discussions, negotiations, sales calls etc.), concentrate on producing action plans. Make it a rule never to emerge from a meeting or discussion without a list of actions either for yourself or for others or both. The action plans should be specific and include a deadline (e.g. 'I will produce a two-page paper listing alternative bonus schemes by 1 September').

3   Make opportunities to experiment with some of your new found techniques. Try them out in practice. If your experiment involves other people, tell them openly that you are conducting an experiment and explain the technique which is about to be tested. (This reduces embarrassment if, in the event, the technique is a flop!) Choose the time and place for your experiments. Avoid situations where a lot is at stake and where the risks of failure are unacceptably high. Experiment in routine settings with people whose aid or support you can enlist.

4   Study techniques that other people use and then model yourself on them. Pick up techniques from your boss, your boss's boss, your colleagues, your subordinates, visiting salesmen, inter- viewers on television, politicians, actors and actresses, your

next door neighbour. When you discover something they do well – emulate them.

5   Subject yourself to scrutiny from 'experts' so that they can watch your technique and coach you in how to improve it. Invite someone who is skilled in running meetings to sit in and watch you chairing, get an accomplished presenter to give you feedback on your presentation techniques. The idea is to solicit help from people who have a proven track record – it is the equivalent of having a coaching session with a golfing professional.

6   Tackle a 'do-it-yourself' project – it does not matter if you are not good with your hands. Pragmatists are practical and, if only for practice purposes, DIY activities help to develop a practical outlook. Renovate a piece of furniture, build a garden shed or even an extension to your house. At work, calculate your own statistics once in a while instead of relying on the printout, be your own organisation and methods man, go and visit the shopfloor in search of practical problems to solve. Learn to type, learn a foreign language.

CONCLUSION

If management development is designed to provide managers with learning opportunities, then the process of learning from experience is an essential ingredient, perhaps the *most* essential. In my view any respectable management development programme should offer explicit help with learning how to learn by doing some or all of the following things:

1   helping managers to know the stages in the process of learning from experience and how their learning style preferences help and hinder them with parts of this process.

2   helping managers to work out how to develop an under-developed learning style so that they can aim to become better 'all-round' learners.

3   providing managers with a safe haven where they can practise developing an underdeveloped style and help learning from experience to be a deliberate, conscious process.

4 helping managers to identify learning opportunities in their current jobs and plan how to utilise them.

REFERENCES

(1) Honey, P. and Mumford, A., *Manual of Learning Syles*, Honey, 1982.
(2) Honey, P. and Mumford, A., *Using Your Learning Styles*, Honey, 1983.
(3) Kolb, D., *Experiential Learning*, Prentice Hall, 1984.

8

Using others to learn*

Roger Stuart

INTRODUCTION

The nature of management training and development

Amongst the many attempts to define management training and
development, the one with which this chapter is in most accord is that
used by Mumford in his Preface (derived from the Training Services
Agency statement[1]).

In accepting this definition, it is important to recognise and
acknowledge that, in fact, learning is taking place all the time –
perhaps implicitly, perhaps haphazardly – as part of a manager's
day-to-day work and life activities. As managers remind us,[2] their
principal source of learning is in and from doing their jobs. Seen in
this light, then, what management trainers and developers are
concerned to achieve[3] is to *aid and abet* that learning through making
it more planned and deliberate; to move managers' learning away
from the implicit to the explicit; to move learning activities and
processes from the haphazard to the more organised; to move
towards more efficient and, ultimately, more effective learning as
demonstrated in workplace performance.

In enacting their roles, trainers and developers have traditionally

---

*First published in *Personnel Review*, vol. 13, no. 4, 1984.

taken upon themselves the responsibility for ensuring more planned and deliberate managerial learning. They have designed and implemented learning events (be they off-the-job in the form of courses, workshops, seminars, etc., or on-the-job as in process consulting, project work, job secondments, etc.) *for* managers. More recently, trainers advocating a management self-development approach (see for example the papers included in Boydell and Pedler)[4] have sought to help managers not by doing things for managers, but by helping them to do it for themselves, viz. to better manage their own learning. Here the trainer role, rather than being what Cunningham and Burgoyne[5] have described as 'expert teacher', or 'learning process manager', becomes that of self-development facilitator'. The latter role includes helping managers to get in touch with, understand, and further develop their learning behaviours so as to move towards more effective self-managed learning (which may or may not include formalised off-job activities such as self-development groups, learning communities).[6]

In support of self-managed learning

It is in support of helping managers to better manage their own learning, particularly as part of their *on-the-job* activities, that some of my more recent work has been directed. Work on managers' learning skills and abilities – which is a fundamental implication of, and a basic requirement for, moves towards self-managed learning – has been rapidly gathering momentum. Not only the author,[7] but workers such as Mumford,[8] Honey and Mumford,[9, 10] Burgoyne *et al.*[11] and Richardson and Bennett,[12] have initiated significant inroads into this area. All have been inspired by Kolb's research[13] and his work on learning styles and behaviours.[14]

Despite a number of studies which call into question some aspects of Kolb's work – for example Freedman and Stumpf[15] – Kolb's basic model (the so-called 'Kolb learning cycle' describing how, through the behaviours of experiencing, reflecting, conceptualising and experimenting, experience is translated into concepts which in turn are used as guides in the choice of new experiences), remains a simple and useful vehicle for helping managers to get to grips with how they learn in and from their everyday experience. Nevertheless, and this only occurred to me comparatively recently, the model *is* limited in the sense that Kolb largely describes what may be called 'solo' or loner's learning, and does not explicitly encompass or say much about learning in a social context.

Solo versus social learning

The picture that emerges from Kolb's work is largely one of the manager making solo journeys around his learning cycle – experiencing, observing and reflecting, conceptualising, hypothesising and experimenting alone. However, the day-to-day activity of most managers is not a solo but a social one, being based in relationships with others in their work situation. Kolb's work does comparatively little to illuminate such relationships, nor to inform the learning which arises directly from and through others.

When I reached this point in my thinking I was prompted to reconsider the approaches that I was adopting in working with people on their learning abilities, and to consider the area of 'learning involving others'. I was fortified in doing so by some comments I came across on re-reading Mumford's book.[8] Thus:

> ... While there are a number of books and articles which tell consultants and advisers how to be effective helpers, there is very little I can find which advises managers on what is required of them in order that they may be effectively helped ... It seems quite crucial that a manager ... should acquire knowledge about what is involved, in his particular case, in seeking and accepting help (p. 174).

It is to this area, in seeking and accepting help with one's learning that is, in *using* (in the best sense of the word) others to help one's everyday learning that this chapter is directed. It presents the product of my initial thinking, research and practice in what is a relatively unworked seam in the world of self-managed learning. It represents a further step forward from Kolb's work and serves to complement the work of Honey and Mumford, and others who are seeking to help managers to further exploit the learning opportunities available in on-job situations.

STRATEGIES FOR USING OTHERS TO LEARN

The data collected

One obvious mode of learning which directly involves others is when they *tell* us things (or in the formalised learning programme 'lecture' to us). This mode of learning is not explicitly captured in Kolb's experiential model. 'Kolb addicts' may, however, view telling as a means of obtaining secondhand accounts of others' journeys around their learning cycle. Thus, others may tell us about their own, previous experiences, observations, conceptualisations and experimentations. One way in which others can be used to fuel our learning is, then, by *asking* them to *share* their own learning with us.

In what other ways do many people use others to help their learning? In pursuit of an answer to this question, I have been researching into the learning of a range of individuals. The formal and structured vehicles of enquiry ranged from questionnaires (administered to individual clients), through 1:1 interviews (with selected subjects) to small group tasks (with workshop participants). This research was preceded and supplemented by rather more informal and less structured 'chats' with colleagues and acquaintances. The formally collected data were obtained from 65 people in all, comprising; 26 management trainers, 15 managers, 10 senior members of the helping professions, 10 management educators and 4 people from miscellaneous professions.

Admittedly this was a small and somewhat skewed sample, the more so because the large majority were fee-paying clients who were seeking to work on their own and other people's learning skills and abilities. Obviously there is a future need to increase the size of the sample, particularly by working with a greater number of managers. Such work is already in hand. Nevertheless, the sample in this study did comprise of real people enacting real learning processes!

The focus for data collection was identification of the strategies each individual adopted in using others to help his/her learning. Some individuals identified one or two ways of using others, whilst other individuals identified rather more, up to a maximum of eight strategies. There was, of course, much duplication and overlap, as well as diversity amongst the strategies identified by different individuals. Equally, some of the strategies were unsurprising, for example:

consulting experts;
encourages one to try things;
helps me clarify my assumptions through questioning why?;
kicking ideas about;
asking for feedback from someone who knows you;
observing a skilled operator in action and copying him.

Others were more novel, for example:
father confessor;
(phantom other) look for a listener, allowing one to talk things
through, talk off the top of one's head;
role play possible future actions;
shows belief in the possibility of improvement;
contracting to provide mutual feedback;
asking self how would Arthur have done this?;
devil's advocate in reverse. Testing my own basic assumptions
when I see them displayed in others.

Whilst some strategies were open and direct, for example:
asking directly for information;
seeking permission to let me try out things.

Others were more indirect, for example:
raising a topic for discussion in the tea-room;
'fix' the agenda for a team meeting.

A wide range of relationship behaviours were reported between 'users' and 'others'. This was to be expected, for as Smith (referring to the needs of adult learners) reports,[17] not only are 'independence and autonomy good', but that 'dependence also has its uses, as does interdependence'. Examples of the diversity of relationships included:

1 *dependency* (a) structures up a learning process for me, (b) directing, (c) sets up opportunities for me to observe;
2 *sharing* (a) helps identify opportunities for trying things out, (b) helps me to anticipate and plan for possible and likely errors, mishaps;
3 *independency* (a) probing, questioning them, (b) looking for passive listening – it prompts one to identify flaws in my thoughts through verbalising them;

Table 8.1
Strategies for Using Others to Learn

Category	Using others as:	Examples
A Clearing the way for learning		
1 Accepting	a means of releasing, dispelling, catharting, allowing the expression of one's negative feelings, thoughts, emotions.	sharing negative feelings; father confessor.
2 Stimulating	a source of energy, spark, enthusiasm.	energising; others provide enthusiasm
3 Confirming	a source of confirmation, reinforcement, confidence, support, encouragement.	seek confirmation to give me confidence; seeking assurance.
4 Sanctioning	a means of permitting, legitimising, authorising, sanctioning one's learning activities.	makes allowances for failure, permits risk taking, seek permission to try things out.
5 Structuring	a means of structuring, shaping, organising one's learning opportunities.	exposes me to new situations; sets up opportunities for me to observe.
B Tooling up for learning		
6 Equipping	a source of understanding of, and methods/ techniques for learning.	shows means of analysis; Provides techniques for learning, e.g. lateral thinking.
C Direct learning interventions		
7 Advising	a source of recommendations, suggestions, guidance, advice, direction.	share their ideas about what to do; advising.

#		Description	Examples
8	Exposing	a means of drawing out, exposing, clarifying one's thoughts, feelings, assumptions.	helps clarify what I think; Looking for a listener. Hear myself talking. God, I didn't know I knew/ thought that!
9	Building	a means of developing ideas; processing, progressing, extending one's ideas.	seek out others on same wavelength to develop ideas; chatting, sparks off ideas.
10	Testing	a means of sounding out, anticipating snags, identifying faults, a source of examination, trial, opinion.	seek objective criticism from others; Use them as guinea-pigs, try things out on them.
11	Confronting	a source of alternative viewpoints and perspectives; challenging, disconfirming.	get them to be the devil's advocate; exposing oneself to thoughts and ideas of other cultures, departments, etc.
12	Feeding-back	a means of reviewing; a source of observations and feedback on one's actions and their consequences.	asking for feedback from someone who knows you; Asking others to observe me.
13	Explaining	a source of help in clarifying, making sense of, explaining what's been happening to one.	helps identify underlying causes; using consultant to interpret/make sense of things.
14	Modelling	a source of examples of behaviour; a focus for imitation; demonstrations, illustrations for one to copy.	watching positive and negative models, shows how to do it, how not to do it; Working with other people, then copying them.
15	Sharing	a source of secondhand, vicarious experience; accessing other's experiencing and learning through listening, questioning, etc.	others sharing their experiences; reading/ scanning the literature.

4 *interdependency* (a) seek out others on same wavelength to develop ideas, (b) joint theorising.

It is important to clarify that the range of these strategies is wholly compatible with a philosophy of self-managed learning. Seeking and obtaining help in one's learning need *not* fly in the face of moves towards self-managed learning. The issue revolves around who takes responsibility for the initiation and provision of that help – the other or the user? An individual who possesses a sound repertoire of strategies for using others is in a strong position to take an active responsibility for getting that help from others, rather than being a responding, passive, perhaps even begrudging and resentful (viz. 'counterdependent') recipient of that help. The connection between using and helping will be pursued later in this chapter.

In all, over one hundred different strategies were reported. Upon subsequent analysis, fifteen categories emerged which serve to organise and distinguish strategies for using others to learn. The categories are listed and defined in Table 8.1, which also includes some examples of strategies in each category.

Categorisation of the data

Before going on to comment on the categories, it is helpful to point to some features of the categorisation itself. Firstly, the categorisation *emerged* out of the accumulated list of strategies identified by individuals in the sample. The categorisation was not imposed on the data. As such, the categorisation has been practically/functionally rather than theoretically/structurally derived. The categories are an abstraction from practice, not an extrapolation from theory.

Secondly, being descriptive of some current practice, the categorisation may well be incomplete, being limited by that which is known and recognised by members of the sample. A number of 'blind spots' may, therefore, exist. Nevertheless, being a summary of real learning practice, the categorisation is proving to have both validity and credibility.

Finally, as with any other categorisation of this type, the actual number of categories isolated is something of a variable feast. The level of aggregation of strategies presented in Table 8.1 does, I believe, cast a useful compromise between fragmented and unmanageable lists on the one hand, and, on the other, being non-discriminative and uninformative. The categorisation is intended to serve to organise the data collected, and at the same time, to be a meaningful framework for informing further enquiry and practice.

The strategy categories

Table 8.1 has been compiled in the hope of being self-explanatory. Nevertheless, it would perhaps be useful to make some further comments. Overall, three broad ways of using others to help one's learning emerged: others as clearing the way for one to learn; others as tooling one up for learning; and others as making direct interventions into one's actual learning processes.

Clearing the way for learning

A whole range of blocks and barriers may exist which act to cut individuals off from productive learning activities.[16, 7] Both the *accepting* and *confirming* strategies make use of others in removing emotional blocks to learning, the former helping the individual to dispel various negative feelings and emotions towards learning situations; the latter to boost an individual's confidence to take advantage of learning opportunities. Closely allied to these strategies is the *stimulating* category within which are found various ways of using others in removing both emotional and, more particularly, motivational blocks to learning. Hence, others may provide the 'inspiration' or 'spark' to learn.

If these first three categories help clear the way for learning by removing intrinsic blocks (viz. those internal to the individual), a further two categories of strategies were identified which worked to remove extrinsic barriers. Thus in the categories of *structuring* and *sanctioning*, others were used both to organise and to legitimise an individual's learning activities, acting on what have previously been described,[16,7] as physical/structural and psycho-social/climatic blocks and barriers to learning.

Tooling up for learning

To learn effectively on-the-job as part of one's work activities requires not just that those activities provide opportunities to learn. Neither, is it enough to be willing and motivated to learn. In addition, effective learning demands that an individual has a range of learning methods and techniques – a 'learning tool-kit' – enabling him or her to take full advantage of the learning situation. The equipping category recognises the contribution that others can make towards tooling-up an individual for learning. Hence, others may be used as a source of 'means of analysis', 'observation methods', 'rational and lateral thinking techniques', etc.

Direct learning interventions

The remaining nine categories presented in Table 8.1 all directly impinge upon people's day-to-day attempts to learn. As such they may be viewed as using others to make interventions into one's journeys around a learning cycle. The approximate positioning(s), of each of the strategies in the individuals' Kolb learning cycles is illustrated in Figure 8.1.

Some of the strategies are represented in each of the four phases of the cycle, for example, sharing and exposing (though the latter is most frequently located in the abstract conceptualisation phase). Other strategies, such as feeding-back and explaining are specific to single phases. Still others, traverse two phases, for example, the modelling and testing strategies. Overall, the majority of strategies reported were used to draw others into the phases of abstract conceptualisation and active experimentation. How peculiar this is to the particular sample used in this study remains a subject for future study. Let us now complete the commentary on each of the nine categories serving as direct learning interventions.

The *sharing* category has already been mentioned earlier in this paper. This strategy involves using others as a source of secondhand learning through asking them to share their previous experiences, etc. Rather more prescriptive in nature, the *advising* category requires others to draw upon that same experience, and to offer guidelines in one's learning.

At the other end of the spectrum from advising, is the notion of a 'phantom other' which was alluded to in a number of strategies in the *exposing* category. 'Phantom other' strategies call upon others to be present, but to adopt a very low profile. That presence provides an

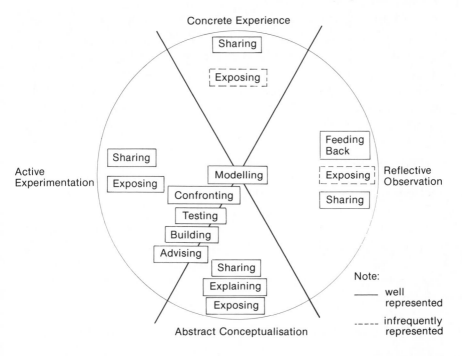

Figure 8.1 Strategies involving others directly in one's learning cycle
Source: Learning Cycle, after Kolb [13]

excuse to think aloud and listen to oneself talking, thereby exposing and clarifying one's thoughts, feelings, etc. Other strategies within this category use others in a more active way, for example 'helps me get in touch with my feelings'.

If one consequence of exposing is to reveal one's ideas, the strategies comprising the *building* category enable the individual to progress those ideas further. Strategies for using others such as 'relying on others to analyse and process my ideas' and 'seek out others on same wavelength to develop ideas', serve not just to expose ideas, but to further develop and build on them.

Testing out is a way of using others not in formulating ideas, but as a means of critically examining them. As shown in Figure 8.1, testing out strategies largely operate in bridging current thought to potential future action. For example, strategies such as 'consulting those likely to see snags, potential risks', and 'using others to pilot ideas for practice', reveals potential reactions. Note the future tense of these testing out strategies, compared to the present and past orientations of strategies included in the feeding-back category. The difference is between what may or will happen and what is happening/has happened.

Feeding back is a category of strategies for using others which is concerned with enhancing learning through seeking information from others on one's actions and their consequences. It includes strategies such as 'Asking for feedback from someone who knows you', and 'Helps me to see the consequences of what I'm doing'.

If 'building' was concerned with the further development of ideas by extending them, often with people of a similar mind, *confronting* represents a radically different collection of strategies. The intellectual opposite of the affective, confirming strategies, using others as confronting involves the active seeking out of individuals of a different mind. Others are used as a means of providing alternative, challenging and even disconforming viewpoints and perspectives. Typical examples in this category include 'disconfirming' argument and debate with others who may not agree, and exposing oneself to thoughts and ideas of other cultures, departments, etc.

Strategies for using others such as 'using consultant to interpret/make sense of things', 'joint theorising' and 'helps identify underlying causes' are examples of the *explaining* category. Others are used as a source of help in making sense of what has been happening to an individual. The explaining category differs from 'sharing', not only in being focussed exclusively upon the abstract conceptualisation phase of Kolb's learning cycle, but also because the explaining is of the user's own experience rather than a recounting of someone else's.

Finally, to comment on *modelling* as a way of using others to learn. This category includes a number of the more novel strategies referred to earlier (viz. 'how would Arthur have done this?' and 'testing own assumptions when I see them displayed in others'). More commonplace were strategies like 'observing a skilled operator in action and copying him' and 'Watching positive and negative models, shows how to do it, how not to do it'. Strategies using others as a source of examples of behaviour tended to link reflective observation with active experimentation (Figure 8.1) and largely by-passed the conceptualisation phase of learning. It is also interesting to note that the 'model' was sometimes unaware of the help he/she was giving to the user's learning.

This latter observation serves to reinforce that what have been described in this section are a wide range of strategies for *using* others to learn. Table 8.1 is *not* a categorisation of helping strategies. All members of the sample, and including the trainers and educators, were questioned not on how they helped others to learn, but on their strategies for using others to help in their own learning.

STRATEGIES FOR USING VERSUS HELPING OTHERS

Notwithstanding the preceding comments, an important, if simple insight for myself and others I have worked with has been to recognise that using others is in fact the opposite side of the coin from helping others. To promote self-managed learning is to turn many traditional learning practices and perspectives on their heads. At issue is not 'how can I, the other (viz. trainer, boss, etc.), help you the learner?' Instead, the relationship is to be looked at from the other side in terms of 'how can I, the learner, make use of you the other?'

As suggested in the earlier citation of Mumford,[8] there are a number of works which advise on how to be an effective helper. In Table 8.2, strategies drawn from the professional helping frameworks of Bolman,[18] Heron,[19] and Blake and Mouton[20] are compared with the using others categories identified in this chapter. It is apparent that there is a good deal of correspondence between the two. This compatability serves to reinforce the validity of the using others strategies, and, it might be added, at the same time confirms the utility of the helping strategies!

All the helping strategies identified by the authors cited in Table 8.2 can be seen to have some equivalence to one or more of the categories of strategies for using others. The reverse is not the case. It is interesting to note that the categorisation of using strategies is seemingly more comprehensive than the helping frameworks, particularly when the latter are considered separately. The eclecticism and richness of the strategies emerging from this study may deliver a salutary jolt to those trainers whose practice is deliberately and explicitly informed by helping frameworks such as those represented in Table 8.2 (including me − for my own practice[7] has owed much to the work of

Table 8.2
A comparison of strategies for using others, and helping others, to learn

USING OTHERS AS	HELPING OTHERS		
	BOLMAN[18]	HERON[19]	BLAKE AND MOUTON[20]
ACCEPTING	(Support)	Cathartic	Acceptant
STIMULATING	////	////	////
CONFIRMING	Support	////	////
SANCTIONING	////	(Directive)	////
STRUCTURING	Structuring	Structuring	Prescriptive
EQUIPPING	(Conceptualisation)	////	Theory — Principle
ADVISING	////	////	Prescriptive
EXPOSING	Questioning	////	Catalytic
BUILDING	////	////	(Catalytic)
TESTING	////	////	////
CONFRONTING	////	Confronting	Confrontational
FEEDING BACK	Providing Feedback	Disclosing	(Catalytic) (Confrontational)
EXPLAINING	Conceptualisation	Interpretive	(Theory — Principle)
MODELLING	Modelling	////	////
SHARING	////	Disclosing	Theory — Principle

////   No apparent equivalence of strategies

☐   Approximate equivalence of strategies

( )   Possible equivalence of strategies

Blake and Mouton.[20] Such trainers may be suboptimising in the help they provide through stimulating, sanctioning, advising, building, testing and modelling. To pursue this theme is, however, to sidetrack from the main focus of this chapter, viz. *using* others to learn. Nevertheless, a consideration of helping strategies is useful in highlighting the diversity of identified categories of ways of using others. And, as I shall point out later in this chapter, the body of knowledge and expertise that has been built up on helping others with their learning is likely to prove a significant resource in pointing towards the further exploitation of day-to-day strategies for using others to further one's own learning.

TOWARDS MORE EFFECTIVE UTILISATION OF OTHERS

The strategies presented in Table 8.1 emerged from data collected whilst attempting to help individuals to identify their own current practice in using others to learn. Presentation of the contents of Table 8.1 to an individual is useful in enabling him or her to look beyond current practice to an expanded vision of the strategies that he/she could be, rather than is, using. In some cases, this greater awareness may be all that is required for an individual to move towards more effective utilisation of others for learning.

In other cases, more work is required if the individual is to move beyond analysis to planning and implementation of strategies for using others. Thus, consideration may be given to the identification of target persons — *whom* to use. When working with clients, I have found it useful to suggest that clients draw a 'map of their using others system'. Represented on the map may be their boss(es), peers, subordinates and any other member of their organisations with whom they have contact as part of their day-to-day activities. It is then possible to identify the principal available channels for using others and also to confront both the real and apparent blockages which are seen to exist to making effective use of these channels. (Incidentally, this exercise can be further capitalised upon if using others to learn is seen as but one specific example of the wider phenomenon of giving and receiving support in organisations. In this connection, I have found the frameworks developed by Hans Noak,[21] to be of great practical value, serving as they do to expose people's attitudes towards giving and receiving support, and the costs of not doing so.)

Cap in hand with an analysis of 'what strategies with whom' may also go a consideration of the *skills* required for effective implementation of each strategy. Here it is important not only to identify the skills demanded of the user, but *also*, the skills demanded of the other person. For example, one contributor to this study identified his use of the strategy 'looking for a listener, allowing one to talk things through; talk off the top of my head'. He saw this strategy as requiring a range of skills, including:

skills required of me	*skills required of the other*
(the user)	has the interest and the time
able to free flow	doesn't want to push his own
able to drop my defensive	ideas
barriers (e.g. status, fear of	doesn't interrupt
appearing non-professional)	doesn't take what I say too
remember to capture the	seriously, e.g. act on it
thoughts on paper as I go	
along	

Consideration of the skills demanded of and the skills actually possessed by the other person is crucial to the subsequent effectiveness of a strategy for using others. It is not very wise to seek of others a form of help which they have not the skills to deliver. A focus upon the skills required by both parties to the strategy leads not only to better diagnosis of the most useful helper for a particular learning situation, but also points the user to the most effective way of gaining that help. Further, such a focus helps to lay the basis for identifying future skill development needs, the satisfaction of which would enable an individual to deploy a greater range of strategies, and to tap a greater number of channels for using others.

My own work has not yet progressed to the point where I am able to adequately respond to the identification of skill development needs by the user. There is a pressing requirement for further work, firstly on the rigorous identification of the skills required for effective enaction of each of the categories of strategies identified in Table 8.1. In addition, a series of skills development exercises should be assembled. In both cases, the literature from the other side of the coin from using others, viz. helping others, is likely to prove a rich source of material. This material will need, however, to be viewed from the perspective not of the giver (for example, the skills of giving feedback), but of the user (for example, the skills of eliciting and receiving feedback). Further work will also be required in locating many of those skills within the day-to-day reality of normal working relationships.

CONCLUSION

This chapter is concerned with strategies for using others to learn, particularly as part of day-to-day activities and relationships. From research into individuals' current practice has emerged a categorisation of strategies for using others; in clearing the way for one's learning; in equipping one for learning; and in making direct interventions into one's learning activities and processes. The richness and diversity of the collective practice of the individuals included in this study is clear. Equally clear is the potential for individuals to make more effective use of others in their learning. Thus, users may seek to broaden their range of strategies for using others; to target their strategies more effectively in relation to the accessibility and skills of the 'other'; and to attempt an improvement of their skills in implementing the strategies. In assisting such development, facilitators may make a further contribution to the promotion of self-managed learning. Now that this point has been reached more work is required in the following areas.

1 extending the size of the sample on which this chapter is based. Not only might more strategies for using others emerge (and I think the affective as opposed to cognitive learning domain appears under represented in this study), but it will then prove possible to develop a better picture of the overall preponderance in usage of some strategies over others;
2 identifying the particular skills required in enacting each of the fifteen categories of strategies described in this chapter;
3 assembling a collection of appropriate skill development activities as a resource for assisting individuals to further develop their skills in using others to learn.

Other areas of enquiry which I believe will be of interest

include discovering whether individuals tend to duplicate or to compensate for their 'solo' learning style (after Kolb[14]) when using others. For instance, do individuals who are strong on 'active experimentation', seek out others with a similar leaning, and for example share ideas about how they might do things differently, or do they seek out others who are strong on 'reflective observation', in the expectation, perhaps of receiving useful feedback on the consequences of their action. The former would be an example of duplication, and the latter of compensation. At a more fundamental level, it would be very interesting to know whether individuals show a marked learning towards solo *or* social learning strategies. And if so, whether this learning is a function of them – the type of people they are – or the situation (for example, job) that they find themselves in, or both.

Less academically, and more in terms of direct usage of the strategies presented in this chapter, I am excited by the potential that the categorisation is showing for prompting in depth discussion amongst members of work teams. I would like to see this avenue pursued further.

Work on strategies for using others to learn cuts into a comparatively unworked seam in the area of self-managed learning. I shall be pleased if this chapter prompts further work by others in a similar vein. I will be even more pleased if they *share* their results with me (Table 8.1, category 15!).

REFERENCES

(1) Training Services Agency (T.S.A.), *A Discussion Document on Management Development*, London, January, 1977.
(2) Burgoyne, J. G., and Stuart, R., 'The Nature, Use and Acquisition of Managerial Skills and Other Attributes', *Personnel Review*, Vol. 5, No. 4, 1976, pp. 18-29.
(3) Stuart, R., 'Training and Development: a natural everyday activity', *Management Education and Development*, Vol. 14, Pt. 3, 1983, pp. 168-9.
(4) Boydell, T. and Pedler, M. (eds), *Management Self-Development. Concepts and Practices*, Gower, 1981.

(5) Cunningham, I. and Burgoyne, J. G., 'Facilitating Behaviour in Work Centred Management Development Programmes', in J. E. Beck and C. J. Cox (eds), *Advances in Management Education*, John Wiley, 1980.

(6) Burgoyne, J. *et al.*, *Self Development*, ATM, 1979.

(7) Stuart, R., 'Maximising Managers' Day-to-Day Learning; Frameworks for the Practice of Learning Interventions', in C. Cox and J. E. Beck (eds), *Management Development: Advances in Practice and Theory*, John Wiley, 1984.

(8) Mumford, A., *Making Experience Pay*, McGraw-Hill (UK), 1980.

(9) Honey, P. and Mumford, A., *The Manual of Learning Styles*, Peter Honey, 1982.

(10) Honey, P. and Mumford, A., *Using Your Learning Styles*, Peter Honey, 1983.

(11) Pedler, M. J. *et al.*, *A Manager's Guide to Self Development*, McGraw-Hill, 1978.

(12) Richardson, J. and Bennett, B., 'Applying Learning Techniques to On-the-Job Development', *Journal of European and Industrial Training*, Vol. 8, No. 1, 1984, pp. 3-7.

(13) Kolb, D. A. and Fry, R., 'Towards an Applied Theory of Experiential Learning', in C. L. Cooper (ed.), *Theories of Group Process*, John Wiley, 1975.

(14) Kolb, D. A. *et al.*, *Organisation Psychology. An Experiential Approach*, Prentice-Hall, 1974.

(15) Freedman, R. D. and Stumpf, S. A., 'Learning Style Theory: Less than Meets the Eye', *Academy of Management Review*, Vol. 5, No. 3, 1980, pp. 445-7.

(16) Temporal, P., 'The Nature of Non-Contrived Learning and its Implications for Management Development', *Management Education and Development*, Vol. 9, 1978, pp. 93-9.

(17) Smith, R. M., *Learning How to Learn*, Open University Press, 1983.

(18) Bolman, L., 'Group Leader Effectiveness', in Cooper, C. (ed.), *Developing Social Skills in Managers*, Macmillan, 1976.

(19) Heron, J., *Dimensions of Facilitator Style*, Postgraduate Medical Federation, London, 1977.

(20) Blake, R. R. and Mouton, J. S., *Consultation*, Addison-Wesley, 1976.

(21) Noak, H., Frameworks included in a 'Support Workshop' tutored by Hans Noak of 'Natural Management', London, 1983.

9

Self-managed learning

Ian Cunningham

The phrase 'Self Managed Learning' (with capital 'S', 'M', 'L') was coined in order to distinguish this approach from close relatives (but relatives which are distinctively different). I was particularly interested in trying to weld together the advantages of various learning modes, whilst at the same time discarding their disadvantages. Some of these learning approaches are:

LEARNING APPROACHES

Independent study

From our work in North East London Polytechnic I wanted to use the idea that individuals can plan and carry out their own learning programmes (see Cunningham, 1981).[1]

Action learning

The value of individual managers assisting each other in their learning (through the use of sets) was clearly demonstrated in various action learning programmes in which I was involved (eg, GEC's Developing Senior Managers Programme; see Casey and Pearce, 1977[2]).

Autonomy labs

Harrison's (1974)[3] work in creating courses where managers were free to do what they liked (almost) impressed me. Restricting the trainer role to providing rich resources and to assisting others in their learning (through counselling and coaching) seemed a healthy stance.

Humanistic education

Rogers (1969)[4] has been an influence on many management developers in the UK, and his passionate advocacy of a 'person-centred' approach provided important philosophical underpinnings for Self Managed Learning.

Holistic education

It seems self evident to me that managers are not disembodied brains (see also Mant, 1977[5]): they exist in physical bodies, they feel (even if they pretend they do not), they value and believe in particular ideals (even though it is not always apparent). Schutz (1979)[6] is one of many writers who have promoted a holistic perspective on learning. His holistic studies MA at Antioch University in San Francisco was one of a number of American programmes I was able to experience at first hand when working in the USA in the late 1970s.

Work-based management development

What I mean by this title is the variety of methods one can use to assist managerial learning without managers leaving their place of work. Coaching, the use of work assignments, job rotation, and apprenticeship are examples of such unglamorous but often highly valuable methods. My experience of consulting in various organisations indicated that these approaches could be the most cost-effective learning modes for much managerial learning. (See Mumford, 1980,[7] for further discussion of this topic.)

OTHER INFLUENCES

As well as influences from learning approaches, Self Managed Learning has benefited from:

    1   developments in psychotherapy which have provided new ideas

on how people change (for example, Neuro-Linguistic Programming – see Bandler and Grinder, 1979[8]);

2   research on the nature of management (for example, Stewart, 1982[9]) which indicates that managing is not a neat subject discipline that can be taught in compartmentalised, standardised chunks;

3   research on brain functioning which shows up the different contributions that the left and right hemispheres of the brain contribute to our ways of thinking (see Mintzberg, 1984[10]);

4   ideas from philosophy about the nature of knowledge and of reality (Bateson, 1973[11] and Watzlawick, 1978[12] were specific influences). The notion that 'reality' cannot sensibly be conceptualised as a concrete entity outside of ourselves is a central tenet of Self Managed Learning. Managers create their own reality and teachers and trainers have to respond to that;

5   Eastern philosophy, particularly Taoism, has provided a subtle and powerful antidote to narrow Westernised modes of thought. This is especially so in relation to the idea that one can work in a both/and rather than either/or mode. I shall comment specifically on this in the next section.

BOTH/AND

In organising SML to get the benefits of the different strands outlined above, I was guided by the notion that we could work in a both/and rather than either/or mode. We did not need to choose between apparent opposites, since many things that are supposed to be opposites are not. Let me pick out one writer (amongst many) who has categorised management education programmes on an either/or basis, and I shall indicate how his reasoning is unhelpful.

Handy (1975)[13] identified what he claimed were the polar opposites in management education – instrumentalism and existentialism. He argued that management teachers had to choose between these two schools. He described the instrumental school as believing that education is subject oriented; that one teaches things to people; that the success of a course is judged on the basis of the person's contribution to society or to an organisation; that reasoning and learning are deductive (practice follows theory); that entry to courses is on the basis of organisational sponsorships only. The existential position he described as concentrating on the individual (and his/her freedom) not on the group. The view of reasoning and learning held by this school, he said, was inductivist (theory emerges from experience). He stated that teachers in this camp disliked assessment and talked instead of feedback. They also preferred to take people onto a course on the basis of personal choice rather than organisational sponsorship.

Handy (1975)[13] argued that it was not possible to 'ride two horses at once' (p. 61), and that all management teachers had to choose one or the other position. The evidence I gathered from my own research (Cunningham, 1984[14]) indicates that effective management teachers/trainers do not conform to Handy's theory.

The people in my research talked very much in terms of working with both poles at the same time. Everyone was, for instance, in some way interested in the development of the person and in the person's contribution to society, their organisation or their area of work. The notion that a management teacher *has* to choose to help *either* the person *or* society (and cannot do both) is nonsensical. For one thing, the notion that 'organisations' and 'society' are objects which can exist separately from persons is difficult to sustain. Secondly, (and conversely) it presupposes that managers can manage outside a social context.

To quote the case of one course in which I have been involved (the Post Graduate Diploma in Management (by SML) at North East London Polytechnic).

1   We recruit individuals as self sponsored *and* as organisationally sponsored.
2   We take assessment seriously, and pass/fail decisions are faced not as a necessary nuisance but as an important judgemental process to be set alongside the less judgemental feedback mode.
3   We value people who are independent *and* interdependent. The course can only work if people *both* consider themselves and work on their own problems *and* consider others and work with them on their problems.
4   The course demands that a person be involved in a learning community as well as pursuing individual and small group work.

5   Course members use subject based knowledge *and* they use their personally created knowledge. Theory and practice are continually counterposed in ways which transcend simplistic deductive-inductive modes.

I have indicated here the notion of a holistic integration of poles. I recognise that there are 'management teachers' who operate according to one or other of Handy's opposites. I have come across messy, self-centred existentialist programmes which have degenerated into chaotic disasters. The history of much of the 1960s/70s radical/humanistic education movement has been that most programmes collapsed because of this unbalanced mode of operating (see Swidler, 1979[15]; Rogers, 1983[16]; Leonard 1979[17]; Deal, 1975[18]).

The nasty degenerate instrumental programmes tend to survive well because of a combination of authoritarian control mechanisms, the exclusiveness and secretiveness of staff, and the investment by course members in pretending that their course is satisfactory (otherwise it would undermine their qualification, and if they have learned the hidden curriculum of instrumentalism they would not want to put their careers at risk).

I realise that what I have expressed above is my interpretation based on my experience of a number of institutions. However, in my research, people time and again expressed their rejection of narrow instrumentalism. They criticised the lack of involvement of such programmes with the lives of course members; the wastefulness of fixed curricula; the lack of effectiveness of standardised taught courses.

SELF-MANAGED LEARNING IN CONTEXT

I want now to put some flesh on the bare bones presented so far. Self managed learning programmes have been operating in organisations as well as in a college context. I shall focus on a college course since it is the longest programme (two years, part-time). The Post Graduate Diploma in Management (by Self Managed Learning) has been operating at North East London Polytechnic since September 1980. Discussion of its inception is contained elsewhere (see Cunningham, 1981[1]). I shall indicate here incidents an observer would actually see or hear, and follow each of these with an explanation of why they would observe such episodes. I hope that this will provide a better insight into the course than a purely abstract discussion.

Observed

New course members arrive on a Friday evening in October for the opening of the Diploma at a residential weekend. They join with existing (second year) course members and do some fairly standard 'getting to know each other' exercises, along with sessions to find out more about the course. So far, it looks very similar to many other management courses. However, as the weekend goes on, differences become apparent. The residential weekend has been organised by a planning group consisting of second year course members plus two staff. This group steers the weekend, but staff, whilst actively involved in particular sessions, are not controlling what goes on. On Saturday a session is devoted to helping first year course members form into 'sets'. The sets are groups of five or six course members along with a staff member and a second year course member (who together act as co-set advisers). The session is disorganised and sometimes chaotic as people try to find a sensible basis with which to group themselves. Eventually they do, and the sets settle down to their first meeting of many they will have over the two years.

On Saturday, all first and second year course members and staff gather together for a community meeting. This meeting discusses and decides upon course issues. It is chaired by a course member, and whilst staff join in on discussions they have only a minority voice in the proceedings. The community meeting decides on who shall be on the planning group for the next residential weekend. It also decides which workshops and other events shall take place before the next residential weekend, which is in the next term.

Explanation

1   Self managed learning is not necessarily an individual activity. Managing one's own learning includes the facility to involve oneself in the learning of others.
2   SML events are sometimes quite tightly structured. The difference between SML and other modes is where the structure comes from. In most college/university run courses, tutors lay

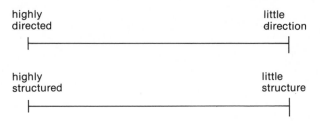

Figure 9.1
Source: The idea is taken from Heron, 1977[19]

down the structure: in SML the structure comes from collective agreement involving course members and staff.

This issue of structuring is important. Just because course members control their own learning it does not make the course unstructured. 'Structure' and 'direction' (or control) are two separate variables, and courses can be more or less structured and more or less directed by staff. This can be shown as in Figure 9.1.

A course can, for instance, be highly directed with little structure. This fits certain T group/encounter group modes where staff dictate a low structure format and do not permit group members to develop more structure. Most so-called 'taught courses' have high direction and high structure: staff impose both content and timetabling (structuring). Certain self-development groups come into the low structure/low direction category: the trainer adopts a low profile on content and structure. The SML mode is unusual in providing a great deal of structure within a framework which has little staff direction over course content. In Figure 9.1 I am suggesting that a total lack of structure is not possible: an unstructured course is a logical nonsense since to have a course is to provide a structure of some kind, even if it is only to arrange a time when people meet together.

3   The community meeting is a key event as it demonstrates the notion of a self managing community operating to make collective decisions about the course. All course members are able to be directly involved in decisions about what goes on, though the community meeting delegates specific tasks to groups (such as the residential planning group).

4   Sets are important in providing support groups besides meeting other needs. Each set is assisted in its operations by the presence of the co-set advisers. Second year course members who want to develop their skills in this area have found it valuable to apprentice themselves to a staff member in order to work with a first year set. The set also gets the benefit of the presence of someone who has been through the first year.

Observed

After the first residential, John, a manager in a construction company, is at home in the evening working on what he should put into his programme of study. He knows he has to write a contract which he has to present to his set for approval. Some aspects of this contract seem much easier to write than others. He has had no problem in covering his past experience, and he has had a reasonable shot at describing his strengths and weaknesses (helped by diagnostic material provided by the college). However, working out learning goals is proving less easy. He knows he wants to advance within his own company, but specifying a balance of objectives is not simple. He decides to take a rough draft of what he has written to his next set meeting in order to get the feedback and comments of others.

Explanation

Paul Tillich called the fatal pedagogical error, 'To throw answers like stones at the heads of those who have not yet asked the questions' (in Brown, 1971[20]). Managing involves asking questions and formulating problems *before* looking for answers and solutions. So for managers to manage their own learning they first need to formulate the questions; the problems.

I define a problem as existing when we cannot go from where we are to where we would like to be simply by action. If I want to know something about company procedures, and these are written in a company manual, I can simply go and look it up. That is no problem. However, if I currently feel unassertive and lacking in confidence (and I want to be assertive and self confident) I may well have a problem. It is probably not at all clear how I can move from my current to desired state. In the Post Graduate Diploma course

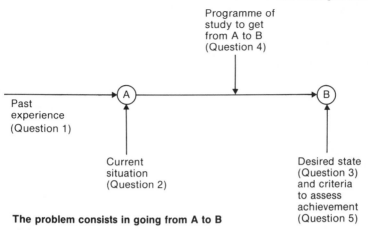

Figure 9.2

managers are advised that they may find it helpful to address themselves to five questions:

1   Where have I been? – what are my past experiences?
2   Where am I now – what strengths and weaknesses do I have? what is the current situation that I am in?
3   Where do I want to get to? – what goals/targets/objectives do I want to set for myself?
4   How will I get there? – what programme of study should I design to achieve my goals?
5   How will I know if I've arrived? – what criteria can I apply to assess my learning?

Most people find this sequence helpful in assisting them to formulate and choose their problems. I say 'choose' because any problem is a choice. If one decides to accept the situation and does not wish to change then there are no problems. It is only when a person *chooses* to change that problems become identifiable. The situation can be shown diagrammatically as in Figure 9.2. This indicates the link with the five questions outlined above.

In Figure 9.2 the person has the problem of going from A to B. The position is chosen on the basis of the person's values and beliefs: it is not an externally defined objective reality. My stance then is to reject what I often hear from trainers and lecturers. 'That manager says he wants to learn X, but that is not the real problem. What he really needs is Y.' The arrogance of such statements is in part based on a notion that 'real problems' exist out there in the world, detached from people. I regard this as an unacceptable standpoint. I may disagree with the goals a manager has set, but that is just my view against his/hers. I believe that I have the right to challenge and question a learner, and in the process they may change their formulation of the problem. However, in SML courses the staff do not have the right to impose *any* goals on learners, no matter how subtly they may wish to do it.

I have argued here for the principle of learners setting their own goals. However there are practical reasons why it is important. The research evidence on managerial learning is quite conclusive in supporting the notion that learning is enhanced if managers consciously set their own goals. Kolb and Boyatzis (1984)[21] quote a number of studies which demonstrate remarkable improvements in learning and performance when managers are given the chance to set their own goals and such changes tend to be independent of how difficult the goals are that people set for themselves.

Observed

John has returned from the set meeting where his draft contract has been discussed. His proposals have been analysed in detail, and many of his ideas have been exposed, under questioning, as being ill-thought out. He had been a bit annoyed at the time, as he felt he had put a lot of effort into his draft contract. However, now that he could re-read his proposals he realised that they were not as solid as he had thought. Just saying that he wanted to 'learn about management finance' and to 'improve interpersonal skills' clearly was not specific enough.

He decided to talk to his boss, because part of the reason he had put in 'improve interpersonal skills' was on the basis of feedback at his last appraisal interview. He now realised that he needed to be clearer about what his boss actually meant by this.

Explanation

1 Sets are often at their most supportive when they confront individuals about what they are or are not doing. This is a good example of how SML transcends the narrowness of Handy's

opposites of instrumentalism and existentialism. Woolly non-judgemental feedback ('I like what you've done') is as inappropriate as destructive judgemental assessment ('You'll never make a good manager'). Supportive confronting involves supporting the person as a person and valuing their worth as a human being, whilst commenting, positively and negatively, on what they do. This can be expressed simply as

support *being* (that is, the person)
confront *doing* (that is, what they do).

2   Part of helping people to manage their own learning is assisting them to specify the precise problems which they wish to tackle. In order to get good answers, one needs good questions first.

3   It is valuable if managers can build into their learning contracts evidence they gain from colleagues, bosses, subordinates and others at work. However, our experience is that much of this evidence is too vague.

We have encouraged managers to go and seek out good feedback, so that they can have a better basis on which to decide what to learn. Sometimes set members (staff or course members) have gone to a person's place of work to assist in this information gathering, especially if the boss or work colleagues get built into the contract as sources of learning.

Observed

Jane has had her contract agreed by her set at the end of the first term, and she now finds she has to start to put her plans into operation. She decides that her desire to learn about basic elements of marketing can best be met by attending a module on this topic, which is already provided on the Diploma in Management Studies. The module is one evening a week for one term. She has been given study leave for one day a week by her employers, so she comes into the college to use the library in the morning, prior to going to her set meeting in the afternoon. She feels she has a problem in running meetings, and looks for books in the library on this topic. However, she comes across an entry in the catalogue of a video tape on the subject. She signs out the tape and views it in one of the soundproof booths provided in the library.

Later in the term she decides to pluck up courage and tackle her fear of computers. She arranges a meeting with a tutor, and he shows her how to operate the microcomputers on open access in the computer room. She realises how valuable it has been for her to have discussed her concerns about computers in the set, as her colleagues were not only able to reassure her about using the equipment, but also helped her to clarify the kind of questions she needed to put to the tutor. She finds that the tutor occasionally gets over-enthusiastic about pushing her into the broader aspects of computer use, but because she is clear about what she wants she is able to steer him back to her needs.

Explanation

1 A person managing his/her own learning can choose a variety of ways to learn what he/she wants to learn.

2 Back-up learning resources are important, though many are ill-designed for easy access by managers. Libraries are often organised to suit librarians, and it can be a problem getting the flexibility and responsiveness needed for SML work.

The use of learning resources in our SML programme is unlike their use in so-called Open and Distance Learning. Most of the latter is not very 'open' at all, being predefined packages which give little or no choice to managers. They are like Tillich's stones being thrown at the heads of managers who have not formulated the questions (and are not going to be allowed to). It is a Henry Ford approach to learning. ('You can have any course you like, so long as it's this one'.)

3 Tutors may also not be ideally responsive. However, part of the skill of managing one's own learning is to manage experts. The experts do have things to offer, and it is short-sighted of managers to ignore this. Managers are, though, rightly suspicious of experts who wish to push their own field of interest too much. To quote Greenberg's First Law of Experts: 'You don't ask a barber if you need a haircut' (Peers and Bennett, 1981[22]). However, if you decide for yourself that you need a haircut, a barber can be useful.

Observed

Jim, a senior manager in local government, meets his tutor from college. They sit down in Jim's office and go through a time diary Jim has kept for the last two weeks. As they analyse his activities, Jim realises how much time he has been devoting to unproductive work. He appreciates now why his staff have complained about the amount of time he is out of the office or otherwise not available to them. He discusses with his tutor ways in which he could reorganise his time to fit more closely with his priorities.

After they have been through the time diary, they discuss how Jim processes paper (since this is another problem he has decided to tackle). Jim calls in his secretary, so that the three of them can consider how to change the filing system.

Explanation

1   SML can be about learning both high level abstract theory and 'nitty-gritty' practical skills.
2   Learning can take place at work, in college (or anywhere).
3   Course members choose one staff member (not the set adviser) to act as a 'specialist tutor' to assist them with specific learning which needs expert help. Ideally the specialist tutor works with the learner over the two years, although in practice people often switch tutors as their interests or requirements change. This special relationship does not preclude the course member from using other tutors on an occasional basis.

Observed

It is a sunny July Saturday afternoon and this is the third residential weekend of the year. Course members can be observed around the building and outside it. Eight people are struggling with a computer-based business game: some are from the public sector, and they are finding the commercial aspects of the game difficult to handle. Ten people are in a seminar on industrial relations negotiations run by one of the tutors. Tom, Jenny and Tim are busy in the computer room, each working on his/her own specific work problems. Tim has been testing out some proposals his employers are about to implement, and he finds a serious flaw in their calculations. He subsequently reports this to his organisation, and they save a seven figure sum by redoing their sums along the lines that Tim suggests.

Arthur sits under a tree in the grounds reading a book on operations research, and every so often he glances at a group of nine people on the lawn who are painting and drawing. They are in a session on integrating left brain and right brain working. Later on, he observes them all lying down listening to a guided fantasy, and he wonders whether he should not have joined that group rather than choosing to work on his own.

Meanwhile, in a darkened room in the main building, a group of seven is watching the film, *The Balance Sheet Barrier*, oblivious of the sunshine outside. Along the corridor Tony, Mike and Sue are using video equipment to practise their counselling skills. Janet, who is on the course, but is also a management tutor in a college, is assisting them, as she runs counselling training courses in her own college.

Down by the lake, well away from the main building, Simon and Carol sit on a bench. Simon is crying: his father died a few days ago. He does not feel up to going into any of the planned activities, and Carol, who is in his set, has agreed to sit with him for the afternoon. Simon is confused because his dominant feeling is one of anger, not sadness, at his father's death. Carol knows that Simon's relationship with his father has been fraught, as it has come up in the set discussions, and she tries to help Simon make sense of his feelings. Eventually they wander slowly back from the lake.

It is now late afternoon and a Tai Ji group is about to start on the lawn, led by one of the tutors. Tim and Jenny leave their computers to join it, along with Simon and Carol. Mike and Sue emerge from their video session to take part and Arthur decides to take a break from his book to do some relaxing meditative movement. At the last residential he had labelled Tai Ji 'too freaky and way-out', but having given it a try he has become convinced of its value.

Inside the building, a session on theorising is being held, and people do various exercises to assist them in being more effective at developing theory from their experiences. In one exercise, course members form into small sub-groups. One person (the problem owner) talks about a problem whilst the others write on cards the concepts used by the person as he/she talks. Together they arrange the cards in a 'concept map' in order to help the problem owner to model the problem. The problem owner is then assisted in elucidating the hypotheses with which he/she is working, so that concepts, models and hypotheses can be linked together as theory.

Explanations

1 Residential weekends provide a range of options to cover what course members request. Sometimes people spend time outside formally organised sessions: this is part of managing one's own learning.
2 The activities exemplify the holistic orientation of the programme. Most people are pleasantly surprised at how valuable it is to attend to their learning needs as whole persons. They find they change intellectually, emotionally, physically, socially and sometimes spiritually. All of this is relevant to management.
3 Course members learn from each other. The course provides a network which allows people to meet others with matching interests and concerns. It also facilitates mutual support in times of personal difficulty.

    This networking often continues after the formal ending of the course. There are facilities for ex-course members to meet up and be in contact with each other. One set which went through the programme 1980 to 1982 continued to meet of its own volition until 1985.
4 The style of the residential is in keeping with a both/and orientation. People work hard and they have fun. They are active and passive. They engage in rational and non-rational activity. They plan rigorously and they respond to serendipitous whims.

I like to feel that our approach is genuinely scientific in the sense that Bateson (1973)[11] has supported. That is, that one counterposes theory and existing knowledge with experience and tests each against the other. I agree with Sirag (1979)[23] that 'the future of physics rests in the hands of those who have an equal toleration for mathematical rigor and free-wheeling fantasy' (p. 18). A similar statement could be made about management.

Observed

The two year course is coming to its end for Mike's set, and they are dealing with assessment, in order to decide on who gets the Diploma and who does not. Mike has already presented various essays and reports to the set, and these have been discussed. He is now at the set meeting at which they are looking at the totality of his work. He first shows a video tape where he is counselling someone, and after that he gives his reasons why he thinks this has satisfied the criteria in his contract on this subject. Other course members and the staff member (set adviser) question him on this, and eventually they agree he has met the required standard. Mike then distributes copies of assessments carried out by his boss and his subordinates on aspects of his performance at work. In discussion it seems that there is doubt on some aspects of these, particularly as to whether Mike has met all his previously contracted criteria. The set agrees that they cannot make a decision on this information, and the task of going to Mike's company to talk to his boss and his subordinates is delegated to two set members. After this discussion, Mike's specialist tutor joins the set, and he reports on Mike's work in the areas of finance and economics. The set quiz him on his report, and eventually agree with Mike and the tutor that the required criteria have been met. The set then consider Mike's other (written) work which they have already seen. They agree that if the two set members seeing Mike's boss and subordinates get the required information, they can proceed at the next set meeting to decide on a pass.

Explanation

It is central to SML that the learner manages the assessment process in conjunction with relevant others. In the context of this college course 'relevant others' means at the very least other set members and the specialist tutor. In the case quoted the person's boss and subordinates were also involved. At no time are judgements imposed externally on the learner: the assessment process matches the initial contracting process in being a collaborative negotiation. I have discussed elsewhere other aspects of assessment: see Cunningham, 1983[24].

CONCLUSION

I have commented on some aspects of one SML course. In-organisation programmes are obviously different in design as, for instance, assessing for a diploma is not involved. In many programmes the creation of a relatively large learning community is not possible, and hence the set becomes much more important. If the programme is of short duration this places increased emphasis on starting the direct learning activity more rapidly.

I have not discussed the staff role here as I have commented on this elsewhere (see Cunningham, 1984).[14] However, I can say that I see this as the crucial determinant of the success or otherwise of SML programmes. Working in this kind of way relies heavily on staff competence, not just in face-to-face activity, such as in sets, but in the design and managing of programmes. If this approach to learning is to expand, the development of people who can staff such courses is going to be the most important factor.

REFERENCES

(1) Cunningham, I., 'Self Managed Learning and Independent Study', in Boydell, T. and Pedler, M. (eds), *Management Self Development: Concepts and Practices*, Gower, 1981.

(2) Casey, D. and Pearce, D., *More than Management Development: Action Learning at G.E.C.*, Gower, 1977.

(3) Harrison, R., 'Developing Autonomy, Initiative and Risk-Taking through laboratory design', in Adams, J. D. (ed.) *New Technologies in O.D.*, University Associates, 1974.

(4) Rogers, C.R., *Freedom to Learn*, Charles E. Merrill, 1969.

(5) Mant, A., *The Rise and Fall of the British Manager*, McGraw-Hill, 1977.

(6) Schutz, W., *Profound Simplicity*, Turnstone, 1979.

(7) Mumford, A., *Making Experience Pay*, McGraw-Hill, 1980.

(8) Bandler, R. and Grinder, J., *Frogs into Princes*, Real People Press, 1979.

(9) Stewart, R., *Choices for the Manager*, McGraw-Hill, 1982.

(10) Mintzberg, H., 'Planning on the left side and managing on the right', in Kolb, D. A., Rubin, I. M. and McIntyre, J. M. (eds),

Organizational Psychology: Readings on Human Behavior and Organizations, Prentice-Hall, 1984.

(11) Bateson, G., *Steps to an Ecology of Mind*, Paladin, 1973.

(12) Watzlawick, P., *The Language of Change*, Basic Books, 1978.

(13) Handy, C. B., 'The Contrasting Philosophies of Management Education', in *Management Education and Development*, vol. 6, no. 2, pp. 56-62, August 1975.

(14) Cunningham, I., *Teaching Styles in Learner Centred Management Development Programmes*, Lancaster University PhD Thesis, 1984.

(15) Swidler, A., *Organisation without Authority*, Harvard University Press, 1979.

(16) Rogers, C. R., *Freedom to Learn for the Eighties*, Charles E. Merrill, 1983.

(17) Leonard, G., 'Frontiers in Education: Past and Present', in *A.H.P. Newsletter*, May 1979, pp. 5-6.

(18) Deal, T. E. , 'An Organizational Explanation of the Failure of Alternative Secondary Schools', in *Educational Researcher*, vol. 4, no. 4, pp. 10-16, 1975.

(19) Heron, J., *Dimensions of Facilitator Style*, British Postgraduate Medical Federation, 1977.

(20) Brown, G. I., *Human Teaching for Human Learning*, Viking, 1971.

(21) Kolb, D. A. and Boyatzis, R. E., 'Goal Setting and Self Directed Behaviour Change', in Kolb, D. A., Rubin, I. M. and McIntyre, J. M. (eds), *Organizational Psychology: Readings on Human Behaviour in Organizations*, Prentice-Hall, 1984.

(22) Peers, J. and Bennett, G., *1001 Logical Laws*, Hamlyn, 1981.

(23) Sirag, S. P., 'Physics Education', in *Newsletter of the Association of Humanistic Psychology*, (May 1979), pp. 17-18.

(24) Cunningham, I., 'Assessment and Experiential Learning' in Boot, R. and Reynolds, M. (eds), *Learning and Experience in Formal Education*, Manchester Monograph, (University of Manchester), 1983.

10

New ways of learning

Don Binsted

This chapter is about important new developments which are beginning to contribute to management development. These developments stem from ideas of open learning, distance learning and new educational technology. Definitions will be attempted, and the new technologies will be described in general terms. No attempt will be made to provide a catalogue of what is available nor to deal with the technical aspects of hardware; but further reading will be suggested. The present situation will be outlined and some possible future developments reviewed. The aim of the chapter is to illuminate the issue for those who will have to make decisions in this area in the not too distant future.

OPEN AND DISTANCE LEARNING: ARE THEY THE SAME?

There is some confusion about the meaning of the terms 'open' and 'distance'. Does the 'open' of the Open University mean the same as the 'open' of the Manpower Services Commission Open Tech Programme? What about the Strathclyde MBA (distance learning version): is that open and distance or both? John Coffey defines openness in terms of removing both educational and administrative constraints. An example of an educational constraint is 'student has to accept the sequence of teaching that is offered'. An example of an ative constraint is 'student must attend in a specific place' 977). [1] The removal of this latter constraint is a cornerstone ustance learning (Holmberg, 1974). [2] The characteristics of 'distance' given by Keegan include removal of Coffey's administrative constraints, together with some other positive characteristics like the use of media. (Keegan, 1980.) [3]

Sorting out the confusion

It is most useful to consider 'openness' and 'distance' as two independent properties, so that four different types of programme can be recognised. Those which are open, or distance, or both, or neither. For example, traditional taught courses fall into the 'neither' category. The Open Tech paper of George Tolley envisaged programmes which were open, but not distance (Tolley, 1983) [4]

One way to distinguish these two aspects is to associate 'openness' with removing educational constraints and 'distance' with removing administrative constraints. Based on the work of both Coffey and Keegan and also current research, and applying these ideas to management development, definitions can be suggested as follows.

Distance learning

1 Involves separation of the tutor and the learner. In this instance the word tutor is used to identify trainers, teachers, coaches, authors, etc.
2 Involves the use of at least one form of media — print, video, computer output, etc.
3 In general is suitable for a solo learner, although it may also be used in small groups of two or more.
4 Needs a delivery system.
5 Works anywhere providing any hardware required is available.

Open learning involves learners having

1 Choice about learning goals they wish to pursue.

2   Choice about sequence, or depth of learning.
3   Choice about learning process and level of involvement.
4   Unrestricted access, i.e. no educational pre-conditions.

Dimensions

Since most examples of open and/or distance learning do not meet the conditions of complete 'openness' or 'distance' it is useful to consider these as dimensions. The dimension of 'distance' would appear to involve the extent of learner's face-to-face interaction with the tutor.

Not distance   Distance

$\longrightarrow$

High tutor interaction   No tutor interaction
and proximity to learner   other than through
                                                    media nor proximity to
                                                    learner

Figure 10.1 The 'distance' dimension

Examples of the extremes are, for 'not-distance', a traditional management development workshop. For 'distance', a self-development workbook (Pedler, *et al.* 1978)[5] or workbook plus passive video (the Henley module on accounting for managers). The new Open University (OU) Business School programme on international marketing contains elements that are at both ends of the dimension. The broadcast or taped video programmes and workbooks are fully distance, whereas the residential weekend is specifically described as enabling learners to test out their own ideas, and to learn from others in ways which simply are not possible 'at a distance'.

The dimension of 'openness' would appear to involve the extent to which the learner's activity is prescribed, compared with exerting choice.

Not open   Open

$\longrightarrow$

Totally prescribed   Totally learner choice

Figure 10.2 The 'open' dimension

Examples of the extremes are: 'no-openness', a standard taught course; and high 'openness', the programme developed at the North East London Polytechnic based on self-managed learning sets (Binsted and Hodgson, 1984).[6] If these two dimensions are put together they suggest a model or map on which a particular programme can be plotted.

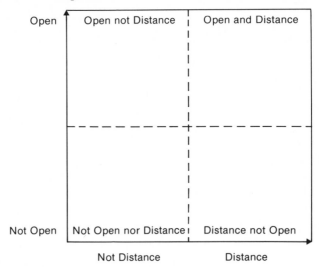

Figure 10.3 The 'open' and 'distance' model

In an investigation for the MSC the programmes and packages then found (January, 1984) were mostly in the 'distance not open' quadrant. Some were in the 'open and distance' quadrant whilst others were really resources for tutors to use with a learner group and are neither 'open nor distance'.

THE NEW TECHNOLOGY

The new technology becoming available to tutors links in with the 'distance' dimension of learning. There is nothing inherent in any technology which predisposes it to be open or not. The technology is about media and creation and delivery of learning materials. Some technology is well established, like the use of workbooks, while some is only at the experimental and 'not-proven' stage in the field of management development. Technology for distance learning (as distinct from technology in the classroom), creates and delivers materials which facilitate learning.

The most common forms of media are:

1 *Print,* in the form of study books (Strathclyde MBA), or workbooks (the Open Business School, Henley, Cranfield programmes). These may include text, graphics and photographs. The advent of word processors has greatly improved the economic production of text.

2 *Linear or passive video,* either broadcast (Open Business School) or on video cassette (Henley, Cranfield programmes, Leeds University coaching skills package). The enormous advantage of video is the ability to show dramatised or documentary interactions and situations. New technology in video production (like the camera/recorder) is helpful but delivery systems (video cassette recorders and TV/monitors) are well established and are available in increasing numbers in the home.

3 *Computer output,* in the form of text and graphics and limited sound (the most common of which is 'peep'). This may be via mainframe terminals (as at work stations) or on single or networked micros. Micros are increasingly to be found in the home. Although new micros are coming on to the market very frequently, the educational programmes to run on computers (courseware) are at the moment very sparse in the management area. However, the limited number that can be accessed at the moment give some idea of the potential of the technology (The Petty Cashier from Daedal, a production line simulation from Ferranti, or the 'Nipper' programme developed at the London Business School (Boot, 1979).)[7] The big advantage of computer-based learning is its interactivity.

4 *Interactive video,* which produces computer generated text, graphics, and sound together with video sequences. In general the more sophisticated (costly) the hardware, the higher the quality of the graphics. There is considerable variation in available systems which link a micro with either video tape players or video disc players. Figure 10.4 shows a schematic diagram of the Felix video system.

Some recent development in this technology offer cheaper

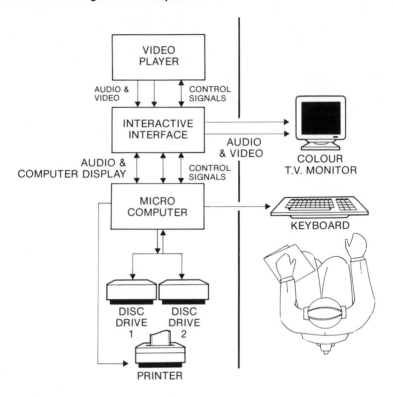

Figure 10.4 The Felix video system

ways of providing a system by using equipment already in the possession of the training department or learner. For example, in the tape based systems IVL provides a way of linking an existing Apple IIe to any commercial remote control video cassette recorder (VCR) to create an interactive video system (available from Dalroth). Felix have the Felix Link which connects any of four micros (BBC 'B', IBM PC, Apple IIe and Sirrius) with a commercial U-matic VCR. Personal Development Projects Ltd have just announced their 'Expert Learning System' which uses a domestic VCR and TV set. They sell a micro which links the components into an interactive video system which needs no disc drives. This is the first system the author has seen that could bring interactive video into the home ownership bracket. A growing library of courseware is now available for this system.

The benefits of tape versus disc is an area of lively debate. There is little doubt that disc offers significant technical advantage for delivery whereas tape has an advantage for in-house production of non-generic courseware.

5   *Other technology*, like broadcast TV via satellite or cable, teletext or view data systems, and teleconferencing all have potential and are alternative ways of delivering materials. An excellent new book gives very extensive coverage of the 'Role of Technology in Distance Education' based mostly on the unique and extensive research and experience of the OU (Bates, 1984). [8]

6   *Authoring languages and systems*, are an important element of new technology. In theory they enable a tutor to program a micro for computer based or interactive video learning. In practice there is a considerable difference between a very easy to use *system* like the Felix Fast 1:6 which offers the tutor a range of options and gently interrogates him, and the more complex *languages* which have to be learned, but may be more flexible. A new interactive video system based on Betamax and BBC B-micro called 'Take 5' offers the best and simplest authoring *system* I have so far found (using low cost components).

New technology has the potential of greatly extending the range of options for creating distance learning materials. Some types of technology may be essential to certain forms of learning (like inter-personal skill development), and may allow learning at a distance which has not been possible before. There are, however, many un-answered questions and little operating experience in the field of management development.

PROGRAMMES AND PACKAGES

Two sorts of open and distance learning material are currently available, and they tend to differ in a number of respects.

Programmes

These are integrated learning activities which form a complete programme of study using some distance learning format. In the examples currently available they average around 100 hours study time. Examples are the Open Business School, Henley, and Cranfield modules. These are similar in a number of respects. They use a multi-media approach of workbooks, passive video and audio cassettes, and the packages are held together with course maps, course calendars, and a number of back-up documents for reference.

The Open Business School models contained marked assignments, and assessment is an optional choice for the learner. The programmes are clearly designed for solo learners, although the Henley publicity does stress the option of using the material in small groups. In both the Open Business School and Henley case, the learner is registered as a student. For Henley this can be at any time during the year, but for the Open University one start date per year is offered. Opportunities are also provided for face-to-face or telephone tutoring, and in the Open Business School programmes, students are expected to attend a residential weekend and tutorials.

Another form of programme found in the research for the MSC already referred to, were examples where organisations had produced their own programmes internally. In these cases much less emphasis seems to have been given to tutor support. The designs of the programmes would seem to reflect fairly strongly the values of the organisations which originated them. An intention of those made in the educational institutions was clearly to produce generic material of wide appeal to as many people as possible. Considerable attention has been given to marketing these programmes. In general these programmes could be described as 'distance' but not very 'open'.

Computer-based and interactive video packages

These are in general of short duration (1 to 2 hours) and generally have a limited but specific learning goal. The designs often show links with what might be called a *training* philosophy rather than an educational one. There are interesting exceptions as in the 'Nipper' program which facilitates reflective learning using the principles of repertory grid. In various ways, packages involving computers are interactive.

An interactive video system has four types of output, text, graphics, audio and video. A computer-only system has only three

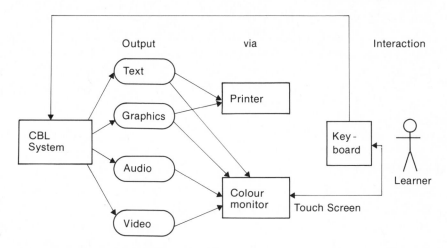

Figure 10.5 An interactive system

since the video output is missing. Input is most often through a keyboard which may be supplemented with a touch screen.

Design basis

A number of design features are discernible in most computer-based learning (CBL), which are borrowed from traditional designs. These include the use of:

Action mazes;
In-tray exercises;
Simulations;
Human interactions (modelling);
Choice and feedback in a task;
Data feedback;
Games;
Giving information and testing.

One obvious possibility is to use computers as programmed learning machines, and some of these principles are discernible in some packages. The question of whether these designs are suitable for management development is at least in some people's mind in considerable doubt. Even more to be avoided is the use the computer as an electronic page turner.

Learner interaction

There are a number of ways in which a learner may interact with a CBL system:

Answering questions;
Reacting to video sequences;
Making decisions;
Feeding in ideas;
Making choices.

MATERIALS AND INFRASTRUCTURE

Mention has already been made of various media and some effects of new technology. It was suggested that these factors might have more to do with the distance aspects of learning. There is undoubtedly much untapped potential and many new developments which need to be made to explore fully the limits of what management development can or cannot successfully achieve at a distance. Research into materials design forms an important part of the research programme in the Centre for the Study of Management Learning at the University of Lancaster. However, of equal importance is the infrastructure in which the material is used. Taking one extreme, of a stand alone programme designed for solo learners which requires little or no tutor support, and contains only self-assessment activities. Such a programme would typically not be computer-based especially if it involved a significant amount of study time. It is easy to imagine the difficulty a busy manager would find in getting the programme to the top of his priority list.

The practical manifestation might well be an inability to actually start or to progress very far when started. Complete lack of infrastructure might thus be a dominant factor regardless of the quality of the materials or media used. Conversely, a defined infrastructure including such things as a course calendar, assignment deadlines, tutorial dates, and completion dates ready for exams, might provide just the trigger for giving the work higher priority. It would appear that in some instances infrastructure may influence the degree of openness experienced by the learner. In any event it appears to be of the greatest importance to consider materials design and delivery, and infrastructure as equally important aspects of open and distance learning. They are complementary aspects and may offset each other. For example, a short stand alone interactive-video package which has a high fascination value may need little infrastructure, whereas a long programme involving dense text in print may need quite a lot. Research should illuminate the situation providing it adequately takes into account the experience of the learner.

There are a number of options for providing infrastructure. It can come from:

1 The producing and/or delivering organisation (Open Business School).
2 The organisation in which the learner works (self-help groups, site supervisors, etc.).
3 The learner (setting deadlines, targets, etc.).

Whether the reader is interested in producing, delivering or buying-in programmes, the message in this section is 'consider infrastructure as much as materials design and delivery'.

HOW DOES THIS FIT IN WITH MANAGEMENT DEVELOPMENT?

There is a growing opinion about the fit between open and distance learning and management development. There are two elements to be considered; *access* to programmes and packages which is predominantly the 'distance' dimension, and *suitability* which is predominantly the 'open' dimension.

Access

On the question of access, a facility where managers can learn at times and paces to suit themselves is a very attractive one, and seems to fit the lifestyle of the manager who may have to work irregular hours, travel extensively, etc. This is particularly the case if the place is either at the desk or at home. This raises the question as to whether the learner is going to do this in his own time. This certainly seems to be an assumption that some work on, and thus rightly claim a saving in cost against conventional methods. The advantage of 'doing it in the comfort of one's own home' can of course have negative connotations for some (what about spouse/kids/dog, etc?).

Suitability

The suitability aspect recognises that managers are most frequently mature experienced people who may not be excited by formal study methods, being predominantly people of action. They may be biased against attending long courses of study, and favour learning from experience, and inevitably look for the practical relevance of learning to their work situation. They may, therefore, be attracted by the use of video, micro computers and other distance learning media, or the flexibility and choice offered in open programmes.

There seems to be some sort of fit between open and distance learning and management people, but whether this potential is finally fully realised will become apparent as new developments are created and researched.

As already stated one issue that is emerging as critical is the infrastructure which supports the learning materials. In one sense the more open and distance a programme or package is, the less the infrastructure will be. This, however, tacitly assumes that the learner is highly motivated and self-disciplined. The problem for many managers may well be that other demands on their time always have a higher priority. Some supportive infrastructure may therefore be vital. In CBL the packages are usually short and can be more easily fitted into other activities. The position of the delivery point may be critical, and this will in turn depend on technology (whether the learning station is a terminal of a mainframe computer at a work station, or in a special location as a learning resource, or on a home micro). Not only is the infrastructure important, the design of the material is crucial as well. Thus the fascination factor of a good interactive video, or the avoidance of dense text without graphics, or the use of commentators on video, who 'jolly you along' (Henley) all appear to be important. A great deal more should be known about this in two years' time.

THE FACTORS AFFECTING GROWTH

There are a number of factors affecting growth of open and distance learning which are all occurring simultaneously, and are thus forcing development at a rate which may seem too rapid. These factors can be summarised as follows:

1   *The MSC Open Tech Programme* There are currently 20 projects which are operational in the management and supervisory field. This represents a total of £7.1M for the development of these programmes. There is no doubt that this is the single largest intervention in the management field, and without this money it is very difficult to see how few if any of these projects would be operational. How many of the projects will finally survive is of course yet an unanswered question, but there is little doubt that this massive intervention by the MSC is one of considerable historic importance. Many people are now involved in producing these programmes who have never been involved in such activity before.

2   *Educational institutions* A number of educational institutions who specialise in the management field have either started or are planning to enter the field. They have a high reputation and subject experts available. The Open University has started up the Open Business School, and with Henley and Cranfield actually have substantial programmes already available. Strathclyde has a distance learning version of their MBA and are setting up a Flexible Management Development Programme. Considerable further expansion is being worked on.

3   *New Technology* Developments by hardware manufacturers are increasing, and some of the first management courseware is beginning to be seen. Hardware manufacturers are coming increasingly into this market, particularly those who produce micro computers and video disc machines. A number of software houses in the educational and training field are producing high grade management courseware. Although the amount of material in the management field is growing it is still fairly meagre. Output from these people includes generic courseware (i.e. programmes that you buy off the shelf), and customarised programs specific to a client. There is still enormous scope for development in this area. Some of these groups offer consultancy, design and training services.

4   *Authoring systems or languages* These allow training staff to

program micros or interactive video systems with little or no previous knowledge of programming or computers. This will enable companies to develop their own sophisticated materials. It does not, of course, solve the problem of designing the material in the first place, which is the key to the quality of distance learning materials, but it enables sophisticated designs to be transferred to interactive video systems.

5 *Television production companies* clearly see the possibility of making and selling high quality video material into this new market.

6 *Being left out*, most management development people are aware of the developments, and are increasingly coming under the influence of markerting activities from providers. The potential is clear but views about what to do first are anything but clear. The need to do something, however, is pressing, so quite a number of organisations are beginning pilot projects, and 'getting their feet wet'.

THE CURRENT SCENE

The situation in the UK is that this is an area of considerable growth and interest (witness the number of conferences in the last two years and those currently planned). But there is very little accumulated operational experience available to provide clear guidance of what producers and researchers are forming. Various networks and research projects which focus on learner experience will greatly help this process.

The MSC must be complemented on setting up a number of support projects which offer help and advice to producers of open and distance learning programmes. Other projects are aimed at producing guidelines for future production and evaluation of the whole Open Tech project. There is, of course, a great deal of experience and research available in areas other than management from for example the Council for Education Technology and the Open University (see 'further reading' at the end of this chapter). A great deal more will be known by about March 1987, when most of the research projects and the Open Tech programme are scheduled to finish.

There is considerable interest in open and distance learning, and enough has been done to demonstrate the potential for management development. Whether this potential is realised will depend on what happens in the next two or three years. The powerful driving forces already referred to may in the end be dysfunctional if development is forced too far ahead of research.

FUTURE DEVELOPMENTS

It is obviously risky to try and predict future developments. However, some can already be seen, as it were, in embryo form. Some of these are:

1 The use of small groups of learners. In many instances the assumption implied in design is that the learner is going to spend most of the time working solo with the materials. This may indeed be a pressing reason for engaging in distance learning in the first place, since the learner may be isolated in some way. However, the use of groups opens up a number of possibilities. Limited experimentation indicates for instance that people using computer-based learning packages seem to learn much more when working in groups of two or three, although this extends the time of interaction. A group of two or three people working through a Henley programme may provide infrastructure and support for each other on a self-help basis.

2 Provision of selection and choice, so that the learner is free to select exactly what she/he wants, and equally miss out exactly what she/he wants. This could be linked with self-diagnostic activities where learners can measure their current level of competence in a particular area.

3 An emphasis on removing other *educational* constraints and moving towards more 'openness'.

4 Extension into the interpersonal skill and affective learning area and the deeper levels of cognitive learning and attitude change.

5 Self-directed groups inside organisations who have a wide variety of open learning materials available 'off-the-shelf' to use at any time.

6   New hardware in the form of micros and video sources, and use of more conversion kits which link equipment already owned to form interactive video systems.

7   More powerful and user friendly authoring languages and systems.

8   Packages for home micros (as distinct from business micros).

9   Utilisation of artificial intelligent and expert systems.

10   Use of Prestel, cable television, satellites, etc.

11   More collaboration between a number of groups or individuals with different expertise since inherently the whole operation of producing distance learning in this field requires a great deal of skill, not normally to be found in one person or one part of an organisation, or even in one organisation.

DILEMMAS FOR THE TRAINER AND MANAGEMENT DEVELOPER

The problems of deciding where to start for trainers or MD people are legion. For example:

1   What level of technology to select, interactive video disc, tape or printed text?

2   What hardware (if any) which will fix in many cases the authoring language and the courseware that can be bought in?

3   Should one buy in generic material, get it specially adapted, make one's own or get someone else to do it for one?

4   Which areas of training to choose and who will the learners be?

5   Negotiating realistic budgets for hardware, software and courseware.

To get started within an organisation, there are a number of steps which I personally believe are essential.

1   Treat the introduction of open and distance learning as an organisation development problem. Work out a change strategy based on a client-centred approached.

2   Find out what is available by contact with producers and hardware manufacturers (exhibitions, promotion meetings, trailer videos), or use the MARIS index and other Open Tech

sources, or go where research and development is being done (for example the National Computing Centre or the Centre for the Study of Management Learning at the University of Lancaster).

3 Put as much thought into the infrastructure to support learning as into the design or selection of material and media.

4 Evaluate a pilot project, particularly using the experience of the learner.

5 Ensure as far as possible that the first pilot succeeds.

Whether the trainer goes to workshops or conferences, hires a consultant, buys in purpose made courseware or generic material or starts on a do-it-yourself basis, the process is likely to involve discovery learning. From observation and conversation in the management field a significant number of trainers and MD people are pondering what to do, and just beginning to get their 'feet wet'.

CONCLUSION

The use of open and distance learning in the management field is being driven by a number of forces already referred to.

What will happen eventually is uncertain, but I have a growing conviction that one of the key factors will be the educational quality of programs or packages which become available. It is unfortunate in one way that so much development is going on simultaneously, and there is a danger that there will not be enough time for all those involved to learn from each others' experience. Even more important is that the amount of research being done is still quite small. The market could be enormous. Henley in their publicity quote a figure of 80 per cent of British managers not ever having had any formal training. Open and distance learning may possibly divert people from the traditional form of management training and development into open and distance learning activities. Since many providers of management education and training have already got that message the result should not be too catastrophic. The other more exciting possibility is, however, that these methods might attract many more people to continue their development in a way which is suddenly much more acceptable to them than the traditional means of education or training. This may also be because the cost enables them to engage in activities which would otherwise be closed to them. If this is the case, and the Henley figure is correct, there is the possibility of accessing a market four times the size of the current one. Thus rather than substituting one form of training or education for another, people may engage in development which they would not otherwise have. It could be the difference between training and no training. If that is the case we could make a significant improvement to the UK's management capability in the next few years.

My personal fear, however, is that if the quality of the materials or the infrastructure in which they are offered is not good enough or in line with what managers need, then the whole approach will become discredited, as so many ideas have become discredited in the management field. The main reason will be that the quality is not good enough. Thus the necessary research programmes to allow high quality material to be produced and intelligently used are of the utmost importance. It is also important to say that intensive marketing could well raise expectations far above reality, and this again would surely be a way to discredit the whole operation. I am in general, however, optimistic that the considerable and exciting potential already visible will be converted into new practice.

REFERENCES

(1) Coffey, J., Open Learning Opportunities for Mature Students in Davies, T. C, *Open Learning Systems for Mature Students*, CET Working Paper 14, 1977.
(2) Holmberg, B., *Distance Education*, Malmo Hermods, 1974.
(3) Keegan, D., 'On Defining Distance Education', *Distance Education* vol. 1, no. 1, pp. 13-26, 1980.
(4) Tolley, G., 'The Open Tech: Why, What and How', Paper No. 1, Open Tech Programme, MSC, 1983.
(5) Pedler, M. J., Burgoyne, J. G. and Boydell, T. H., *A Manager's Guide to Self-Development*. McGraw-Hill, 1978.
(6) Binsted, D. and Hodgson, V., Open and Distance Learning in Management Education and Training, *MSC Positional Paper,* 1984.
(7) Boot, R., 'The Management Learning Project: Final Report to the Director London Business School', 1979

(8)   Bates, A. W. (ed.), *The Role of Technology in Distance Education*, Croom Helm, 1984

FURTHER READING

Beech, G., *Computer Based Learning*, Sigma Technical Press, 1983.
Dean, C. and Whitlock, Q., *A Handbook of Computer Based Training*, Kogan Page, 1983.
Duke, J., 'Interactive Video. Implications for Education and Training', Council for Education Technology Working Paper, 22, 1983.
Heaford, J. M., *Myth of the Learning Machine, The Theory and Practice of Computer Based Learning*, Sigma Technical Press, 1983.
Lewis, R., *Open Learning in Action*, CET, 1984.
Neil, M. W. (ed.), *Education of Adults at a Distance, Open University*, Kogan Page, 1981.
O'Shea, T. and Self, J., *Learning and Teaching with Computers, Artificial Intelligence in Education*, Harvester Press, 1983.
Parsloe, E., *Interactive Video*, Sigma Technical Press, 1983.

SOURCES OF INFORMATION

Centre for the Study of Management Learning (research only),
Gillow House,
University of Lancaster,
Lancaster. Tel: 0524-65201, ext. 4855

The National Computing Centre Ltd,
Oxford Road,
Manchester,
England M1 7ED. Tel: 061-228-6333. Contact: Janet Rothwell

The Open Business School,
The Open University,
Box 76,
Milton Keynes MK7 6AN. Tel: 0908-71231. Contact: Brian Lund

Henley Open Management Education,
Greenlands,
Henley-on-Thames,
Oxon RG9 3AU. Tel: 049-166-552. Contact: Aldwyn Cooper

Strathclyde Business School,
130 Rottenrow,
Glasgow G4 0GE. Tel: 041-552-7141. Contact: Rob Harrower

Wirysystem Ltd (for Felix hardware and courseware),
32 Hill Rise,
Chalfont St. Peter,
Bucks SL9 9BH. Tel: 0753-885549

National Interactive Video Centre,
27 Marylebone Road,
London NW1 5JS. Tel: 01-935-8190. Contact: Angus Dalton

Manpower Services Commission,
Open Tech Unit,
Moorfoot,
Sheffield S1 4PQ. Tel: 0742-704996

Personnel Development Projects Ltd,
Unipenta House,
4 High Causeway,
Whittlesey,
Peterborough PE7 1AE. Tel: 0733-204727

Ivan Berg Software,
Dunluce House,
4-8 Camfield Gardens,
London NW6 3QT. Tel: 01-328-3341

11

The learning spiral

John Morris

BRINGING WORK AND LEARNING TOGETHER

'I know I learn a lot from doing things, but if there's something I need to know, it seems sensible to take time off work so I can learn about it.' If the busy manager can be heard to say this, the training and development specialist can breathe a sigh of relief, and go ahead with carefully designed learning-programmes, shaped around clearly defined learning-needs and paths to their achievement.

Of course, learning by doing will remain the keystone of all programmes of training and development: the acid test of effective investment in learning is whether the learning can be applied. But there seem to be many reasons why 'working' and 'learning' should be distinguished from one another, if only to enable successful learners to remain aware of how their learning has been achieved, so that they can be more effective when they turn their hand to coaching and counselling their successors.

The problem seems to be this. How can one clearly distinguish work from learning, and yet find ways of bringing them together skilfully and deliberately in a self-managed flow of learning from experience? In helping managers to tackle this problem, the various models of learning styles have been immensely useful. Probably the best known approach is still that of David Kolb (Kolb *et al.* 1979).[1] This takes the form of a four-phase diagram, each phase neatly contrasting with another in an elegant cross-formation. If you want to see your preferred style of learning, you complete a simple questionnaire and see yourself clearly represented on the model. You can then compare yourself with other people, of different ages, sexes, occupations and so on.

Good models are for focusing our attention on something that interests us, not for covering everything in their domain. It is a tribute to the model that it has fostered variants on it; some would say improvements. It has also attracted sharp criticism: in my view, another tribute. I came to the model rather late, from a background in social and developmental psychology. My appetite had been sated with the rich fare of psychological research into learning processes (in fact it had given me acute indigestion). Human learning turns out, as you can imagine, to be a fantastically complex affair, made even more complex because our study of learning is itself a process of learning. Or rather, a complicated hierarchical network of processes. When rich food fails to satisfy, something simple and salty is refreshing, and may prove far more nourishing. For me, the Kolb model met this need. His later work in developing the model shows how soundly based it is.

But I also found the Honey and Mumford model (1982)[2] very attractive, especially in working with busy managers in short events. The words describing the phases were simpler than Kolb's, though they were turned into types of managerial behaviour rather than phases of learning. Activist, theorist, pragmatist, reflector: everyone can readily recognise these. I found the questionnaire meatier than Kolb's. Add to all this a club in which members could pool their scores and experiences of working with the approach, and we have a learning model which takes its own lessons seriously.

A further model of learning, in the form of personal development, has been recently developed by Bert Juch (1983)[3]. Juch locates his learning model in a rich context of other studies, drawn from many fields. For good measure, he embeds his research investigation in a personal history, showing how he came to develop the model and what his experiences have been with it.

I have found these models illuminating and useful, but have also found it helpful to use another, which is close to them in its structure, but is more 'organisational' in its focus. Organisations are systems for getting work done, by dividing it up (usually very efficiently) and then putting it together again (notably less efficiently). The learning model that I have been using links directly to an organisation for doing work.

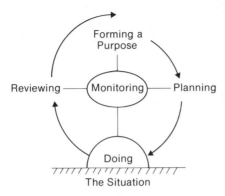

Figure 11.1 The learning spiral approach

Just a word or two now on why I call the model a 'spiral' (Figure 11.1). I join with Juch here. It is really a preference for an open metaphor, rather than a closed one, like 'cycle' or 'style'. Juch talks of 'whirling cycles within a lifelong spiral' (p. 24) I find it useful to think of turnings in a spiral rather than sharp discontinuous levels of learning. But I cannot deny, from frequently repeated experience, that some of the turns can be very abrupt!

From Figure 11.1 it can be seen that at the bottom is the earthy activity of 'doing' (that most flexible of terms), grounded in a situation. Above it are the classic managerial activities of planning, monitoring, and reviewing, and above that – forming a purpose. If I had to find an extended phrase to include these phases of learning, it would be something like this: Learning from trying to express a *purpose* in action within a situation: *planning* being the shaping of an appropriate action, *monitoring* being the control of action as it occurs, and *reviewing* being the comparison of the action with the purpose. The model has the virtue of being easily transposed from the individual level to the group level, and to the organisational level. Since I am interested in linking individual, group and organisational levels of learning, it has been useful to have a model that seems to move so readily from individual to organisation.

Another useful aspect of the model is that it enables one to see very clearly an unfortunate side-effect of the conventional form of organisation. I call it 'splitting the learning'. (See Figure 11.2). This obviously happens because of the manifold advantages of the division of labour, as against the organisational advantage of singleness of

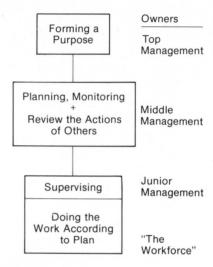

Figure 11.2 Splitting the learning

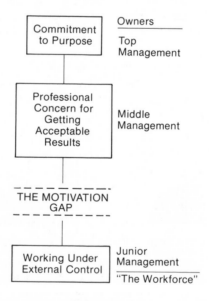

Figure 11.3 Splitting the commitment

over-all purpose (survival, for example, or growth). But when we look at the implications of the division of work for the continuity of learning, it is clear that the devices used within organisations for turning purposes into action may not be those that occur in individuals when strongly felt purpose is expressed in action. *By and large, conventional organisations replace strong feeling, which is the individual link between purpose and action, with tight control.* This produces one of the most depressing effects of this kind of organisation – a splitting of commitment that results from a splitting of purpose from performance. I have called this 'the motivation gap' and have conservatively placed it below the managerial level of planning, monitoring and review. But many groups of managers I have worked with suggest that the motivation gap is often above that level, so that one commonly finds a highly motivated board of directors signalling their purposes wildly but ineffectively to a distinctly unmoved group of executives. (See Figure 11.3).

There seems to be a powerful and attractive way of getting purpose and performance close together again. It is the direct-action approach. (See Figure 11.4). The purpose is embodied in a leader, rather than a mere owner, or director. The leader, full of the energy that flows from purpose, makes direct contact with those who take action, cutting across the managerial layers, and especially those with a concern for planning and review. One finds this commonly enough in small, entrepreneurial businesses, and in 'real-time management', celebrated for its hair-trigger response to emergencies.

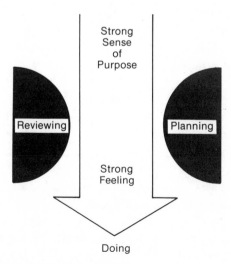

Figure 11.4 The direct-action approach

Unfortunately, the by-passing of planning and review can have dire effects on many kinds of action. New products and services may take years to gestate, and will never appear if direct action rules. Routine performances may need to be carefully assembled and rehearsed, but will be ignored or under-valued by direct action. Direct action is splendid when it works, and often disastrous when it does not. It is all or nothing. And it certainly has no time for fostering learning, for enabling it to become conscious and reflective. Such qualities are seen as pernicious, as the forerunners of 'paralysis by analysis'.

Is it possible, then, to find other ways of countering the fragmentation that is all too common in the conventional organisation, with its disastrous effects on an energetic flow of learning? Can we combine work and the whole spiral of learning? Clearly, to do so effectively requires an unconventional organisation, one in which purpose can infuse performance without loss of planning and review. One way in which this purpose can be achieved is in the deliberately small world of a development programme, in which learning comes from project work. Not project 'exercises' or project 'recommendations' but real development work, in which needs are met and there are changes for the better.

In a development programme, based on live projects, the energy that flows from purpose needs to be shaped into coherent activity through a process of continuous planning, monitoring and review. Instead of these 'managerial' activities being operated through a formal procedure of decision and control, the people who are engaged in the operational work of the project are able to relate their experience to the guiding purpose, *which is very much in themselves*. If we still wish to use the invidious term 'control' (invidious only when it comes to controlling people) we could say that the project is a continuing experience of self-control in the light of a guiding and energising purpose. This stands in the sharpest possible contrast to the conventional organisation, in which the work done by the 'workforce' is based on the distant and often inscrutable purposes of owners and investors, mediated by complex and often contradictory control procedures.

The development programmes I wish to comment on now have been part of the work of the Development Consortium, which is a recently established venture in management development, hived off from Manchester Business School (though still based there) with the aid of the Foundation for Management Development. It is independent and self-funding, existing to foster initiatives in action learning and other forms of development work that seek to bring work and learning into the same set of activities. Unlike the usual management centre, it does not have a fixed staff, apart from the two managing partners and an administrative partner. It works wherever possible with practising managers as the learning consultants and advisers. If other staff are needed, they will be brought in for a specific programme. The basic unit of work is a development programme, usually consisting of several linked projects.

We often think of a consortium as an ad hoc association of several substantial businesses coming together to manage an important project. The Development Consortium is a more informal association, bringing together individuals, rather than institutions, in development programmes of many kinds. They have included corporate strategy workshops with a major public corporation, senior development workshops for a leading textile firm, action learning programmes with the Co-operative Wholesale Society, participation in the design and staffing of the Senior Management Development Programme of the water industry, action research in new work options for mid-career managers, and a linked series of action learning programmes for the Manchester Social Services Department.

What do all these diverse activities have in common? They all take the form of development activities, rather than educational programmes or training courses. They all struggle to identify complex issues of real concern to the managers taking part, and they are all closely associated with managerial work, rather than being clinically uncoupled from it.

There is another thing that these activities have in common. They all follow through the whole learning spiral, often through several turns of the spiral. They relate purposes to performance, planning to review. They question purposes in the light of experience, rather than force experience (or reports of it) to conform to fixed purposes. They recognise that an effective development activity must find its own strong purpose, since it is exposed to so many sources of disturbance that lack of purpose will swiftly lead to its dissolution.

But any further search for common factors in diverse activities would probably be mistaken. One great value of development activities is that particular issues can be addressed in all their uniqueness. What might prove useful, however, is to note some of the experiences that seem pertinent to getting the learning spiral to work. The experiences are not pointed enough to be called 'lessons', and they are not solidly enough based to be claimed as 'evidence'. But they may indicate questions for later consideration.

DEVELOPMENT CULTURE IN WORKING COMBINATION WITH DOMINANT CULTURE

Development projects bring two cultures closely together. These are the dominant culture and the development culture. The dominant culture is the set of values and ways of doing things that predominate in the organisation: the tone usually being set by the central group of top management (or, in owner-managed enterprises, the owner). In a successful organisation, the dominant culture will usually have strong developmental aspects, but these have to fit in to many other day-to-day requirements and pressures. The development project, on the other hand, has a licence to establish a development culture, and certainly a practical necessity to do so, if it is to be effective in achieving its task.

Much of the literature dealing with developmental failures reveals situations in which the two cultures came into collision and, in the short run at least, the dominant culture won.

In the activities of the Development Consortium, the two cultures are brought together from the beginning, because a steering group is invariably part of the programme design. The steering group contains senior line managers from the organisation or organisations taking part in the programme. They are members of the dominant culture, faced with the challenge of enabling the two cultures to work together to mutual advantage. The development culture knows all about mutuality: thrives on it, in fact. Not so the dominant culture. Most dominant cultures are greatly concerned with the maintenance of the existing pattern of authority, often exercised through a clearly-defined line of command. The task of balancing the two cultures provides a powerful learning experience for members of the steering group, and a continuing insight into the challenges posed by each to the other.

COMING TO TERMS WITH TRIBES

Of course, there are far more than two cultures living within the organisation. There are also the powerful sub-cultures of the main business activities: marketing, sales, production, distribution, finance, accounting, technical services, personnel. Many of these sub-cultures have been lovingly nurtured by professional education and training. Some of the professions provide traditions, career paths, rewards (and punishments) of great power and long standing. They cut across the dominant culture of the business, often providing opportunities for development, and sometimes unintentionally producing inertia, confusion and cynicism.

It does not seem too fanciful to see these sub-cultures as the sustaining elements in organisational tribes, and whenever I have discussed this notion with groups of managers, they have accepted it readily (particularly where other tribes are concerned). Indeed, in many an organisation, the tribes and their mutual antipathy are taken for granted; a fact of life. Yet the experience of working with 'multi-tribal' project teams suggests that tribes are to some extent conventional metaphors, rather than all powerful realities. Tribal loyalties can quickly be set aside when a demanding and engrossing task is in hand.

Successful businesses seem to be able to bring the tribes together in a durable confederation, with the larger commitment of securing the success of the business as a whole. In a sense, the whole business comes to resemble a small nation.

HUNGER FOR UNDERSTANDING OF STRATEGY

Managers who are working on projects quickly find themselves looking beyond their usual boundaries. Partly this is because development projects are chosen to widen their perspectives, and are invariably successful in achieving this. But it seems also to be a matter of getting a sense of how the organisation as a whole is moving, and perhaps a hope that this will provide a set of useful guidelines for one's daily work, and a reasonably clear context for the project work.

There is also a sense in which 'strategy' becomes a synonym for 'the over-all purpose of the business'. Development work encourages questioning, and questioning sooner or later becomes a questioning of purpose. 'What are we doing this for anyway?' 'How does this fit in with the other activities going on?' As the questions become wider, one can see them as expressing a real hunger for an understanding of the over-branching purposes of the organisation.

The sheer sense of urgency that project work engenders – or perhaps it is rather a sharpened sense of organisational opportunities – leads to confrontations which are focused on the feasibility of current organisational stances. In one of our programmes, managers in a project-set accused top managers of leaving a 'strategic vacuum' within the business. When this was discussed, the top managers argued that the 'vacuum' was one of the many signs of the intractability of an old, highly ramified business with structural abysses a century old. The question for them was: How do we slowly form a strategy that can gain the commitment of all the varied interest-groups shaping the business? Within the heightened consciousness of the project-set, fresh from disturbing extrapolations of future business threats, this 'slow but sure' approach seemed unacceptably complacent.

It is characteristic of development work that it encourages these issues to be raised, and perhaps coped with. And it reminds us that the hunger for an understanding of strategy is part of the deeper need to couple performance with a durable sense of purpose. Performances, however efficient, are not self-sustaining, especially when one begins to question them. At this point, the issue of leadership arises.

LEADERSHIP

There seem to be many kinds of leader. One well-known political figure was reputed to have said recently: 'I don't understand all this fuss about leadership. You just tell people what to do and they do it!' Another kind of leader would see this as domination, acceptable only in emergencies, and even then building up a formidable weight of resentment and subversion.

My experience in project teams brings out a familiar insight: leadership flows from demonstrable commitment to purpose, which releases energies that focus attention. For those who share the purpose, this kind of free-flowing energy is attractive: the person imbued with purpose becomes a readily identifiable focus, an embodiment of what needs to be done. Because a project team is a kind of small world, capable of following through the whole learning spiral (usually several turns of it) in a manageable timescale, the presence of leadership is usually easily recognisable. Because the purpose is so clear and readily available, all members of a project team commonly find occasion to act as leaders, according to skill, sensitivity and circumstance.

KEEPING IT SIMPLE

In a major programme in the public sector, a visiting speaker from an entrepreneurial business made a great impact with his succinct and salty list of Do's and Don'ts for successful management. One of the best received of these was 'Keep it simple, stupid!'

We can understand why senior managers from an uncomfortably visible part of the embattled public sector should hunger and thirst after simplicity. All the more when the relevant Department of State complicates life for these managers by imposing its own notions of simplicity on their planning and operations.

Yet it seems clear that success in most activities depends on holding the essentials of the business in mind (and at heart) as a set of vital priorities. 'As complex as you must, as simple as you can' emerges as a lesson from work in development projects, where it seems at times that almost everything is relevant to the project work, yet pressures of time and resource impose severe limits.

LEARNING FROM BEST CURRENT PRACTICE

Reg Revans (1983)[4] identifies a tendency of experienced managers which can seriously limit their capacity to learn from a wide range of contacts: eager acceptance of the charismatic influence of other managers seen as being successful. He argues that this tendency must develop into willingness to use one's own powers to the full, and have them questioned and stimulated by others. The result of this transformation is that any impulse to literal imitation of someone else's success is turned into emulation on the basis of one's own distinctive strengths. The manager then becomes able to learn from failures as well as successes, and from a whole host of contacts, irrespective of formal status.

It is interesting from this point of view to look at the lessons drawn from two recent studies of best current business practice: the McKinsey study of American firms '*In Search of Excellence*' (Peters and Waterman 1982)[5] and the British study '*The Winning Streak*' (Goldsmith and Clutterbuck, 1984).[6] Despite some interesting differences between the two studies, successful companies emerge as those with a strong, distinctive culture, represented by the top management. They are firmly based in products and services in which they have a widely recognised competence, and which the managers know how to manage. And they all have a distinctive ability to do a number of simple things well. But many of the simple things pull in different directions and have to be skilfully balanced.

From the descriptions given in both books, it is clear that successful companies have dominant cultures with a strong and continuing thrust towards development, particularly to doing things better than others. They succeed in countering their own tendencies to fragmentation by a great variety of devices: early fostering of general managers, high visibility of top managers and their priorities, internal promotion, continuing attempts to work with their members on the basis of mutual advantage, strong emphasis on informal communication, semi-autonomous business units, and careers open to their talents.

One might wonder what semi-autonomous business units are doing in a list of ways of countering fragmentation. It is the fragmentation of learning and commitment that is of concern here, and small business units, with a close association of purpose and performance within the working group, come very close to providing a natural flow of learning from business experience.

Many of these ways of countering fragmentation are only open to top managment, and not the whole of top management at that. In order to effect the kinds of changes in structures and systems that many of the successful companies display, one would need a substantial mandate for re-organisation. But this is only because we are seeking a solution to fragmentation on an organisational scale. If we reduce the scale, it is possible to see possibilities for bringing the key phases of the learning spiral energetically together on *any* scale of human activity. The release of energies and creativity in those who choose to leave formal employment in order to start in their own businesses is striking, yet commonplace. The recent emphasis on self-development programmes enables individuals to look carefully at their working roles in order to find opportunities for 'negotiated change' in line with their under-used skills and interests. It is perhaps not surprising that many of these individual self-help materials focus on the same issues as the sophisticated studies of corporate strategy: identifying one's strengths and weaknesses in relation to external opportunities and threats, mobilising one's resources setting priorities, and developing the capability of continuous learning from experience.

It seems to me, then, that all the ways of countering the deep-seated drive to organisational fragmentation link up with one key theme. *The task is to turn as much work as possible into development work, without seriously unbalancing the organisation and wasting resources.* It is worth recalling at this point, that we have not been arguing for the 'direct action' approach, though that has an intuitive appeal to most of us, with its sense of energy and commitment. The whole argument has been for opportunities for us to move purposefully through the *whole* learning spiral, with our own purposes providing the energies.

The learning spiral, seen as a whole, gives due place to planning and monitoring and review: all of them highly conscious, deliberate, responsible activities. The planning of development work must take into account its effect on other work. If this is not picked up in the planning phase of the learning spiral, it should be evident at the monitoring or review phases. Those development activities that incur avoidable costs or unbalance the system of which they are a part need to be carefully checked against their initial purpose. Was the purpose over-ambitious, or naive? Since the purpose itself is part of a set of purposes, it can itself become the focus of learning. While it may sound like gobbledy gook if we read it quickly, it is nonetheless perfectly reasonable, and indeed often necessary, to form the purpose of looking at the ways in which one of our purposes keeps causing trouble, for us and others.

I have talked about 'turns in the spiral' where others have talked about 'levels of learning'. Part of conscious learning is to become consciously critical of our purposes, and able to relate them to more comprehensive and coherent purposes. It may sound odd and confusing to talk about 'learning to learn'. But we can easily recognise that one of our purposes can be to manage our own learning; to become aware of how we are currently learning, and to find ways of improving it. If we do not manage ourselves, we will find no lack of other people willing and eager to manage us, to their own advantage.

Not all development work has to be cast in the form of a project (though there is nothing to stop us seeing our own learning-activities as personal projects: it sharpens the mind). Most enterprises, however enterprising, use the term 'project' rather sparingly, to describe major initiatives or 'one-offs'. And yet every really successful organisation is full to bursting with development work, because people have become members of a culture which places great emphasis on doing things well, and then doing them better.

To return to the title of my chapter: if we want to get the learning spiral to work, we must treat it consistently as a *development spiral* focusing on the endless opportunities for development work, from the smallest improvement in working practices or product quality to the most cosmic 'great society' that our collective imaginations and skills can devise. In development work, small or large, the divided activities of work and learning, purpose and performance, long separated by conventional forms of organisation, come together in a continuing process of changing for the better.

REFERENCES

(1) Kolb, D. A. *et al. Organisational Psychology*, 3rd edition, Englewood Cliffs, New Jersey, Prentice-Hall Inc., 1979.

(2) Honey, P. & Mumford A., *The Manual of Learning Styles,* (self-published, 1982).

(3) Juch, A. H., *Personal Development*, Chichester, John Wiley & Sons, 1983.

(4) Revans, R. W., *The ABC of Action Learning*, 2nd Edition, Bromley, Kent, Chartwell-Bratt, 1983.

(5) Peters, T. J. & Waterman, R. H., *In Search of Excellence*, New York, Harper & Row, 1982.

(6) Goldsmith, W. & Clutterbuck, D., *The Winning Streak*, London, Weidenfeld & Nicholson, 1984.

Part IV
MANAGEMENT DEVELOPMENT IN ACTION

12

Creating in-house programmes

Bruce Nixon

My central interest in recent years has been to discover how to make in-house management development really effective. In my view management development has huge, if largely unfulfilled, potential for organisations. This chapter is about that quest in one particular organisation.

Sun Alliance is a traditional, city-based, financial company whose origins date back to 1710. It is a very successful organisation, especially when assessed by financial criteria. Organisations such as this function in a world of increasing and unpredictable change. These are conditions in which management development with its emphasis on leadership, teamwork, strategic management, effective problem solving, flexibility and adaptability should have a great deal to offer.

My experience is that managers in this type of business are typically down-to-earth and practical. Their attitudes to management development are usually cautious although they often become interested if they see a practical pay-off. They are not given to experimenting and are put off by approaches which seem theoretical or smack of 'navel gazing'. A management style which emphasises control and discourages risk-taking and openness often gets in the way of excellent performance and the full development of potential. The severe pressures of the market and continued changes in systems and technology make tremendous demands and restrict the time available for management development.

Paradoxically, it is often when important changes are taking place that managers are most reluctant to spend time on management development, team development or organisation development. The pressures are such that they have to be absolutely convinced that there will be a practical pay-off. Unless they have experienced the benefits previously, they are likely to feel that it is an unnecessary indulgence to take time out to plan crucial changes despite the potential benefit of better decisions and higher commitment. Such approaches are contrary to familiar patterns of conducting business in a large organisation. Therefore it requires an unusual degree of independence and openness to act in contradiction to accepted ways of managing.

These conditions at first look difficult for a would-be innovator in the field. Yet in fact they provide an excellent discipline for the management development practitioner who is determined to work close to his customers and provide services of real value.

As a Training Manager I do not believe I am in the business of education. To my mind, what matters in a business environment is that performance is improved and potential developed. I am in the business of helping managers create a winning business. In my view the task requires concentration on approaches which focus directly on improved individual, organisation and business performance. It also requires great care not to cause adverse reactions which may jeopardise months or sometimes years of patient work. Care is needed not to suggest that the search for improved performance implies criticism. The difficulty here is that the potentially most effective approaches may seem more threatening than traditional methods. To talk in generalities or work on anonymous case studies and role plays is far safer than to work on one's own actual difficulties or opportunities and to make a commitment to change. Yet the risk must be taken if there is to be a worthwhile pay-off. The practitioner must create the conditions in which that risk will be taken.

I was delighted to read the recent study (Peters and Waterman, 1982)[1] of the characteristics of America's most successful companies. Amongst the most exciting quotations in this work is a statement by Thomas J. Watson Jnr., son of IBM's founder:

I believe the real difference between success and failure in a corporation can very often be traced to the question of how well the organization brings out the great energies and talents of its people. What does it do to help these people find common cause with each other? How does it keep them pointed in the right direction despite the many rivalries and differences which may exist among them? And how can it sustain this common cause and sense of direction through the many changes which take place from one generation to another?

These problems are not unique to corporations. They exist in all large organizations, in political and religious institutions. Consider any great organization — one that has lasted over the years — and I think you will find that it owes its resiliency, not to its form of organization or administrative skills, but to the power of what we call *beliefs* and the appeal these beliefs have for its people.

This, then, is my thesis: I firmly believe that any organisation, in order to survive and achieve success, must have a sound set of beliefs on which it premises all its policies and actions.

Next, I believe that the most important single factor in corporate success is faithful adherence to those beliefs.

And finally, I believe that if an organization is to meet the challenges of a changing world, it must be prepared to change everything about itself except those beliefs as it moves through corporate life.

This is the nature of the challenge for management development practitioners. It is to help the leaders of an organisation bring out 'the great energies and talents of its people' and to find 'common cause with each other'. Hence, the learning I am interested in has taken place when managers are functioning better, taking more responsibility, acting more powerfully, flexibly and appropriately, pulling together as a team and, in consequence, the performance of the business is substantially improved. My experience is that the most exciting and effective way to bring this about is to help managers discover the full extent of their potential by successfully working on the actual problems and opportunities they have. I believe many practitioners who work with organisations either as employees or consultants have come to similar conclusions and are adapting their work accordingly.

However if the in-house practitioner is to be equipped to meet this exciting challenge, he or she will particularly need:

1 the skills to function as an organisation development consultant so that he or she can work with organisations and not simply with individual managers;
2 the skills to work with attitudes that block both excellent performance and the development of potential;
3 patience to work strategically over a long period.

The skills to work with attitudes are too rarely available at present. Yet attitudes can block managers and hence organisations and the people they employ far more profoundly than deficiencies in knowledge and skill, especially when they affect the leaders of a business. It has been said that the limitations of a leader become the limitations of an organisation. We need to increase our understanding of how to help managers in this crucial area (Nixon 1980[2], 1981[3], 1982[4], and 1985[5]).

This chapter describes our efforts in Sun Alliance over a number of years to find out how to put these beliefs into practice. It frankly describes our successes and our mistakes and how we have gradually got nearer to what we believe are fully effective approaches.

TRADITIONAL APPROACHES

Our early efforts in the first half of the seventies largely consisted of traditional courses, systematically designed to achieve defined learning goals mostly expressed in terms of knowledge and skill. We provided courses for different kinds and levels of management, making use of external programmes for more senior levels. We offered a wide range of seminars on various management skills or topics. Such programmes have attractions: they provide substantial and tangible evidence that 'something positive is being done'. Also they can be mounted relatively quickly as they are often not based on much analysis of what is actually needed. However, this visible activity is not always matched by corresponding improvements in performance. I am not decrying this sort of programme. It has a value, especially for young, newly-appointed managers or older men and women who, appointed because of their professional competence, have never been taught the basics of management. Courses such as these have a place in the management development programme of a well-run business. However, such programmes usually suffer from severe limitations.

1 There is often insufficient research to find out what managers really need to learn.
2 The courses deal mainly with knowledge and skill whereas changes in attitudes and beliefs are frequently more important if performance is to be improved.
3 Individual and organisational goals are not properly set and not enough time is devoted to planning application.
4 There is insufficient attention to individual needs and participation may be relatively low because of a high participant/tutor ratio and rigid course design.
5 The content is often regarded as too theoretical and not relevant.
6 There is insufficient organisational support for participants, on return to the job, to apply what they have learned.

Consequently, transfer of learning to the job is poor and often little or no change in job performance results from a heavy investment in time and money. One only has to listen to one's customers to discover this. There is a great hunger I believe for something that will be helpful. Consequently if tutors are competent 'performers' and courses are well-organised there may well be favourable immediate reactions from participants. Top management may well be pleased and reassured by the visible activity. However, disillusion often sets in as it is realised that no real benefit has been achieved in terms of bottom line pay-off or other measures of success back in the organisation. If in reality little has changed back on the job, this is extremely disturbing to any conscientious manager or trainer as this truth dawns after the initial euphoria has worn off.

The traditional approach may be represented diagrammatically as shown in Figure 12.1. In other words, the design focuses on developing knowledge and skill and pays scant attention to goal setting, overcoming attitudinal blocks, or making things happen back in the job.

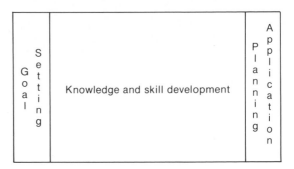

Figure 12.1 Traditional courses

A FIRST ATTEMPT AT A NEW APPROACH

The evidence that the traditional approach was not sufficiently effective came from participants and their managers and could not be ignored. Many managers in Sun Alliance had by now experienced some basic management education or training and the group at the end of the seventies was looking for economies.

We cut back these programmes and largely discontinued the practice of using external courses. Nevertheless, new managers were still being appointed and we urgently needed to devise a more effective way of training them. In 1978 we sought the assistance of Mel Berger and with his help designed an entirely new approach. This has been described more fully elsewhere (Berger and Nixon 1981[6] and Nixon 1981[3]) but I will summarise it here.

The new programme which started in 1978 was developed initially for newly-appointed section heads in UK branches. It was designed to address the weaknesses of earlier programmes. The tutoring methods and the structure of the programme recognised that if changes in performance are required it is not sufficient to work on knowledge and skill. Attitudes, energy and planning implementation also need to be included. We found Figure 12.2 helpful, both in the design and the execution of the programme. The focus of traditional methods has been in quadrant (1). It was valuable for tutors to help each participant diagnose where his own blocks to improved performance lay and to help him accordingly. Tutors were trained to work in all four areas and not just in the first quadrant as in conventional programmes.

(1) Knowledge and Skill	(2) Attitudes
(3) Energy	(4) Planning Application

Figure 12.2 The basis of the design

We started our practice of holding trainer development workshops in order to equip tutors with a full repertoire of skills. At that time our methods were partly influenced by Bioenergetics. This approach provides a framework for working on attitudes and energy. A strong belief in bioenergetics is that people will be healthier and more effective if they allow their feelings to a greater degree than is generally encouraged in organisations. It recognises the importance of physical movement and the expression of feeling in releasing energy and creativity. Clearly we had to adapt these approaches in ways which were 'safe' and acceptable to the people involved.

Our belief is that if real changes in performance are to take place a substantial period of time is often required. So we designed the programme to take place over a period of six months. The programme consisted of three short workshops of 3-4 days duration. Each workshop was preceded by an individual briefing meeting with the participant and his superiors to establish both organisation and learning goals. Each workshop was followed by an 'application phase' in which the participant implemented changes planned during the workshop. Workshops were structured as shown in Figure 12.3. We made sure the content was practical and relevant by using each participant's own work as the main content to be worked on either by role playing or problem solving. We attempted to restrict 'inputs' to the simplest models or handouts usually designed with the help of tutors who were current line managers. These inputs were introduced only when relevant. To ensure that there was a high degree of attention to individual needs, participants worked mainly in groups of three or four, each group having one tutor.

Diagnosis	Goal Setting	Development	Planning
Assessing participants' needs.	Setting participants' organisation and learning goals.	Working on knowledge, skills, attitudes, energy. Working on actual job problems.	Planning application.

Figure 12.3 Workshop structure

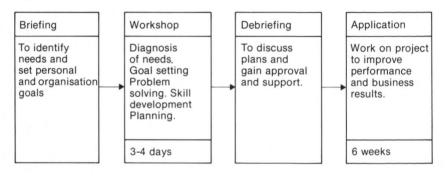

Figure 12.4 Programme structure

There were three workshops in each programme: Workshop I dealt with planning, organising, controlling and time management; Workshop II leadership and communication; Workshop III staff development. The programme structure was calculated to maximise the chances that learning would be transferred to the job and that changes and improvements would actually result. (See Figure 12.4). As there were three workshops in each programme this pattern was repeated three times over the total period. Finally, there was an evaluation to identify the changes that had taken place and what effect these had on business results such as new business, cash-flow, costs, throughput. In practice the results were impressive and in many instances added up to considerable sums. In a number of ways we tried to ensure that there would be a high degree of support for the participants on their return to the job. We selected some of their managers to be tutors who would help design and tutor the courses;

there was a high degree of consultation with their managers about the design of the programme; we also trained their immediate superiors to coach participants during the application phases.

This programme continued until the end of 1980 when organisation changes brought it to an end. By then something like 100 managers had been trained. In many respects it was very successful. The majority of participants and their managers were delighted with the results. Many individuals made enormous strides in their personal development as managers. However, a few participants found the programmes overly demanding or threatening and were unable to respond.

We used the pause to reflect and review our approach. Our main conclusions were:

1 We had not been fully successful in getting the branch management to 'own' the programme – to a degree they saw it as 'ours'.

2 The quality of support from superiors varied too much.

3 The 'high confrontation; high support' tutoring style had proved overly confronting for some who needed a gentler, more supportive approach to help them make changes in their performance. Despite great care, in one or two cases these methods got the programme a bad name and damaged our credibility in some quarters.

4 The programme was very tutor-intensive, requiring tutors to carry out briefings and one tutor to three or four participants. This workload was exhausting for the professional trainers involved and limited our capacity to reach sufficient numbers of people.

5 The programme only addressed issues in the control of individual participants, all of whom were at a relatively low organisational level. Its design provided consultancy and support for individuals. It was not possible to work directly on problems involving whole teams or other members of a team because they were not there. This was a severe limitation in tackling vital issues.

6 The programme worked at too low a level. Some issues could only be resolved at much higher levels.

7 We concluded that despite our efforts it was still not sufficiently

tailored to different organisations and was still too knowledge and skill orientated.

In conclusion, it was still 'ours' not 'theirs'; it was still individual not organisation development and it was still separate from the top.

ANOTHER ATTEMPT

Our blueprint

I had been much influenced by David Casey who did some work with our team in the mid 1970s. His ideas and methods (Casey 1974[7] and Braddick and Casey 1981[8]) reinforced my belief that management trainers and management development practitioners have much to learn from organisational development consultants. In developing our new approach, my colleagues and I were considerably influenced by our recent experiences as a team of working with our consultant, Michael Simmons. Michael had been working with us for 2-3 years helping us improve our effectiveness within the organisation and work on increasing our personal competence. His methods (Nixon 1981[3]) drew on open systems consulting and counselling methods, the latter having their origin in the work of Harvey Jackins (Jackins 1980[9]). These counselling methods offered a gentler, less confronting method of tutoring, which, when appropriately adapted to a business situation, proved more effective in helping participants to learn and to make changes.

We have found this form of counselling, called 're-evaluation counselling', extremely valuable in helping managers where attitudes block excellent performance and the development of their potential. The assumption is that people are naturally intelligent, creative, flexible, zestful, co-operative and powerful. If they do not act in this manner it is because something is getting in the way. This may be something in the present or it may be an obsolete 'pattern' which has its origin in the past. Counselling can help the individual re-evaluate his or her experience, understand how the obsolete 'pattern' prevents him or her from functioning effectively and enable him or her to make decisive changes. The approach places responsibility for development and for deciding and acting with the individual. It also encourages people to value and trust themselves and their colleagues.

These aspects are healthy contradictions in organisations where the culture often acts in contrary ways and discourages people from taking responsibility for their development, supporting the development of others and exercising leadership.

By the time we started our new initiative, in 1981, Home Division had re-organised the branch network in the UK and the Republic of Ireland into nine areas. After gaining the support of the senior manager responsible for the nine areas we divided them between the four members of the management development team. Instead of attempting to design a national programme we approached each of the area managers to find out what would be most appropriate for his area. In view of our previous experience our intention was to:

1 Work at the highest level we could.
2 Use our skills to provide consultancy and training consultancy – not to do the training ourselves, but to equip others to do so.
3 Tailor our work to each area.
4 Focus even more directly on helping management make changes and improve performance.
5 Wherever possible work with whole groups – not individual managers.
6 Use our increased understanding of how to help managers learn by using less confronting and more supportive methods.
7 Build widespread support in each area by training as many managers as possible in tutoring and counselling skills, which they could use either as tutors or in their day-to-day role as managers. In effect to build a community of people all aiming to provide excellent leadership and support for positive and success orientated management.
8 Get out when we had got things going; leave it to the management to carry on and move on somewhere else.

I think it would be untrue to say that this strategy was entirely clear when we began, but it became clearer as we progressed and learned from experience.

Each of us set out to negotiate a contract with one or more of the area managers. The form of this initial work is shown in Figure 12.5. After a preliminary talk with the area manager, if it was agreed to proceed, we would consult individually with his senior management to collect data from them and gain their support for continued work.

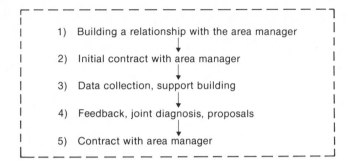

Figure 12.5 Contracting

Our aim was to help members of the team:

1   review the current situation;
2   build a vision of how things might be;
3   identify both obstacles and things that were going for them;
4   plan how to achieve the goals they envisaged.

We would then feed back their collective view of the situation and how it could be transformed and propose a contract to work with them in whatever ways were most appropriate. After this initial stage, six alternative forms of working emerged as shown in Figure 12.6.

In practice

I should now like to describe how this 'blueprint' worked out in practice by writing about the two areas with which I was most intimately concerned.

Area X

In Area X I had worked closely with the area manager a few years earlier, when he was a branch manager elsewhere, in developing the approach described in the previous section. In short, I had a customer who understood and supported our approach. Hence, when I suggested starting by working with him and the senior members of his management team, he readily agreed and gave me the strongest backing.

I followed model (A) in Figure 12.6, and began by talking privately

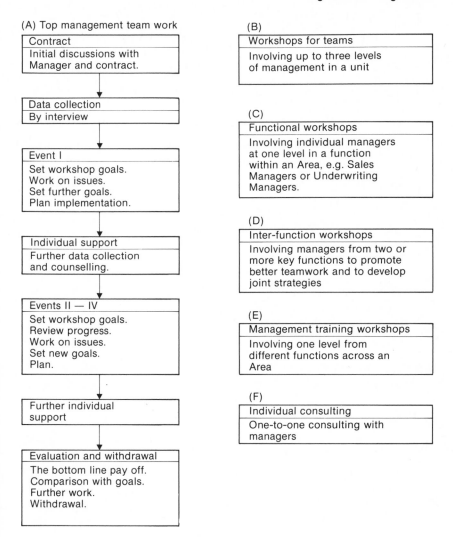

Figure 12.6 Alternative forms of consultancy

to him and members of his team. A number of issues emerged quite clearly. These were:

1 The area manager's management style. Certain aspects were praised but other aspects were thought to cause problems.
2 Communication. As one of the team said 'The biggest single problem is communication.' The management team were not

open with each other about problems. They were reluctant to say what they thought and hence get problems solved openly.
3 One key manager in the team was said to be under-performing and not clear about his role. His team was not united.
4 Certain other key individuals at various levels were not fully effective.
5 Sales and underwriting were not co-operating fully.
6 Virtually all the junior managers needed help to clarify their roles as managers, develop their management skills and take more responsibility.

I fed this data back to the area manager and his team. With great courage, in my opinion, they confirmed that this was a correct diagnosis and agreed to embark on a 12 month programme to work on the problems which had been identified.

In brief this consisted of four 2-day quarterly meetings for the top team (following pattern (A) in Figure 12.6) and a 2-day meeting for the manager who was said to be under-performing and his team. This was followed by two further meetings. The initial meetings were sufficiently successful for further work to be arranged as follows:

1 A meeting between the sales and underwriting management to resolve problems hindering their full co-operation (pattern (D)).
2 Training for selected managers in how to run management training workshops and team events.
3 Programmes of management training for each of the principal management teams in the area. Most of these followed pattern (B) in Figure 12.6.
4 Some individual consulting or consulting with pairs also took place.

The aim of all this work was to transform a loss-making situation by increasing business, cutting expenses and improving cashflow. These goals were achieved.

By the end of 18-24 months nearly all the initial objectives of the programme had been achieved by one means or another. I use the latter phrase because in a few cases job changes or early retirement were the solutions finally reached, whereas a training consultant often hopes that changes in attitudes or skill will achieve the goal. It is also true that in some cases I felt disappointed because my clients chose not to continue working with my help on certain key issues which they had declared to be of great importance at the outset. However, a consultant has to learn that the client, not he, is in charge! There was a resistance to working on these key issues and I was unable to find a way of making it safe enough for them to do so. Also I was (inappropriately in retrospect) disappointed when I was told after 18 months that my help was no longer needed and they wanted to carry on on their own. I am now of course delighted, as I left an area which was more skilled and better able to tackle its own problems.

Furthermore the area had a group of management trainers, skilled in counselling techniques, who would be able to give each other sustained, reciprocal support for each others' continued development. What more could a consultant wish for if he has the maturity and self-confidence to see his withdrawal as a positive and necessary step?

Area Y

Area Y was entirely different. It is a much larger area with five instead of the two branches in area X. Also the area manager and his branch managers did not have the experience of working closely with me in the previous programme. Indeed, in one crucial branch a few managers had unfortunate experience of the earlier programme. Hence when I tried to follow model (A) it simply did not work. I collected a good deal of data about problems in two of the branches and fed it back to the management teams concerned. However there was not enough confidence or trust and to my great disappointment neither team was willing to continue. I found this intensely frustrating as I was convinced I could have helped them. However it was not to be – or at least not in the way that I anticipated.

Although at this stage it was not possible to work at the top of the organisation (which I believed would be the most effective way) there was plenty of work to be done with first level managers. The area manager wanted all of them to receive management training throughout the area. He gave excellent support for work to start at this level. Indeed his continuing support and involvement throughout the programme was absolutely crucial. He provided strong leadership, sold the programme to other managers and secured their commitment and involvement.

I started work by arranging for three managers to attend our trainer development workshop which taught them basic counselling skills following the model of Gerard Egan (Egan 1975). This included one relatively senior, young and extremely determined manager who had considerable credibility with the area manager. After attending this workshop he became a 'convert' to our methods. This proved very significant subsequently in gaining the area manager's confidence and the support of other managers in the area.

The three managers and I then developed a simple design for training the first level managers. It was a simplified version of the workshop programme described above in the section about our 'First attempt at a new approach'. It consisted of two workshops. The first helped participants clarify their roles as managers and then identify and work on the key changes, in their work or themselves, they needed to make to improve their performance. The second workshop was a follow-up to review progress and do further work on developing their skills and improving their performance.

The success of the first workshop programme was such that altogether five programmes were arranged; many more managers were trained to conduct them and subsequently similar workshops were held for the middle and senior managers in the area. A number of managers at various levels found the counselling skills they acquired were invaluable in helping themselves, their colleagues and subordinates. As in area X, by the time I withdrew, there was a significant network of managers skilled in tutoring and counselling methods who could continue management development in the area. At that point a substantial programme of further management development work was planned for the next 12 months. In this case, the work had started at the bottom, taking form (E) and spread into forms (B), (C), (D) and (F), largely making use of their own skilled resources. Although no work taking form (A) was planned some of the problems identified at the beginning were being solved, particularly in the branch where the 'convert' was located.

Similarly varied patterns had emerged in the other areas. Broadly speaking, in some areas the work started at the top and spread down; in others the reverse took place. In two of the nine areas very little progress was made mainly because sufficient support at the top was lacking. At the end of approximately 18 months a considerable amount of management development had taken place. In the nine areas as a whole a very considerable resource of managers skilled as tutors and counsellors had been created. This constituted a valuable support network for formal and informal management development. In the majority of areas there was a considerably enhanced appreciation of what management development could achieve in terms of increased managerial effectiveness and hence improved performance. The ownership issue had been dealt with correctly and most of the areas wanted to and were capable of continuing their own management development with only a small amount of outside support.

Conclusions

We had developed flexible approaches which combined elements of both consulting and training, recently described as 'Consultraining' (Hornstein and MacKenzie 1984[10]). In most cases it was very effective in helping managers tackle problems, improve their effectiveness and improve business performance. In the few places where little progress was made it was because we were unable at that time to secure active support at the top or we did not have sufficient resources.

However, although the new programme was enthusiastically supported by the area management with whom we were involved, it was not always understood elsewhere in the organisation. We had not yet been able to secure much work in head office departments. As the organisation is relatively centralised, the absence of their involvement and strong support was a handicap. It was difficult to explain to top management a programme of which they had no direct experience that was much less structured and visible than more traditional approaches. Head office managers, also lacking experience of the programme, were not in a position to assure them of its advantages.

In addition, a programme which was relatively unstructured emphasised development (rather than control), teamwork, vision building and strategy planning and countered established patterns was likely to take time to be accepted.

In retrospect it would have been wiser to have made opportunities to involve head office managers and top management more fully than we did. We are now remedying this deficiency by extending our services to head office departments and all the divisions of the group. In the case of the two largest divisions the service has been devolved and each now has its own training manager with appropriate resources.

We discovered that there is indeed a demand for more traditional courses to complement 'consultraining'. They are required particularly for newly-appointed managers and in certain basic skill areas. Such programmes have the advantage that they bring together managers from different divisions of the group. Traditional courses are much more visible to top management with whom it is so vital that the training function builds credibility. Therefore we are now providing a management skills programme which offers courses to managers in all divisions. We have overcome the disadvantages of traditional courses by using the experience we have gained in programme structure and course design. Reality is never so simple that only one way is appropriate. In the same way as public courses often lead to in-company business, our expectation is that the goodwill resulting from this programme will lead to a demand for OD consultancy and 'consultraining'.

We are hoping to develop 'action learning sets' (Revans, 1971) for managers with high potential, drawn from different divisions and functions within the group. We envisage this as a 'Winning Managers Programme', in which small groups of managers will meet together under the guidance of a skilled consultant, several times a year to assist each other in developing their competence and improving their strategic performance.

REFLECTIONS

The conclusions I draw are as follows:

1 A professional's values, beliefs and needs fuel his energy and define the unique character of his work.

2 When these are close to his client's, exciting collaboration is relatively easy. When they diverge it can be a struggle. Professional work depends on his being fully aware of these differences and never allowing his values, beliefs or needs to interfere with putting his client's needs first.

3 For the professional who is employed by an organisation, the

whole management are his clients — all of them, at all levels and not just those with whom he has the greatest affinity or those with whom he is immediately engaged. An in-house practitioner neglects the others at his peril.

4   The implication of this is that effectiveness requires the greatest respect for all his clients, the utmost flexibility and a great variety of approaches, some of which may diverge from his own preferences.

5   Security may be gained from knowing how to do things and indeed the professional is often expected to know how to do things. Yet real professionalism often entails not *knowing how* but 'letting go' and *discovering how*.

6   There is a genuine difficulty about gaining work with top management. The culture in British organisations is such that it is extremely difficult for top managers to be open about their problems or needs especially with each other. Hence progress in this area is likely to be slow. Progress is likely to be helped as they gain positive feedback from and appreciate the benefits to managers reporting to them and see the pay-off for their business.

We have come a long way since 1978. We have made considerable progress. We still have a long way to go. Eventually, I hope to write a sequel to this work.

REFERENCES

(1)   Peters, T. and Waterman, R. H. Jnr., *In Search of Excellence — Lessons from America's Best-Run Companies*, Harper and Row, New York, 1982.

(2)   Nixon, B., 'Recent Trends in Management Development', *Industrial & Commercial Training*, September, 1980.

(3)   Nixon, B. (ed.), *New Approaches to Management Development,* Gower, 1981.

(4)   Nixon, B., 'Last Chance for Management Development', *Industrial & Commercial Training*, September, 1982.

(5)   Nixon, B., 'Some Effective Ways of Working with Managers', *Industrial and Commercial Training*, July/August, 1985.

(6)   Berger, M. and Nixon, B., 'Management Development That

Works', *Journal of European and Industrial Training*, Vol. 5, No. 3, 1981.

(7) Casey, D., 'A Diagnostic Model for the OD Consultant', *Journal of European Training*, Vol. 4, No. 1. 1974.

(8) Braddick, B. and Casey, D., 'Developing the Forgotten Army — Learning and the Top Manager', *Management Education and Development*, Vol. 12, Part 3, 1981.

(9) Jackins, H., *The Human Side of Human Beings — The Theory of Re-evaluation Counselling*, Rational Island Publishers, Seattle, USA, 1980.

(10) Hornstein, H. A. and MacKenzie, F. T. 'Consultraining: Merging Management Education with Organisation Development', *Training and Development Journal*, January, 1984.

13

Action learning – a questioning approach

Jean Lawrence

> Learning and progress accrue only when there is *something* to learn from, and the something, the stuff of learning and progress, is any completed action. *In Search of Excellence*, Peters and Waterman (p. 134) 1982.

> There isn't a logical difference between how American and Japanese managers think about decision making but the weight of experience in decision making can be very different. The Japanese tap into their experience to inform their understanding. They regard their day-to-day corporate experience as a learning lab from which they may acquire wisdom. *The Art of Japanese Management*, Pascale and Athos (p. 112) 1981.

McKinsey and Co., with whom the writers above were associated at the time, are not known for their enthusiasm for action learning. But their statements express truths, gleaned from their own experience, about the approach we are to explore.

Reg Revans has been working with managers in action learning since his very early days in the coal mines. But there was a long gap in UK activities while he worked in other countries, and no one here caught up with his thoughts, until a group of us began to work with him (as a 'set' in action learning terms) to promote this 'new approach

---

*I am grateful to my partner John Morris for the suggestion that I write in a questioning way about the questioning approach! – and for much else over the years!

to management education' here in 1971. He had, 3 years before, developed the Belgian programme, as the first action learning based programme of management development.[1] Action learning is relevant to all the issues of the day – and many of the day after! – but here we are concentrating on its application to management development.

Out of our experience together we formed ALP (Action Learning Projects) International and, after about a year of 'talking about action' in our meetings and seminars we were fortunate to be able to take action[2] developing a management development programme for GEC. This programme, the first in the UK, is fully described in *More Than Management Development*[3] mainly by GEC managers. I remember that the 'crunch' in the process of contracting for the programme (some eight months later) came at the Reform Club – and at that time I, a woman, had to enter via the basement! I believe we *all* learned from that – a good many changes were made!

Since then action learning has spread round the country and almost every management education institution claims to be doing it somewhere in the mix of their activities. Some other organisations have also developed ways of working with the ideas. It seems to be 'done' in a wide variety of ways, some of which are described in *Action Learning in Practice*,[4] by practitioners. I want in this chapter, to use some of my own experience of management development programmes over the years to try to discuss some of the questions I am often asked. I remember that as I went through that original set experience in our group of 10, meeting once a month or so, I had as many sceptical questions as I now hear from others – and still new ones occur to me.

Questioning – more and more discriminating questioning – is at the heart of action learning. The reciprocal process in a set is not feasible in a book but let us move now to some more or less discriminating questions and try out the approach as best we can.

ISN'T IT JUST LEARNING BY DOING?

It is learning by doing – but not 'just'. We learn by doing from the cradle on. In action learning, we go further by making arrangements, often very simple arrangements, to enhance the opportunities to learn from our experiences, and to speed up the process. The arrangements create a structure within which people can explore their own experience and that of a few like minded others, as they move cautiously further and further into new and challenging activities.

The small basic structure is a 'set' – a group of 5 or 6 people who work to test and question each other until each is much clearer about what he wants to do and why. Each member knows that after he has taken his next step it will all be re-examined with him in order to learn from that particular event and to plan, with him, the next possibilities. After the discussion he will, by himself, choose the next step – and the work of the set will proceed in this way until the set disbands. The support given by the set provides quite a different picture from the 'learning by doing' concept, which is often used in relation to infant and junior learning. Here the child tries something, fails, tries something else and proceeds to success in this way, supported mainly by the teacher. In management the work that is pursued in action learning is important and failures can only be tolerated marginally. The support of the other members of the set minimises the possibility of serious failure, and tests plans for 'trials' so thoroughly that even minor failure is unlikely. The support comes mainly from the set not from the 'teacher'.

So in this 'set process' step-by-step analysis is undertaken and each move is brought into consciousness by reviewing it and exploring its significance. Day-to-day events are exposed and understood in their own right, but also as part of the rather lengthy process of getting change to happen. In its turn, this interpretation and digestion of the small events week by week, can be understood by each individual as a part of the progress he and the others are making in their learning. Perhaps even more individually and deeply the experiences can be consciously accepted as part of the person's own growth. Each can 'reorganise his own experience' as Revans has it or 'reframe his problems' as Braddick and Casey[5] suggest. Individual behaviour can be observed in the group. Gradually as the set matures, insight can be gained into the way each member behaves in back home situations, and into values and attitudes which have a vital influence on effective management.

When changes in behaviour occur and are noticed by a member of the set, others can provide support with their own recollection of his or her previous ways of behaving. There is then agreed evidence of

earning — and encouragement to hold on to the change.
ıg is by no means confined to the sets. In the part of the
ion in which the 'set member' works, many managers may
ake a new view of the task — and also, perhaps, of the way
to tackle a problem of this kind.

A client (later a managing director) in a senior management
exchange programme, wrote that he had benefited both from the
work he had done with the visiting participant and from his contacts
with his own staff member working in another company. 'This
company has undoubtedly benefited enormously at all levels at which
(the visiting participant) has had contact and where the concept of
action learning is understood. I for one would welcome further
involvement in what I believe to be the most practical and useful
Management Training Programme that I have had the good fortune
to be involved with.'[6]

ACTION LEARNING SEEMS TO HAVE A LANGUAGE OF ITS OWN

Can you explain some of these terms? — *P & Q, problems and
puzzles, clients, sets, set advisers.* They come from Revans' writings.
P & Q and puzzles and problems refer to a basic distinction of great
importance in action learning. 'P' is programmed learning, available
knowledge. 'Q' is questioning where there is no certain answer —
question flows from question and more than one response can be
accepted as sensible. One of our difficulties in tackling some of the
intractable economic social and political problems that beset us, may
be in part that while our education system is more and more full of
'P', our lives are more and more full of huge issues only susceptible
to the processes of 'Q'.

Puzzles have a solution however difficult it may be to find — we
will all agree with it when it is presented. Problems — and opportunities — are the stuff of action learning. We can work on them in
a variety of ways, come to many different conclusions, all open to
discussion and disagreement.

These concepts can be used when we face any dilemma — how
much P & Q? — is it a puzzle or a problem? In this chapter I shall be
talking only about action learning in management development, but

it is relevant to all kinds of problems — on the shopfloor, in hospital wards, in communities — and work in these areas in the UK and across the world has been described elsewhere. [7]

I should like to quote here a recent example of the relation between P & Q in management. If my problem is to find a way to create some activities to improve the public relations of the water industry, I can ask many experts about public relations techniques, analyse the cost, look at how it is done in other industries, nationalised and private, and in other organisations — gather as much 'P' as I can (and incidentally a good many new questions). But no book will help me to see how to persuade X (a senior manager) what should be done, nor reassure me that it is indeed X who should be persuaded first, nor whether to write a report, nor why I find it difficult to decide to call that particular meeting together — which, on the face of it, looks eminently sensible. Nor indeed will the book define the odds on my losing my hoped for promotion if I do stir up the wrong kind of interest in high places in the issue. Problems of this kind involve uncertainty and the questioning process in the sets gradually ensures that a wide variety of directions are carefully explored, leaving, at each stage, the project champion to make his own decisions, justify them and then live with them.

Much has been written about *sets* (Revans *et al.* 1983[8]). I have said something about the process in responding to the last question, and in the comparison with consultancy later on. For me *action learning* has three essential characteristics — the participants work on real work (not exercises or cases), they learn from each other by a questioning process (not from teachers) and they carry through the work to implementation (not just to a report or analysis, recommendation and planning).

The logical outcome is a structure in which a few people work together on one or more real tasks until they have made a visible contribution to progressing their problems, and have themselves inevitably changed in the process. Their work has included their recognition of these changes and their derivation. We call these structures 'sets'.

Project champion, is the name I have given to a set member who is working on a particular task and is learning from it. "Championing" is described in Peters and Waterman, 1982. [9] The task he is working on has many of the characteristics of other projects, but in addition

223

there is a continuous effort to make the learning explicit.

Clients are the problem-owners. They are the people who at this moment, want an answer. Clients will pose the problem, and will be available to hear progress and to support the implementation as they agree a way forward with the project champions. They remain responsible for what occurs but will be greatly influenced as the project champion develops his investigation, his hypotheses and experiments, and then asks the clients' agreement on a plan of action.

Nominators or sponsors select the participants for the programme and usually play a part in selecting the problems to be worked on.

The set adviser is the person who helps a set to work well, and is interested in promoting the achievements and in particular, the learning, of the members of the set. This role has been described in a number of articles by practitioners[10] and the work of the set adviser is referred to later in this chapter. Set advisers can be, and often are, consultants or trainers but other managers can fulfil the role, especially if they themselves have participated in an action learning programme.

The programme provides an envelope in which all this can occur legitimately and provides added learning opportunities through co-ordination of meetings and interaction of sets. The arrangements may also help participants to enter more quickly into learning and to take back with them into their 'normal' lives what has occurred, with minimum attrition. The re-entry problem in the form familiar to course organisers is virtually unknown. The form of the programme should reflect a clear understanding of the agreed objectives, and is discussed fully in a later section.

IT ALL SOUNDS VERY OPEN ENDED

How do we know what we are becoming involved in? Isn't it a political hot potato? It is open ended, but we can manage the process. We can agree carefully what we are trying to do and for whom. We can be clear about our priorities — for example, are we focusing on developing individual managers for later promotion, or on changing the culture of the organisation? Are we developing a level of management in their present jobs, or re-organising a department in the face of a change in its environment? Often we are concerned with more than one objective. Several goals will be achieved in the programme — managers will develop and changes will occur in the organisation — and work will be done on the specific agreed tasks. But it helps if those who are setting it up are clear at the outset about the balance of aims.

We can reduce the uncertainties still further. We can foresee some of the likely outcomes of the programme. In general we can predict who will be affected and how we will try to meet the objectives we have set ourselves. Additional beneficial results, which we could not predict, may occur, as they did in GEC.[11] Admittedly we cannot foresee with any clarity the outcome of the tasks the participants take on — as we cannot when we tackle real problems in our own jobs. This difficulty is inherent in the kind of problems we have chosen to tackle. Authority for action, however, always remains with the client. The participant will always be no more than transient in his commitment to that work — unless arrangements are changed towards the end (and in my experience, that would be very unusual). His task is to learn how to get action to happen where he has no direct authority but strong commitment as a project champion. In 'own job' projects he has direct authority derived from his 'normal' client, his boss. But he will probably designate part of his work, probably new work, as the focus for attention, and agree this with his boss and his colleagues. He may risk trying out new ways of working in this designated area and will be scrutinising, with the set, each step as he takes it.

Clarity of agreement about the nature of the task to be worked on, how it is to be evaluated, and what resources are available, are all necessary at the beginning — but even more important is the recognition that these matters are likely to be renegotiated as the work progresses. Unlike 'filleted projects', found in some training courses, real work will take a path that cannot be forecast with confidence. The definition of the task may change as more information is made available. The subsequent renegotiation often includes a change in the focus on a particular manager as the 'client' for the work being done — the 'owner' of the problem. As the problem is explained and symptoms are identified which lead to diagnosis of the 'real' problem (itself perhaps a temporary diagnosis) all may agree that the ownership has in fact changed, and a new 'client' is named.

Politically it can be a hot potato, if there is a lack of confidence that change will be accepted if it is promoted from below. It is necessary that top people — those whose decisions can encourage or forestall most important changes in the policies or shape of their organisations — believe that things will change, with their agreement, as a result of the programme. Often this does mean the exercise of political skills by those who, within the organisation, are introducing action learning. The process of introduction in itself, may provide considerable learning for the organisation and, unavoidably, for those who introduce it. As in all developments, timing is important. Often as the likely results are understood the chief executive will take the lead.

Even then a lot of preliminary work may be needed to help senior managers to appreciate that what is being embarked upon is not just another training course where the manager's 'knowledge in the head' will grow. The manager returning from such a course may have very little effect on the work of the organisation. Signing a cheque and putting forward a name, however carefully selected, is not enough to promote learning and the changes in the organisation, which are inevitable if learning has taken place.

So yes, action learning does require top management commitment to organisation learning — and therefore change — and if this seems like a hot potato, there should perhaps be a number of ways of cooling it! But it is *not* a charter for chaos.

The meat of the programme is all that occurs after this top management commitment is obtained. Those involved can be trusted to work on it with no more hiccups and difficulties than are involved in any change process. Probably there will be less difficulty here because so much attention and analysis is focused on these particular changes, in order that maximum learning is achieved.

WHERE DOES ACTION LEARNING MAKE ITS BEST CONTRIBUTION?

Does its whole success rely on the choice of 'problem'? Its most valuable contribution is to increase general management skills at all levels. Not to make an accountant technically more competent at manipulating data but to help him to influence others from his expert base. Action learning will tackle how he can get his ideas across; let him see the value of his role more clearly; lower the fences round his department; indicate better ways to make his data useful to his peers, his staff and his boss, and help him to recognise that it is valid to work on unclear human organisation problems using as much skill and care as he usually spends on reaching his technically correct answers.

This can be achieved for every manager at every level. One manager (an MD) recently said he had not realised he could give attention *of the same kind*, to personnel matters and the way people behave, as to his business problems of marketing, finance etc. till he met action learning, in a lecture by Revans some years ago. He now has his entire management staff working in mixed groups on his business problems and monitoring their learning.

Action learning is not useful for increasing technical competence, nor for increasing knowledge about management. Talking *about* management, gaining new knowledge that he may need or think he needs, can be done in a thousand ways more effectively than through action learning. It is useful only if the need is for more effective managerial action.

In business schools and colleges a great deal is done to improve knowledge, techniques and particularly analytical skills. I recall that after Manchester and London Business schools had been running for 5 years the Owen report [12] said that while they were very effective in teaching these skills, they did little to help their students work with people, or with the implementation of decisions. It was difficult to see, at the time, how they could, but that was the nudge I needed to pursue action learning with vigour. I got in touch with Revans then.

At Manchester, I was building on experience already gained through a growing commitment to use projects (a huge variety within the species) in our programmes. Joint development activities were a feature from 1971 and 'stretched' courses with projects woven into the programmes began in 1972. The first 'stretched' courses provided group project work for operational managers in manufacturing units other than their own. Twenty days' work was spread over four months. The organisation had originally asked for a three week management course. Action learning including a full phase of implementation still seems to be almost impossible to integrate into a business school or college except in lengthy qualification programmes, e.g. MBA part-time programmes. At least three institutions in the UK and one in Ireland offer these long programmes based on action learning using real problems in organisations centrally in their work.

If the special contribution is in the area of general management and we are to learn by taking action then we need 'whole business' problems or as near to that as we can find. Since we are not involved in passing on or applying known answers, the choice of problem is vital to success. [13] Often a list of problems can be generated with ease. It seems that the better the organisation the greater the number of real problems that are on their agenda. We need to select problems that will stretch the participants we have in mind. These will often be the ones which would normally be on the desks one level above. They must certainly be inter-departmental, not already studied and reported many times, and be of appropriate size for the length of programme. The most difficult criterion to handle concerns the obvious requirement — reality. If it is real, how can it fit into the pattern of a programme? If it is implementable — a feature of a real problem — how does that relate to urgency? If we want something done — to make a contribution to this problem — can we wait 6 months starting next March or May perhaps?

One way of working at these issues, and ensuring the connection between the reality of the work that is to be done and the central concerns of the organisation, is to work through a steering group. Garratt's programme manager [14] may be an alternative; here he is a designated member of the steering group often called programme co-ordinator. Line managers concerned with getting things to happen, join with developers, and perhaps external consultants, to take responsibility for the form of the programme. They select the participants, and the 'projects' and ensure that a 'client' is identified for each, sometimes a member of the steering group. The first part of their work ends with one page descriptions of projects written by clients and a list of participants ready to enter a programme whose broad design they have agreed.

The distribution of problems to individuals or groups can be done in a variety of ways. In many programmes the clients present the problems publicly to all the participants and all the other clients, the tutors and training staff. Usually more problems are presented than are required so that real choices are available. In the consortium programme, after the presentations, the sets go away by themselves to discuss the possible projects and come up with their individual choices. They had already developed criteria for choice which included not working in their own company and working in an area of management with which they were not familiar.

If participants can choose the task they will work on and with whom they will work we can expect high motivation to work and learn. Some say, though, that this is not like real life. My experience is that quite often participants can choose their own projects and sometimes their sets. For group projects they may be able to form their own group. More frequently groups and sets are formed by the steering group. In GEC each participant was allocated his project and his set by the central management development manager. In more recent programmes, much more choice has been made available to participants.

In a complex programme where there are many groups or sets the process of choice can be fairly chaotic and should in my view be encouraged to be lengthy. The explanation of choices, the criteria on which they are based and the stresses that are generated are, or can be, an important part of the learning process. It is the first occasion in the programme where participants have to live with the results of their choices. That will occur on many occasions later, but perhaps at no point with such immediate and clear results for the participants themselves. Later in the programme a review of the choices made can provide useful personal learning, not least about organisational pressures and culture.

As the set work begins the role of the steering group changes to monitoring the progress of the programme, being visibly interested in the results of both the project tasks and the learning, but not judgmental about the way each project task is being achieved — that is the job of the client and the set, with the help of the set adviser. An important role of the steering group is to 'hold the ring' and to manage effects in the organisation which may be inimical to the continuation of a series of programmes.

Examples of potentially damaging effects have included demanding too much time from top managers too soon, over burdening a single department with reports and change proposals, or giving working papers to interested staff without due clearance. After the start the steering group will be supporting particularly the credibility of implementation, ensuring that their colleagues, above and below them as well as at their own level, do actually expect that changes will result from the programme. This may later include informally helping clients to get items onto the agendas of influential meetings. A strong factor in enabling programmes to continue is that acceptable changes are made, especially those benefits top management did not expect to occur. This seems to be true even when other objectives e.g. manager development, are important, often more important.

Steering groups for programmes change their roles after a few programmes. They may be thought to be a good forum for working on wider management development issues, putting organisation strategy and development together, or they may take responsibility for other particular groups, e.g. graduate intake, and reconsider with their new joint experience, appropriate methods of development for them; or they may say, 'this is fine for those top level managers, what about those one level down?' and work step by step towards a full role in management development.

HOW CAN WE ARRANGE EXCHANGE PROGRAMMES?

We have heard of exchange programmes where senior people work in other organisations. How is all this arranged? Like the porcupines making love, – with difficulty. Many current top managers have experienced a period of secondment, an opportunity to work in another industry, country, organisation or role, and all seem to look back on it as a highly developmental period. A manager moving to a new job has a short but exciting learning period and often in retrospect recognises the struggles as having been highly developmental. The trick is to give more people these opportunities without disrupting current performance in the sending or receiving organisations. Gone are the days when someone whether good, useful or promotable, can be 'spared' for an extended period; or when someone with few skills in the work, can be accommodated and take the place of a hard pressed good performer, in order to learn. Job swops, secondment, job rotation are even more difficult in the current climate and although they may be feasible for junior managers usually cannot be contemplated at relatively senior levels.

But there *are* real problems to be tackled, issues to be explored, in every organisation at every level. The more managers are hard pressed by change and cost cutting, the more there are opportunities for special effort to be applied to important one-off problems. If the work is real, it has to be done somehow. So projects, tasks, can be tackled in a special way and managers can learn from that experience, bringing with them to the task, the advantage of good managerial experience. In addition project exchanges do not have the same difficulties as job swops – the effect of ignorance of the precise field of action is limited. Indeed the project champion often stimulates a new view of the problem because of this ignorance. If it is thought that a consultant from outside, or the line managers in their normal roles can get to a better solution and get the change made more easily and quickly, surely this should be carefully considered; then the only remaining issues are who learns from the process, and how are managers to be developed here?

Some time will be required from the current managers working as resources in the area of the project, but that will be essential, anyway if the work is to get done at all. The kind of work required of them may well be different. For example, they may be involved in initial information – giving, then authorising, and arranging resources for implementation. In other circumstances they would perhaps be managing the data gathering, doing the analysis, developing alternative strategies and scenarios, and planning and monitoring the implementation. The 'project champion' participant is likely to take on these activities. As the project progresses he will be authorised to do so. He may need more junior people to help him – they would have been equally necessary in other circumstances.

There are then, few difficulties in finding problems or in expecting results in terms of changes and managerial learning. The difficulties arise from the lack of inter-organisation communication channels and the problems of getting like-minded companies and institutions to take decisions together, matching their participants and dovetailing their requirements in terms of time. There is a role here for an established organisation to provide an 'exchange' of information on needs and opportunities at this high level, and to play a part in managing such a network of programmes. The Consortium Programme (sometimes referred to as the Rolling Programme) in 1975-8 met this need, providing a top level exchange programme which involved nine UK organisations. It failed to continue after three years because it could not extend its base to involve enough organisations so that very high level participants would be available regularly for each programme. At the time, none of the organisations involved would contemplate basing the programme in an institution, particularly a Business School, believing, rightly in my view, that it would be emasculated by institution pressures. A steering group of the participating companies organised the programme in hotels and conference centres, and I provided a focus for communication at Manchester Business School.

I was somewhat anxious about letting go the central administration, fearing dilution of the sharp edged and seemingly risky activities we were involved in. I feared pressures to make it too tidy and simple so that the learning opportunities provided by the uncertainties of tackling real problems (not filleted ones) would be diminished. I had seen too many projects make progressively simpler to fit course, staff and institutional requirements. Staff enjoy preparing projects and learn enormously in the process; often, quite unintentionally, at the expense of the learning of those they mean to teach. Managers too are often concerned about the acceptable risks within their own organisations. Administrators like things to happen in a regular convenient pattern and prefer not to have to adapt too frequently to the demands of real life. Things have changed in the decade since then. As understanding of how to manage this kind of programme has increased the anxieties have faded. The risk of promoting and administering a network of programmes of this kind from an institutional base should surely now be taken.

In the current climate more and more institutions are recognising that work is the best base for learning and that managers learn best by managing difficult situations, (taking on new jobs, starting new ventures, changing organisations are easy examples in many managers' experience). A catalytic organisation promoting a partnership between those who wish to speed the change towards learning while working, and those who represent the vast army of organisations in which managers work, would provide a way of helping the porcupines to be productive. We still need an aphrodisiac in British management learning – maybe just an encouraging arrangement would do!

ARE THERE GROUP PROJECTS IN ACTION LEARNING?

The Belgian programme was based on individual project work. More recently I have heard of group project work in this connection – is that really action learning? Yes, for me it can be. These programmes *can* meet my basic criteria – real projects, learning from each other and implementation. But because the set work is different it is more difficult to hold the programme at a high level of learning and thus the tutor/set advisor role is even more demanding. Implementation, though achievable, is often less focused. Participants learn in their groups from the activity while in the programme but often a few (not often the whole group) continue to be marginally involved after returning full time to their jobs.

Set work in group project programmes differs considerably from set work in individual programmes. The group itself is not a set, though its members probably come from a wide variety of backgrounds – and should, in my view, always be working on 'new' work. The individuals in the group are working towards a single objective and exploring their part in progressing the work. This kind of group is in danger of becoming only a good and useful taskforce, so learning has to be a clear and important objective. Unless they define their individual roles very clearly, the pressure the group can put on each individual, and he can put on himself, is not of the same order as that in the individual or paired project set. When the group works well, the work and learning are brought together by a process of critical examination of what is being done and an exposure of the difficulties. Members of the group question each other from their own experiences.

There is a qualitative difference, however, between this kind of questioning and the questioning of an individual who is entirely responsible and at risk in his own project. The individual needs the questioning of other members of the set who will not share the direct responsibility for what happens on that project, but reciprocally need his help for their work. To get the benefit of these open confronting questions born of an equal need for help, we have experiemented recently in group project work with putting two or perhaps three project groups together for a day to work in a set. In these sets, time was allocated so that one group would question the other about their project and then reciprocate. The orginal groups had been formed of people who had no recent experience in the area of their group project. When this joint set meeting occurred, fairly expert people in the field of the project from the other group, were able to question those who were struggling to find effective ways of progressing their unfamiliar work. Some of those asking these questions from their expert positions would also be involved in the implementation of the project work at a much later stage. This enhanced the benefits of the cross-group questioning. The sets were huge but the participants seemed to be able to cope with that by working as a team in their own groups, asking questions of the other group. We also created mixed groups towards the end of a group programme to share their experiences of the learning processes in the groups. These experiments will be repeated.

Intergroup meetings are akin to the meetings with other programmes (in Belgium and Sweden) arranged in the Belgian, GEC and Consortium programmes. The level of commitment in sets and in action learning programmes creates difficulty in sharing, especially early in the programmes. It takes a very mature group to attend as much to the outside world as to the inside.

More work needs to be done to experiment with increasing the learning group to group, set to set, and programme to programme. Much of the learning in one set on one, or say five projects is at present lost to others. Perhaps more use of delegates or representatives may help?

FORMS OF PROGRAMMES

Is it true that top management programmes are always full time exchanges? Are other forms appropriate only to other levels? No, there are other versions for top managers and many variants to meet different needs at different levels. It is true that a full time exchange programme, probably running over six months, must involve a number of different organisations in making a high investment in the development of single members of their workforces so it will be likely that participants will be limited to very senior influential managers. In the UK these programmes have involved managers likely to be appointed to company, division or group boards, and in many cases this has happened. So we can expect this form to be used only at top level. But the reverse is not true, very senior managers can be developed in programmes with a different design, particularly if the objectives are different, e.g. the priority objective is team building in a board.

The form of a programme is very much dependent upon the

Table 13.1

Choosing the form of management development programmes in action learning

Example	Organisation		Task		Time	Notes
	One or Several	Own or Exchange	Group or Individual	Own or Other		
GEC	One Group several coys. & customers	Both	Individual or Pairs	Both	P/T F/T	(a)
Consortium (or Rolling) Prog.	Several	Exchange	Individual	Other	F/T	(b)
Social Services	One	Own	Group	Other	F/T	(c)
Large Mnfg. Co.	One Dept.	Own	Group	Other	P/T	(d)
Water Industry	One (10 regions)	Own	Group	Other	P/T	(e)
Large Retail Org.	One	Own	Individual	Other	P/T	(f)
Small Family Trpt. Co.	One	Own	Individual	Other	P/T	(g)
Manag. Action Group	Several	Own	Individual	Own	P/T	(h)
Africa (Planning only)	Several	Own	Individual	Own	P/T	(i)
Quality Circle	One	Own	Group	Own	P/T	(j)

purposes being addressed. There is an enormous range of choice. Action learning is well placed to meet three main objectives (a) management development; (b) organisation change and development and (c) task achievement. Tasks will be tackled and some progress will be made whatever choices are made about the form. The main influence will come from the priority given to one or other of the first two objectives, management development or organisation development, though both will no doubt occur to some extent. Numbers involved and the level of investment in money, time and support facilities, may also play a part.

Decisions about the form will include whether other organisations should be involved or the programme should be entirely domestic and how limited within the domestic world; whether work should be taken on individually or whether there would be more benefit to be gained by working in a group. Managers may be challenged to work in an area of management of which they are ignorant or on a familiar task, and there may be good reasons for them to work part time.

Often a priority for organisation change may influence form in the direction of own organisation, part time and perhaps group work. While a strong need for manager development suggests perhaps individual work, several organisations, exchange and full time. But many variants are possible to fit many different organisations' needs. Sorting out these issues and gaining commitment to the form can be a fairly lengthy process. Some examples are given in Table 13.1.

The GEC programme (a) was full time but not an exchange programme though there were some exchanges between companies in the group. It also included a number of other variants of both organisation and task. [15] In GEC managers were 'one below eye level' because Sir Arnold Weinstock regarded his 100 or so managing directors as 'eye-level' — they had face-to-face contact with him. So it was a senior programme involving high level projects worth six months' full time work.

The Consortium programme (b) [16] was also full time but involved 'exchange' projects. Its aim was to develop top level managers. It required a considerable investment in time and money and participating companies regarded it as an alternative to say, Harvard.

The Social Services programme (c) was devised to develop managers at a particular level but also to increase mutual understanding of the work of the various departments and functions. The large manufacturing company (d) wanted to raise the competence of its managers in project management in one department and to share some understanding, knowledge and skill from one specialist area in the department to another. Similarly, an 8 months part time programme in the water industry (e) is intended to develop 24 individual managers in each programme, as well as to increase the common appreciation, across the regions, of what goes on in the water industry. This programme includes two taught modules – they were in fact the starting point for the programme and the project work was built round and through them.

In the large retail organisations (f) some gaps at the top were foreseen and development of selected senior individuals was regarded as urgent. The complexity of the organisation, its long history and current reorganisation indicated an internal programme. The need to develop a few very senior managers suggested individual projects. In the small transport company (g) the whole management team needed development both as individual managers and as group. The new MD, a family member and an MBA, felt overtrained compared to his managers, and wanted them to gain some understanding of the whole system of the small company and to develop towards board roles.

The Management Action Group[17] (h) is director and managing director level, each manager working in his own company and meeting for a day every 5 or 6 weeks. After an introductory week, the programme, in this case, consists only of the set, and a series of set meetings. The set has met consistently for 3 years and has survived a number of job changes/promotion among the set members. The members continue to come because they find the thought provoking day away fruitful – and worth the cost.

The result of the analysis is the same for the action planning in the African planning programme (i) which involves twenty or more managers from different African countries each time. But as explained in the last section in this chapter there can be no implementation within the African programme.

The final example, for interest in the comparisons, is quality circles. As can be seen from Table 13.1, the form differs strikingly from the other programmes. This may be appropriate. As I see it, quality circles are a very low risk form of action learning related to everyday work, and the priorities in the objectives are likely to be different.

Whatever the form of the programme, it goes through a similar process from introductory work and identification of the projects to investigation and analysis, testing the arguments and ideas. At around the mid-point there is usually a pause and a very stringent evaluation of the proposals before moving further into action. Then the second half is concerned with experimenting and implementation, review and disengagement, and later reviews.

In the single long running set at director level, (h) each member goes through this cycle many times as he defines for himself new tasks and projects. A new task usually overlaps with the last one which is by then perhaps in the early stages of implementation.

DO YOU NEED OUTSIDE STAFF IN THE GROUPS/SETS?

Why can we not do it ourselves? I am not sure you always do need outsiders except at the beginning. But even those whose training and professional interest is in how people work together and how groups work or fail to work, find it quite difficult to be one of a working group which is making its ways of working explicit and open to examination and interpretation. I have found this to be true for myself when working with social workers, psychologists, development managers and trainers. An outsider, who, essentially, is not involved in all the processes leading up to each participant facing this new experience which is to be real and evaluated, can work without the level of anxiety, discomfort, and defensiveness present in the others. He/she can help members of the set towards the open, communicative, risk taking, thoughtful, caring, imaginative, reflective behaviour which is needed. Then there is a chance that the realities of working relationships, the members' areas of ignorance and the many constraints on action, can be exposed and accepted, and the difficulties overcome. Not that the outsider is free from anxiety. But this kind of anxiety − about starting a familiar process with new people − is well recognised and can be managed, so it is not likely to impede the work. It is important that someone has as his priority the way the set is developing as a challenging supportive working unit, while others have quite different priorities in these early stages. They may be more concerned with finding a way of surviving in the set, understanding what is expected of them, dealing with doubts about the value of the experience just beginning, wondering why they were nominated for it, and sorting out why the outsider is not teaching or leading in the conventional sense, says very little, and does not 'keep order' in the set.

The outsider, the set adviser, is not the same as other members of the set but need not be from outside the organisation. A supervisor or colleague may feel confident to fulfil the role though he or she will have additional difficulties in dealing with the set's expectation based on their own past experience. An internal trainer or manager from another department or function or company in the group will have fewer difficulties on that score. This arrangement has often proved successful especially after the first programme. Preliminary work on understanding the role (both intellectually and emotionally) is of course necessary. Nothing can replace the experience of being a set member, as a starting point. Working in a set alongside someone experienced in helping sets to start and to work well is one way to gain further experience; another is to work with a set alone but alongside a more experienced person working in another set. Then a discussion of each meeting can take the form of a review of the role and how it was taken up in each set. It is usual, in my experience, gradually to transfer the work to internal staff in the later programmes even if external experienced staff are used at first.

Once work has started, the set adviser will re-examine with the set his usefulness on a number of occasions (though not at every meeting!) and may withdraw as the programme progresses. The difficulties of implementation are frequently under-rated and the set may well need the help of a set adviser for at least part of this process. There is often a role in helping to legitimise micro-politics at this stage. Often the set adviser has more varied (but recognisably secondhand) experience of organisations, their structures, culture, power systems, than members of the set and may be able to help by providing frameworks for analysis. This may be less appropriate in mixed sets where there must already be considerable experience of organisations. Even today, there is less written about implementation than analysis and the function of helping the set members to generalise their experiences may be especially valuable.

It is possible, particularly at this later stage, that the balance between attention to task completion and making learning explicit can move too far away from learning in the absence of a set adviser.

This phenomenon varies from set to set and pressure from the client system is usually part of the reason for over-concentration on the task at the expense of monitoring the learning. The task can drive out learning as it so often does in ordinary managerial life.

IS IT ONLY SUITABLE FOR THOSE ABOUT TO BE PROMOTED?

We are involved in developing managers to be more competent in their own jobs — there's little chance of promotion at the moment. Would Action Learning help? Yes. Action Learning is an enormously flexible approach in terms of the needs it can meet, as long as the need is not met just by familiarity with techniques or a 'programmed learning' approach.

The design of the programme and the choices made about the form it will take (see Table 13.1) will be highly influenced by the need to develop people in their own jobs. It does not necessarily mean an individual project/own job/own organisation/part time programme. There might be a strong case for 'team building' where group projects or exchanges within a department might be indicated. In a recent Social Services Programme this was the situation. There was a strong need to understand others' jobs and roles. Group projects where there was no recent specialist experience in the group, featured in the programme. A side effect was a much increased understanding of the difficulties and constraints in top jobs previously seen as remote — names had been known but not persons; and responsibilities, far from the sharp end, were little understood.

The top people were enormously impressed by the unusual initiatives taken by those further down the system and appreciated their own previous neglect of these resources within the organisation. Nothing changed in terms of promotion but there was an identifiable change in the way those in the organisation worked together.

ISN'T IT JUST CONSULTANCY?

No. In consultancy the consultant's learning is incidental to the task in hand and the client should be alert to ensure that it never takes priority over task completion and client organisation learning. In many assignments organisational learning is likely to be in the form of acquiring digested expertise from the consultant (very near to 'P'). The consultant appears as an expert in the field in which he/she is to work and has often been asked to help because his 'P' in that situation is higher than that of the internal managers. Good consultants work hard to reduce the organisation's dependence on them (and spend less energy than most of their colleagues on preparing the ground for the next – and continuing – jobs) but their own learning is not part of the design. At the worst, the experience can be likened to an excellent oft repeated lecture, and at the best, as in 'teaching', the edge of the subject is explored mutually and the excitement of learning is shared, but unevenly. The client's learning both in quantity and rate is highly influenced by the consultant, as it is by the teacher.

In action learning the excitement of learning is built in from the beginning, both in the set and in the client organisation. There, perhaps only after the very early stages, the deep exploratory questions a good manager asks generate the excitement of shared insights and learning. The stuff of the set is this questioning and the excitement is inevitable as the challenge of exploration is pursued. The participant who, in the parallel situation, is the consultant, has to struggle with his perennially questioning colleagues who will explore every argument or idea he puts forward knowing he has no expertise with which to blind them. They do not assume that he is right or likely to be right. They know they are uncertain in their own work and need this examination process to give them confidence but have high trust that with the help of the set he *will* get it right. When he returns to his client organisation again he is subject to questions and exploration for they too are sceptical and cannot completely rely on his expertise. Once again back in the set, he will be supported in whatever difficulties he has with the client system – 'it's the same for all of us in our different ways, we are all struggling' – and given the confidence, with ideas thoroughly re-examined, to go back and continue. 'Comrades in adversity' indeed, as Revans has it.

As he survives this process he no longer fears dealing with peers who have expertise he does not have, but values their contribution. Nor does he doubt his ability to influence work where he has no formal authority.

HOW DOES IT END?

The participant cannot implement it completely, can he? In earlier project work aimed at the development of learning within courses, the implementation phase hardly existed. The project would typically end with a report and recommendation to the client, often a teacher, standing in! The process of getting an organisation to accept not only the recommendations but actually to make the changes, challenges the project champion and the other members of the set. The project champion has done the work in developing the ideas but has a limited time in which to see the implementation begin and to make sure it is progressing well when he leaves. He has to foresee the real difficulties he will encounter and cope with determination with those he does not foresee. The recognition of political pressure and the need to work with the power system, is often a revelation to people who have worked only within a function. They may have seen the structure in which they work encouraging sniping across the boundaries, without any obvious opportunity to use the real relations between groups within the organisation to achieve important progress. Now they can find new ways of influencing change.

It seems that it is hard for participants as they approach the end of a programme to see how to disengage from their project work. The idea that implementation has occurred is difficult to accept when they know that a final report has not been written, they have already decided that will not help, that the final memos have not been sent, that the person they think should be appointed is not actually in place. It seems helpful to suggest that implementation has occurred when the participant leaves the organisation in which he has been working on his project, or leaves the project work itself, in such a state that the work is more likely to progress than to cease. The reverse is frequently true in organisational life — change processes can easily be killed off. If the project champion is no longer there to hold the boundary and the change relies on him, organisation forces can collude to stop it. The organism rejects the foreign implant and rapidly reverts to normal. However, if the project champion in an action learning programme has done his job well, he will have arranged that enough powerful people in the system are involved in the work on the project with him, so that his disappearance is hardly noticed and the energy remains with the powerful group, they or one of their number becomes the project champion. The powerful group ensures that the work is unlikely to be able to be scrapped by organisation forces of rejection, lethargy or resistance to change. The organism itself is mutating and the 'external' influence become irrelevant.

The programme does not end there. Usually the sets review their work a few weeks before they are due to return to their normal jobs or to leave the programme. This review provides an opportunity to look back at the experience and to work at the process of disengagement from the project work. They can also face up to re-engagement in a normal managerial role full time and wonder what will change, and for how long. Often career planning features in this discussion. Differences as they experience them, between the person who entered the programme and the one who now leaves, are identified and evaluated.

Later reviews, perhaps one month and then six months after they return also give programmed opportunities to see the direction of changes in the light of their experiences, and to support those for whom the direction is not always seen as entirely positive.

HOW CAN ACTION LEARNING BE FITTED INTO THE REQUIREMENTS OF TRAINING PROGRAMMES/COURSES?

On the face of it, it can't! It is not possible at one and the same time to say, 'Within this programme of x weeks, we are teaching you management, you are receivers, we are givers, we will arrange for you to go through some clearly defined exercises. Each of them can be evaluated in terms of the performance of the giver and the ability of the receiver to respond in a predicted way by performing well-defined tasks'. And also to say 'We are here to help you to interpret your intentions and your actions within a programme bounded only by time, place and agreement on a task – an objective for work over an extended period, maybe 6 months.'

Nevertheless, as Revans has so often said, 'P' is also necessary. It is possible, though difficult, to combine 'project experience' 'work experience', 'projects', etc. with a taught course. The combination of such disparate activities carries the danger that the programmed activity drives out the unsure, unplannable leaps into reality. The integration of the project work into the programme, so that it does not stand alone as an 'add on' or 'something other', is difficult *and* essential. It will always be second best to promoting an action learning programme on a base of previously understood and well integrated 'P', e.g. if new graduate intake are taught *about* management, perhaps 2 or 3 years later an action learning programme can build on this early knowledge and experience. The programme can then be based wholly on the performance of real work and carried right through to implementation and review.

Where the attempt is made to combine action learning with taught modules, much of the real work has to be done in the design stage. This is true of all programmes involving experiential work. It is difficult to achieve integration within the staff group so that staff in taught sessions and those in experiential work (where they are not the same people) all feel a responsibility for the success of the total programme. Time will be allocated so that they will have worked together sufficiently to appreciate the way the whole programme will develop and where the 'joints' may at first creak. Also they will have noted, how in management games or perhaps structured behavioural exercises, the excitement of highly programmed and carefully arranged sessions (arranged not least in order to provide excitement) can compete and usually win, in gaining the temporary allegiance of learners.

Less programmed work with its intrinsic excitement but apparent lack of shape and defined ends, cannot survive alongside the short term demands of clear deadlines in a business game. Given space and careful introduction, and clever timing of sessions within a programme, commitment to real project work is easily gained and grows with increasing understanding of the realities in which the learners are involved. Then the energy and excitement know no bounds.

In many institutions this is the way that real project and eventual action learning work, may be introduced. It usually means dismantling a programme so that it is spread over a period of perhaps six months (or in degree programmes, an academic year) with the whole group meeting for an introductory period, other residential phases, and a review period just before the 'end' of the programme. In this way work done in organisations can begin at the beginning of the programme, be supported by all the 'course' work and 'end' as the results of the work are embedded in the organisation when the programme ends. That it grows and does not wither as courses are repeated, requires high skills (political as well as professional) on the part of the 'introducers'. It can so easily become a routine problem: 'the part of the course that is seen as difficult'; 'it's a bit of a nuisance to set up'; 'perhaps we can simplify it this time'; and thus you can lose most of the learning.

Staffing such a programme seems to present minor practical difficulties. Often here, groups will work on a single project. The groups can be left to tackle the work without help; but often the intention is to facilitate their work and raise their level of awareness of the learning opportunities presented. 'Tutors', used to tutoring exercises, business games and teaching in formal sessions, perhaps on the same programme, find it difficult to justify being 'out' for a day with a group where the group is doing the work and does not need direction. The tutor is being asked to be a set adviser and the last thing he will have the opportunity to do will be to tutor. Perhaps he will say very little in the day, but what is said at that one moment may have great value. Often in practice, tutors find other priorities take them away and groups are 'visited' less frequently than might seem useful. One group recently reported 'our thanks also to our "tutor" – they call it distance learning, I believe!'

ARE THERE HEAVY REQUIREMENTS FOR SKILLED RESOURCES?

This is a difficult question. Taught courses are perhaps being regarded as the norm, and measurement of the resources used in them is frequently controversial. Senior courses might perhaps be 9 or 10 weeks long. Planning them is not very demanding on resources once a pattern has been set, though very high on resources the first time through. Running such a course might require a director (perhaps half time), a 'teacher' each day on average, and quite demanding administration backup.

For an action learning programme of similar calibre there is more work each time at the planning stage, though first time round it would certainly not require more resources than the taught course. When the programme runs, administrative backup is markedly less but of a high order – remarkably adaptive for instance. Participants meetings are short and infrequent and residence is hardly a feature. Participants are not usually away from home and do not need 'looking after'. Few materials are circulated or prepared and most of those which are needed are provided by the participating organisations. Academic or trainer resources are required on a much higher staff/student ratio, say 1/6th rather than 1½/30 but for far fewer days. The requirement will vary considerably with the design but perhaps it will be 15 to 20 days instead of 60 days; and normally there is no need for a separate extra course director. The 'programme manager' may well be a manager in the organisations concerned, a member of the steering group and has usually worked on the development of the programme. Some specialist help may or may not be required for say 5 days overall. In many programmes, particularly after the first time, set advisers are drawn from a wider field than just academics or trainers.

So from the academic/administrative side for a group of 30 there may be little difference in resources in man/days. A taught programme can increase its intake above this figure with very little more staff time, and perhaps little loss of value – though many would question this. In action learning more people means more sets of 5 or 6 people and each set needs a member of staff (academic or manager) for some days – perhaps 15 or 20 days. Increased numbers may also provide enhanced learning opportunities, because more groups can learn by sharing their work on the projects, and be stimulated by the set work in other sets. Administration may be slightly strained by the increased comings and goings. An individual project programme of this size needs more setting up and more administration while 30 projects are running.

The main difficulty in embarking on such programmes, for the academics, trainers and administrative people (apart from any role change) is that the patterns of work are so different from those required for the normal course offered by any institution. Booking whole days and 3-day meetings, often off the premises, for a number of staff (possibly coinciding) may interrupt the academic's other plans and not fit with terms or avoid rush periods on other courses etc. So the demands may seem greater than they are and are often said to be so. Course or programme prices must be realistic so that those involved feel equally rewarded – institutionally or personally – not for the number of words said but for their personal involvement in the work.

Client organisation staff are much more involved in an action learning programme. The participant will typically be working on his job part time and on his project part time (perhaps one day per week) for about six months. His colleagues in his department, division, or company may be involved with his work. Someone senior, probably a chief executive, will have become involved at the beginning of the programme discussions to ensure that change-action is expected and accommodated.

Development managers become partners, with line managers and perhaps outside help, in the 'design' of the programme, and take the risks involved. But they and their staff working in the programme in any way will be unable to deny that they have learned themselves, and most feel that, first time round at least, it is an important developmental experience, so the resources in the organisation are enhanced and strengthened. Many clients and colleagues associated with the programme have made similar statements. But it must be recognised that the process of (joint) development of the programme does use resources and tests the reality of the commitment to management development and this form of organisation change.

HOW IS ACTION LEARNING RATED?

Most of the popular training approaches are low on risk and high on consumer satisfaction. How does action learning rate? It is much more difficult to get an immediate standing ovation! We have all heard the lecture which consists of little more than a series of anecdotes, many of them humorous, received enthusiastically – some of the jokes are memorable.

We are asking good competent managers to face difficult problems which may be well outside their normal competence, perhaps in another organisation, with the spotlight on them and often they will believe that their future careers will be much affected by their performance. We offer them nothing more than each other and expect an act of faith.

By the end of the programme, we can hope for enthusiasm. They will be aware of what they have learned, and may have seen changes in behaviour in themselves and others. They may have achieved a task and seen a change (probably 4 or 5 changes) of some importance begin to take shape, and know they had considerable influence – for they will have followed closely the work of all the others in the set. They will have taken high risks on entering the programme and have felt themselves at risk many times as the work progressed and they will have survived in good order. A very few leave the programmes part way through and a few emerge unmoved and unscathed, as reported by one participant in the GEC programme. [18] There must be similar experiences on taught programmes, though physical withdrawal (as opposed to mental or emotional withdrawal) occurs equally seldom and leaving unscathed is not always highly visible.

The risk for trainers and developers is higher in starting out in action learning. Most trainers enter a programme not having worked with a set and they convince their management on the basis of theory (Revans) and 'it seems to have worked there' – and often they seek the help of an experienced ally. Fortunately, most people though not all, are now aware what they are taking on and prepare the ground carefully getting help as they need it, and sometimes very early in the process. The steps to be taken have been carefully outlined in an 'action manual'. [19] The idea seems so simple; put a few people together, get them to take on a task or tasks, and let them get on with it. But most institutions have too many rules and procedures, too many sensitivities about authority and too much vagueness about their own purposes and their expectations of others, to find that comfortable.

So it is complex – to give a degree of authority, to let loose an open mind on a problem not in his own backyard, and to work to get his mind more open, his behaviour more innovative, does involve risk. The rewards can be huge, an encouragement to moves in these directions in the culture of the organisation, as well as achievement of changes in each single problem area; and more competent managers using more imagination and strategic thinking, more easily able to get things done once decisions are taken and more able to make good actionable decisions.

Consumer satisfaction is not usually a problem at all. Most programmes are repeated (eg 7 of the 9 in Table 13.1) where there is still a need. The difficulty, in 'market' terms, is in maintaining the integrity of the product so that learning remains equally as important as task.

ACTION PLANNING AND ACTION LEARNING

We do action planning at the end of our courses. Why do you think that this is not action learning? The last time I had this question I was talking to a colleague who works in action learning, about the work I have been doing in Africa. At the Centre there, technically well qualified senior managers come for 5 or 11 week courses in general management. They come from all the developing countries, almost all from Africa. They work in groups of 5 or 6 throughout the programme, meeting for one period each day, so they know each other's country, organisation, job and personality quite well towards the end of the programme. We then convert the groups from integrated task groups working on exercises and assignments in the programme, to sets ready to work on action planning.

Each member of the set presents a real problem (not a puzzle – these should have been dealt with in options) he is particularly concerned about. Reflecting on the work he has done on the programme he now wishes to prepare a plan to progress it. The set works in the normal way for say one and a half hours on each problem and after his session the member goes away to sum up his new ideas. These are re-presented and examined in the set, and each member takes a last look at the revised version of the action plan in the same way just before the members leave the programme. All the work is done in the sets, the same groups in which they have worked together for many hours throughout the course. The work seems valuable and is regarded as an extremely useful part of the programme. The staff have now incorporated this process in all their programmes.

But this action planning in the set cannot, because of a geo-graphical spread of thousands of miles, be concerned with implementation. There is a hope that 'things will happen' and support by letter, telex and telephone is available from the Centre and from set colleagues, but the invaluable working through implementation step by step with the support, analysis and evaluation of the set cannot be experienced. As they leave we wonder about the future course of action actually to be pursued by that manager who has to tackle keeping a secure boundary round his research centre, with squatters seeking life-giving water from his water source; or that other who must tackle the nepotism from above him which ensures that one of his four divisional managers who does not perform (or even arrive for work very regularly) cannot be moved – and the set's analysis here was extremely imaginative! Or the one whose responsibility is to provide the government with the income from the farmers on his coffee project but knows that the money is demanded from the farmers by the 'patriots', 'terrorists', on the border, on pain of death – and he is equally at risk if his own demands are too harsh! Managerial problems take on a new dimension, and the lack of support during early implementation stages, a new importance.

Action learning requires this testing of the pious hopes and case study solutions arrived at in the early stages of the sets. However well done, however discriminating the questions and the analysis, we know that the really learningful challenges will occur as we move to change things. Vested interests will be threatened, someone's *amour propre* upset, the dominant power culture will react, and the resulting processes have to be carefully managed. Powerful people will have to be convinced of the value of the plan, persuaded to co-operate, or be overpowered by the carefully selected band of allies the project champion has collected together.

In many sets it is in this area that most insights are gained – not necessarily mind blowing revelations, but a growing understanding of how the power system works and how it can be worked with, to achieve change. One's own immediate structure and the system within which it is embedded often seem quite invincible, but others in the set can, by careful persistent and sympathetic questioning, identify chinks and open up new pathways. Checking assumptions and testing boundaries can have surprising results. Unfortunately, little of this valuable questioning, persuading and risking, is available within the supportive environment of a programme that does not include implementation.

THOUGHTS ON ENDING

As I have struggled to write this chapter responding to questions remembered over the years, such clarity and insights as I have experienced have come as they always seem to, in two different ways. Sometimes we see a new simple way to look at something – an incremental eye-opener, which helps learning. Members of a set have called these the 'nuggets in the gravel', others say they take home from each set meeting one or two ideas they can apply next week. At other times the simple nudge of a question occurring as one responds to another, can change the way we see ourselves and be a permanent, unrepeatable eye-opener!

Questions always lead to more questions, and perhaps more discriminating questions! It seems unlikely we will be able to make progress on the vast organisational problems in businesses, governments, and society without developing the skills of asking and responding to more and more discriminating questions. It is certain that we will not find in any book an answer on how to distribute food to the starving; how to enable computers to arrange to do the heavy, dangerous and repetitive work without causing hardship to people; how to ensure that we give adequate health care to all new born babies; or how to house even our present population.

NOTES

For basic ideas and practice in the UK over the last 15 years;

Revans, R. W., *ABC of Action Learning*, Chartwell Bratt, 1983.
Pedler, M., (Editor), *Action Learning in Practice*, Gower, 1983.
Casey, D. and Pearce D., *More Than Management Development*, Gower, 1977.

Reg Revans' writings in *Action Learning – Its Origins and Growth* and in *Action Learning – Techniques for Management* give a comprehensive guide to thinking about wider applications of the principles, with examples of practice worldwide.

REFERENCES

(1) Revans, R. W., *Developing Effective Managers – A New Approach to Management Education*, New York, Praeger, 1971, includes a full report of the Belgian Programme.
(2) Op. cit. p. 54-55. A distinction underlined in the frequently ignored chapter on the theory of action learning.
(3) Casey, D. and Pearce, D., *More Than Management Development – Action Learning at GEC*, Gower, 1977.

(4)   Pedler, M. (ed.), *Action Learning in Practice*, Gower, 1983.

(5)   Braddick, W. and Casey D., 'Developing the Forgotten Army: Learning and the Top Manager', *Management Education and Development* vol. 12, no. 3, 1981, pp. 169-80.

(6)   Letter to author re Consortium programme, from John Bird, then Chief Executive, Private Systems Business, Cable & Wireless Ltd., 14 October 1976.

(7)   Revans, R.W., *Action Learning, New Techniques for Management*, Blond & Briggs, 1980 (and 4 above).

(8)   Revans, R. W., *The ABC of Action Learning*, Chartwell Bratt, 1983, pp. 50-54. Many others refer to the processes in sets, often while discussing the Set Adviser role, eg Casey, D., 'The Emerging Role of the Set Adviser in Action Learning Programmes', *Journal of European Training*, vol. 5, no. 3, 1976, adapted in *Action Learning in Practice* (as in 4 above) pp. 205-16.

(9)   Peters, T. J. and Waterman, R. H., *In Search of Excellence*, Harper & Row, 1982, pp. 208-9.

(10) For example, Casey, D. (as 3 above), Harries, J. M., and Pedler, M. in Chapter 17, 18 and 19 in *Action Learning in Practice* (see 4 above) and my early personal exploration on pp. 96, 97 of *More Than Management Development* (3 above).

(11) Mike Bett, then Personnel Director, GEC, writes of the need for improved communications – 'probably the most important lesson those involved have learned' in *More Than Management Development* (as 3 above).

(12) Owen Report, Business School Programmes, The Requirements of British Manufacturing Industry, London, BIM, 1971.

(13) Revans, R. W., *Origins & Growth of Action Learning*, Chartwell Bratt Ltd. In Chapter 31 Revans writes of choice of Projects, Clients and Fellows (participants) and I now see he uses 'a questioning approach' to start the chapter!

(14) Garratt, R., Chapter 2 especially pp. 32-3, in Pedler, M., *Action Learning in Practice* (4 above).

(15) A list of the projects and the way they were tackled is given in App. III, page 139-44, and the variants discussed pp. 19-20 and summarised to nominators, p. 132-3 in *More Than Management Development* (3 above).

(16) 'The Self Developing Manager', a description of the Consortium

programme printed by Cable & Wireless, a participating company, to help to recruit other organisations. Available from International Foundation for Action Learning, c/o IMCB, Castle Street, Buckingham.

(17) 'Management Action Group' was originally spawned by the Management Action Programme sponsored by Manpower Services Commission and operated by EMAS Ltd.

(18) Casey, D. and Pearce, D., *More Than Management Development* (3 above) Chapter 7 by David Carr, 'It didn't work for me'.

(19) Pedler, M., *Action Learning in Practice* (4 above), Appendix 1, by Pearce, D., 'Getting Started – an Action Manual', especially pp. 266-8.

14

Experiential based learning

Rick Roskin

Few organisations fail to have a statement in their annual report to the effect that their most valuable asset is their people. Yet often they pay little more than lip service to the idea. However, those that are committed to the personal growth of their employees include management development as a priority objective. But there are trade-offs to consider according to Wexley and Latham (1981).[1] It costs money to train employees. If this is not seen as an investment, then the impact on organisational effectiveness may be great because of the failure to develop staff.

To achieve effective management development one must be aware of the many approaches available to facilitate the process. This is especially true since instruction tactics should parallel the demands of the learning environment. Although the methods of adult education are best known in the 'people management' area, they are equally critical to all be they finance or computing. In fact, the technical areas of management probably stand to gain the most from a clear understanding of the various experientially based learning methods along with their associated strengths and weaknesses. As Stuart-Kotze and Roskin (1983)[2] state:

> The lesson to be learned from Japan is not a technological one, however. What the Japanese managers understand, and what we seem to have forgotten, is that people make a difference.

The importance of the contingent application of instructional methods is underlined by Sashkin (1982).[3] Although emphasising the participative model, he says that the 'it all depends' approaches to management are the most realistic since we must realise that with the behavioural sciences we are into an area of 'probability science'.

Literally every review of personnel effectiveness emphasises the importance of management development being integrated within the total organisational system and properly administered, for instance, see Von Glinow et al. (1983).[4] The significance to the individual and the organisation of effective management development means that we should be aware of Experiential Based Learning (EBL) approaches. The variety of methods within the EBL framework makes a definition difficult, however, underlying most experiential based episodes is a degree of induced ambiguity to test the participant's reaction. Generally, certain learning boundaries are attempted to help with the internalisation of the experience and subsequent application. In other words, it is common for a theoretical base to be provided as a framework for the experience. Then, within it, the learner is motivated to test out his or her beliefs or abilities. The facilitator eventually co-ordinates the event by attempting to highlight what happened and integrate the outcomes within the model. Those that were involved are effectively used as consultants and provide valuable information as regards what they experienced. The process very much parallels the Kolb et al. (1984, p. 31)[5] four-stage cycle of learning and problem solving:

1 concrete experience is followed by;
2 observation and reflection, which lead to;
3 the formation of abstract concepts and generalisations, which lead to;
4 hypotheses to be tested in future action, which in turn lead to new experiences.

The authors have developed a Learning Style Inventory (LSI) which measures one's relative emphasis on the four learning needs which constitute the earlier mentioned cycle. They argue that no one style is better or worse than another; nor is a balanced profile necessarily best. Rather, the key to effective learning is to be competent in a particular mode when it is required.

EXPERIENTIAL BASED LEARNING EXAMPLES

Later in this chapter we will be discussing different general categories of experiential based learning, however, a few specific examples of EBL would be useful at this stage. Perhaps the work of Maier (1973)[6] is the best known to many people, particularly his role playing designs. They consist of situation incidents with associated roles to be performed by participants. The objective is for the participant to behave in a manner appropriate to the designated role. From such interaction it is hoped that the dynamics generated will lead to greater empathy and knowledge retention on the part of those involved. One of the most famous of these role plays is called the 'change of work procedure'. In it the foreman, Gus, must resolve the conflicting demands of management's man (a time and motion expert) who suggests how each employee should work, and the desires of his own group for autonomy. By involving the student in various roles they become more aware of the difficulties that confront employees in the work setting.

Business game simulations are another approach to translating theory into action. These simulations may be computerised. Participants generally operate on teams and make decisions within a competitive environment. The quality of their decisions determines the success of their group against others. But there is more to learn than simply filling in forms. Most of those involved indicate a vast source of learning through their involvement with others. The human side of enterprise becomes an important factor even when decisions require technical expertise. The previous descriptions are but two of many approaches since EBL methods draw upon a vast array of techniques, processes and theories as outlined by Roskin (1978).[7] Each independent procedure has strengths and weaknesses. Each will be successful or not depending upon four fundamental underlying factors:

1 The learning objective
2 The learner
3 The facilitator, and
4 The environment.

In simplistic terms one must initially decide whether the primary objective is to develop cognitive enrichment or skill-building. The second consideration is the nature of the learner; age, background and motivation. The third consideration is the inherent knowledge and skills of the facilitator. Finally, one must be aware of the influence of environmental factors such as the commitment of those who must use the EBL and its effect on other parts of the system.

The most effective combination of the four factors for experientially based learning occurs where the objective is to develop application skills; where the learner has achieved the ability to integrate experiences into a meaningful mental and action model; where the facilitator has sufficient ego strength and knowledge to be able to cope with unprogrammed responses that occur from the interactive nature of the orientation, and where the environment consists of a relatively autonomous unit of committed EBL practitioners.

THE AUTHORITY VACUUM

Since a fundamental basis of the experiential approach is to place the learner within an environment of moderate uncertainty, it must be assumed that most can readily cope with ambiguity, otherwise such situations would be seen as attempts to force exposure and as such might lead to withdrawal. Unfortunately, many individuals have a much lower tolerance of ambiguity than they realise or than is necessary to provide a meaningful experience.

The problem is that the average individual has been so culturally 'shaped' to be a quasi-robot that they almost 'abhor a vacuum'; a situation where past experience or prescribed rules are not available. They have been whipped into shape by many forces to become an 'expert subordinate' rather than a leader or one who accepts and encourages change. This idea is reinforced by Argyris (1960)[8] who argues that:

> Most human problems in organizations arise because relatively healthy people in our culture are asked to participate in work situations which coerce them to be dependent, subordinate, submissive; to use a few of their more than skin-surface abilities.

If one were able to review the average individual's life span of experiences, the previous circumstance might become more understandable. As a child, they did what their parents wanted – or else they might be deprived of love. In school, they found that rules and regulations were to be followed precisely – or else they might be faced with corporal punishment. If they went to university – the bastion of intellectual freedom – they conformed, or else they might not pass. Upon reaching employment age, they learned to do what the boss said – or else they might be fired. They could not even escape the feeling on Sunday if they felt they must follow religious dogma – or else their final resting place might be rather warm. And, so pressurised by people, events, rules and regulations they adapted to living with the 'or else' feeling.

But the individual must eventually succeed in a range of un-certainties. As Herzberg (1966)[9] puts it:

> The fourth characteristic of psychological growth is effectiveness in ambiguity. The world is ambiguous and perhaps probabilistic; uncertainty pervades our living experience.

It is the problem of the need to induce ambiguity for learning purposes and the tolerance level of the learner and facilitator which poses some design difficulty when attempting to achieve an effective equilibrium (since some ambiguity must be introduced but not too much). Since not all individuals cope with ambiguity equally well, it is understandable that their experiences vary even within the same condition.

It is, therefore, important for facilitators to diagnose their own needs and abilities, to assess the probable needs and abilities of the learners and from there to develop an appropriate experiential design.

DESIGN DETERMINANTS

A number of issues need to be considered by the designer including the learning objectives, those of the participants, their own ability and environmental influences.

The Objectives

Are the objectives and desired outcomes clear? Too often experiential exercises are designed simply to use up some time. When this occurs they are usually perceived as little more than 'parlour games with new names'. Without meaningful integration within an overall learning strategy, they will be an ineffective crutch. The use of random exercises is bound to prove confusing and frustrating to participants. Therefore, where a series of structured events are to be utilised, there should be a careful plan concerning the order of introduction and method of linkage. Further, some back-up or peripheral exercises should be part of the kitbag to help handle possible related needs of participants.

To design a successful experience there has to be some specific rationale behind the process. A common thread of reason must tie it together within a priori determined boundaries. Without such discipline, so-called responses to the needs of the individual become reactive. Analysis of the process becomes distorted through the cloud of uncertainty of those who have little conceptual theory to grasp. Therefore, theoretical inputs, while normally being short in duration, are fundamental to a successful outcome of the learning design.

Application

A number of years ago I was involved in a seminar for middle managers of a pulp and paper company. The group consisted of about fifteen engineers. I decided to begin it with a so-called ice-breaker. It was a classic called 'Test Of Direction Following Ability'. There are about twenty sentences on a sheet of paper. The first one says 'Do nothing until you have read all statements'. Then down the page are a series of commands such as:

1 Write your name in the top right-hand corner.
2 If you have reached here yell out 'I have'.
3 Count from one to ten out loud.

This continues until number twenty which says 'Now that you have reached here do only number one'. Of course the majority neglect the first instruction and feel rather foolish at the end of it all having publicy broadcast their error. In the case mentioned, one of the senior engineers asked, 'What the hell had the dumb exercise to do with the course'. A logical question. From that point on it took a great effort on my part to convince the others that everything we undertook did not have a trick to it.

The learner

The adult learner is different from the child. Knowles (1972)[10] argues too many instructors use their own childhood experiences at school as a model for teaching (the pedagogical approach). In general terms, the following factors should be taken into consideration when designing experiential based events:

1 Adults see themselves as relatively independent.
2 The adult desires a sense of self-accomplishment and determinism.
3 The adult is motivated through diagnosing his/her own needs.
4 The adult likes to actively participate in his/her learning experience.
5 The adult likes to be involved in self-evaluation through opportunities to compare performance to norms.
6 The adult has experienced a great deal and considers that experience an essential basis for future learning.
7 The adult tends to evaluate learning in relation to its applicability to day-to-day living.

Consequently, experiential learning designs must include the following learner oriented factors:

1 Inclusion of the learner as a resource person.
2 Active participation of the learner in the programme.
3 The use of evaluation as a basis for problem-solving orientated improvement.

In summary, what is being suggested is that within the programme design it is often useful to have participants generate some of their own related difficulties and some expectation as to what they hope to learn. In the first instance, the facilitator may be better able to use specific methods to problem solve if made aware of real life difficulties of participants. The second instance allows for there to be a meeting of minds on what the course will be (including the facilitator's area of competence) and to make certain that levels of aspiration are not unrealistically high.

Application

The introduction of the four P's of experiential teaching design will facilitate the appropriate instruction approach. They are:

1 *Presentation*: each segment should begin with the introduction of some theoretical support for the event by way of a short input by the instructor. Most commonly, the lecturette will include a model or some simplified way to remember the key points.
2 *Participation*: participants will then engage an activity so as to be able to 'experience' the objective of the event. The prior input by the instructor should increase motivation.
3 *Processing*: the instructor will then use the experience to glean data from the event including the feelings and opinions of those involved, thereby, actively using them as 'consultants'. This is the critical stage because if the exercise is not usefully discussed, then it will lack in validity.
4 *Publication*: finally, the results will be written to flipchart or blackboard for all to see and all to take relevant notes.

The previous four steps are cumulative and must be followed to maximise the power of the learning experience.

The facilitator

An effective facilitator in EBL designs must possess two different abilities. Firstly, they must have a comprehensive knowledge of their subject area or course *content* and, secondly, they must be able to develop an appropriate learning *context*. The context of such an approach is that of process analysis. Without skilful interpretation of group and individual interaction and solid theoretical back-up, many possible benefits will be lost.

It is essential to make strategic interventions in the dynamics to emphasise and underline the range of learning alternatives available to participants. Often they are so embroiled in activities as to make observation of the hoped for experience difficult. The necessity of reacting to many different individuals with many different needs means that facilitators must be secure in their knowledge base and process intervention strategy. It means, as well, that they must have the courage to own up to not always having all the answers.

Finally, many experiential situations, by their very nature, are generators of controversy and/or uncertainty. It is important for the facilitator to think carefully about the nature and frequency of interventions in the learning process. Often, it is beneficial for participants to *work through* their own problems rather than attempt to gain the support of *the answer* from the seminar leader. Unwise seduction can be detrimental to their effectiveness in future situations where expertise may legitimately be needed.

Application

I was involved in a programme to improve communication within a hospital. A series of management development programmes had been arranged by a university for whom I worked. One of the instructors had much greater experience teaching university students than working adults. When confronted by a head nurse who disagreed with a communications concept he became agitated. Instead of using the 'shared experience' as a living laboratory, he turned to her and said 'You want to know what makes me right and you wrong! I've got a PhD in communications – what have you got?'

The environment

Research indicates that situational influences are more powerful than individual personality. Hence, where programme elements are interdependent, it is essential that facilitators agree upon the overall philosophy of experiential based learning, otherwise they are likely to see such effort, at best, as ineffectual and, at worst, as subversive. In both cases, it is probable that they will behave as catalysts for change if the programme is implemented, or as agents of the status quo where it is not. Such activity takes a short time to find its way to the learner and provides little positive reinforcement. The operational problems of any learning environment are difficult enough without dissension within the ranks as to the efficiency of experientially based learning designs.

Application

A colleague and I have developed an instrumented seminar called Mach One – short for Managerial Achievement. Occasionally, we have attempted to train trainers to be able to present the seminar. Frequently, management development specialists over the age of forty have a sensitivity or T-group training background since that approach held a great deal of currency in the sixties.

Our experience in convincing individuals from the sensitivity training school to follow our well-tested design and not 'fiddle with the knobs' has had varying degrees of success. During one programme, one of our instructors engaged a participant in a conversation about his feelings concerning communism – well away from the course rationale. Mach One does not have time built in to handle such diversions, especially when the participant escaped from a communist country. The trainer was accused of 'sharing his ignorance' by the participant who mounted a table to gain greater presence and underline his point. The trainer changed into his 'T-group mode' but we had to move on before the issue could be fully resolved.

EXPERIENTIAL BASED LEARNING DESIGN

A great number of learning approaches and specific learning vehicles are utilised today. However, most can be defined as one or a combination of the six noted below:

1 Paper and pencil instruments
2 Unstructured group dynamics
3 Instrumented group dynamics
4 Video feedback
5 Computer augmented feedback
6 Field experience

Each has particular strengths and weaknesses (see Table 14.1) which should be considered when deciding upon their application.

Table 14.1
Experiential based learning designs

	Paper & Pencil Instruments	Unstructured Group Dynamics	Instrumented Group Dynamics	Video Feedback	Computer Augmented Feedback	Field Experience
STRENGTHS	Inexpensive	Powerful facilitator of self-awareness	Active participation	Irrefutable feedback	Behaviour quantification	Role socialisation
	Easy access	High participant commitment	Face validity	Quick feedback	Complex feedback	Reality testing
	Easily replicated	Sense of community	Diagnostic capability	Motivational adherence	Skill building and research branching	Learner commitment
	Standardisation	Quick pay-off	Skill building	Repetition	High participant commitment	Learning goal compatibility
	Comparable norms	Enhancement of self	Replication	Observation of theory into action	Comparative data base	Adaptive interaction
	Specific identification					
WEAKNESSES	Face validity	Depth of intervention	Theoretical underpinnings	Movie star syndrome	Cost	Control problems
	Participant motivation	Necessitates highly skilled trainer	Participant parlour game mentally	Few strong process models	Accessibility	Evaluation problems
	Reliability	Difficult data collection	Time	Expensive access	Feedback comprehension	Academic faculty commitment
	Learning transference	Limited instrumental objectives	Trainer skills necessary	Time consuming	Numbers game	Statistical data base
	Fatal flaw syndrome	Replication limitation	Forced categorisation	Peripheral generation	Time consuming	Completion time

Pencil and paper instruments

These are used in almost all experiential designs to some extent. Occasionally, data is gathered from participants and analysed to develop group related measurement dimensions making the process organic.

Quite often, training indices are used for 'quick and dirty' comparisons of group norms. While individuals are warned about the fact that the results should not be considered predictors, many people find it difficult to disregard a result so derived, especially where the facilitator has some organisational power over them.

The widespread use is based upon a number of reasons including the fact that they are inexpensive and normally easily accessible. When standardised tests are utilised they provide some valid, comparative norms and allow research opportunities since replication is possible. Perhaps, most importantly of all, they allow for relatively quick and specific identification of where individuals stand in relation to others.

Since many are wary of paper and pencil analyses, motivation can be a problem because many do not consider information gained in such a manner as valid. One other consideration bears mentioning. It is that designs which identify individual 'fatal flaws' often do not provide a regimen for solving such shortcomings. In failing to do so they are not particularly helpful to the individual in transferring their findings to the back-home environment.

Application

Results from tests seem to have almost mystical meaning in the eyes of recipients. This is even more the case when a computerised printout is used. On one occasion, in our desire to make the use of a management style test more user-friendly, modifications to a computer program had been made. However, the old program had been used, with the results being incorrect because of this. Participants had largely 'bought into' the erroneous data when a revised output was given to them. They then bought into the new results as well.

I have scrambled astrological heading types and found that many people agree with the attributes assigned to them notwithstanding

content. What largely determines beliefs is acceptance of the underlying theory, theorists, and/or seminar presenters.

Unstructured group dynamics

This approach to experiential learning is based on number of
variations-on-a-theme of sensitivity training. While this is still
relatively popular in 'helping service organisations' and for individual
growth, it has lost vogue in most industrial settings.

As a powerful design to bring about increased self-awareness on the
part of individual interpersonal skills, it usually has high participant
commitment from those who have personally opted to attend such
sessions. A quick pay-off normally results and individuals gain
satisfaction from the group support that develops.

In most situations, identifying and reinforcing the worth of the
individual irrespective of particular skill-achievement is, from the
human potential perspective, quite valuable. However, in many
situations the demanded emotional investment on the part of the
individual goes beyond that which is necessary to bring about an
appropriate learning experience. Many such programmes lack
specific instrumental objectives and the nature of the dynamics –
usually with limited model boundaries – means that data collection is
difficult if not dysfunctional to the very basis of the process.

Finally, the intensity and complexity of unstructured group
dynamics means that highly skilled facilitators are required to ensure
success.

Application

During a week-long T-Group I attended, a participant cried the whole
time. She was a young girl of twenty-four who had been recently
married. After about the third day I realised that I had less empathy
than I had first thought.

Since I am a university professor, I attempted to take notes as
events unfolded. I was accused of breaking the confidentiality of the
group and had to stop.

One of the trainers involved us in a non-verbal exercise relating to
trust. The idea was to fall backwards into someone else's arms. He
was rather portly and for some strange reason chose a diminutive girl

as his partner. As she was unable to hold him, he tumbled on to her causing minor injury to her and severe injury to his credibility.

While I learned a few interesting things, I was at a loss as to how I would communicate them to my boss.

Instrumented group dynamics

The use of various instruments such as indices, simulations, cases and other instrumental activities serve as the basis for this approach to experiential learning.

The objective is either to test or allow a comparison of individual opinion or behaviour within reasonably specific objectives. Hence, a theoretical idea is made to come alive by generating activities which relate directly to the concept under question. Participants are then able to see how they operate within the boundaries of the experience which is being generated. Because individuals are actively involved in the learning process, ideas are readily internalised and boredom is decreased. Furthermore, activities can be developed to relate directly to participant experience; therefore, most programmes have good face validity.

The data generated can be replicated by repeatedly using a specified combination of instruments. Standardisation of the programme or instrumentation can facilitate the diagnosis of individual and organisational effectiveness. Since instrumented group dynamics can be used to develop simulated work environments, and because participants are actively involved, the approach is particularly useful for skill-building purposes. It is essential, however, that the activities themselves – the context – do not usurp theoretical underpinnings – the content – otherwise activities tend to lose much of their value.

Another consideration is the time element as many activities take considerably longer to operate than the simple one-way lecture approach. However, when the time to comprehend the concepts and quality of comprehension is considered, there may be little real difference.

This method tests facilitators both before the event when they have to develop new approaches or carefully integrate already invented instrumentation, and after the event when they have to guide the analysis of generated data. Finally, some concern is expressed about the fact that many instruments somewhat artificially force individuals

267

to make choices among fewer alternatives than the real world might offer, or than might be available within their own repertoire.

Application

The use of instrumentation allows the structuring of events so that there is equity in terms of the amount of attention everyone gets. However, while a variety of activities are possible during long seminars, there can be a sense of repetition and a lack of commitment towards giving everyone fair opportunity.

One design I have used requires participants to act as team members four times and as a manager once during simulations. On one occasion, the last simulation was ruined by one team when they broke into the main seminar room late one evening and hijacked the simulation material. Since data was entered into a computer and results calculated based upon the whole week, serious damage was done to the integrity of the output. A substitute simulation was quickly derived but it could not emulate the careful rationale, nor the efficacy of the original, which had been tested through years of research.

Video feedback

Video recording provides the basis for powerful, rapid feedback to the participant. And the nature of the process tends to motivate individuals towards the acceptance of learning objectives and commitment thereto. Since the record of activities can be stored and replayed, individuals are able to see the nature of their personalised learning curve. Learning possibilites are enhanced by the fact that individuals can spend time thinking about their own performance — how they might improve it, etc. — without having to worry about concentrating on feedback since it is available repeatedly at the flick of a switch.

Importantly, participants can see whether or not theory is translating into action. Further, they can gain a much broader understanding of things such as group dynamics since they need not operate as a participant observer (possibly confusing process with content) because the experience can be repeated through replays with different focuses of attention possible each time.

Some considerations to be aware of when using video feedback are that, initially, participants suffer from a 'movie star syndrome' finding it difficult to concentrate on the process under review since other irrelevant activities gain the centre of attention. This may be caused partially by a lack of strong process models particularly orientated to the video medium.

The cost of such equipment tends to somewhat limit access. However, most electronic technology is decreasing in price rapidly. Finally, the procedure can be time consuming since several playbacks are usually necessary to maximise learning.

Application

The artistry was impressive. The camera panned around the table catching the smoke from cigarettes wending its way towards the ceiling. Then, from an almost impossible angle, the view was that which a bird would see if it hovered over the table. Next, a keyhole shot, giving a sense of the invasion of privacy. This is what I viewed after assigning classes to attend our Centre For Audio-Visual Education. The objective had been to obtain some footage regarding group decision making. What I had neglected to do was inform the producer, in precise terms, the goal of the exercise. Consequently, his psychological set had driven him to 'do a Fellini'. The reaction of the students had been to become 'actors' playing to the director's requests. It was an interesting exercise but the data generated had little to do with what I had in mind.

Computer augmented feedback

The power of computers can be used to provide data based feedback to participants. Hence, with appropriate experiential models and simulations, behaviour can be quantified in a manner which is much more complex than most other systems provide, and computers allow for both learning functions and research branching. They also provide a comparative data base with the possibility of statistical analysis. Since data based feedback normally necessitates a fair amount of form filling by participants, they will be more committed to accuracy when they believe the output to be of significance.

Many programmes are available which are interactive in nature and allow for different levels of learning, speed and remedial action. However, computers are often being used within experiential based learning environments more as an adjunct than as a focus of the design. In other words, they serve the purpose of data collection, manipulation and feedback of that information.

Some limitations of computers include the fact that they can be costly to use and are not as accessible as many other learning systems. However, the rapidly decreasing cost of microcomputers and their increasing power means that they are quickly becoming cost-effective. Depending upon their function and the nature of the design of the programme, it may take a fair time to input the data and then receive the output. Once the information is available some considerable guidance may be required from the facilitator to help the participant comprehend the significance of the numbers. They should not be seduced into disregarding other aspects of the learning experience believing that the cold, black print of the output to be infallible.

Application

Unless the objective of a learning design is to understand computers, they should be used as a tool and not as a goal in themselves.

A key phase of a management seminar I operate occurs during the last afternoon when instructors give feedback to participants about how they might achieve more in their back-home environment. At the same time, the microcomputer is receiving the final input so that it may begin its job of analysing the data and printing out a hard copy of the results.

During one seminar, in the early stages of our using a microcomputer, it malfunctioned. I hurried to a computer store to try to solve the problem, but to no avail. Then I made several transatlantic calls to check out the software – all with no success. In the meanwhile I had lost valuable time and was unable to give the normal amount of feedback to the participants. Furthermore, I was somewhat unnerved by the events and the quality of the feedback suffered because of this.

Field experience

The design consists of placing the learner in the actual environment they may have eventually to operate within. As a result, role socialisation can take place rather rapidly as the candidate becomes familiar with the values and norms of the job and organisation with which they are involved. It also provides them with a real life laboratory to test theory against practice.

Since EBL designs are experientially orientated the field experience approach is compatible with the learning objectives. This generally means greater commitment on the part of the learner as they can quickly identify whether or not they have chosen the correct career path.

The process provides a two-way communications channel between 'those that teach and those that do' which can bring about appropriate adaptation in a rapid fashion. Consequently, the correct theories can be chosen and developed while the actual practice can be modified where new theory would improve results.

Some of the limitations of the approach occur when questions of control surface. Often discussion centres around who is running the show – the trainers or the practitioners. Arising from this conflict is the question of evaluation. What distribution is allocated to academic success or failure and what to field experience?

Confrontation between those who value the academic pursuit of knowledge, devoid of practical application possibilities or experience, may lead to decreased commitment of those on both sides of the fence.

An important consideration is that many EBL approaches have not adequately utilised their field experience data base to show statistically that they are superior, in some situations, to other learning approaches. Also, many have not made data collection a significant part of the design. Finally, they generally take longer to complete than straight theory designs, although once comprehension and application skill is considered, this may not be true.

Application

The university where I work has a 'sandwich type' programme in which students must participate in several work terms before graduating. As a mechanism to maintain academic control, students are required to complete a report. This report is frequently suggested by employers and given final approval by them. It is then marked by a faculty member.

A case arose wherein an employer considered a report to be satisfactory, while a faculty member did not. After rereading it a number of times, as required by regulations, the mark remained unchanged.

The employer was incensed by the result since he had evaluated the report as very good. He informed the university that if they did not change their view of the report he would hire no more students for work terms.

THE MAIN ISSUES

The fundamental issues that must be addressed and assessed when considering the experiential approach to learning can be summarised into five C's: control, capacity, congruence, competency and commitment.

Control

A significant consideration when deciding upon the probable success of experiential learning is the question of the facilitator foregoing some control. Since the basis of the approach might loosely be called learner-directed, it is paramount that the facilitator delegates an unusually large degree of authority and responsibility to the learner for their own success. This, of course, does not mean abdication of the important role of providing an environment to facilitate learning but it does mean allowing the learner to make mistakes except where such errors can be quickly and readily discussed without contamination of the design, or where such mistakes may have serious consequences.

Some facilitators are surprised when confronted with the control issue, to find themselves as threatened by the loss of the normal anchors of power, as the learners are with their new found responsibilities.

Application

A fundamental concept in the management literature is the

importance of being able to cope with ambiguity and uncertainty.

Several years ago, I developed a theory and a series of exercises pertaining to this issue. It suggested that there are two fundamental strategies which can be pursued: absorption, which entails the use of experience and problem-solving abilities, and avoidance, which entails the use of forward thinking and planning.

To demonstrate the concept to some managers, I presented the theory to them at a seminar during one hot summer afternoon. An associated exercise consisted of a blank sheet of flipchart paper. They were told to get on with the task and I would collect the results in ninety minutes time. That was all the direction they received. I returned later to see how they had 'coped with ambiguity'. One team had discussed how they handled such conditions at work and had written up some application principles for back-home. The other team said they had opted for 'avoidance' and lain out in the sun for the entire time!

Congruence

It seems important that the facilitator models the behaviour that they are espousing. Hence, experiential based designs generally call for owning up to feelings, delegation of some control and taking the stance of alternative provider rather than expert; or more correctly, acting as a resource individual with regard to content while maintaining the expert role as context designer. The problem for many of us is that our past experience has been that of the pedagogical model and hence we appear to be 'on the boundary' both in terms of developing the educational environment wherein the 'student' holds a major role as responsible learner and as regards presenting ourselves as the expert source of information.

Margulies (1978)[11] discusses this problem rather succinctly, but in terms of the consultant's role which really parallels that of an experientially based facilitator.

In fact, the great difficulty that faces the facilitator is attempting to more than straddle a number of conflicting positions. As a corollary, success may be determined by their ability to provide for the rational side of nonanalytical, verbal, problem-solving and linear thinking needs while at the same time being sensitive to the intuitive side such as the non-verbal, emotional, more esoteric and even mystical approaches to learning. The great problem is that they must somehow integrate or synthesise both poles – the technical and the process approaches lest they be seen as indecisive and ambivalent.

Margulies suggests that one way of coping may be to operate 'on the boundary'. In this case, the facilitator would be a marginal adherent to the psychologically opposed teaching approaches identified as pedagogical versus andragogical. Boundary positions are determined by the amount of time the individual uses each approach and by the importance of each position to them. Depending upon their own personal resolution of the optimum pursuit and what the environment will allow, there may be considerable personal stress, tension and personal conflict. Such influences make it more difficult for them to operate congruently and, as a consequence, they will be less effective in the eyes of the learner since that learner must suspend disbelief.

Dilemmas facing those operating 'on the boundary' include:

1 Involvement – to what degree does the facilitator provide the answer?
2 Responsibility – to what degree is the facilitator charged with the duty to assure success of the learning outcome?
3 Acceptance – to what degree can the facilitator feel personally comfortable when he/she must reach a balance between never being totally accepted or totally rejected?

Application

During my doctoral education in England, a famous American management development specialist was invited to present to some top British managers. His background led him to believe that the event would be most successful if the design allowed for significant involvement of the managers.

Almost immediately it became clear that they were there to listen to the Guru and were not 'up for' a general 'pooling of ignorance'. Upon realising this, he went on to use a Mary Poppins analogy to try to get a point across. By the afternoon tea break only a third of the participants remained. When asked why they were leaving the majority said they had not paid to hear other managers – they had paid to hear the 'expert'. By the time this message was clear, the Mary Poppins analogy seemed inappropriate.

Capacity

To foster their development one must assume that both the facilitator and the learner are capable of increased learning in experientially based designs, otherwise they are merely 'public works programmes for educators'. While this is true in some situations it is not the case for most. Over and above the relationship between desired learning outcomes and methodological issues are the personality characteristics of the facilitator and the learner. For if experientially based learning is to succeed, both must have at least a moderate ability to tolerate ambiguity. This holds true because such designs are often centred on the developing of 'safe emergencies'. Extreme reaction can lead to withdrawal from learning in the case of perceived threat or no experimentation where the individual feels little stress.

Perhaps at issue here is an effective selection method to determine which type of individual is likely to perform best in which type of educational design.

Application

In over fifteen years of management development experience, I have been involved in only two situations where participants left a programme prematurely. In the first case, the individual had brought his wife to the ski resort where the course took place. She became bored in the evenings since the design continued late into the night. His departure, while being disruptive, allowed us to discuss the type of feelings experienced by a team when a member leaves.

On another occasion, an individual disappeared without informing anyone. Despite support from his team and the training staff he was unable to cope with the situation and returned home.

After devising a series of questions to help screen applicants, we have yet to develop the perfect application form; but there are some important considerations:

1 Is the person coming of their own volition?
2 Is the participant alone or are they accompanied by others who are not involved in the programme?
3 Has the participant identified any psychological disorders?
4 Is the nature of the programme clearly identified in brochures, including usual hours of operation?

5 Are the facilities 'up to scratch' including lodging and food?
6 Is the programme design likely to be different from that which the participant has experienced in the past?
7 Will the design allow for a mixture of participants of teams consisting of those who have attended other seminars and those who have not?
8 Does the design build slowly towards the necessity of increasing emotional investment?
9 Are the trainers capable of handling the emotional, as well as technical side of human dynamics?

Competency

The new competency orientated educational designs are generally more compatible with experientially based learning. This is a result of the range of possibilities available for testing as to whether learning is translating into both knowledge and skill. Pedagogical approaches are generally geared to cognitive learning, whereas, andragogical orientations are very successful at skill induction. Since EBL methods range from simulations to practical field experience, assessment of competency is comparatively easy.

Application

In the late seventies the American Management Association became concerned about the direction the Master of Business Administration degree was taking. A review of the research by them indicated that the use of scholastic records, intelligence scores, etc. was an unreliable yardstick of managerial potential. Furthermore, they were unhappy with the focus of business schools, away from application skills, towards theory. This, combined with rigid class scheduling, restrictive transfer credits and a lack of recognition of any professional success, frustrated many managers.

To overcome these problems they introduced the Master of Management (MM). This programme includes a series of specific competencies, instruments to measure them, educational designs to parallel specific objectives and an internship component.

In England, the International Management Centre from Buckingham (IMCB) has tried to bridge the gap between theory and action (Wills and Day, 1984).[12] The distinctive objectives of the Centre are to:

1   Root programmes in the organisation
2   Use real, not artificial examples
3   Apply learning to practice.

The authors quote Ruskin to indicate their philosophy: 'what we think, or what we know, or what we believe, is in the end of little consequence. The only thing of consequence is what we do'.

Commitment

The question remains as to whether EBL can be successfully integrated into a system where all constituents are not committed. The answer is, in part, dependent upon whether the various subsystems are interdependent. Where they are relatively autonomous, EBL methods can be introduced on an independent basis. However, interdependence can cause tremendous problems if most people in the system are not proponents of EBL. Since it is often viewed as radical, serious resistance must often be confronted. In fact, its philosophy is not radical being simply to provide a hands-on approach to learning. It is the contextual boundaries of the learning process which differ rather than the content.

Using a computer as an analogy, one could suggest that the pedagogical approach focuses upon the memory banks — stored information — and that the EBL approach focuses upon the software programme that turns that information into meaning and application skills.

Application

The introduction of frequent management development programmes into organisations has led to a 'flavour of the week' attitude on the part of many employees. This stems from a lack of long-term planning and integration into the corporate culture of new or revised programmes.

To overcome this type of valid criticism, we often take concepts and redesign them so as to use organisational terminology. As an example, the Mach One programme mentioned earlier, uses a pool of twenty-seven general job demands to evaluate a manager's job. However, during the second stage of the programme, the pool of job elements are revised from the general to the specific. In other words, the pool is developed from tasks which are identified as being directly associated with the organisation using the programme.

CONCLUSION

Perhaps the best indication of the power of well designed management development programmes is the Japanese model, termed Theory Z by Ouchi (1981).[13] Rather than depending upon business schools as sources of trained personnel, they frequently recruit high school graduates. These graduates are then put through a lifetime of company orientated management development programmes that, according to Sullivan (1983)[14] teach them, among other things, how to co-operate with each other. The method includes both technically (e.g. quality circles) and socially directed objectives (e.g. exercising control through employees internalising corporate values). The manager is the teacher; the employee the student, and the organisation the environment.

The effectiveness of corporate orientated management development is supported by Illich (1971)[15] who argued that formal education systems tend to immunise students from learning. That much of what we know is picked up in less formal settings; particularly the more important aspects of living. The increasing division of labour according to Jones (1982)[16] forces many people to seek self-expression outside the classroom or work environment. Yet carefully designed management development programmes could harness such energies and provide an advantage to both the individual and the organisation.

IMPLICATIONS FOR MANAGEMENT DEVELOPMENT MANAGERS

EBL can be a powerful ally. Yet it must be integrated carefully within a development strategy which takes into account the relationship between participant need, the organisational goals and appropriate technique. Too often so much attention is paid to the content of management development that the process is overlooked. Clearly, the process is an important consideration, for content will not be effectively retained if it is inappropriately presented. To achieve the ideal situation, the management development manager must assess the nature of participant needs, and the skills of those involved in the educational facilitation role so as to choose the best learning design. He or she must also be aware of the many different EBL methods available so as to be able to make an informed decision.

It would appear that the most appropriate organisational design is that of an 'organic learning system' containing actors who are continuously learning from the environment, as well as through appropriate corporate management development. Experientially based learning (EBL) design is a significant and useful approach to fulfilling the previous goal. As a technique that focuses upon the process of interactions, it is particularly useful in bringing about increased self-awareness. It nurtures empathy as well, since participants often become enmeshed in roles that may be unfamiliar to them.

It is a methodology that strives to accelerate the type of learning that accrues through a lifetime of experience on the pretext that the environment within which we live does not afford us the luxury of time. Instead of grey hair constituting the necessary time frame, its philosophy is that 'grey matter' efficiently used is better. And by placing the learner in an often exaggerated situation to magnify what might otherwise have to be learned through the 'school of hard knocks', they obtain maximum results with minimum pain.

REFERENCES

(1) Wexley, K. N. and Latham, G. P., *Developing and Training Human Resources in Organizations*, Scott, Foresman and Co., Glenview, Illinois, 1981.
(2) Stuart-Kotze, R. and Roskin, R., *Success Guide to Managerial Achievement*, Reston Publishing Co., Reston, Virginia, 1983.
(3) Sashkin, M., *A Manager's Guide to Participative Management*, AMA Publications Division, New York, 1982.
(4) Von Glinow, M., Driver, M. J., Brousseau, K. and Prince, J.,

'The Design of a Career Oriented Human Resource System', *Academy of Management Review*, vol. 8, no.1, 1983, pp. 23-32.

(5) Kolb, D. A., Rubin, I. M. and McIntyre J. M., *Organizational Psychology: An experiential approach to Organizational Behaviour*, 4th edition, Prentice-Hall, Englewood Cliffs, N. J., 1984.

(6) Maier, N. R. F., *Psychology in Industrial Organizations*, 2nd edition, Houghton Mifflin, Boston, 1973.

(7) Roskin, R., 'Determinants of Experiential Based Learning Design', Presented to the National Conference on Programmatic Uses of Experiential Learning in Professional Education, Dallas, Texas, 24-26 May, 1978.

(8) Argyris, C., 'Individual Actualization in Complex Organization', *Mental Hygiene*, vol. 44, April 1960, pp. 226-9.

(9) Herzberg, F. R., *Work and the Nature of Man*, The World Publishing Co., 1966.

(10) Knowles, M., 'Ways of Learning: Reactive versus Proactive', *Journal of Continuing Education and Training*, vol. 1, no. 4, May 1972, pp. 285-7.

(11) Margulies, N., 'Perspectives on the Marginality of the Consultant's Role', Proceedings of the OD '78 Conference – A conference on current Theory and Practice in Organizational Development, San Francisco, 16-17 March 1978, University Associates, 1978.

(12) Wills, G. and Day, A., 'Buckingham's new action learning business school – how well does the theory work?' *Journal of European Industrial Training*, vol. 8, no. 6, 1984, pp. 3-4.

(13) Ouchi, J., *Theory Z*, Addison-Wesley, Reading, Massachusetts, 1981.

(14) Sullivan, J. J., 'A Critique of Theory Z', *Academy of Management Review*, vol. 8, no. 1, 1983, pp. 132-42.

(15) Illich, I., *Deschooling of Society*, Penguin, London, 1971.

(16) Jones, B., *Sleepers Wake!: Technology and the Future of Work*, Oxford University Press, Melbourne, 1982.

FURTHER READING

Margerison, C. J., *How to assess your managerial style*, West Yorkshire, MCB Publications, 1979.

Revans, R. W., *The origins and growth of action learning*, Chartwell-Bratt, 1982.

Sashkin, M. and Morris, W. C., *Organizational Behavior: Concepts and Experiences*, Reston, Virginia, 1984.

15

Using the outdoors

John Teire

In recent years a growing number of companies have been making use of the outdoors as part of their management training and development. They are finding that courses with projects based on physical activities present their delegates with a challenging variety of managerial situations which cannot be matched in the lecture room. Those taking part soon realise that they are learning quickly and directly from their own experiences. The outdoor projects demand qualities of leadership, teamwork and managerial skill, and when combined with review and discussion, are a powerful training medium. The lessons learnt can soon be applied back in the workplace.

Yet, to be effective as a training method, the outdoors must be used appropriately. The activities themselves, be it climbing, canoeing or any other, are a means to an end. They need to be linked with theory, discussion and review to make the most of them.

Course design is also important, and depends upon your training objectives. What are you setting out to achieve? How does it relate to other company development activities? How will you follow it up in the workplace? As a way of answering some of these questions and sharing information on the use of the outdoors, this chapter is written as a case study on the development and running of such a course for a particular company. It covers the background, the course itself from a participant's point of view, and subsequent follow up in the company.

THE BACKGROUND

Like many others this company is experiencing changes in markets, technology and traditional ways of doing things. Product life cycles are shortening and there is a need for greater flexibility. Not surprisingly this has had an effect on the people and on their training and development needs.

Over the past few years the company has evolved a management training programme to cope with these changing times. This has aimed at broadening management understanding, increasing the awareness of working with and managing others, and developing specific skills and knowledge for the industry. I have been involved in parts of this, and after a while it became clear that the managers who received a grounding from the programme were now ready and eager for a next step which would take their learning further. With this in mind, the training manager and I sat down together to explore the possibilities.

THE OBJECTIVES

A next step for us had two main objectives. The first was to build on previous courses, particularly in the area of taking personal responsibility in management, and understanding and working effectively with other people. The second was to look at the process of change and how individual managers were coping with it. It was also our objective that any further development activity should be a participative one, and should give delegates a practical and relevant challenge from which they could learn.

The many ideas which we generated just did not fit together into a neat jigsaw puzzle. They kept moving around as we tried to get hold of them. But we realised after a while that this was quite alright, as it is just the same in any company. It is impossible to have a complete and unchanging picture of what is going on there. Instead we found that we had ended up with a set of concepts which we felt were important and which we wanted to build into a week's programme. To do this we needed a basic structure and a range of activities which would highlight the concepts in an experiential way and show how they were inter-related. At this stage we had more or less decided on a residential week somewhere off-site.

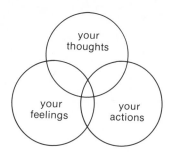

Figure 15.1

THE DESIGN

One of the first concepts we wished to make use of was the relationships between a manager's thoughts, feelings and actions, as shown in Figure 15.1.

Many training courses concentrate on the delegate's thoughts by giving him new ideas and telling him systematically how to carry them out. A few, but not many, take into account the manager's feelings which affect him so much, and a growing number are looking at the 'action' part by using outdoor projects and physical skills. We wanted to bring these together in a more balanced way which would also show up the inter-relationships.

This was particularly important for helping the manager understand his own reactions. One of the problems which many of us have in managing is ourselves, our set patterns of behaviour, our fixed ideas and our conditioned feelings about things.

We needed activities which would be unusual for the delegate and would challenge these different elements – thoughts, feelings and actions. Through the challenge he might see and understand his own reactions better. We decided to make use of the outdoors with sailing, canoeing, rock climbing, horse riding, orienteering and trekking. But the outdoors itself was not the only objective. We also decided to use the great indoors with painting, and relaxation exercises. Many of these would challenge the manager's preconceived ideas of what he could and could not do, as well as allowing him to see how his feelings affected his actions. We all have unused potential; often unused because of the unnecessary constraints which we impose on ourselves.

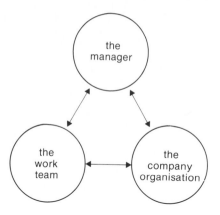

Figure 15.2

Another concept we wished to use was the interdependence that the individual manager has with both his work team and the company organisation. (See Figure 15.2.) So many times these are taken in isolation from each other, and the ways in which the needs of each of them are related are not seen at all. This is particularly so when we add the third of the concepts, that of the *task* and the *process*, where the task is what we are doing, and the process is how we are going about it, often with little awareness. Both of these concepts, we felt, were important for understanding and working effectively with other people, which was our other objective. Any increase in the manager's awareness of these two would not be a bad thing! It occurred to us that the most direct way for those taking part in the programme to learn about these two would be for them to have some responsibility for the organisation of the week's structure as well as for the daily tasks of living together.

Within the limits set by the resources available, the delegates could have the task of designing part of the week's programme and balancing and co-ordinating the many different and often conflicting needs. This would include planning the week's menu and buying and cooking the food each day. The course would have a budget to do this.

It was important for us that the delegates be given a choice in what they did and in the roles that they took. This meant that although there were many activities and projects available, no one delegate would have to do them all, and different delegates would have done different things during the week. Some of these were group activities, some were for the individual, and some involved everybody. By giving the delegates a range of tasks and activities from which they could learn but also giving them some responsibility for organising and managing themselves, we hoped to create a realistic and challenging environment.

So, as a basic structure, we decided on a residential course of six days duration with twelve to fifteen delegates at a training centre in North Wales. The choice of place was important but only in how it fitted in with what we wished to achieve. Taken together, we thought, these would give ample opportunity to explore the last of our concepts, that of managerial *responsibility*. In so many cases we can see when things are going wrong, but we are not prepared to do anything about it ourselves. It is easier to blame someone or something else, than to take a little risk and have a go ourselves.

THE EXPERIENCE

The theory has already been stated. But what actually happened? The personal account which follows is by Dave, a participant in the programme, reflecting his own experiences. Right at the beginning he had decided to keep a diary of the events, and extracts from this are given here.

Before the residential part of the programme a meeting was held at the company for the training manager and me to introduce it to the delegates and to start them off. We explained the thinking behind it, the range of possible activities and the need to do something about food for the week! They held a second meeting by themselves two weeks later.

Although twelve delegates shared the week, and took part in many common tasks, there were at least twelve different courses going on at the same time. Most days there were two to four groups doing different projects only coming together to take stock, review and re-organise as necessary. To put the diary into context, bear in mind that the Monday morning was set aside for detailed planning and organisation of the week (started a number of weeks earlier at the two meetings on the company site), Thursday was a full day's project outdoors on the hills which involved everybody, and Friday evening was reserved for some creative entertainment. The rest of the time was organised by the delegates.

DAVE'S DIARY

This first meeting is held to discuss what the course is about and what is likely to happen. We make little progress. It has a debilitating effect on my responsibility cells, at the same time stimulating my mouth cells. During the meeting I make a number of promises to myself. These are:

1 that I will keep a diary
2 that I will not put myself in a position where I could be elected as the MD and
3 that I will try to practise the art of *responding* rather than *reacting* to situations.

The meeting goes on and we talk about food (my subject!). There is an overwhelming apathy about this. I quote, 'Don't bother, beans is fine'. This strikes at my very parts. I offer to be quartermaster, (my mouth again). Again there is overwhelming apathy, but an acceptance upon my threat of withdrawal. Things begin to look up as the meeting continues. Stan asks, 'who wants to go sailing?' This sounds more like it. We provisionally organise a sailing party. After more talk we agree to meet again in two weeks.

A very different atmosphere at this second meeting; lots of talk. I had circulated a menu and a shopping list but there is no response from anyone except Bob who says 'why can't we have fresh meat?' Despite the three commandments I react, and instantly wish that I had not. Not as easy as it sounds, this responding thing. Suspicion is rife that the whole course is a big 'con' and that any arrangements we make will be reversed and we will be told to 'get out of that'. I begin to believe this. It all sounds too good to be true. I receive lots of help and enthusiasm from people outside the course who do not see the black cloud. Maybe there isn't one.

I think of some activity and prejudge it, for example canoeing, there's no way I am going in a canoe. Conversely I think of an activity which I would enjoy and my imagination pictures me climbing impossible cliffs or canoeing in fast flowing mountain streams. I must admit I feel somewhat frustrated at not having a finite situation to unravel, and problems to overcome. Others are in a similar frame of mind but are prepared to tackle the situation as it happens.

After our second meeting the suspicion deepens. Why don't the garage know anything about the hire cars we shall need to get us there? Why are the catering people delaying our order? Why is there such a large queue at Tesco?

Sunday

The sun shines. We arrive in good order and, first of all, pick the best beds. A touch of remembrance of thirty years ago at school. John and George do not arrive although the others do. Is it all a con? We eat, we lock up the centre and we go to the pub like schoolgirls whooping. We say we don't care. I think that we do. We get back and they still haven't arrived. What next I wonder. Then they do arrive. There is lots of duvet stuffing, pillows, laughter and silliness. Did we know that they would come? Of course we did. The very idea!

Monday

We have an 'unstructured breakfast' and it is a huge success. Brian has been doing an imitation of a Kamikaze pig all night. He and I will not last the distance, I swear. There will be an unexplained accident . . .

When the range of projects is announced I feel dread at the thought of undertaking some of them and a thrill of excitement towards others. This is crunch time. Do I go for what I feel I would get something from, or wait and see what the majority split is?

I choose the latter and then realise that this group appears to have forgotten all the advantages of group discussion. I become aware that there are definite sub-groups, those prepared to go along with the majority without any input, and those anxious to get on with it. I try to respond to the situation but find I cannot find anything to respond to. This task is more difficult than I thought. As I look out of the window I can see a man over the wharf from me. He stands, building a fire in an old ship ventilator in the autumn sun. It is Monday, 10.30 a.m. I do not envy people but I might envy him. I expect that he thinks that 'process' is what you do to peas. I think that he is right.

I lose interest in the proceedings but, noticing that others are the same, I decide to make a suggestion. This time a pen lands in my lap with a voice saying 'get on with it, Dave'. I feel relief. At last I can do something useful.

Once at the board things move. Suggestions are constructive and the situation assumes one of order. People air their views and a programme materialises. It is evident that some are unable, or un-willing, to make decisions. It also appears that certain activities are under discussion, but the less appealing ones such as cooking and washing up are not mentioned ... Perhaps they think these will go away if ignored. A separate chart is drawn up for each day and individuals enter their requirements under specific projects. This saves a lot of argument and debate and I feel that I have achieved something.

The afternoon's activity of orienteering is a chance to achieve some concrete objective. Everyone is involved, in small groups, and we need to give attention to target setting, communications, and dealing with limited information. We also have to judge the capabilities of each team member.

The exercise benefits everyone. My colleagues take it in turns to direct and we progress at a cracking pace. Mistakes are made and assumptions prove incorrect, but overall we all feel a sense of achievement.

We get back having correctly completed the task. One group, considered to be expert, comes in one hour after everyone else. Until they arrive we all have a laugh at their expense. When they arrive, we say nothing, and mumble about 'having to go round the course anti-clockwise is difficult'. We are two-faced and charitable. We return and have a good meal. It occurs to me that it is the same ones who are charitable who also say that the meal is good. I cannot unravel that.

The evening discussion is very similar to the morning session. However, the division of the larger body into the smaller sub-groups is an interesting exercise. We divide ourselves into discussion groups to review the events of the day. I bend the resolutions that I had made and change groups three times. Does this mean that I am trying for selection rather than being selected? Some of this is gratifying, but not all. I think this only applies to me. I do not care. Yes I do. Why? I end up with three people I know and like. Fine. The different groups separate and we talk and laugh.

I feel happier in this closer environment, but nevertheless, I am finding difficulty coming to terms with some of the statements being made. After some time it becomes apparent that the group need help but can I offer the kind of help that would be constructive and would the group benefit? I decide to soft pedal, concentrate on two members and then to meet the obstacle on my own ground at a more opportune moment. This works and a relationship is beginning to form, to which I can offer a useful contribution. It is getting late. The door opens and Ken comes in in his pyjamas saying, 'what's all the noise?' He says he can especially hear my voice. If only he knew that two hours earlier I would have apologised. I say 'hard luck, mate' and I am ashamed later. But at that moment I can justify what I say as a response. I ought to make efforts in this direction, but suspect I will not.

We go to bed, giggle at the snores leaking from next door and fall asleep. Brian and his pig gain the benefit of divine intervention. He lives till morning.

Tuesday

Sailing today. I am up alone at 6.30 a.m. and listen to the shipping forecast. They say 'Irish Sea, gale force 9 is expected soon. Good'. Bad, it is cancelled. First thoughts, let us go quickly, we are all packed up for the day. Too late. We have breakfast and then meet to replan. I find myself trying to establish a consensus and then remember my promises. I stop and observe.

We are doing better. People are making an attempt to listen. How are we managing this change of plan? Some adapt easily, others are stuck. Is this a time to respond? No, not now. Peter is doing fine. Do not cramp his style. We do not need two leaders. Good stuff, this self management, when we do it well.

I take on the challenge of a canoeing project with a team of four. Do what you are unsure of, said the tutor. It is better for your learning. Well, here goes. What an eventful day it turns out to be. There is no handholding with this one. In at the deep end, so to speak. We are given three possible projects with information on weather conditions, tide times and a guide to the progress we could make if we work well together. None of us has had any canoeing experience before. We set to and sort out our objectives for the day and select a project which we feel will give us a challenge.

During the day my ideas about canoeing are turned around. How fixed opinions can get in the way. Watch out for this. I find that I can do much more than I would have dreamt. We have lots of problems to overcome as a team, and spend as much time on dry land, discussing and deciding, as we do in the water. My problem person from last night is in the team, and I make a special effort. It works.

A pity we miscalculate the falling tide and can only get back to the centre by carrying the canoes through the wood. We do look silly.

My return is met with a headache. A belaboured cook is panicking over supplies. I respond easily and fix it. Am I improving? I take time to write to the kids. There is lots they do not know about me (and the reverse). Will I live long enough? Wish my dad had. I write to Joan. Warm feelings. Good.

Another good meal. Did I misjudge the feelings and capabilities of my colleagues? How could I have found out? That is something else to ponder on.

After dinner we discuss the day in our small groups and I find that my fears of the impression I give are well founded; I think this is my major task; to take a 'step back', to be aware of its effect.

We go to bed and I find that I am also a Kamikaze pig. Am I on the start of a learning curve?

Wednesday

A sound night's sleep and I awake feeling refreshed. Will my legs work when I swing them out of bed? They do. Relief, and I get as far as the showers to wake up the rest of my body. The breakfast group has been up already, and smells of bacon and eggs come drifting up the stairs. At breakfast there is much talk about yesterday's activities. I hear a lot from the group that went rockclimbing. This is my project for today. I listen and take it in, being aware of forming ideas which would only cause problems. What comes across clearly is the extent to which people become involved in their projects and how this practical approach sorts the theory out and brings us face to face with our own abilities. The tutors seem to be there for guidance, safety and advice when necessary, but most of the time we are having to sort ourselves out. What things have I avoided in the past? More importantly, what things am I avoiding in the present?

Rock climbing today. What a surprise. We all enjoy it. A different team and different personalities to contend with. And different skills to take into consideration. Paul is 17 stone, and with his positive attitude is turning out to be the star of the course. He causes us to slow down and pay attention to each other. Do I ignore others at work? How am I to know? Am I learning to stand back a little more, instead of rushing in? Our day is one of working closely together, while pushing through fears which come from our minds. I see similar fears getting in my way at work. Are they in my mind? Must investigate further when I return. One incident in particular strikes me. On one section of our climb, Brian sits down and refuses to go on. We spend twenty minutes with him, giving support. With no effect. It is only on our way back that he says he needed a kick up the backside to move him. Remember not to be stuck with just one style of dealing with people. Be adaptable. Also, we can learn from what we do not do as well as from what we do.

In the evening we review the day's projects and then change the groups around to discuss the 'entertainment' for Friday evening. I catch myself falling into the lead. Before bed a small group do some relaxation exercises. Not for me. I go to bed very tired and try to learn my monologues for Friday evening, but never get beyond 'Now Pa, who had ...', because I fall asleep.

Thursday

Today is our all-day project for everyone. We wake and I just know that the preparation of the packed lunches will be left to John and myself. How wrong I am. All hands set to. There is no 'organisation', but everything is completed swiftly and effectively.

There has been a build-up to Thursday as the highlight of the week. As a result there is considerable enthusiasm, and judging by the alacrity with which we leave the centre, everyone is determined that we are going to do our utmost to succeed. But to succeed in what?

We set out separately in the discussion groups used in the evenings. Good. Our group follows the rules and enjoys a self-righteous feeling. Soon, Bob becomes impatient with John's map reading but we get on well and arrive at the first rendezvous point with another group and everything is going well. Bob asks us to monitor the way in which he interrupts people. We do so in style.

We manage to rearrange the groups quickly as required for the task, and I launch a brief sermon on 'no competition'. I just do it and enjoy it, but as I seem to be banging on, I shut myself up. Everybody is confident. We pick up more gear and flog on back up the hill. John cannot manage going up hills. Smoking? I carry his bag and try not to feel smug and I believe I may need similar help later. From then on I carry double packs to assess capability.

Wales is like a documentary; it show all the best bits. Super, I fall in a bog! I'm very wet and I imagine the rest of the group thinking 'go on, make a joke out of that!' I do; it is not always easy. At lunchtime we meet up with the other group and all are happy. It is only when the majority of people are formed up that I realise one is missing.

Leaving the others, I retrace my steps to find a member of the team sitting at the bottom of the hill. He has severe muscle cramp and does not have enough strength to climb the hill. After some discussion I carry him piggy-back taking care to put him down before we come into view of the others, to save embarrassment. Neither of us speaks but words are unnecessary. Then I go back for his kit. This is another of those instances that the memory retains for the rest of your life. Words are inadequate to describe how I feel. Perhaps I am too sensitive.

Later, during the 'rescue', tempers fray and we manage in a totally unco-ordinated way. Wetness dampens the spirits and puts people under pressure. The heavy pack reminds me that I am coping. I realise that my pressure is not knowing whether I can manage, and I try not to be boastful when I can. We arrive back with some steam left and our original group are so elated we decide to walk back. We enjoy it, but wonder what effect our behaviour has on the others. I hope they understand. We all arrive back and everybody is happy again. It worked well.

There is more panic in the kitchen, over milk this time. Steve does a Dave and fixes it. Is the pleasure it gave me the same for others when I do it? I hope so.

At the evening review we come back to our disorganisation at the 'rescue'. It is bad news. On reflection, if I had not been determined not to take on the 'MD' role and overpower the situation, things may well have been different. I conclude that this was neither an honourable objective or a very sensible one. It must have contributed.

There is a certain contentment to be found in letting things happen all around you, and spending time observing whilst the *now* spirals into chaos. But during reflection the contentment fades away. Worse still, we cannot relive this afternoon.

Friday

I wake up with yesterday in my mind. How our understanding of a situation can change when we stand back! For me, yesterday was all about groups working together, and the responsibility each of us has. I can see it going on at work amongst the different departments, and how we blame each other instead of doing something about it. There is a lot to learn here.

Sailing today, rearranged from Tuesday because of the weather. Stan is a man transformed. We are due to be out for the morning only and the others are expecting us back at the centre for lunch.

Yet at lunchtime when the question is asked 'Do you want to carry on?', we live the biggest lie of the week. In the afternoon, discussions are planned to finalise the evening's entertainment. Steve and I have put together a couple of sketches, but these need rehearsal and polish; also, we have not consulted any of the other groups. If we stay at sea, these discussions cannot take place. We debate as a group, and come to the conclusion that we will stay at sea but inform the centre via ship to shore radio. What have we done? We are enjoying ourselves, the evening's entertainment has taken second place and perhaps the other groups will put something together without us. More to the point, we have avoided the responsibility of involvement and put our own interests before that of the others.

The sailing is of great value and brings out qualities in people which I had never suspected. We see each other in a new light and are amazed at what we achieve in a short space of time. It is not until we approach the centre in the evening that unspoken thoughts of apprehension are apparent. In the centre we narrate our day's experiences, carefully avoiding the evening's entertainment. There is a disgruntled atmosphere and I am aware of annoyance about our absence during the afternoon.

The evening meal is superb. The cooks have put in a terrific effort. The organisation as well as the quality cannot be overlooked. I think that if a small number can organise themselves, why are larger numbers incapable of the same?

The evening approaches and I can see that everyone is conscious of not having fulfilled the suggestions put forward earlier in the week. As groups chat, most people are hoping that by ignoring the situation it will go away. However, as we know deep down, there is no avoiding the inevitable.

Someone has a few direct words with Stan about how the sailing trip, which started at the first meeting many weeks ago, has had an effect on this evening. Stan is quiet and thoughtful. This leads me to offer him the monologue I had prepared. We go into another room and Stan is very nervous but willing to have a go. He does and it is magic. He is very good and I am pleased afterwards when he thanks me. This changes the mood and the 'entertainment' gets under way, I do a hastily put together sketch with some others about the week, we play some games and enjoy the general air of relaxation which develops. I regret that I am the first to crash out. I do not want to break up the party but I go limp from my head downwards. Good sleep.

Others have the stamina to stay on into the early hours discussing many matters of a personal nature which have come to them during the week. There is a good feeling of togetherness.

Saturday

Everyone is busy cleaning, scrubbing and getting everything ship-shape. The remarkable thing is that none of the activities is pre-planned. We all know what wants doing and, when one job is finished, people look to see what else is required. This is what it is all about — working as a team.

When the work is complete, group photographs are taken, we say our goodbyes and offer thanks before leaving. Each of us is deep in thought as we travel many miles without talking, each remembering the week as each wants to remember it.

REFLECTIONS

On the journey back, the training manager and I had many thoughts buzzing around. Had it worked? Did we get the right balance? Had the delegates seen the underlying reasons? What will be the effect in the coming weeks? One thing we were sure of — it had been a full and rich week with many experiences for the delegates to learn from.

By the time we arrived back, we had talked ourselves into a few early conclusions. First, we were surprised and pleased that the delegates had taken to self-catering and had produced such a high standard of cooking; giving them the responsibility for this had been the right thing. Secondly, the decision to leave the choice of projects to the delegates had been right. We had not wanted to force them into anything, or to organise the week for them. Giving them this responsibility had thrown up many valuable organisational problems. Thirdly, not seeing the outdoors as the main reason for being there but making use of it as an aid to learning. Finally, on the overall structure of the week, we felt that we might have achieved a better balance by restricting certain activities to particular days. Surprisingly for us, the conclusions from the delegates were that we should not change anything. The point they made was that to learn, they had to struggle, make mistakes, create their own problems, and enjoy their own successes. If only, they said, they had believed at the time that we really were giving them the opportunity which we said we were! However, these are my thoughts. What about Dave's?

'My first reflections after the week were about how we all anticipated problems and assumed that these would be created by interference from the outside. This turned out to be completely unfounded. Most of our problems wer self-generated! Far worse than the real thing. How much of the time are we doing this?

'Of my longer-term reflections, one thing has become very significant. This is about the three promises I made. The first was to keep a diary – which I did. The second was not to get elected MD. This proved to be particularly selfish during those times when I could have contributed more. I tended to listen and watch. A balance between the two is more desirable.

'Promise number three, to respond rather than react, proved difficult. However, with practice, this has become easier and has had a significant effect on those around me at work.'

SOME TIME LATER

Since the course which Dave wrote about, we have brought together delegates from a number of courses to share views and experiences. The structure of this day was for the participants to work in small groups and then to present summaries of their discussions with flip charts. These fell naturally into the three areas of before the course, during the course, and after the course, and the charts (Figures 15.3, 15.4 and 15.5) give the main points of general interest which emerged.

One thing which struck me about them was the absence of the activities which the delegates were taking part in on their courses. Many people who are considering a course which makes use of the outdoors have a natural concern that it should be relevant to the manager's job and to the company. Often, they have difficulty in appreciating the link between, say, an orienteering or a sailing activity, and the day to day problems back in the company. Here, the delegates have concentrated on the learning which has come from the activities, rather than on the activities themselves, which indicates that it is the resultant learning which is important and relevant.

The flip charts here are like most flip charts produced by syndicate groups for presentations to other delegates. They give the essence of their discussions, and the presenters fill them out with examples. Perhaps you could use your own experience of similar situations to see the meanings behind the words.

IN ADDITION

In addition to the comments which emerged about the course and about the value which people found it to have afterwards, the review day itself was well received. The delegates said that it acted as a refresher and gave them further insights from each others' experiences back at work. From this meeting and from a questionnaire we sent out a few observations about using the outdoors came into my own mind.

Why the outdoors?

Potentially we can learn from all situations, so what is the particular value of the outdoors for management training? Three things emerge. Firstly, it is realistic. The problems, decisions and experiences are not hypothetical. Secondly, it is a challenge to our conditioned ways of thinking and seeing. The unusual circumstances (for most of us) can shake us out of our ruts and cause us to see things more clearly. And

<u>BEFORE THE COURSE</u>

<u>FOR OURSELVES AS INDIVIDUALS</u>
* WE HAD A MIX OF FEELINGS AMONGST US ABOUT THE COURSE.

* THERE WAS ANXIETY ABOUT THE UNKNOWN, WHAT CHALLENGES WOULD
THERE BE? WOULD I BE ABLE TO COPE? WHAT ROLE SHOULD I TAKE?

* THERE WAS EXCITEMENT ABOUT THE OPPORTUNITIES IN STORE, WE WANTED
TO MAKE THE MOST OF THEM.

<u>OUR PRECONCEPTIONS OF THE COURSE</u>
* THESE VARIED FROM PERSON TO PERSON.
* SOME OF US WERE SUSPICIOUS AND THOUGHT WE WOULD BE 'SET UP'
DURING THE WEEK.
* SOME OF US SAW IT AS A 'PRACTICAL' FOLLOW-ON FROM THE PREVIOUS
COURSE.
* OTHERS WERE ANTICIPATING INTERPERSONAL, LOGISTICAL AND
ORGANISATIONAL PROBLEMS TO DEAL WITH.

<u>AS A GROUP</u>
* WE FOUND THE PRE-COURSE PLANNING MEETINGS WE HELD
OURSELVES TO BE VERY VALUABLE.

* IT WAS NOTICEABLE HOW WELL WE ALL GELLED TOGETHER
— GROUP EMPATHY.
* THERE WAS A FEELING OF WANTING TO 'GET IT RIGHT' AND
MAKE IT WORK.

Figure 15.3

<u>DURING THE COURSE</u>

<u>MOTIVATION</u>
* THERE WAS A HIGH MOTIVATION BY INDIVIDUALS TO 'HAVE A GO' AND ACCEPT CHALLENGES.
* INDIVIDUALS AVOIDED THOSE ACTIVITIES WHICH THEY CONSIDERED TO BE TOO HIGH A PERSONAL RISK.
* THERE WAS AN UNSELFISH, SUPPORTIVE ATTITUDE. AMONGST ALL THE DELEGATES.

<u>LEADERSHIP</u>
* WE WERE HOPING FOR 'LEADERSHIP' TO EMERGE.
* THROUGH THE WEEK WE SAW EACH OTHER IN VARIED AND CHANGING ROLES WHICH WE HAD TO MANAGE.

* INDIVIDUALS WERE ADAPTABLE IN THE DIFFERENT ROLES THEY TOOK....

* .... AND THERE WAS A NATURAL AND SOMETIMES SURPRISING SELECTION OF LEADERS AND FOLLOWERS IN DIFFERENT SITUATIONS AT DIFFERENT TIMES.

<u>TEAMWORK</u>
* AS THE WEEK PROGRESSED WE BUILT UP TRUST AND SUPPORT WITH EACH OTHER.
* THIS LED TO GOOD TEAMWORK AND MORE WILLINGNESS BY INDIVIDUALS TO HAVE A GO.

.<u>OTHER THINGS OF VALUE</u>
* OUR REVIEWS AND DISCUSSIONS BEFORE AND AFTER THE ACTIVITIES.

* THE WIDE CHOICE OF ACTIVITIES WE HAD.
* HAVING TIME AND SPACE TO ONESELF PERIODICALLY - RESPECTING THIS NEED IN OTHERS.
* LEARNING TO RECOGNISE OUR LIMITS.

Figure 15.4

AFTER THE COURSE
(A NUMBER OF MONTHS BACK AT WORK)

FOR OURSELVES AS INDIVIDUALS

* IT HAS CLARIFIED AND REINFORCED THE PREVIOUS COURSES.

* THERE IS AN INCREASE IN OUR SELF-CONFIDENCE.

* WE HAVE A BETTER UNDERSTANDING OF OUR OWN ABILITIES.

* IT SHOWS THAT A POSITIVE ATTITUDE CAN LEAD TO SUCCESS.

* OUR MANAGEMENT OF TASKS AND DECISION MAKING IS IMPROVED.

FOR OUR RELATIONSHIPS

* WE HAVE MORE UNDERSTANDING OF, AND PATIENCE WITH, OTHERS

* THERE IS AN IMPROVEMENT IN THE METHODS AND ABILITIES OF MANAGING OTHER PEOPLE.

* WE NOW BRING SITUATIONS OUT INTO THE OPEN TO RESOLVE THEM.

* WE HAVE AN INCREASED AWARENESS OF THE RELATIONSHIPS IN A TEAM (INCLUDING THE FAMILY AT HOME)

FOR THE COMPANY

* DIFFICULT PROBLEMS ARE NOW TACKLED AS A ·RESULT

* THE SHARED EXPERIENCES AND COMMON LANGUAGE ARE LEADING TO BETTER COMMUNICATIONS.

* IT IS POSSIBLE TO SEE HOW A COMPANY STRUCTURE CAN AFFECT PEOPLE'S BEHAVIOUR.

* THERE IS A REALISATION THAT WE, THE PEOPLE, ARE THE COMPANY.

RESERVATIONS

* SOME PEOPLE MAY 'MISS THE POINT' OF IT ALL

* OTHERS MAY TREAT IT AS A HOLIDAY.

* THE OUTDOOR ACTIVITIES MAY NOT SUIT CERTAIN TYPES.

Figure 15.5

thirdly, it involves our actions and our feelings, as well as our thinking apparatus (which often only gets in the way). The learning is not *about* the outdoor activities. It is about ourselves, individually and in teams, and about how we react in these different circumstances.

What is your purpose?

The design of a course like this depends upon your reason for doing it. Is it teambuilding, do you want to improve an existing team, or perhaps gell a new project group? Is it individual development, drawing out the potential of the manager and giving him understanding and confidence? Is it organisational understanding, seeing how people can learn to work together effectively? Or is it for the improvement of relationships amongst departments; for developing leadership skills; for understanding change? Knowing your purpose is important for knowing how to design your course at the beginning. Each of these objectives is possible, but the way in which the activities should be used will vary. The activities are not an end in themselves, but are a means to an end (or even a means to a beginning!).

Where does it fit?

The purpose and design of a course also depends upon your other training and development programmes. Is it a first off for the delegates? Does it follow on from another course? Does it lead in to another phase?

The course described here was designed to build on previous courses which develop awareness, understanding and skills of managing and working with others. It was because of this that we gave the delegates responsibility for their course and their learning. For other situations, the initial design could well be different. In this case the participants seemed to take up the opportunity readily.

Keeping a perspective

Lastly, keep it in perspective and do not get carried away with the physical activities alone. Although we have made use of the outdoors here, we have also made use of other things for learning too. There were the pre-course meetings, the self-catering, the indoor activities, the delegates' time alone, the many one-to-one talks, the group discussions and the timely reviews.

All of this certainly does not mean that everything ran like clockwork on the courses. You may remember from Dave's diary that at many times just the opposite was the case. But really this does not matter. The purpose is not to 'get it right'. Again, I should like to leave the last words to Dave.

Life is not long enough to keep retracing the path and discussing where we should have gone. The experience of going is the real lesson ... Perhaps the greatest gift is the ability to stand away and view yourself and the situation from the outside. Being self-critical achieves little on its own. Changing the criticisms into actions is satisfying and reaps its own rewards.

FURTHER READING

Chris Creswick and Roy Williams' Paper on *Using The Outdoors For Management Development and Teambuilding* (FDITB 1979) is one of the earliest reviews. They discuss the range of applications and explain the progression during a typical course.

Alan Mossman's Paper on 'Ways of Using the Outdoors For Manager and Management Development' (*Management Education and Development,* vol. 14, no 3, pp. 182-96) differentiates between manager and management development in the outdoors and describes the differences between the management training and self development approaches. This paper concludes with a fairly comprehensive bibliography of good and bad reports on OMD.

John Bank has recently written *Outdoor Development For Managers* (1984) Gower. Bank discusses the what and how of OMD as well as presenting a number of company case studies and an outline of the work of many of the providers.

Alan Mossman talks to providers and users of Outdoor Management Development on *Personnel Training Bulletin* tapes issues 21 and 22 January and February 1985, from Didasko, Huntingdon, Cambs.

16

Management development in the Thomson Organisation

Don Rose

The Organisation is entering a new era. The scale of financial resources which are likely to be available are so large that the impact will not just change the size of the Company or just increase the scale of its operations, but is likely to change its future and its prospects in a fundamental way.

It is necessary therefore to plan new policies now, both to ensure that we can grow and develop, but also to enable us to anticipate changes often of a profound nature which are likely to change many of the ways in which industry is going to have to operate in the next decade.

The policies relating to how we develop and use our human resources will need, in the future, at least as much attention, and assume as much importance as financial policies have done in the past.

The year was 1979 — the words portrayed an organisation that, as a result of the availability for new funds for investment, was poised for growth. The ways in which it had gone about the task of developing managers were no longer defensible. There was the need for a new approach — a new approach that would shed the casual response of the past and be tied more specifically to strategic business objectives.

THE ORGANISATION

By definition in its annual report 1984:

International Thomson Organisation Ltd is a leading international information and publishing business with strong interests in travel and natural resources.

The group is listed on the Toronto and London Stock Exchanges. Total assets are around £1,053 million and the numbers employed are over 22,000.

The organisation was created in 1959 by a reverse take-over of Roy Thomson's Scottish Television franchise, Scottish Television Limited, by Lord Kemsley's newspaper group, Kemsley Newspapers, which left Roy Thomson with 70 per cent control of total business. At the beginning of the 1960s, its principal interests were:

1   The *Sunday Times*, the leading quality Sunday newspaper barely profitable and fighting hard to maintain the circulation lead it had just assumed.
2   A group of regional morning, evening and weekly newspapers predominantly situated in the areas of our more traditional industries – in Wales, Lancashire, the North-East and Scotland. Most of these publishing centres were poorly housed and operating with old and often inadequate plant and machinery.
3   Scottish Television Limited, the exclusive commercial television franchise in Scotland.

With this mixture of activities the organisation was potentially vulnerable in the medium term on three counts:

1   Half its profit was generated by Scottish Television whose franchise was due for renewal in 1964. Because this had become, as Roy Thomson forecast, a highly profitable venture there was every expectation that the government would want to take a larger share under any new contract. It was also becoming politically sensitive for newspaper companies to own major television interests.
2   A high proportion of the company's revenue came from advertising, rendering it particularly vulnerable to the vagaries of the economic cycle.

3   There was a clear danger of legislation to control ownership of media, which could inhibit the company's growth and expansion in its main businesses. Only four years later such constraints on the acquisition of newspapers were imposed by the Monopolies and Mergers Act.

Faced with this vulnerability, the management set a new course for the organisation. At this time the company's main resource was its people rather then the strength of its balance sheet. It had become renowned for its expertise in the selling of advertisement space. So much so, that recruitment advertising by other employers at the time placed a premium on people who had been 'Thomson trained' and quite brazenly used the phrase in their recruitment advertisements.

DIVERSIFICATION

So it was, with relatively limited financial resources, that the company embarked upon a programme of diversification. It was logical that that programme of diversification should extend into other forms of publishing – magazines, books and data bases. Alongside its newspaper division, a new division Thomson Publications was formed in 1964 to accommodate these new publishing ventures.

With hindsight, the move into leisure has been rationalised as a strategic move but it was purely opportunistic, a characteristic of management at that time.

Through the amalgamation of the tour operating interests of Skytours, Riviera Holidays, Gaytours and Luxitours from 1965, Thomson Skytours was formed in 1970. The company became known as Thomson Holidays in 1972. Sunair and Lunn Poly were acquired that same year and the latter now operates over 200 retail travel outlets under the Lunn Poly name.

In 1984, 1.40 million British holidaymakers travelled abroad on holidays planned and operated by Thomson and one in five package tourists travel with the company. Their destination ranged from the popular sunshine resorts around the Mediterranean to the Caribbean and USA, East and West Africa and the Atlantic Isles, north to the Arctic Circle and eastwards to Siberia and Japan.

The sales agency for the Post Office Yellow Pages directories was seized and developed. Our newspapers in Scotland at Edinburgh and Aberdeen made a natural partnership with an American Oil Consortium seeking a UK based company to advise and handle its social responsibility programmes when the North Sea was tapped for oil. A partnership that was to alter significantly the development strategy later.

By the mid-1970s, after a programme of diversification what was the result? Television interests had been shed. The Regional Newspaper division published from as far north as Aberdeen, westwards to Belfast and Cardiff, to Reading. It had become the largest provincial newspaper publisher in the United Kingdom.

Thomson Publications owned such fine publishing houses as Michael Joseph, Hamish Hamilton, and George Rainbird, publishing among many illustrious authors, people like Georges Simenon, Nancy Mitford, Dick Francis, Harold Wilson, James Herriot, David Niven and Henry Kissinger. The most notable of its consumer magazines were Family Circle, Living and Illustrated London News. Its trade magazines covered quite specific business markets with trade papers like Construction News, Big Farm Weekly and New Electronics. Its data bases were handled predominantly by Derwent Publications Ltd. The field of educational publishing was served through Thomas Nelson and Sons Ltd.

The leisure interests were market leaders – Thomson Holidays, Britannia Airways, Portland Holidays and Lunn Poly. Thomson North Sea looked after the company's interests in oil, gas and forestry. The Yellow Pages sales agency was successful and a secure business.

WHERE NEXT?

Over 18 years the programme of diversification had achieved growth, growth built upon high borrowings at initially low interest rates. As interest rates rose, management had to turn its efforts toward cash flow and cash control. The argument was decentralisation and little thought was given to co-ordinated people policies. Everybody was very busy keeping their heads above water. Each division did its best to keep its management through ad hoc decisions on remuneration in response to individual demands and the effect of the market place.

But then came oil! It generated cash. There was now time to pause, stop and consider. What were to be the fundamentals in using this new money:

1   To pay off our borrowings and accelerate new capital investment in our traditional business.
2   To define a strategy for growth.

The oil revenues were great and the initial temptation was to redefine the shape of our businesses and plan to become a major oil company.

The temptation was put aside. The decision was to put the bulk of our investment into the burgeoning information technology sector, where we had much experience as publishers, continue to develop our interests in the leisure sector, the holiday company and the airline, while maintaining our interests in oil and gas.

We planned that much of our thrust in development was going to be North America − for two main reasons:

1   The business was unbalanced internationally with 98 per cent of our earnings coming from the United Kingdom with its historically very low growth rates.
2   The scale of the investment that we envisaged would not have been accomplished in the United Kingdom without running into severe monopoly problems.

NEW MANAGEMENT DEVELOPMENT POLICY

This then is the general background in which a new policy relating to management development was created. The business strategy was based upon two simple assumptions.

1   The money for development would be available − that assumption was virtually certain to be fulfilled.
2   The more important assumption was that the people would be there to carry through the strategy.

It was the second assumption that caused the chief executive most concern. As he at the time simply expressed it − if we have not got the people, then quite simply I have to change the strategy.

Where were we to start? A large organisation, decentralised into quality divisions, a brand new group personnel function. There was a history of appraisal activity and some functional management training.

What sort of management did we have and how good were they? How many good managers were there?

The management audit

We borrowed a discipline from our financial friends and instituted an audit — a management audit. Quite arbitrarily, it was declared that the top 250 managers across the organisation were to be seen as a group resource. Their careers and their development would be managed from the centre. It was decided that the chief executive of each division would come to the group headquarters for one day each year to discuss the quality of his people. So that the meeting would have a discipline, a simple administration procedure was adopted — two pieces of paper for each person.

1   A succession plan is what it is called. Who in the short and longer term are seen as natural successors to senior appointments? A valuable piece of paper, not to be underestimated.
2   An appraisal form — two sheets of A4. There were no columns to be ticked, there were no pre-formed options to choose from.

We wanted the chief executive to think about his people. We did not want him to reproduce the appraisal that existed as an individual at divisional level. They were to be thoughts about achievement, performance and potential. The appraisal form for the management audit was an additional discipline. It was a form full of white space that had to be filled with words.

The initial reaction was mixed, as it was expected to be. At the first audit meetings, there was evidence of lack of application, basic suspicion, reticence at providing information about people and a mistrust of the process and what it was about and hoped to achieve.

It has taken time, but five years on, duplications of those pieces of paper and the reticence in providing information about people has disappeared. The audit has become part of the natural management of the business. No action was taken on the information that was gathered until everybody felt comfortable with the process.

Findings

1 The main board was ageing – an average age of 58 years.
2 There were similar problems of ageing at divisional board level.
3 We had a reasonable crop of product managers i.e. newspaper managers, airline managers, magazine publishers, but our growth strategy called for business managers who could seek commercial advantage to the full in any opportunity.

The most urgent problem was the selection and preparation of the next generation of main board directors. We wanted to be sure that when we appointed the next generation of main board directors they felt fully equipped and lacked no competence in the management of business. It is surprising how many people carry areas of incompetence with them as their careers progress.

Problems . . .

There were several problems to tackle:

1 We wanted to create an opportunity for them to talk freely about their needs. Appraisal systems are useful but never get at the full truth. Within any organisation there is always a sense of unease and reticence when it comes to discussing an individual's strengths and weaknesses.
2 These were busy people running large businesses and they could not be away from the businesses for too long.
3 As main board directors their task would involve strategic issues – strategic issues of a policy nature for the business as a whole, not just newspapers, books or holidays – the total business. How then to develop these strategic policy-making skills?
4 They had to have an understanding of developments in the outside world that were changing the context in which policy making was being carried out.

These problems are not new but the solution evolved was and still is novel.

. . . and their solutions

A group of 15 senior executives were chosen from the management audit. It seemed that, on past performance, executives whose career had been one of solid achievement and who had shown an ability to 'think' about their businesses had the most potential to take on the role of director of the main board where the emphasis was strategy and planning.

It was decided that they would be brought together as a group with their own tutor. They clearly appreciated the nature of the exercise – the two-fold objectives. Firstly, that they were being placed in a goldfish bowl and that the activities would form part of the selection process. Second, that the exercise was also educational and developmental.

Finding the tutor for the group was not easy. We needed someone of maturity, who was approachable, easy to talk to and an academic heavyweight. To compound the problem, he would have to give the majority of his time to the group. A proverbial needle in a haystack! The majority of the established business schools looked at us in horror when we described our needs. Previously, as an organisation, we had run open courses at the Oxford Centre for Management Studies. Uwe Kitzinger, the director, found our man. He coaxed Professor Douglas Hague away from the Manchester Business School. Douglas would join the faculty at the Oxford Centre where outside of an annual Strategic Leadership Course, he would commit himself fully to the 'Thomson Group'.

The programme was launched in 1980. Douglas was given access to the Group's personnel files. He met and talked to the members of the group individually. Douglas sought to strengthen the individual skills of each member of the group by linking each one to a tutor from the Oxford Management Centre who would provide personal tuition on topics that each individual saw as being particularly important to him. Whenever possible the learning had to be 'live'. For example, two of the group visited a number of important British companies to cross-examine their strategic planners in the way that those organisations carry out such planning.

Besides dealing with the needs of each individual member, there was also to be a concentration on the needs of the business. It was argued that the business did not exist in a vacuum. The business environment was constantly changing. All members of the group would need to understand these changes and their influences economically, socially, politically, and technologically.

Each year, because these were busy people, three three-day seminars were organised where the whole group would discuss, debate and argue with experts in those fields. The experts would come not only from the UK but America and Continental Europe − the brief was to bring in the world's top talent from wherever those with that talent worked.

The third element in the programme was the most exciting. The group were asked to evaluate the organisation's long term plan − its strategy. When the group was ready Gordon Brunton, the chief executive, and the current board sat in the hot seat and the group interrogated them about the thinking in the plan and its proposals (no restful experience). Arising from this we agreed that there were three aspects of the plan that needed more study. They divided into smaller groups and through the summer of 1982 the people worked away at these three topics. Douglas worked with the groups, bringing in experts who were able to give further advice where needed.

When they were ready, they made their presentations to the main board. A depth of thinking and investigation was applied to topics of particular interest to the organisation.

1   The possibility of expansion in the Pacific Basin.
2   The development of the organisation's customer bases.
3   The policy for divestment.

Five of the group have been appointed to the main board and it is interesting that despite having achieved those appointments, they did not want to lose the facilities that the programme had provided.

At the beginning of this year, as a result of our management audit, nine of the members of the group of fifteen were taken out of the programme. We had considered them over three years, and the potential that had selected them for membership of the programme had not stood up to the test.

There is now a group of six, five appointed to the board and one not as yet. It was appreciated that this type of education could not be turned off like a tap. The business environment is constantly changing − so the group will come together for one week a year to update the information given in the three day briefings. They still use

Douglas as their 'Father Confessor' — a bond that is of value to the individual and to the organisation.

There were similar problems at divisional board level. Much the same activity as has just been described for the development of main board directors has been done at the Henley Management College. Again it must be emphasised that we took our business to Henley because there we found another Douglas Hague in the guise of Professor David Farmer. Since 1982 David Farmer has been responsible for a group of 28 senior executives culled from the management audit, who were seen to have the potential for divisional directorships. David Farmer acts as their 'Father Confessor' dealing with individual skill, or training needs, and where possible involving the individual's manager in the process. David spends time visiting the individual at his place of work so that he may more readily understand the business problems, pressures and restraints that influence the individual manager's performance and progress.

Whilst there is a strategic overtone to the programme it concentrates more heavily on the measurement of business performance and market opportunities.

For the Thomson Organisation, what has been described in this chapter has been an adventure; an adventure in management development that is exciting and which abolished the boundary between the business school classroom and business — in essence a management development programme tuned finely to the needs of individuals and the business they are to manage.

Part V

ISSUES IN MANAGEMENT DEVELOPMENT

17

Management development and organisation development

Graham M. Robinson

This chapter reflects the writer's experiences of working in the fields of organisation and management development since 1965. During that period the conviction has grown that the distinction between effective organisation development and effective management development is artificial to the point of irrelevance. The distinction only has significance in considerations of relative ineffectiveness. Both are dependent upon the closeness of their association with clearly developed, articulated and sustained organisational strategies, to which the members of the organisation, including the organisation and management developers, are deeply committed. Both are dependent upon a process of thorough situational analysis, diagnosis and appropriate action. Both are dependent upon the skills, competence and credibility of the practitioner on the one hand, and upon the confidence, commitment and sense of ownership of the client manager or group on the other.

The focus of the chapter is on the orientation of the client manager towards the contribution of the specialist or practitioner. It is argued that this orientation has often been more positive and, as a result, more effective in the case of management development. There is seen to have been a greater sense of identification with the norms and values of management development than with those of organisation development (although the latter have had a significant influence on the former). Organisation development, it is argued, has tended to import values to the client organisation which owe more to the expectations arising from the application of scientific discipline to management practice as a result of the business school revolution of the sixties, than they do to the strategies and values of the client organisations themselves. As a result there has been a tendency, in Europe at least, for organisation development to be an externally 'owned' process, identified with particular practitioners, academics and consultants, rather than as a process vital to the internal functioning of the organisation itself. While, to a lesser degree, the same has been true of management development, leading towards the 'flavour of the month' trend, there has been a much closer sense of management identification with the concepts of management development, even if only in the negative sense of saying 'we ought to do more of this'.

The success, in the 1980s, of those writers who pursued the holy grail of 'excellence' has served to emphasise the importance of common values and strategy to successful organisational performance. The chapter concludes by referring to a study which suggests that a majority of European corporations (private and public sector) are weak in both these areas. If these findings hold true, it is argued, management development should be taking a lead with groups of client managers in forcing the clarification of organisational strategies and values. In so doing, the emergent values may well not match with those underlying organisation development as described in the literature. However, the irony is that the genuine and lasting development of the client organisations that the practitioners seek may be achieved only as a result of such a process – which is political, confrontative and pro-active rather than scientific, consultative and advisory.

THE BACKGROUND TO CURRENT MANAGEMENT ATTITUDES

Management development is perceived as 'an attempt to increase managerial effectiveness through planned and deliberate learning processes'.

Client managers have tended to have fairly clear views about management development within their organisations, and they have usually had few problems in making a distinction between their perceptions of management development on the one hand and management training on the other. While the latter has been perceived as a process necessary to the acquisition of the skills associated with a particular management level or role (for example, budgetary development and control), management development tends to be viewed as a broadening, educational process by means of which the individual is initiated, shaped or fitted to the attitudes, values, rites and rituals of successively higher levels within the organisation. As such, management development may or may not encompass formal training, and it may be self-managed (many organisations attach especially high value to processes of management self-development, even to the extent of welcoming back the prodigal manager who, having resigned 'to gain experience in another environment', now returns to the fold with renewed vigour).

To an extent, then, client managers would relate management training to a process by means of which the individual acquires the skills associated with a specific management job or level. They would tend to regard management development as having much more to do with career development and progression.

This difference in perception tends to be thrown into much sharper relief in organisations where responsibility for management training is assigned to the training function, while management development is assigned as a personnel responsibility. This distinction is further reinforced where there is, real or perceived, competition between the two functions over which is accountable for what and as to where the senior status lies.

Whatever the situation in a specific organisation, there would appear to be a general consensus among client managers that both management training and development are a 'good thing' and that their organisation probably has not done, or is not doing, enough in these areas.

The views of client managers towards organisation development are quite different. For a start it tends to be less immediately meaningful to managers outside the personnel and training functions themselves. In response to an illustration or example of a piece of organisation development work, client managers will tend to respond with a reference to the name of a particular consultant or academic who 'once did some work with the company along those lines', rather than indicate any familiarity with, or expectations of, organisation development per se. As a result organisation development tends to be known in terms of what particular practitioners do, rather than as a process or discipline with which managers are naturally familiar.

An interesting phenomenon among human resource specialists is the use of the initial letters OD in discussions relating to organisation development processes and practice. Unlike other management specialisms developed over the past twenty years, the initials do not appear to have been picked up by client managers themselves. Thus, while it would be quite unremarkable to hear an experienced line manager make reference to O & M (organisation and methods), OR (operations research) or to DP (data processing), the letters OD roll rarely off the tongues of the same type of individual. Similarly, personnel and training people rarely, if ever, make reference to MD or MT to refer to the areas of activity mentioned earlier in this chapter.

This use of the label OD and its association with specialisms such as OR may provide a clue to one of the significant areas of difference between management development and organisation development, and this difference relates to management's sense of identification with and ownership of the two processes.

In the 1960s, operations research was perceived as having a particularly significant contribution to make to the resolution of highly complex management problems in conditions of high uncertainty and risk. It had already made dramatic contributions in the military field during the Second World War, when inter-disciplinary teams of scientists had applied the scientific method to the analysis, modelling and resolution of previously intractable problems. At about the same time in the sixties, a number of reports were circulating in the USA which were highly critical of current business school practice. Such practice was, at that time, highly dependent upon 'crude, non-rigorous, highly specific descriptions of particular businesses. There was little if any generalisation across many businesses to formulate a set of general principles that could apply to many situations' (Mitroff and Kilmann, 1984).[1] The successful application of scientific method to the resolution of complex management problems offered by the OR people contrasted strongly with the perceived inadequacies of the business schools. The latter, argue Mitroff and Kilmann, over-reacted, consciously trying to emulate the academic departments that had spawned the successful scientists and technologists. They 'hired' newly accredited PhDs from prestigious universities who had been trained in the so-called 'pure' (i.e. untainted by practical application) sciences and academically respectable disciplines, e.g. computer science, economics, industrial engineering, mathematics, political science, psychology, sociology. As a result the academic respectability of the business schools went up enormously.

The expectations that organisations had of the scientists in the OR teams, both in the university departments and in 'user' organisations in the private and public sectors, were extremely high and many successes were scored (for example, the development of Critical Path Analysis and PERT). Not unnaturally, therefore, the suggestion arose that what was being achieved by the natural scientists in OR should be capable of being emulated by the behavioural scientists. Initially, this emulation took the form of the development of Human Factors Groups within the OR teams (in the UK within the British Iron and Steel Research Association (BISRA), and the National Coal Board, for example) and direct consultation from the universities and research institutes, such as Birkbeck College and the Tavistock Institute. In the USA, specialist behavioural science teams sprang up at the interface between business and academic institutions to examine the specific contribution that behavioural science could make to the development of these organisations and, thus, organisation development, OD, was born.

There was a fundamental difference in the antecedents of management development and organisation development. Management development was always a process 'owned' by the organisation itself. It may not have been done particularly well, but the manager within the organisation could identify with it as a process that had specific meaning for him, within the context of the norms and values of the organisation by which he was employed. Organisation development, on the other hand, was more specialised, more specific and, in aspiration at least, more scientific. It tended to be the domain of the business schools and the research institutes rather than incorporated into the organisation itself. Although not writing specifically about organisation development, Mitroff and Kilmann provide a possible insight as to why the values and concepts of organisation development have rarely been incorporated into the organisations that it was meant to be serving:

> 'A Ph.D. straight out of graduate school who had never in his or her life even been near a real business organisation, could teach, write, and do research on business and management. While they thus achieved greater prestige in their own network, they increasingly lost touch with the business community and the world at large. Intentionally or unintentionally, they shut out from the halls of academia the very reality they were supposedly in the business of studying'.

The Mitroff and Kilmann argument may tend towards the extreme and, as noted above, they are not referring to organisation development as such but to the relationship between the business schools and business in general. It does, however, provide a backdrop for the image of the organisation development practitioner as 'outsider'. The practitioners themselves have tended to prefer this role, as facilitator and change agent, as consultant and catalyst, as opposed to that of integrated participant in the hurly burly of the organisations which they have aspired to develop.

With the dramatic economic changes of the 1980s the increase in uncertainty at all organisational levels and a reduction in confidence in the ability of Cartesian logic to come up with the right answers to the complex problems of organisational and business life, there is a good deal of questioning of the contributions offered by all the specialisms which developed so rapidly and with such promise in the sixties. Line managers tend to be suspicious of operations research, other than in those areas of complexity where it has an established track record (vehicle scheduling, stock control and re-ordering, life cycle forecasting etc). It tends to be perceived as 'esoteric, backroom stuff', highly mathematical and largely beyond the comprehension of the managers whom it is there to serve. O & M, on the other hand has lost some of the gloss that it had in the sixties, not least because its emphasis on rationalism leads to a natural (though not always fair) association with rationalisation which in turn means 'putting the squeeze on my department'. Organisation development has suffered in its turn from its identification with outsiders to the organisation. Its emphasis on humanist values has had a rough ride in organisations forced by economic necessity to experience the massive employee shake-outs of the late seventies and early eighties. At the same time there is a much greater awareness of the limitations to the skills that managers have at their disposal to enable them to tackle the challenges that the new circumstances present. Therefore, of the four specialisms mentioned (operational research, organisation and methods, organisation development and management development), more is probably expected of the latter than of the others. As a manager, it is I who am looking for help in raising my capability to deliver against frightening levels of demand and expectation. It is I who need that support in order to maximise my chances of survival. It is my head on the block. I am apt in these circumstances to ask very forcibly the question 'what's in it for me?' By and large, the answer is more likely to be sought from the management developer than from the other specialists with less personally perceived concerns.

ORGANISATIONAL DEVELOPMENT FRAMEWORKS

Before pursuing the theme of similarities and differences between organisation development and management development further, it would be helpful to be clear about the particular frameworks within which organisation development has endeavoured to operate. The word 'frameworks' is used rather than 'definition' or 'frame of reference' because the field has become too imprecise, in the view of this writer at least, for any one of the many attempts at definition to be entirely adequate. Bennis (1969)[2] described organisation development as 'a response to change, a complex educational strategy intended to change the beliefs, attitudes, values and structure of organisations so that they can better adapt to new technologies, markets, and challenges, and the dizzying rate of change itself'. Such a description places organisation development at the apex of the organisational pyramid. It is strategic, it is concerned with values and it is concerned with structure. If organisation development interventions are to be effective in terms of Bennis' description, then they must be made with the full participation and commitment of top management. Beckhard (1969)[3] wrote:

In an organization-development effort, the top management of the system has a personal investment in the program and its outcomes. They actively participate in the management of the effort. This does not mean that they must participate in the same activities as the others, but it does mean that they must have both knowledge and commitment to the goals of the program and must actively support the methods used to achieve the goals.

Perhaps less elegantly but with a shrewd eye for the realities of organisational life, Reddin (1977)[4] wrote: 'When change agents tell me that they plan to attempt a change from the bottom up, I remind them of the military dictum that the penalty for mutiny is death'.

But is this insistence on top management involvement realistic? In the current climate such involvement is usually the result of massive and usually externally induced change, such as merger, take-over or bottom line crisis (British Leyland, British Airways, ICL all provide examples where such involvement has been the springboard for organisation development type interventions). But in the majority of organisations, the demands of running the operation in a difficult, but not necessarily catastrophic, environment may make the demand for such involvement unrealistic. Bennis himself goes on to suggest that his description of organisation development may be to provide 'an abstract and perhaps, useless, definition'. In order to clarify his position, therefore, he goes on to provide four examples of organisation development in practice:

1 Team development
2 Intergroup conflict resolution
3 Confrontation meetings
4 Feedback

Each of these examples is concerned with 'process' issues having an impact on the effectiveness achieved by particular work groups, either internally or at the interface between groups. Each is also concerned with the intervention of a third party 'change agent' or facilitator. Margerison (1978)[5] writing ten years after Bennis picks upon this latter point to suggest a simpler framework for organisation development than that of the earlier writers: 'The term "organisation development"... means the skills and methods used by people to facilitate organisational improvement.'

While Margerison's description may reflect what organisation development has often become (and may provide an explanation as to why client managers have a hard time in recognising the term 'organisation development' at all), it has lost two key elements of the Bennis and Beckhard requirements. The first of these is strategy and the second is top level commitment. While their aspirations may have been too high (reflecting Mitroff and Kilmann's concern about business schools' distance from organisational realities), Margerison's description opens the door to the cynical comment that organisation development is what organisation developers do when it is successful. When it is not, it is what the client manager did and, therefore, is not organisation development.

A useful framework probably lies somewhere between the two and needs to include a reference to the areas of knowledge, the particular skills and methods the organisation developer would characteristically employ. Margulies and Raia (1972)[6] go a long way towards meeting this requirement when they state that 'organization development borrows from a number of disciplines, including Anthropology, Sociology, Psychology and Economics. It generally involves the use of concepts and data from the behavioural sciences to attempt to facilitate the process of planned change'. The toolbag is specified with the references to the disciplines upon which organisation development practitioners draw, and the stress upon planned change goes some way to meet Bennis' emphasis upon organisation development as a strategic activity (though it would not be argued here that a strategy and a plan are one and the same thing). Margulies and Raia go on to write that:

> organisation development is essentially a systems approach to the total set of functional and interpersonal role relationships in organizations. An organization can be viewed as a system of coordinated human activities, a complex whole consisting of a number of interacting and interrelated elements or subsystems. A change in any one part will have an impact on one or more of the other parts ... organization development itself can be viewed as a system of three related elements – values, process and technology.

They then provide examples of what these three elements might comprise. These examples are summarised here.

Values

1 Providing opportunities for people to function as human beings rather than as resources in the productive process
2 Providing opportunities for each organisation member, as well as for the organisation itself, to develop to his full potential
3 Seeking to increase the effectiveness of the organisation in terms of all its goals
4 Attempting to create an environment in which it is possible to find exciting and challenging work
5 Providing opportunities for people in organisations to influence the way in which they relate to work, the organisation, and the environment
6 Treating each human being as a person with a complex set of needs, all of which are important in his work and in his life.

Process

1 Data gathering
2 Organisational diagnosis
3 Action intervention.

Technology

1 New ways of organisational learning
2 New ways of coping
3 New ways of problem solving.

The set of values provided by Margulies and Raia are essentially humanist in orientation. This provides another clue to the externalisation of organisation development from the organisations within which it is practised. The values as listed are desirable to most people, but the experience of organisational life in the eighties has not done much to suggest that these values are shared within the organisations themselves. More difficult still, because organisational members can identify with them at an individual level, they are easily espoused by the organisation in formalised expressions of its values ('Our greatest asset is our people and their unswerving commitment to Company goals'). But, to paraphrase Argyris (1974[7] and 1976)[8] the values in use are demonstrably different. 'Despite the best endeavours of Senior Management the economic pressures have meant that we have had to release five hundred valued members of the work force'. Thus, the experience of organisational members during the eighties has tended to be at odds with the stated values of organisational development. That experience has reflected a swing to much more functionalist or pragmatic values concerned with being clear about the organisational task, and the resources required to achieve it, in terms of staff (or, increasingly, subcontractors), equipment, finance and time. These values place emphasis upon effective and efficient delivery as opposed to the values of human growth and satisfaction.

This is not to disagree with those who argue that it is possible to have both sets of values represented and, hopefully, shared within the organisation, but to suggest that the emphasis placed by organisation development practitioners upon humanist values places them in a frame of reference that is essentially external to that of their client organisations. In the seventies, as the pressures of impending recession increasingly made themselves felt, the discussion was frequently to be heard as to whether the organisation developer should remain professional and independent of the politics and in-fighting within organisations in which individual and corporate survival were becoming dominant themes, or whether they should regard themselves as part of the process and be there in the thick of it. In the eighties and beyond, it can no longer be a matter for debate – the value position of the practitioner will have to be made clear.

Galbraith, (1977)[9] does not start from the same, humanist, standpoint that characterises the writers referred to so far. He is, however, very much in tune with the systems orientation espoused by Margulies and Raia and places great emphasis upon the importance of strategy, in common with Bennis. But perhaps the most significant difference in style in Galbraith's work from those alluded to previously is the sense that he is writing for the manager who owns the problem rather than for the organisation development practitioner who can analyse the problem. Indeed, he refers to organisation design as the key issue and not to organisation development:

Organisation design is conceived to be a decision process to bring about a coherence between the goals or purposes for which the organization exists, the patterns of division of labour and interunit coordination and the people who do the work. The notion of strategic choice suggests that there are choices of goals and purposes, choices of different organising modes, choices of processes for integrating individuals into the organization, and finally, a choice as to whether goals, organizations, individuals or some combination of them should be changed in order to adapt to changes in the environment. Organization design is concerned with maintaining the coherence of these choices over time.

These choices are fundamental and confront the manager with increasing frequency.

Writing some time later, Galbraith (1983)[10] develops his systems orientation further to indicate that organisations 'consist of *structure, processes* that cut the structural lines like budgeting, planning teams, and so on, *reward systems* like promotions and compensation, and finally, *people practices* like selection and development'. This approach is considerably more in harmony with the prevailing, functionalist orientation that is characteristic of the eighties management style, than is the humanist approach characteristic of Bennis, Margulies, Raia etc. His emphasis upon the notion of choice and, in particular strategic choice, would also find favour with Mitroff and Killman who berate the business schools and their academic antecedents for their post sixties emphasis upon training students to tackle exercises rather than to solve problems.

> It is vital as a culture that we come to appreciate that there is a vast difference between structured-bounded exercises and unstructured-unbounded problems ... In a phrase we have bred a nation of certainty-junkies. We have trained the members of our culture to expect a daily dosage of highly structured-bounded exercises. The difficulty is that the problems of organizations and society have become highly unstructured and unbounded.

Their reference to certainty-junkies will strike a chord in the hearts of management trainers who are asked so frequently to 'dispense with the theoretical stuff and give us some techniques'. All too often the expectation seems to be that provided one has the analytical ability to take a problem apart and break it down into its constituent parts, it will be possible to examine it logically and resolve it with precision. Unfortunately, the resolution of organisational and managerial problems tends to be less about elegance and simplicity and a great deal more about subtlety, ambiguity and choices.

'TELL ME SOME GOOD NEWS FOR A CHANGE'

In the 1930s the sale of comics, escapist 'penny dreadfuls', sky-rocketed. The same period saw the rise of Hollywood and the Busby Berkley musicals. Both had as much to do with the harsh realities of an economically depressed industrial society as the 'Fame' musicals have to do with youth unemployment in the 1980s. Both situations do require a catharsis, a discharge from the unremitting gloom of the dole queue and the company insolvency stories. It is not surprising, then, that the studies of excellence and success from the McKinsey Group (Peters and Waterman, 1982[11] and Deal and Kennedy, 1982[12]) and others (Goldsmith and Clutterbuck, 1984[13] Kanter, 1984[14]) have proved to be so successful. The intention is not to suggest that these works are to management in the eighties, a precise equivalent of the penny dreadfuls and Hollywood to the unemployed of the thirties. There are, however, certain parallels. Peters and Waterman do leave the reader with a warm feeling for the anecdotes of successful organisations awash with style, shared values and champions. They do not, unfortunately, leave that same reader with any prescription for action if that reader happens to be the manager of an organisation which is manifestly unsuccessful or in a declining industry.

Nevertheless, The McKinsey 'Seven-S' model offered by Peters and Waterman has some close affinity with the systems model offered by Galbraith:

strategy
structure
systems
staff
skills
shared values
style

The elements of the McKinsey model are very similar to Galbraith's (for people in Galbraith, read staff and skills in Peters and Waterman, for systems read processes, for part of shared values read rewards, and add style). Both emphasise the importance of strategy as a cornerstone in fostering corporate success.

But Peters and Waterman make no reference to organisation development as such, though they do refer to one or two practitioners by name (including Bennis). Writing for an audience of managers, the concepts, values, even the name of organisation development, do not enter the pages of the best selling book on management practice in the last decade. Once more, this would appear in keeping with the view of organisation development as an externalised process as opposed to an accepted area of effective management practice to be internalised within the organisation.

The key to unlocking this situation lies in the strategic focus emphasised by Bennis, reinforced by Galbraith, and central to the McKinsey 'Seven-S' model. Unless the organisation development process (and, indeed, the management development process) is closely related to, and in keeping with, the organisation's driving strategy it cannot be effective. This may well mean that the practitioner may have to forego the lucrative assignment where the strategy espoused (or used) by the client organisation is inconsistent with those humanist values referred to by Margulies and Raia. He will certainly have an obligation to make them explicit, change his values, or play Iago to his client's Othello.

STRATEGY AS THE INTEGRATING THEME

Professor Phillipe de Woot (1984)[15] has sounded a loud cautionary note about the enthusiasm among European managers for the findings of the McKinsey group and, by implication, for Goldsmith and Clutterbuck in the UK as well. He points out that the assumption underlying their approach is that most companies are overmanaged in what they refer to as the 'Hard S's' (strategy, structure and systems). They have developed these to an extent where the individual manager is reduced to being an administrator of a decision system rather than being required to be a decision taker, and certainly not a risk taker, himself.

The writers on corporate excellence concentrate their attentions on reviving interest in the so-called 'Soft S's' (staff, skills, shared values and style) which, one might think, should be regarded as a shot in the arm for the humanist values of organisation development. But, argues de Woot, this only makes sense if the underlying assumptions of over-management and over-control are correct. In the European context he finds little evidence to suggest that they are.

The results of a six year research programme headed by de Woot suggest that very few European organisations practice the basics of strategic management which are a prerequisite for corporate success regardless of whether the management emphasis is hard, soft, or balanced. An organisation committed to these basics would demonstrate that commitment through elements such as clarity over corporate goals, systematic management development at *all* levels, and a range of sophisticated decision support processes and systems. In the absence of these, he argues, to jump upon the *In Search of Excellence* bandwaggon may be meaningless or downright dangerous for an organisation lacking in professionalism and 'tightness' (clear operating procedures, control systems, levels of authority etc.). Such 'tightness' needs to exist not only at the centre but throughout all of its operating units. No large company can be truly innovative and entrepreneurial (let alone intrapreneurial) if it has not developed a highly professional base for its total operation. He warns against interpreting this professionalism too narrowly, stating that 'tightness based only on financial controls is totally inadequate since it gives the headquarters no ability to provide strategic direction and to communicate fruitfully with its off-shoots.

Such is the state of apparent backwardness in Europe that de Woot found:

1   that a number of top managers did not believe in defining clear objectives, and making them explicit throughout the company. 'I am not the Pope,' he quotes one as saying. Such companies, he reports, suffer from 'Shakespearean' intrigue and instability;
2   that top management frequently fails to set a strong lead;
3   and that employees 'are often slaves to external social values, rather than to the organisation's culture.'

Once more the critical finger is pointed at the negative consequences of adherence to values that are external to the organisation itself, whether these external values are those of society at large, or those of the academic community, as claimed by Mitroff and Kilmann, or those humanist values claimed to be at the heart of organisation development by Margulies and Raia.

In the absence of a clearly expressed strategic framework and an associated and consistent organisational value system to which their contribution can relate, organisation and management developers alike are likely to share a common experience of floundering around in a sea of apparently random, at best feudal, managerial behaviour. In such an environment, development, whether organisational, managerial, group, or individual employee based, is likely to be characterised by a series of fits and starts and sudden changes of direction resulting from the importation of new techniques having all the characteristics of the flavour of the month.

If de Woot is correct, and experience would suggest that at least he is on the right track, it is clear that the thrust of both management development and organisational development in Europe should be towards the specification, clarification and communication of organisational strategies and values. In order to be effective in this role, the developers have to earn the right to contribute. They have not always been particularly successful in so doing, not simply, as Mitroff and Kilmann argue, because they have used inappropriate models imported from inappropriate cultural and value sets, but because they have not had the corporate 'clout' to be heard. Perhaps the two things go together.

ON THE HORNS OF A DILEMMA

To summarise, for organisation development interventions to be effective they must be consistent with and contribute to the strategies and values of the organisations within which the intervention is made. However, it has been suggested that most European organisations pay scant attention to managing strategically, preferring to adopt a more reactive, seat of the pants approach. This unsystematic approach creates a vacuum which is filled by the importation of values and quasi-strategies from outside the organisation, for example, from government statements, from business schools, from external change agents or from internal specialist functions, such as personnel or training. But because these are imported values and do not form part of a 'tight' whole, they are fragmented and essentially ephemeral. Beckhard's response to this situation, presumably, would be to argue that this is precisely why organisational development interventions should only be made with the involvement of top management. Unfortunately, experience suggests that the internal specialists rarely carry the corporate 'clout' to make effective interventions at that, top management, level. Therefore, when the need for such an intervention is recognised it is more often than not assigned to an external advisor who owns another set of values . . . and the process is perpetuated. The resolution of the problem must lie within the organisation itself, and a resolution is essential to corporate survival for the non-European competition does not appear to share this problem to anything like the same degree. 'If we do not create a managerial revolution,' warns de Woot, 'we will wake up one bright morning and discover that . . . we have become under-developed or colonised. By then it will be too late.'

It is interesting to note that similar concerns are expressed among management developers. For example, Critchley and Casey elsewhere in this book (Chapter 23) argue against the conventional approach to team management development. A view which would suggest that before a management group can seriously address such issues as strategy formulation or the determination of key tasks, it is first necessary for them to build a degree of openness and trust. Critchley and Casey argue that, on the contrary,

> high levels of openness and trust are only rarely needed, and management groups get most of their work done very well without them, preferring for safety and comfort to remain relatively closed, and, covertly at least, distrustful. To ask such groups to make a major cultural shift, to take such big risks with each other as to be fully open and trusting, requires some mighty cogent justification . . . if their purpose is to be of real value to their clients . . . they (should) start by encouraging their clients to clarify the role and purpose of the management group in question, to identify the nature of the tasks which they need to address as a group – complex puzzles or real problems, and then to consider the appropriate modes of working, and the skills and processes that go with them. When we have reached this stage,

most of us have the skills and technologies to provide what is needed. What is often left out is the diagnostic work which gets us to that stage.

CONCLUSION: RESOLVING THE DILEMMA

If management development is effective it will result in positive organisation development, with effectiveness being measured in terms of enhanced organisational capability. It has been asserted in the earlier part of this chapter that management development is more generally recognised by in-company management as a 'good thing' than is organisation development. This is because highly stretched managers can usually identify a potential personal benefit to themselves from an effective management development process. This benefit may not necessarily be obtained directly: 'My boss should go on this programme' is a statement not unfamiliar to the management trainer.

It was also asserted that expectations of management development programmes, with some notable exceptions, tend not to be very high. However, the very fact that management development as a potentially 'good thing' is a commonly shared value in organisations gives the management developer a significant 'leg-up'. It is eminently sensible for the management developer to ask the question of senior management: 'Management development for what?' Indeed if the question is not being asked, then the organisation ought to be seriously questioning the value of having management developers any way. The answers to the question should lead, step by step to a clarification of the role and purpose of the management group. This is the investment in the diagnostic process argued for strongly by Margulies and Raia, and so frequently neglected in practice as observed by Critchley and Casey.

Presented with the results of the diagnosis, the next step needs to be placed firmly in the hands of the management group itself, and that is a questioning of the group's contribution to the achievement of overall organisational strategy, aims and objectives. If the answer is not apparent, then, either the group has misjudged its role and purpose, or the strategy, aims and objectives are unclear. Whatever the reason for the situation in a specific instance, the group, which owns the problem, should push and push hard for its resolution. In this the members of the group must be supported and encouraged by the management developer. He cannot afford to sit on a professional fence for, if he does, he will have earned the comparatively low expectations so often expressed. If, on the other hand, he does get involved in the uncomfortable process of questioning and re-appraisal that will result, he will have made a significant contribution to a genuine process of organisational development. Such a process will not of necessity incorporate the humanist values espoused by writers such as Margulies and Raia, it may even bring about the management revolution felt by de Woot to be so vital for European economic survival. Some practitioners who go down this road will no doubt wish that they had heeded Reddin's warning that 'the penalty for mutiny is death'. But whatever the outcome for the management developer, going through the process should make a significant contribution to the two things that all the writers referred to in this chapter seem to be agreed upon and that is that genuine organisation development is contingent upon the espousal of clearly formulated and communicated strategies on the one hand, and internally developed shared values on the other. When this is achieved, the similarities and differences between management development and organisational development will be meaningless, because we shall be talking about one and the same thing.

REFERENCES

(1) Mitroff and Kilmann, *Corporate Tragedies*, Praeger, New York, 1984.
(2) Bennis, *Organization Development: its nature, origins and prospects*, Addison-Wesley, Reading, Mass. 1969.
(3) Beckhard, *Organization Development: strategies and models*, Addison-Wesley, Reading, Mass. 1969.
(4) Reddin, 'Confessions of an organizational Change Agent', in *Group and Organization Studies*, International Authors, B.V., March, 1977.
(5) Margerison, *Influencing Organizational Change*, Institute of Personnel Management, London, 1978.

(6) Margulies and Raia, *Organization Development: Values, Process and Technology*, McGraw-Hill, New York, 1972.

(7) Argyris and Schon, *Theory in Practice: increasing professional effectiveness*, Josey-Bass, San Francisco, 1974.

(8) Argyris, *Increasing Leadership Effectiveness*, John Wiley & Sons, New York, 1976.

(9) Galbraith, *Organization Design*, Addison-Wesley, Reading, Mass., 1977.

(10) Galbraith, 'Strategy and Organization Planning', Pub. in *Human Resource Management*, vol. 22, nos. 1/2. John Wiley & Sons, Spring/Summer, 1983.

(11) Peters and Waterman, *In Search of Excellence*, Harper and Row, New York, 1982.

(12) Deal and Kennedy, *Corporate Cultures: Rites and Rituals of Corporate Life*, Addison-Wesley, Reading, Mass., 1982.

(13) Goldsmith and Clutterbuck, *The Winning Streak*, George Weidenfeld and Nicolson, 1984.

(14) Kanter, Rosabeth Moss, *Change Masters*, George Allen and Unwin, 1984.

(15) de Woot, 'Le Management Strategie des Groupes Industriels', Economica, Paris, 1984. Quoted by Christopher Lorenz, *Financial Times*, London, 26 November, 1984.

18

Handling cultural diversity

David Ashton

The impact of cultural differences on work organisations, their operations and effectiveness has become a popular subject during the last few years. Some of the reasons for this increased interest may lie in a more general move which recognises the importance of 'soft' data as a basis for explanation of differences in the performance of organisations. But interest may also have grown because a number of practitioners have been able to develop approaches which have made progress on real problems associated with cultural differences in work organisations.

In this chapter, we are going to start by defining culture and cultural differences, and then look at the key ideas that have been developed in this field over the last 15 years. With these key definitions and concepts in mind, we can then go on to examine the relevance of such approaches to learning in general, and development programmes for managers in particular. We shall consider the impact of the cultural differences both on the determination of appropriate content for development programmes and on its learning styles and strategies. The final part of the chapter will be concerned with a key developmental benefit which can arise when cultural differences are present in a development group.

KEY CONCEPTS AND APPROACHES

In this brief review of relevant concepts it may be best to start with some exclusions. By culture, we would refer to those *national* differences which affect, among other things, the way in which people work together. There has also been a growing interest in work performance arising out of specific differences in *organisational* cultures. However, this latter body of knowledge relates to a very different set of original concepts and will not be a subject of focus within this chapter.

Perhaps the single most important figure in the development and analysis of cultural difference in organisations is Gert Hofstede (1980).[1] While working within a large multinational company, he undertook a study of national differences among large numbers of employees in more than 40 countries. His definition of culture is based more on an anthropological approach – he describes this group identity as 'a collective programming of the mind'.

Hofstede analysed his data across all his countries in which he carried out his investigations, and identified four key dimensions which provide maximum differentiation between national cultures. Figure 18.1 identifies each of these dimensions and gives some examples of individual countries which have extremely high or low scores on these dimensions.

It may be helpful just to say a few words of explanation about each of his dimensions:

Individualism – This reflects the extent to which a society focuses on the importance of the individual rather than the group within the society.

Masculinity – Hofstede has assessed this by looking at the extent to which general roles in a society are allocated along traditional male/female lines.

Power distance – This covers the extent to which inequality is accepted by less powerful people in a society.

Uncertainty avoidance – This dimension focuses on the strength of concern about order and security in a country.

Hofstede's data has enabled him to 'place' countries on these particular dimensions – although it is difficult to explain, to everyone's satisfaction, the reasons for the positions of particular

Country examples high score	Dimension	Country examples low score
US Australia Britain Netherlands	Individualism	Pakistan Guatemala Taiwan Indonesia
Japan Germany Mexico Italy	Masculinity	Netherlands Chile France Sweden
Nigeria Malaysia Panama India	Power Distance	Israel Denmark New Zealand Britain
Portugal Uruguay Belgium Japan	Uncertainty Avoidance	Singapore Denmark Hong Kong Britain

Figure 18.1 Key dimensions of cultural difference

countries. However, careful reflection does yield some interesting points. On the whole, wealthy countries do tend to have a high index score on the individualistic ethic – although there are one or two which, like Japan, are clearly exceptions. Other countries which have apparently little in common in terms of culture and heritage *do* score highly on one particular dimension. For example Germany, Mexico, Italy and Japan all score highly on the masculinity dimension – in these countries, therefore male values are likely to dominate in their organisations. Hofstede reports some general trends for all countries in two of the dimensions of cultural difference – thus, tolerance of power distance is reducing in all countries, and concern for uncertainty avoidance is increasing in most countries.

The impact of these cultural differences, expressed in these key dimensions, is not necessarily clear when we look at the level of the work organisation and other factors which support or modify these cultural differences and need to be taken into account. From the point of view of the development programme it is important to understand different societal approaches to individual and group learning, in order to anticipate the likely responses of an individual from a particular society to a new learning experience in his work organisation.

André Laurent (1980)[2] identified national differences among individuals' views of their business organisations. He found the North American and North European employees tended to take a more instrumental view of business whereas the Latin countries of Europe took a more 'social' view of the work organisation. Laurent defines the 'instrumental' view as emphasising the rational organisation of tasks — and the manager's role is defined by these tasks and his functional responsibilities. Within this overall view, boss subordinate relationships would tend to be seen as impersonal; authority is associated with role or function in the organisation. The social view, by contrast, emphasises that the business is a group of people who need to be managed. The manager's role is therefore defined by social status and his authority comes from personal and functional attributes. In a social organisation, subordinates are expected to be loyal and deferential to their bosses — in return for more personal relationships and support.

Little has been published on culture and organisations which directly examines the impact of national differences in development and training. It is of particular interest to note here the recent work of Seddon (1985),[3] who identified the dangers of applying a western organisation development approach to African business organisations. In particular Seddon noted several contrasting assumptions, in two key areas:

Approach to development: In Western organisations, the employee takes responsibility for his or her own development. African employees manifest greater dependence in relationships and hence expect all development opportunities to be identified and arranged for them. They also would not wish to lose face by encountering novel, and therefore risky, situations. Neither would they understand the Western conception of a conflict between employers' and employees' needs.

Tactics of development: Western learning designs are likely to encounter problems in Africa. African employees require highly structured interventions which do *not* assume openness in relationships.

Seddon argues that the host culture is better regarded as a potential strength, rather than a hurdle to be overcome, and development approaches should take account of this.

In reviewing the work of Hofstede, Laurent and Seddon, two broad conclusions emerge. Firstly, national differences *do* matter and should be taken into account when constructing development programmes. Secondly, we are only just beginning to understand all the issues and problems of improving our decision making in this area of learning and development.

CULTURAL DIFFERENCES AND THE CONTENT OF DEVELOPMENT PROGRAMMES

Against the background of the key concepts of cultural differences, it becomes a matter of practical concern to take account of such differences when designing and running development programmes for multicultural groups.

A first area of concern is the *content* of such programmes. Hofstede (1980)[4] wrote an article questioning the transferability of American theories. Given that American motivation theory is likely to focus on the *individual* employee, he argued that such an approach would be wrong if straightforwardly transferred into a collectivist society — where it is more effective to work on the motivation of *groups* of employees. Seddon's (1985)[3] experience in Africa would support this view.

In the design of a multicultural development programme, it is essential to look carefully at each of the major *subject* areas of the programme, in order to understand the cultural limitations of the concepts and approaches which may be inherent in each subject. The extremes can be readily spotted — for example, it is unlikely that key economic concepts, and their application to the workings of the national economy, or the major structural characteristics of an industry, will vary from one country to another. At the other extreme, however, it is highly likely that approaches to employee relations will vary — because of legal and political as well as social and cultural differences, on a country-by-country basis. Between these two extremes lie the rest of the fundamental subject areas of management. We would suggest that it is more than just the human resources field which may be affected by cultural differences.

In a general way, the following contingency approach may help in the determination of subject content:

1 Identification of a key concept or framework
2 Identification of normal contingency factors associated with the application of that approach
3 The additional consideration of the impact that national differences may make upon the application.

Here is one example to show how this approach might be implemented.

Productivity

Productivity is apparently a universal theme and a wide range of applications have been reported on a specific productivity approach known as quality circles. To date, however, the literature has tended only to give individual stories and to develop 'folklore' – that is, subjective and often journalistic accounts of successes and occasional failures. Clearly the quality circles approach was initiated in a specific cultural context. It seems to have been an American idea, but developed within a Japanese group oriented context. Equally, it is clear that not every national context of employee motivation and productivity improvement is similar to that of the Japanese. Among the contingency factors to be considered, therefore, would be an identification of key characteristics of Japanese attitudes to work organisation – this would take account directly of national cultural differences. These differences would be assessed against the key features of the *other* national cultures, in which the quality circles approach might be applied or recommended.

Finally, if the approach seems to be worth examining in these new cultural contexts, then cultural differences should be part of the application discussions – in order to encourage awareness of their likely impact on the effectiveness of quality circles as a productivity 'solution' for the development programme delegates own work context.

In one sense, the quality circles approach is an easy example to make – since the majority of readers will not be Japanese (!) and, more significantly, they will be very ready to acknowledge the cultural differences of Japan from their own societies. It is the author's experience, however, that almost *all* management and business subject areas and specific techniques should be approached on the contingency basis outlined above, when decisions are made about course content on multicultural development programmes.

CULTURAL DIFFERENCES AND LEARNING METHODS

Management development is an area which has been closely associated with innovation and experiment with learning methods. Many of these have come about because of the apparent inappropriateness of formal, one-way methods, like lecturing, as effective means for helping experienced managers to learn. But these newer methods have tended to develop in English-speaking developed countries – particularly the United States and Britain. They often involve extensive participation by the management students, including exposure of personal feelings and values, which are not usually shared by working colleagues except in the development context. It will not be surprising therefore that some of these methods are initially found difficult by people of other cultures where the importance of role differences and more formal methods of education and training may be strongly stressed. Indeed approaches to learning and social interchange may be markedly more restricted and less relaxed in some of the English-speaking countries. Such cultural differences do not rule out the use of these more participative methods in management development, education and training. But they do mean that the manner and timing of the introduction of these more participative methods must be extended where cultural differences feature among delegate managers.

In introductory sessions, therefore, it may be important, with a multicultural group, to give everyone the opportunity to contribute – particularly in terms of talking about their own experience and the differences of their own national and business situations. Once these individual views and some insight into these individual differences are established, it may be relatively easier for both delegates and trainers to handle the differences and to understand the likely limitations on the contribution of individuals. Such participation by *all* delegates at the beginning of a multicultural programme becomes critical to their effective participation in later stages of the programme. But time *must* be given for all of these individual contributions to be brought out and it must be done in a non-threatening way. The primary objective is to enable all people to contribute, rather than to rigorously test their ideas. Such preparation and initiation is a necessary start for effective learning in a multicultural management group.

There will of course be other opportunities to build on cultural differences and their impact on business as a means of learning in a multicultural group. Thus, for example, discussions about the business environment could build around mapping exercises where individuals are given the opportunity to lay out their own 'national maps', which identify the important factors in their own business environment – increasing trade unions power, inflation, government controls, or whatever. These 'maps' explain what is important to enable the effective operation of their organisations in their national context.

There is also some argument for ensuring good opportunities in a multicultural programme for small group discussions. These must not however be set with such tight time limits that the predominant language group – most often the English speakers – dominate because the task must be able to be achieved within great time pressure. Smaller groups do make it much easier for individuals to make contribution in somewhat uncertain circumstances.

Obviously, having realised the impact of learning methods on cultural differences among delegates, it is particularly important to judge the pace of the first few days correctly. Trainers must also provide opportunity for individuals of all national backgrounds to make contributions, and for these contributions to be recognised by their peer delegates, as well as accepted by the teaching staff. At that point, cultural differences may become less important – individuals will have a confident and positive base on which to build their fuller participation and response to the range of learning methods which may be involved in the rest of the programme.

CONCLUSIONS

Much of this chapter has been concerned with the differences and by implication the difficulties that cultural diversity may make to effective manager education in effective manager development. It would be wrong however to deal with cultural difference primarily in this negative light. Again, from the author's (Ashton 1984)[5] own experience, for mature and successful managers of whatever nationality, comparison of themselves with other and different managers is a particularly valuable means of learning. The process of comparison has to begin with 'What I am' or 'What our company or system is'; this is likely to provide a basis of self-understanding as a starting point. This can be built on through discussion with other managers who are equally effective in their own circumstances, yet offer remarkable contrasts in the way in which they approach their work and the goals and priorities which they set.

Practising managers are more often impressed and learn better from others with effective but different working models for their own managerial roles, than they do from textbook theories – and it is right that this should be so. A multicultural group offers such richness because of the diversity of approach and assumptions of the individuals and businesses concerned, that, if the communication barriers of inherent cultural differences can be overcome, then the potential plus which comes from the richer and varied bases for comparison, can offer a genuine advantage and key additional feature for development and learning in a multicultural context.

Clearly this cannot be achieved quickly; programme designs must take account of slower introductory sessions and of a greater need for all to participate in the initial stages. But if that foundation can be achieved and confidence be given for all to participate, then the richer bases of comparison may provide a more effective and stronger development by the end of a development programme. The insidious assumption may be that the theories and approaches of the trainers, or of the parent company, provide the most effective universal way of approaching management and business problems in all countries. Clearly this is not true and this form of 'acculturalisation' must be resisted. It would only be an ineffective and accidental form of colonisation, which was detrimental to the effective operation of organisations in different national contexts.

REFERENCES

(1) Hofstede, G., *Culture's Consequences*, Sage, 1980.
(2) Laurent, A., 'Once a Frenchman always a Frenchman ...', *International Management*, June, 1980.

(3) Seddon, J. W., 'Issues in Practice – The Education and Development of Overseas Managers', *Management Education and Development*, Spring, 1985.

(4) Hofstede, G., 'Motivation Leadership and Organization: Do American Theories Apply Abroad?' *Organizational Dynamics*, Summer, 1980.

(5) Ashton, D., 'Cultural Differences: Implications for Management Development', *Management Education and Development*, Spring, 1984.

19

Developing local nationals

John Crosby

The aim of this chapter is to provide the reader with an appreciation, in some detail, of how one multinational company undertakes its management development work. Although many of the processes which will be described apply to United Kingdom, Expatriate and Third Country National staff, the focus here is primarily upon developing local nationals for advancement in their own companies.

Broad conclusions, by definition, have no place in opening paragraphs. Similarly it would be inappropriate to ascribe an academic thesis to the work which will be described as it represents a process which has been developed in a series of practical steps and refined by experience. Nevertheless, if there is a philosophy which can be derived from our company's experience it is that management development activities are fully effective only when they are integrated with other strategic planning processes undertaken by a board and that, within a multinational company, they should rest upon personnel systems which operating companies have devised (within a broad policy framework) to meet their local needs and circumstances. Within the personnel function itself, the management development system requires input and collaboration from most of its sub-functions: effective management development activity is not the sole prerogative of management development specialists.

COMPANY CONTEXT

British-American Tobacco Company Limited (BAT Co.) is a multi-national tobacco business, with over 60,000 employees, and is now part of BAT Industries whose interests also embrace paper, retail operations and financial services. It is primarily an overseas company with operations in 52 countries; only one of its subsidiary companies is located in the United Kingdom. Because of the company's philosophy and also because the substantial home base typical of most other multinationals is absent, it has developed a decentralised and devolved form of management. Thus, in terms of management development (as well as of the personnel function as a whole) companies are expected to be as self-reliant as possible; as already indicated, they have discretion within broad limits to develop their own procedures to reflect operating circumstances and their national culture. In this respect, BAT Co. is the antithesis of some US multinational companies in which, for example, appraisal procedures and personnel records would be standardised around the world.

COMPANY VIEWPOINTS ON MANAGEMENT DEVELOPMENT

1 Planned managerial development is vital to the success of our business. In a mature and highly competitive industry – without unique patent/protected technology or access to scarce natural resources – the quality of management is a fundamental strategic issue.

2 We recognise that a multinational company has special responsibilities to contribute to the national economies in which it operates and that the development of properly trained and experienced staff is one of these.

3 It is our belief that 90 per cent of management development takes place within a manager's own company and work context. Although home and overseas courses have an important role to play in the process, our philosophy of development is rooted primarily in the identification of potential followed by carefully planned job movement to provide the experience necessary for progressive advancement to senior posts.

4 We expect our operating companies to provide their management staff with basic training in management techniques and company business knowledge and to develop effective succession planning processes. The head office involvement in these two activities is normally limited to providing specific help (when requested) in developing new training procedures and to monitoring planned succession arrangements for board level and senior specialist posts within the companies.

THE ELEMENTS OF MANAGEMENT DEVELOPMENT

Selection

To begin with the obvious (therefore a point sometimes overlooked), the ultimate effectiveness of management development activities must be closely linked to the quality of incoming managerial staff from graduates/young professionals upwards. We have therefore agreed with our companies that their recruitment policy should be to recruit candidates for managerial posts whose abilities (or developable skills) not only match current requirements but also have the potential to meet future job needs. In parallel, our companies have adopted a mutually agreed framework for selection: the main elements of this are the use of written job descriptions and specifications, an operating company-wide methodology of interviewing, the training of selectors at all levels in the chosen methodology, the use of group selection techniques when candidates numbers warrant, and the conduct of validation studies to pinpoint cases of success and failure in selection. It is important to stress that, within this framework, companies have discretion to use the forms of job description, interviewing techniques, psychological tests etc. which they feel are most relevant to their local circumstances.

Where requested, training in advanced selection and interviewing skills can be provided by the head office personnel function in the United Kingdom, either within the operating company or (as is becoming more typical) on a regional basis. A key pre-requirement before any form of personnel-related training course is offered is that one or more local personnel management staff must be prepared to continue the work with reducing help from the centre.

Appraisal

Appraisal is regarded as an integral part of management development and companies are expected to devise forms of appraisal to suit their local circumstances. The actual documentation used within our companies varies significantly therefore in length and content. Equally, the style of appraisal discussion will vary from country to country depending upon the directness of questioning and comment which is culturally acceptable. To ensure both a minimum standard and also that certain key points are covered, the following guideline has been adopted by companies. It is typical of the form of guidelines which the head office personnel department discusses and agrees with companies on all important personnel issues, including employee relations and remuneration which are not discussed in this chapter.

Policies

To use the performance appraisal process as a basis for ensuring that there is full agreement between a manager and his subordinate about the principal objectives of a job and the tasks to be achieved. It should serve as the main means for assessing performance against agreed work objectives and for identifying training and development needs.

Strategies

1 Define principal objectives/goals to be achieved and the standards/means by which attainment is to be judged.
2 Review performance against the previously-agreed principal objectives/goals and measures.
3 Identify training, experience and development needs in the light of an employee's current and next likely post.
4 Define any external circumstances which have helped or hindered materially the achievement of agreed objectives.
5 Record an individual's career aspirations and any features which could restrict his/her promotability.
6 Provide internal training courses for managers in the techniques of appraisal interviewing.

The need for strategy 5 was learned the hard way some years ago: one key employee in an overseas company had been developed progressively for a local board-level post. When the post was offered, he refused to take it on the grounds that his social and family ties to his provincial town had become such as to make it impossible to accept a promotion which involved a relatively modest geographical transfer!

Succession planning

Although the period may seem unrealistically long, we find in practice that sensible decisions about training, development and job movement of identified candidates of potential for senior posts require something up to a ten-year planning span. Whilst the crystal ball becomes a little hazy towards the end of a projected ten-year period, the discipline of forecasting is vital. We have therefore developed with our companies a form for 'Organisation Forecast and Succession Planning' (Figure 19.1). This allows planned promotions, retirements and organisation/job changes to be recorded against each managerial post, together with an indication of firm or potential future candidates. Envisaged new posts are also charted.

In parallel, an Individual Career Plan document (Figure 19.2) has been introduced in recent years to record both biographical and work experience data of identified candidates *and the action which is planned for them.*

The use of both documents (OF&SP and ICP) could become mechanistic were it not under-pinned by positive management action. To this end, an agreed set of strategies exists as indicated by the following guideline extract statements.

Identify and analyse the professional and managerial knowledge and experience content of the key posts which are critical to business success (Board, head of function and senior specialist levels).

Identify the subordinate jobs and experience opportunities available within the operating company (considering also opportunities within the Operating Group at large with the help of Head Office) which provide logical progression to the key posts.

Identify candidates at all levels within the management

Issues in Management Development

STATUS CODES (Col. 4)   PERSONAL CODES (Next move – Col. 7)

I   — International (Expatriate)   Rt   — Retirement

TCN — Third Country National   Pr   — Promotion

L   — Local National   D   — Development/Company requirement

LN   — Local Non-national   X   — Transfer — indicate destination

C   — Contract   ?   — Not known

JOB TITLE JOB HOLDER	JOB Gp.	JOB HOLDER					REPLACEMENTS	
		Nationality	Status	Born	Current Appt.	Next Move	Code	Name
(1)	(2)	(3)	(4)	(5)	(6)	(7)	(8)	(8a)

Figure 19.1 Organisation forecast and succession plans

REPLACEMENT CODES (Col. 8)

P   —   Planned

E   —   Emergency

O   —   Other Candidates

COMPANY:

DEPARTMENT

DATE COMPILED

19	19	19	19	19	19	19	19	19	19	REMARKS
(9)	(10)	(11)	(12)	(13)	(14)	(15)	(16)	(17)	(18)	(19)

Figure 19.1 (cont)

Name	Present Appointment	Date of Present Appointment	19	19	19	19	19	19	19	Nomal Retirement Date
Nationality	Job Group — J / P									

International Status
Yes/No/Willing to accept if offered
(delete whichever is inappropriate)

Date of Birth: Place of Birth:

Marital Status:
Children: Sex: Date of Birth:

Education:

Previous Experience:

Group Service:
Date   Job   Company   Grade

Languages:
Training to Date:

Ultimate Estimated Promotablity within Company/within
Tobacco Division (delete whichever is inappropriate)

General Manager

Head of Function

	Estimated Grade	Potential
General Manager		
Head of Function		

Potential Posts

R = Readiness for Promotion   A = Availability for Promotion

Job Title	Job Group	Location	Overdue Readiness	Now R	Now A	1–3 years R	1–3 years A	3–5 years R	3–5 years A	5+ years R	5+ years A

Training Proposals/Plans:

Development Proposals/Plans:

Action

Special Aspects to be Borne in Mind:

Proposed by Head of Function:
(name and initials) Date:

Recommended by General Manager:
(name and initials) Date:

Figure 19.2 Individual Career Plan

352

structure who have potential to meet the requirements of key posts and plan their career progression.

Once an individual company board has reviewed and agreed its succession plans, head office becomes involved in respect of nominated candidates for local director and major head of function posts. Awareness of and a concern for the appropriateness of succession planning for such posts, together with associated proposed development plans for potential candidates, is clearly regarded as a BAT Co. Board concern and the subject is on the agenda of two Board meetings annually. Succession planning is therefore fully integrated into the vital planning processes of the company and is subject to the same regular examination, detailed scrutiny and commitment as are other key business activities.

Once plans have been agreed, the role of the head office personnel function is to keep under review the development of identified candidates with the companies concerned, to arrange central training courses and programmes where it is impractical to expect these to be run locally, and to facilitate developmental transfers/secondments between operating companies as well as periods of attachment to head office when opportunities for relevant experience do not exist or are restricted locally.

Management training and education

Companies undertake managerial and functional training of their staff, using in-company or external national facilities depending upon the size and sophistication of the business and country. Nevertheless, there remains a positive role for the head office to organise courses in respect of both functional and general management training and up-dating. Arrangements include:

1 *Specialised functional courses both in the UK and on a regional basis.* In the personnel field, for example we have developed our own 'Training for Training Managers' course in recognition of the absence of such facilities in many countries. This course, typically of three weeks duration, ranges from the identification of training needs to the writing and handling of tobacco-industry based case studies. Increasingly, it includes consideration of the uses which can be made of video facilities.

2 *Functional appreciation courses outside a manager's immediate knowledge area*, such as 'Finance for non-financial managers' and 'Marketing for non-marketing managers'.

3 *General management courses*, arranged by BAT Industries at its Chelwood staff college, the most important of which are:
(a) *The management training course* Designed to acquaint younger managers with basic management skills, including human relations skills, and also with the main features of our industry.

(b) *The management development programme* Designed to provide managers with 'management education' in the broad aspects of business and with recent/developing trends and activities which can affect both their own and their companies' future operations.

(c) *The business manager programme* Designed for seasoned managers who are candidates for general management positions (or for a major head of function post) at home or overseas. This programme is conducted on a project basis.

(d) *The senior management programme* Designed on a conference basis to allow general managers and heads of function in major companies to examine strategic issues affecting BAT Industries' interests and also possible developments to its existing policies and practices.

In any one year it is not uncommon for up to 150 BAT Co. managers to attend Chelwood programmes; the vast majority are local nationals employed in our overseas subsidiaries.

In the human resource field, BAT Co.'s specialised courses not already described include a performance appraisal workshop to assist companies to identify for themselves the appraisal needs appropriate to their situation; an appraisal advisers training course (designed on programmed learning principles) to equip selected company employees to guide their colleagues in both the interviewing and goal/objectives setting aspects of appraisal; a remuneration practices course which covers job analysis, job evaluation, salary surveys and salary structures.

Assessment centre techniques

We have been experimenting in the United Kingdom with the use of assessment centre techniques and have now developed a two days programme which we call an 'Individual development programme'. Through the use of various exercises and psychological tests, participants have an opportunity to ascertain for themselves what are their present strengths and weaknesses, against the norm of a general manager's post in an operating company and to re-examine their aspirations. Results of an IDP are communicated in detail to participants and to accountable line managers, and ultimately are fed into the overall succession planning process.

Experimentation has shown us that it is not appropriate to extend participation in the programme to managers whose first or working language is not English. However fluent their spoken and written English may appear to be, they are likely to be at a disadvantage when a large amount of complex written material has to be absorbed in a limited time and also when faced with the cut and thrust of group discussion. An equally important point is that observers may well be inhibited in making judgements where they feel (however unspecific their feelings) that demonstrated performance using English language may be below that which an individual could display in a home context.

In the long term, assessment centre techniques will be imparted and commended to operating companies and it will then be their decision as to whether or not they are appropriate to their local needs and culture.

Staff movement and management development

To help companies expedite the development of staff, the London Head Office has a fundamental role to play in finding suitable development opportunities on a worldwide basis. Secondments to acquire specific knowledge or expertise are typically of 3/12 months duration. Transfers, which involve the performance of a substantive job which is able to provide developmental experience, are typically of 2/3 years duration. Examples of the latter form of movement include a Sri Lankan to Hong Kong, an Indonesian to Sri Lanka, a Malaysian to the United Kingdom, a Chilean to Central America and a Mauritian to Zaire.

In parallel, there is a role to play in identifying managers in overseas companies who may be prepared to accept a long term international career outside their own country. The problems of international staff movement are growing in as much as many countries are imposing ever-more rigorous limitations on the granting of work permits and the remittance of earned income (even when a direct exchange of staff is involved). Equally important, one can no longer assume that the domestic circumstances of managers (or their perceptions of the quality of life in many countries) are such that they would necessarily welcome geographical movement. Nevertheless one still has to try if management development opportunities available within a multinational company are to be optimised for the benefits of both the staff concerned and the organisation as a whole.

GENERAL OBSERVATIONS ON MANAGEMENT DEVELOPMENT

It is always tempting — but the temptation is to be avoided — to draw conclusions of general application from one company's experience. However, we believe that the following elements have contributed to the success of our management development activities. They are:

1 *The integration of succession planning with other planning processes undertaken by the boards of both BAT Co. and its operating companies.* Succession planning is therefore regarded as a key management process rather than as a special domain of the personnel function. As indicated earlier, the subject is on the agenda of two BAT Co. Board meetings annually and is preceded by detailed examination of projected appointments, transfers and development plans by individual directors with the assistance of the personnel function.

2 *Devolved discretion to operating companies, within mutually agreed guidelines, to develop the format of procedures most appropriate to their company and national context.* Effective management development must be the responsibility of line managements and they should be able to feel some 'ownership' of the methodologies involved.

3 *The recognition that management development is an integral*

(indeed an inextricable) part of the personnel/human resources function overall as it impinges on most of the function's specialist activities, including those such as the underlying philosophy and design of remuneration policies which have not been discussed in this chapter.

This last element perhaps deserves additional comment. Whilst, for example, management development and training specialists at various levels will be expected to take the lead in identifying training and experience needs and in making proposals on means of meeting management training and education requirements, they must closely relate to and co-operate with colleagues responsible for other human resource aspects such as recruitment, manpower planning, appraisal, assessment centre work and remuneration. Put another way, their contribution will be optimised if they are able to take a generalist as well as a specialist view of situations. The philosophy which is implied in this approach to management development is that it is most effectively conducted when all activities which contribute to the recruitment, growth, retention and motivation of staff are considered collectively and complement one another.

A FINAL COMMENT

Although hiccups happen inevitably in any management process (such as downturns in identified managers' performance or unexpected illness/turnover which can create the need for highly accelerated development of individuals) – and no management process works as smoothly as it is described in published form – I think that we can claim to have been successful in developing our managers. The proof must be there in the bottom line and in the extent to which we grow and retain our senior management population.

20

Women managers

Judi Marshall

When I first reviewed the literature on women managers, I was surprised to find so many articles asking whether men and women are *really* different. Most of the authors were trying to prove that they are not, so that women could be endorsed as suitable management material. In the main they were able to find data to meet their purposes, for example on leadership behaviour. But this is only part of the story. It is more appropriate to view men and women as both the same and different, as sharing fundamental aspects of human existence but approaching them from distinctly different bases and from different social positions. Certainly research shows that women and men can *behave* similarly as leaders, but it also reveals differences in their initial approaches and in how their behaviour is responded to by others (see Bartol, 1978,[1] for a review). Women tend to emphasise people management over task structuring, whilst men have opposite priorities; women are often inhibited in exercising position power because other people reject or undermine their use of authority, stereotype them in devalued female roles, act dependently towards them and so on.

As an opening to this chapter I shall argue that we currently need to concentrate on men and women's differences rather than acclaim their undoubted similarities as a necessary phase in movement towards true equal opportunities. In the remainder, I shall discuss the training and development initiatives currently arising from an identification of women's separate needs.

SIGNIFICANT DIFFERENCES BETWEEN WOMEN AND MEN

There are two interlinked bases for my assertion that women and men are meaningfully different. The first involves theories of archetypal patterns, in terms of which women broadly represent a different range of potential human characteristics from those of men. The second involves the recognition, to which my work in this area soon led (Marshall, 1984),[2] that because of inequalities in social power, men's characteristics have traditionally been valued more than women's, and so have shaped organisational life. These frameworks help identify women's development needs and show why these are currently so important.

Male and female values

Various theoretical frameworks distinguish between male and female values as two potentially complementary viewpoints on the world reflecting an archetypal polarity. This is especially clearly expressed in the Chinese concepts of yang and yin, and has close parallels in Jungian psychology. Drawing on these sources, the male pole is characterised by self assertion, separation, control, focused perception, classifications, rationality and contractual arrangements; the female pole by interdependence, merging, acceptance, awareness of patterns, wholes and contexts, emotional tone and personalistic perception. Male and female values are qualities to which both sexes have access, rather than the exclusive properties of men and women respectively. But through physical makeup, orientation, and to a certain extent social learning, women are grounded in the female pole and men in the male pole. As managers, women draw, to varying degrees and in individualistic ways, on a base of values which distinguishes them from men. Individual development involves balancing the capabilities of one's grounding with appropriate aspects of the other perspective. This offers a more flexible array of abilities than does either set of values alone. But this is to some extent an ideal picture.

Social power

In its recent history, Western society has emphasised male values, and these have shaped its organisations, cultural norms, language and so on. Female forms are relatively devalued and underdeveloped. This is such a pervasive aspect of our culture that it is unusual to identify ways in which women differ from men without the assumption being made that women are somehow at fault. All too easily men become the unquestioned norm to which women's behaviour is compared, and any deviations seen as unusual and therefore to be penalised.

In this chapter, 'differences' are not viewed as faults of either sex. Rather they are aspects of our cultural and gender heritage which can be used either productively and creatively or inappropriately and degeneratively. It cannot be assumed, for example, that what men do in organisations is somehow 'right'. Their management styles and career patterns reflect a narrow range of possible options. There are disadvantages of which men themselves are aware. Established ways of working contribute to job stress, and may eventually lead to coronary heart disease; hierarchical forms of organisation restrict development opportunities for all but a small group of 'successful' people. (Although there is no room to do so here, it is worth questioning whether we know what men's development needs *really* are.) It is possible, however, to overidealise female values in contrast. Openness to the environment can have its degenerative forms of being overwhelmed, invaded and dependent.

The social dominance of male values has inhibited the development of complementary, female alternatives. This is shown culturally by an emphasis on individualism, competition and control, and limited attention to interdependence, collaboration and acceptance. Along with other commentators (for example, Capra, 1982[3]), I see the re-emergence and elaboration of female values as a significant aspect of a current re-vision in society, with potential benefits for men and women alike. But unless they are taken seriously and allowed considerable scope for experimentation, they will continue to be constrained by the current pattern of culture. Women's separate development is, then, an essential element in any social evolution, and so is the focus of this chapter.

Women's development needs

Many women now want to join in the world of employment and benefit from the financial rewards, achievements and personal growth it offers. They are joining a largely male world. In doing so they have conflicting needs. Until recently, equal opportunity initiatives concentrated on gaining acceptance for women, and emphasised their capability to work similarly to, and as well as, men. A moderate level of success in this direction has been achieved. But the foundations of women's identity as managers are different, as are their experiences of the organisational culture. These issues are now becoming central as they determine the shape of women's approach to work. The analysis of women's current development needs below highlights the difficulties they face as a result of these conflicts. It is important to remember that these are balanced by many satisfactions and opportunities for achievement which women also value. I shall draw for illustration on research with middle- to senior-level women managers in the retailing and book publishing industries (Marshall, 1984).[2]

Many women managers are operating from values, assumptions and perspectives which reflect their female grounding but are not widely represented or accepted in organisational life. This creates conflicts and pressures, and many describe themselves as working in 'hostile environments'. In their everyday work and career prospects, women are continually affected by inequalities in social power, although usually these are in the background rather than foreground of their experience. These become most apparent when women are placed in 'one-down' positions because of their gender, find that others reject their use of authority power because it contravenes stereotypes of femininity, or they are passed over for promotion despite appropriate qualifications and experience. It is common, for example, for female managers to be mistaken for the secretaries or assistants of male colleagues, to find that their opinions go unheard in meetings or be denied development opportunities such as assignments abroad because it is assumed they would not cope. Maintaining their own self-image and confidence, and managing relationships with others, thus become high priorities.

As women's characteristics do not correspond to images of 'good' management, they are encouraged to play down their femaleness and to copy male models of behaviour in order to succeed. Many have done this to great effect, and developed capabilities which would otherwise have remained dormant. But this often leads to conflict between their work and personal self-images. Some established managers are currently acutely aware of what they have given up in order to succeed organisationally. They are looking for more female-compatible ways of working. This is particularly reflected in dilemmas about management style and career management. The low key, person-oriented management style which many favour is in sharp contrast to the competitive, independent, achievement-oriented model they see around them. It can make them personally vulnerable, prove ineffective in competitive environments and limit their chances of promotion. The managers I interviewed wanted to blend aspects of several approaches together into a more robust style. Most were hesitant about the choices of 'using their femininity' and 'adopting male tactics' they could immediately identify, as these might not fit their self-image or allow them to build co-operative relationships with others at work.

Some women managers are looking for different ways of fitting employment into their lives from the standard, life-long career pattern. Many also want it to serve purposes other than conferring social status. Those I interviewed considered a wide range of factors including intrinsic job challenge, their health, relationships and their sense of personal identity in any decisions they made about work. Female values thus shaped their engagement with employment. Some had rejected promotions which threatened these priorities. Being employed was one highly significant role amongst several for them, and they wanted 'to lead a balanced life', but found this difficult.

Research evidence suggests that women bring a different range of viewpoints to management. Gilligan (1982),[4] for example, distinguishes between two moral codes, one used more consistently by men and the other by women. The male moral system views the world in terms of rights and principles, which can be defended and used as the basis for decision making. The female system perceives life as a network of social relationships, with the individual at its centre. Right and wrong become relative and pragmatic, dependent on the situation. Gilligan concludes that women 'speak in a different voice', a view that is widely held amongst linguistic analysts too (Spender, 1980).[5] Other authors identify variations in cognitive style. They detach intuition from its associations with emotional guesswork and offer a definition in terms of subjective and contextual awareness which has much to offer management thinking. It is however usually difficult for women managers to get their perspectives heard if they differ from established frameworks, and this may eventually undermine their own faith in them.

Despite the high needs for alternative strategies expressed above, women have few sources on which to draw for fresh ideas. Their traditional roles of housewife and mother have become compromised in the recent moves towards work as a significant role. But at work there are few competent female models to aspire to. Even those women who do survive in organisations without copying dominant styles remain invisible, their learnings and accommodations kept private. Stereotypes of hard, lonely older women managers are so powerful that most of the people I interviewed did not want to stay in management until retirement in case this happened to them. This dearth of role models is partly because female values remain in the background of organisational life and do not impact its public face. It is also because women have tended not to identify or mix with each other at work. To gain acceptance, particularly at senior levels, they have identified with their male colleagues rather than with other women. Women also therefore need opportunities to share their perspectives, experiences and ways of coping, but without organisational penalties for doing so.

The analysis of needs above reveals five main development priorities for women. They are:

1 extending their range of job skills, especially those of self expression;
2 enhancing interpersonal and management skills, with particular attention to power issues;
3 developing strategies for being effective in and influencing current organisation cultures;
4 reviewing what they want from employment;
5 doing all these in ways which allow them to express female aspects of their identity.

Shared development needs

This chapter has taken the perspective of highlighting differences, and so has little to say about the many development needs which women share with men. These are particularly in the realm of specific skills or general management training such as MBA programmes. In fact it is impossible to exclude as potentially relevant any area of training, as long as sufficient attention is paid to the sex of trainees and issues of gender are discussed as relevant. Rather women need to gain access to a wide array of training, on which they are under-represented relative to men, and to see promotion opportunities ahead of them to make their experiences meaningful.

These areas are, however, relatively unproblematic as development opportunities if the woman manager is secure in her own self-image and needs, and is able to appraise and act effectively within the organisation culture. If these foundations for organisational identity are in doubt, her engagement with more skill-oriented training is likely to be unclear and possibly half-hearted.

Different approaches to development opportunities

In fact, women's attention to development so far has given priority to issues men, whose choices about employment are less apparently problematic, might view as 'background'. This contributes to differences between men and women in how they approach development opportunities. From my own experience and discussions with other trainers, it seems that women tend to bring their whole selves, their full range of life roles, to any activities and want to be changed by their experiences. Men in contrast, present themselves as organisational people, looking for relevance within a particular area of expertise, and doubt whether radical change in adult life is possible. One consequence is that women may need help to integrate learning into the other life areas it impacts. Assertion training, for example, may improve their management skills but create temporary havoc in relationships at home. Trainers will need to be alert to, and prepared to work on, these wider repercussions.

MANAGEMENT DEVELOPMENT PROVISION

There is now a wide range of courses and other development activities directed at women managers. A valuable source on new offerings is 'Women and Training News', produced by The Co-ordinating Group for the Development of Training for Women, Manpower Services Commission. The activities covered below are not solely relevant to women, but do directly address their concerns. In some areas such as assertion, men are now showing an interest in training initiated for women; in others, women's training shares a label with men's but typically takes a different form in practice. It is important to recognise that the patterning of social power which has helped shape women's development needs can also hamper appropriate attention to them. For this reason training structures are as significant as specific course topics. These aspects are dealt with separately.

Training structures

Networking

As they become more aware of the world of work and concerned about their places in it, many women are looking for people of 'their own kind' to mix with. They also often feel cut off from established channels of communication and information sharing. Various motives have led to a growth in women's networks and associations, some official like the European Women's Management Development Network, others informal; some with a specified constituency such as women in publishing or computing, others looser groupings of people who have common perspectives. Broadly based networks offer members reference points outside their immediate work context, and news on current developments. Informal networks within a company or locality serve other, more supportive, functions as well.

As these activities grow, women are exposed to possible role models as well as friends and contacts. Coaching by mentors higher up their organisations has been a vital factor in many successful women managers' profiles. Networking offers more lateral coaching relationships. Some organisations are deliberately creating opportunities on induction programmes for new female recruits to meet established women managers, making such relationships more possible. Advice to trainers and members on creating and fostering networks is also now available.

Women-only groups

Although we are experiencing their re-emergence in society, female values remain fragile and their development tentative. They need protection if they are not to be swamped or overridden by their robust male counterparts. Similarly in their development, women need the comparative safety of working in women-only groups. Here participants can to a certain extent suspend dominant cultural stereotypes, and explore and compare experiences which either men do not share or which affect them differently. Even patterns of conversation make this more difficult to do in mixed company. Men and their opinions tend to take primacy, and either leave women out or assign them to supportive roles. This pattern occurs even in mixed sex discussions of *women's* issues. Men often speak for women with a clarity the latter are reluctant to contradict with their more diffusely formulated ideas. In women-only groups participants can concentrate on understanding and supporting each other, and finding clear expressions of their own needs, rather than on competing for attention. They are also more able to take risks.

Women-only groups and networks vary across a wide spectrum in terms of their ways of working and the issues they address. Some act as support groups, talking through attitudes, motivations, problems and choices, gaining new perspectives and sharing ways of coping. Some are organised on a company or occupational basis and have a clear objective of professional development. They run seminars on particular management skills, invite guest speakers and so on. Some represent women's viewpoints to their organisation or industry. Recent initiatives in assertion and management effectiveness training have done much to establish women-only courses as viable and valuable activities. Their number is rapidly increasing, despite debate and some criticism. Amongst other things this reflects a growing identification amongst women, and in this way too provides new models of possible working practice.

Women-only groups are not, however, appropriate forums for all issues and for all times. Sometimes conflict within the group is suppressed, and harmony becomes more important than allowing a diversity of views. This may mean that members leave rather than address their issues within the group. Managing conflict is an important area that women need currently to work on, both in relationships with men and with each other. Many reject men's competitive attitudes as a model, and are looking for alternatives which combine co-operation and self-assertion.

Many men find women-only activities bewildering and threatening, and it is not easy to introduce them into organisations. Once a group is set up it is not unusual for individual men to make powerful bids to join or to find out what is being discussed. Any group which has the function or desire to report back to the rest of the organisation on topics of general relevance must consider how the boundary can be managed in this direction too. These 'safe spaces' need, then, careful management and attention.

Flexibility

A keynote of women's development needs as outlined above is exploration. Predetermined course formats are not usually sufficiently flexible to meet this requirement. There is a trend therefore to schedule free time on courses during which members can work individually or in small groups on topics of their choice, using trainers as resources or guides. The diversity that women bring to courses is also accommodated by attention to contracting at the start of the course and as it progresses. Typically participants are asked to write down three things they want from the course, three things which will stop them achieving these objectives and three things they have to offer. These are then displayed publicly. Contracts help participants clarify their expectations, and give trainers an opportunity to state clearly which the course can and may not meet. Contracts can be reviewed part way through the course to monitor progress. They help increase the course relevance and tailoring, and demonstrate participants' responsibility for their own learning. They are more common on women-only than on other training courses. Perhaps misguidedly it is usually assumed that men are a relatively uniform category in terms of training needs and styles.

Dispersed training

A crucial need identified above was for women to increase their competence in potentially inhospitable organisational cultures. Once and for all training is seldom the best solution to such issues, but many trainers are forced into this format by tradition, participants' difficulties in getting time away from work, financial constraints and so on. Some courses do, however, meet at regular intervals for several weeks or months with opportunities for members to test out their new skills in between. This format has been especially successful for some assertion and self-development training.

Self-development groups

Opportunities for maximum flexibility are offered by self-development groups for women. Some examples along these lines already exist, and the Manpower Services Commission has recently funded a significant initiative to set up and evaluate such groups (see Boydell and Hammond, 1985, in MEAD special edition).[6] A group meets at regular intervals, with a trainer acting as facilitator. Participants manage their own process, identify their individual and collective needs, and plan and run a programme of activities to address these. The emphasis is on holistic development, covering work in the context of other life areas, and recognising the interdependence of thinking, feeling and doing. Initial evaluations are that such groups can be highly successful, and support their members in significant work and personal learning. Managing the group's development and decision making themselves gives participants valuable experience, and opportunities to experiment with more varied styles and strategies than they use in their own jobs.

Training topics

Assertiveness

The single most significant and impactful training topic for women so far has been assertiveness. It directly addresses their inferior position in terms of social power, and offers ways to reclaim personal and organisational power. Assertion training helps women develop their self-confidence and their interpersonal skills, including their ability to express and honour their own perspectives, even when these do not conform to established organisational norms and ways of thinking. Participants are usually concerned to find work styles which reflect their female grounding and reject behaviours they find too aggressive or competitive.

The basic principles of assertion training are: respect for self and others; equality; responsibility for one's own needs; maintaining appropriate boundaries between oneself and others; and choice —

including when and whether to be assertive. Typical exercises involve practising various assertive techniques such as dealing with anger, accepting or giving criticism and saying 'no'; role plays of problem situations; explorations of non-verbal behaviour and its implicit messages; and distinguishing between assertive, passive and aggressive behaviour. Dickson (1982)[7] provides a valuable primer.

Some organisations have recognised the benefits of assertion training and are now offering it widely. Many courses however go on outside companies as part of women's development for themselves, but with obvious job implications. Most current courses are for women only, but an increasing number of mixed courses are being introduced. Assertiveness is an essential first rung of management effectiveness training for women. The near future is likely to bring more refresher and advanced offerings to consolidate its contribution.

Management effectiveness

Several higher education establishments and training organisations are now also running 'Management Effectiveness' courses specifically for women. Some have a base in business knowledge and skills such as finance and marketing. Others cover an established range of skills such as time management, negotiating, stress management and decision making, but take on a distinctive flavour because their participants are women. In sessions on stress, for example, conflicts between different life roles and the pressures of working in competitive environments usually figure as concerns. These courses generally recognise the importance of participants' identity issues to their approach to work, and include activities to clarify personal needs and build confidence.

Redefining management skills for women

Once women pay attention to management skills in this way many established values and assumptions are brought into question. A focus of attention at the moment is the revision of notions such as leadership, management style and management effectiveness from a more female-compatible perspective. This is happening in some courses, but is for now more a conference topic amongst management trainers. Some tentative models are already emerging from this process, including courses on selected topics identified as key skills for women such as influencing. More important than guidelines or prescriptions, is the freedom women are being offered through some development opportunities to explore for themselves and achieve their own uniquely appropriate blend of female and male values from which to operate.

Life planning and career building

Another early training concern amongst women was life planning, and this is still a major priority. The basic format of reviewing one's past history, assessing strengths and weaknesses, identifying un-fulfilled ambitions and so forming plans for future development is already well established. Women bring several distinctive concerns to these activities, and their own pattern of life phases. The early thirties are emerging as a critical time for many as they review their career progress and wonder whether to have children. Balancing career with a home life is a continuing focus of attention, becoming especially significant in choices about whether to marry, have children, move, take promotion or change jobs. Whether to interrupt their career at some point is a particularly difficult decision. Some companies are now offering 'returner schemes' to allow extended leave for parenting, with opportunities for keeping in touch through occasional training or work experience. Although such measures are helpful the dilemmas and plain practical difficulties remain.

For many women these choices are related to how ambitious in conventional terms to be. The managers I interviewed had notions of career which drew on a more female base of values. They wanted a sequence of satisfying and challenging jobs, but upward progression was less important to most of them than leading a balanced life. They were prepared to become self-employed, change occupation or work part time in order to meet other goals. Very few could rely on another person for support, any new directions therefore had to be financially viable. Many of the established women managers I meet are using life planning to explore these possible options, often putting their whole lives in the balance at a particular choice point. Some are wondering whether the strain of working in organisation cultures they find inhospitable is worth the benefits, and are looking for companies which are more influenced by female values. Whatever their choices, women cannot guarantee that anyone else will shape and manage their careers for them. Many life planning reviews therefore offer highly directed advice on career building. They openly declare that to succeed in organisations, women have to be exceptionally clear about their objectives and persistent in pursuing them. Some women reject these ideas and point to their own success through more opportunistic progress.

Sexuality

An area which is beginning to receive training attention, and will most certainly expand, is that of sexuality at work. Courses on sexual harassment are becoming available, aimed at a mixed audience of advisors to victims and victims themselves. As women and men more often work together as equals, individuals are more exposed to dilemmas about sexual attraction. Some women are concerned about the management of sexuality in intimate working relationships, and looking for opportunities to explore their feelings and strategies in this area. This may well become an additional topic in assertion or management effectiveness courses.

Men and women as colleagues

The initiatives covered so far have concentrated on building bridges between women and the organisations in which they work. Work-shops which take 'men and women as colleagues' as their theme offer a more direct opportunity to influence organisational cultures. Typically participants work in both single and mixed sex groups reporting back in full session. Attitudes to work, sex role stereotypes, management styles and so on are not only discussed but put to the test in role plays and problem solving activities. Training objectives are enhanced understanding of the similarities and differences between women and men, individual learning about one's own attitudes and behaviours, and awareness of how organisational structures and cultures carry and enforce norms and values about gender. When workshops draw several employees from one company, it is hoped that further exploration and development will happen on their return to work.

Such workshops require considerable skills from the trainers involved. Sex differences in power, language, values and emotional expression all figure prominently in the discussions themselves and need careful handling if some participants are not to feel misunderstood or even damaged in the process. But the dialogue such arenas offer is a vital next step to developing women's and men's relationships at work and so must be fostered despite its challenges.

CLOSING REMARKS

In this chapter I have charted women's development needs and training provision as they are at the moment. In these terms, we live in times of considerable change. In the USA where affirmative action legislation is extremely powerful, there is now said to be a backlash against paying separate attention to women. In the UK too there are signs that some men resent concentration on women's needs, and are prompted by it to voice more concerns of their own. This is a potentially healthy move if men and women can avoid getting locked into competition for attention and concern. The argument that because one sex suffers disadvantages or difficulties at work, the other cannot legitimately question them is not very convincing. The main danger is that current power differences and cultural patterns will so shape development activities that women's perspectives will remain muted. To guard against this we need both separate development for women to strengthen their perspective and confidence, and joint development through dialogue between women and men.

REFERENCES

(1) Bartol, K. M., 'The sex structuring of organisations: a search for possible causes', *Academy of Management Review*, October, 1978.
(2) Marshall, J., *Women Managers: Travellers in a Male World*, Wiley, 1984.
(3) Capra, C., *The Turning Point: Science, Society and the Rising Culture*, Wildwood House, 1982.

(4) Gilligan, C., *In a Different Voice: Psychological Theory and Women's Development*, Harvard University Press, 1982.

(5) Spender D., *Man Made Language*, Routledge and Kegan Paul, 1980.

(6) *Management Education and Development Journal*, Special Edition, 'Men and Women in Organisations', Spring, vol. 16, no.2, 1985.

(7) Dickson, A., *A Woman in Your Own Right*, Quartet Books, 1982.

FURTHER READING

'Women and Training News' via Ann Cooke, Department of Management Studies, GLOSCAT, Oxstalls Lane, Gloucester.

21

The role of the management trainer

Alun Jones

An increasing number of practising trainers in the United Kingdom are beginning to adopt the language of the organisational development consultant and are moving into the kind of work that is more to do with directly intervening in the organisation than with the traditional activities associated with trainers. Increasingly in the training literature the terms 'intervention' and 'training consultant' are appearing. [1]

The problem is that a large proportion of trainers and of training in the UK is still traditional in nature. Few trainers have any training in the behavioural sciences and most are strongly based in the specific technology of their industry. Their basic practical or academic training is concerned with that technology and their 'training in training' has often been grafted on, sometimes at a minimal level. They have learned by experience about training within their particular industries, and this has continually reinforced a specific 'industrial skills' emphasis in their activities and outlook. This is to be compared with the strong assertion by many professional organisation development consultants that competent intervention must be based on adequate training in the behavioural sciences. [2]

Whichever view is taken, it is apparent that, although trainers in the UK as elsewhere are moving into this field of intervention, there is a vast gulf between the majority of trainers and the organisational consultant. This is understandable as it is clear they they are out of very different stables. Further, although there is a growing body of knowledge and experience about organisation development consulting there is yet little systematic work and literature available about training development and training consulting. And what there is gives an impression of being an extrapolation from the world of the behavioural scientist and the OD consultant.

However, a number of recent research projects have begun to chart this relatively new training territory.[3, 4, 5] These studies have started from the traditional activities of trainers and the traditional processes of training and have then begun extrapolating into the fields of organisational intervention which many trainers are exploring. The intention is that this charting will link up with the growing and well-established field of organisational development.

Some new models and frameworks have been built up which capture and give some conceptual form to the experience being gained. From then it is becoming apparent that management trainers themselves have some learning to do.

LEARNING TO INTERVENE

If trainers are to become more interventionist within organisations, and to make a more direct and significant contribution, then a number of changes are necessary.

Change in the basic 'model'

It has been suggested that much of training in the UK and the activities of trainers have been built upon an 'educational' model (see Figure 21.1). The key to such a model is the strong primary contract between the trainer and the individual trainee. It is left to the trainee to make a subsidiary contract with his/her organisation to apply and utilise the new skills (learning) they have acquired, just as the educational system leaves it largely to individuals to apply within society the education they have acquired.

Thus a transfer and application problem is created by the nature and the methods, and often by the location, of the training. It can be seen from training literature that many trainers and researchers are

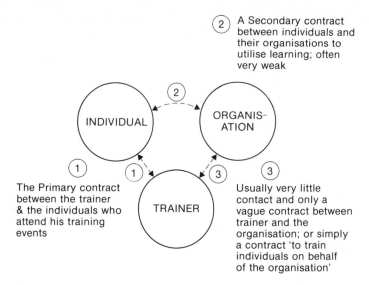

② A Secondary contract between individuals and their organisations to utilise learning; often very weak

INDIVIDUAL

ORGANIS-ATION

②

① ① ③ ③

TRAINER

The Primary contract between the trainer & the individuals who attend his training events

Usually very little contact and only a vague contract between trainer and the organisation; or simply a contract 'to train individuals on behalf of the organisation'

Figure 21.1 Education model

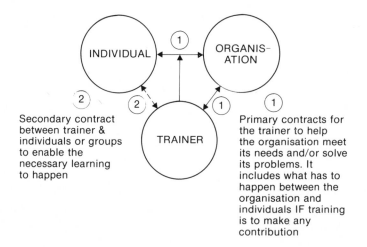

INDIVIDUAL

ORGANIS-ATION

①

② ②

① ①

TRAINER

Secondary contract between trainer & individuals or groups to enable the necessary learning to happen

Primary contracts for the trainer to help the organisation meet its needs and/or solve its problems. It includes what has to happen between the organisation and individuals IF training is to make any contribution

Figure 21.2 An organisational model

well aware of the problem and are taking steps to alleviate it (see recent work at Lancaster by Burgoyne *et al.* and at Glasgow by Huczynski and Logan[6].

The problem can only be solved by changing the underlying model or assumptions on which the whole training activity is based. It demands the trainer 'intervening' more into the organisation itself. He will need to make the primary contract with the organisation and not merely 'provide training' on behalf of the organisation — for few organisational problems are as simple as that. The contract needs to embrace how the learning is going to be applied and utilised, and what else has to happen in support of the training. Probably more important in this organisational model the trainer is concerned to arrange a primary contract between the individual trainee and his organisation, represented often by the immediate manager. The secondary contract is there for the trainer to help bring about the learning that is required as a part of the primary contract. In summary the training, and thus the trainer, takes on more of an organisational emphasis and focus than an educational one. (See Figure 21.2.)

Change in the role of training

It follows from a change of model that a change in the role of training within the organisation will also be required if training is to become more interventionist.[7] Thus a shift needs to be made from merely providing skilled manpower to becoming involved in mainstream organisational processes and problems. The trainer will help to identify where new learning is required and where it will contribute; and then help to cause that learning to happen in a wide variety of ways — not only by providing a specialist 'teaching' service.

Getting involved in mainstream and vital activities and processes which have a direct effect on the organisation's fortunes and performance will have implications for the status of the training function and its place within the organisation for a change in role is an interactive process between what the organisation is willing to accept and what the trainer is able to provide.

Change in the emphasis of activities of trainers

To fulfil this more interventionist role there will also need to be a change in the emphasis of the trainer's activities. The obvious one is that he will have to operate more in the organisation, in departments and in working groups, and less in the training department or training school or room. He will need to put more emphasis on diagnosing the organisational need in depth and in translating it into learning requirements. There must be a better balance between activities aimed at acquisition and those aimed at application of skill, i.e. trainers will need to extend the boundary of their learning interest outside the training room. And this will lead to activities more concerned with evaluating eventual and practical results, and less with assessing the result of the training sessions. The outcome will be a better balance of activities concerned with the whole learning process within the organisation and not mainly with improving the training technology and training expertise within the training department and 'schoolroom.'

Change in skills of trainers

These activities, if they are to be carried out effectively, will demand skills which will be new for very many trainers. [8] Some of them may be termed 'intervention skills' but many are a normal part of any systematic training process. In other words, they are skills which many trainers have not been called upon, or allowed, to apply as a part of their normal activity. In other cases they are special skills within the trainer's armoury which the average trainer has not developed to any significant degree of expertise. Trainers who have established a vital and effective role within their organisations have often achieved this by developing and applying skills which result in more effective intervention and penetration into their organisation. These skills they have applied within a clear and consistent training process which most trainers recognise. If this is to be the experience of more trainers, and if training is to make a more effective contribution in more organisations, then two requirements appear to be necessary:

1 For trainers to develop a more strategic and organisational view of their training activities; this will include the need for trainers to extend their own boundaries of both time and space.
2 For trainers to become more aware of, and then to develop, the training skills which have greatest effect in intervening and penetrating usefully in organisations.

The following section offers an attempt to create a framework or taxonomy of training interventions so that individual trainers might identify and learn how to make a more significant and worthwhile contribution to their organisation's functioning. The third section suggests some practical applications of the taxonomy.

A BASIC TAXONOMY OF INTERVENTIONS

From studies of the experience of trainers who have been developing a more interventionist role, either from outside or as an integral part of their organisation, it is possible to put together a process or cycle which describes the peculiar activities and skills a trainer can contribute to the organisation as he develops a more interventionist stance and role.

The activities can be grouped in a taxonomy under clearly defined areas, although in practice they are neither as neatly grouped nor as chronologically tidy as the list might suggest. They are an extension of the well-known training cycle to which a number of new and crucial activities have been added.

Helping to diagnose the need (diagnosing)

This is both broader and deeper than merely identifying the training need, which sometimes degenerates into 'suggesting the training solution' or 'devising the training plan'. It involves activities which help to diagnose what altogether is required and what part training (or learning) can play in bringing about what is required. It deals in organisational terms and currencies and not in training jargon. It is concerned with organisational needs, goals and problems and not with training activities.

Determining the specific contribution of training (translating)

This is a key link for the trainer and demands a 'translation' of business and organisational needs and objectives into learning needs and objectives. It is probably one of the most vital activities in enabling 'training' to make a real contribution and intervention into the mainstream business. It is an activity many trainers are not often involved in nor skilled at. Yet it is one which the trainer misses out at his peril. It is the key activity where the trainer's strategies (if he has any) can be directly linked with current and future organisational strategies and plans.

Designing learning strategies and methods (designing)

The skilled trainer will bring about a great deal of the required learning through his contacts with managers and their staff in helping them diagnose what is required. Nevertheless an important part of his expertise is also to design training programmes, events or situations to enable learning to happen effectively. Some of this may well need to be achieved away from work in a classroom involving groups of managers and staff. This activity most trainers are well-experienced in as it is the focus of many training of trainers' courses. However great strides have been made in designing the learning which trainers need to keep abreast of.

Developing and organising training resources (resourcing)

A growing aspect of the trainer's managing skills, as opposed to his direct training skills, is his ability to develop all the resources required by the learning design. Thus he will use line managers and supervisors quite often to instruct or train, rather than using specialist trainers or instructors. His role in developing managers, supervisors and others to train their own staff involves him in some critical intervention strategies. In this area of activity his ability to influence the allocations of resources will be measured by the resources he can attract. The need to be in the organisation's networks of decision making will guide him in maintaining close contact with key managers, especially those in charge of finance.

Bringing about the acquisition of learning (implementing)

This is separated from the next step in the process because it still tends to be the practice for many trainers to concentrate mainly on the acquisition of new skill and knowledge. Separation, although it may seem artificial, may help to emphasise the point that both acquisition and application are equally necessary in the process. But it depends where the trainer, and his organisation, draws his boundary. Traditionally his expertise has been to help people acquire skills in a training environment. He ought to have skills there; but the learning that is required may have to be achieved on-the-job, within the context of the day-to-day organisation. The trainer will then have to concentrate his activities in the manager's 'court' and not in the comparative security of the training room.

Enabling the learning to be applied and developed (enabling)

If much of the learning has been achieved on the job then acquisition and application are hopefully achieved together. If, however, training has been brought about in a training situation away from the organisation the trainer will need to give a great deal of attention to helping staff apply what they have learned in their job contexts. Many trainers see this as outside their responsibilities. And unfortunately many managers would have it so. An important series of activities to do with application and development of learning on the job is necessary if the trainer is to achieve more effective intervention and effectiveness in organisational terms. His contacts with managers and his own personal credibility with them will play an important part in this aspect of his work.

Catalysing support action (catalysing)

Closely linked with this activity in the departments of the organisation is the influencing that will almost certainly be necessary to ensure that other things happen within the organisation as well as individuals achieving learning. This activity should be one of the results of diagnosing the need effectively, as that should have revealed the need for a variety of actions and decisions, as well as training ones. Whether or not the trainer acts as a catalyst or stimulus to see that these other things happen will depend partly on his influencing skills. But many other organisational factors will apply here, including competitiveness and inter-organisational 'politics' and rivalry. One important factor is whether managers will allow the trainer to work alongside them as a resource.

Evaluating organisational results (evaluating)

Most training literature on evaluation concentrates on assessing the training activity in training terms. It is often retrospective. But an effective intervention activity concentrates on evaluating the whole of the strategy against the diagnosed need. Often it will involve the managers themselves in evaluating results, assessing what has been learned and applied and what else needs to be activated. In this it is a similar activity to helping them diagnose needs and demands similar skills of data collecting and interpretation. Again, it will be carried out largely inside departments and not in the training room.[9]

These eight categories form a cycle of training interventions which take the trainer more and more outside his traditional boundary of training. Like any cycle it can be entered at any point, and so the trainer's ability to use and develop whatever opportunity is offered as a change to initiate an effective training intervention applies at all points of the cycle.

Usually the cycle begins as the result of some kind of stimulus, either from outside or inside the organisation. Sometimes the trainer himself will provide the stimulus to heighten the awareness of a real need. But he will be on dangerous ground if he merely manipulates the organisation to want his 'solution'. Logically, wherever the cycle starts, the trainer will get round to helping to diagnose the need appropriately and as comprehensively as possible. So this training intervention process can act as a guide to the trainer to ensure that his activities are progressively interventionist and likely to penetrate the organisation. For it is 'inside' the organisation and its processes that the trainer needs to contribute if his activities are to become increasingly effective. This can be illustrated in diagrammatic form as in Figure 21.3.

PRACTICAL APPLICATION OF THE TAXONOMY

How can this taxonomy be applied in practice? Trainers involved in management development have found it useful to divide the taxonomy into three parts: developing every opportunity offered and helping to diagnose the need and translating it into what learning is required clearly form the pre-training activity. In the vernacular it has been called 'getting it right'. The next three categories of the taxonomy: designing, resourcing and implementing are about planning and doing the training, whether in the training department itself or inside line-departments. Those three together can be called 'doing it well'. And the last three, enabling, catalysing and evaluating, put together form the post-training activities, which,

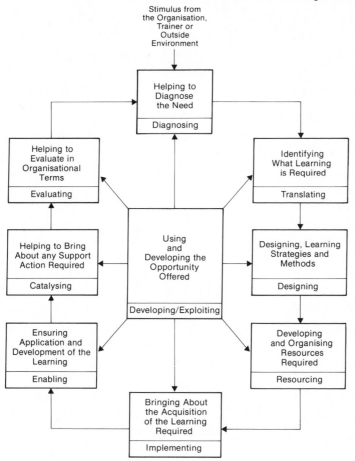

Figure 21.3 The training cycle

when carried out effectively, are all about 'making the training stick'. So in practice it has been useful to look at the taxonomy in three parts particularly where the management trainer's primary role has been to provide training events and programmes:

'GETTING IT RIGHT'→'DOING IT WELL'→'MAKING IT STICK'

Within these categories there are a number of activities which management trainers can follow in order to help them to be more interventionist, starting from their well established programme providing base. Let us examine them one at a time:

Getting it right

Most experienced trainers will admit that the most challenging task they have is to maintain the relevance of their training programme in meeting real organisational needs. Four activities seem to be key:

1 *Building up networks*: in order to develop and exploit opportunities within the organisation the trainer needs to expand his networks of key managers. This will enable him to be on the spot or at least available when problems arise rather than 'out there' in the training department, busily running programmes which may have lost their cutting-edge of relevance.

2 *Organisational understanding*: he needs to spend much more time understanding the context of the problem or the organisational demand within which training or learning is required to make a contribution. His understanding of the organisational need will be a key factor in his ability to translate this into a relevant learning objective. It will also be crucial in his designing learning that managers can actually use and apply.

3 *Before and after*: he needs to spend more time clarifying with managers what has to be done after the training programme both by the learners and their immediate bosses, and others around them at work. The transfer and application problems need to be tackled before the 'training' happens. This will ensure the programme is seen as a part of a total and continuous process and not as an isolated event.

4 *Contracting*: encouraging and 'training' participants to write out contracts about what will be expected to happen on and after the training event and how it will be assessed and measured has been found to be a significant intervention activity. It goes without saying that these contracts need to be the result of enough discussion between participants and their 'bosses' to ensure understanding agreement and commitment. The trainer needs to influence this essential process.

Concentration of effort on these 'getting it right' activities will help to ensure the relevance of the training that is going to go on. As a by-product it can also prepare the learners to want to use the training programme or event for their own purposes and to see it as a part of their own on-going learning process, i.e. to take more responsibility for managing their own development. As trainers are required more and more to demonstrate the value of their activities to the organisation 'getting it right' is becoming an imperative.

Doing it well

Even in this well established traditional area of designing and running training, trainer roles are changing. Three rapidly developing aspects of these changes are worth highlighting here:

1 *Learning to learn*: many trainers have moved the emphasis of their training programmes away from their own skills of teaching and leading towards enabling managers to become more conscious of their own ways of learning. The work of Kolb and Honey and Mumford [9, 10] has developed techniques for making managers more aware of the styles and the preferences of their own learning processes. Developing this awareness within training programmes enables managers to begin to see 'training' as a resource which they need to manage themselves, rather than something a trainer does to them.

2 *Learning to transfer*: a great deal more can be done in most training programmes to encourage and enable managers to apply the learning that they have been achieving. In one way this is just simply a practical application of the learning cycles mentioned above in that managers within the programme are asked to reflect upon what they have been doing, to come to conclusions about it, and to plan to test it out in their work situations. Instead of leaving action planning to the last session of the programme it becomes an integral part of every part of the programme. Managers collect their actions together as a final summary of their 'strategy for action' when they leave to go back to work. And so the trainer lays emphasis on application back at work throughout the programme, rather than simply on acquisition of knowledge and skill while on the programme.

3 *Learning together*: although there are obvious benefits in managers learning more about management and about themselves in stranger groups away from their own organisation,

they also need help to learn together with the managers they have to work with. More and more trainers are designing programmes for family groups of managers. Vertical groups, including a variety of levels or grades in the organisation and multi-disciplinary groups across departments form the more usual training-group. The managers who have to manage together are thus also enabled to learn together. In this way, through dealing with critical masses of managers within the same organisation sharing similar learning the transfer problem of getting the training *into* the organisation afterwards is very often overcome.

Again these developing 'do it well' activities for trainers who are becoming more interventionist are focused on managers taking responsibility for their own learning and making it effective in their own managing situations within the organisation.

Making it stick

The trainer who is developing a more interventionist role within his organisation can carry out a number of activities which ensure that the training he has been organising sticks in the organisation. All of these activities look outward into the organisation and demand the trainer crossing the boundary between his department and the rest of the organisation:

1   *Following-up*: if the trainer is going to have any direct influence at all over what happens after participants leave his training events he must organise follow-up activities. Preferably these are done in person but in some cases he may have to resort to the telephone or written communications. The follow-up is not concerned with helping the participants to learn more about the training event they have left; its main focus is applying the learning within the organisation. It is a catalysing, enabling role where the trainer is concerned to talk not only to the participant, but to his boss and the people around him. It may mean not only dealing with training problems using training jargon and currency, more likely it will involve him in talking about the real issues within the departments in which the participants work. More important, getting involved in these

kinds of discussions about processes within the organisation enables the trainer to see more clearly other training needs which managers may have. In this way it becomes an integral part of the next cycle of 'getting it right'.

2 *Fulfilling contracts*: it is essential that the trainer gets commitment to the participants and their managers reviewing the contracts they made prior to the training event. He can encourage and stimulate this to happen simply by asking for information about the *results* of the discussions about contracts. If he can get involved in these discussions as a part of his follow-up then this obviously puts him in a good position for further influence and intervention. It goes without saying that the trainer must there be talking in the manager's language and not in training language. Many trainers are finding the value of subcontracts between pairs on the same programme. This enables managers to experience the process of using colleagues as training resources and not simply looking to the trainer for counsel and help. Where the management development programme is based on one organisation or one department this subcontracting clearly lends itself to action learning sets, tackling real problems and issues within the organisation.

3 *Evaluating results*: evaluation has been found to be one of the most powerful techniques for both intervening in the organisation and making training stick. Clearly it has to be concerned with the results of the training in organisational terms and not with how well the training event was conducted. Further, it has to be carried out by participants and their managers and not by the trainer – data is for their use in applying the learning, making use of it and getting value from it within their own departments. This is a very different focus for evaluation activities from the more traditional ways of evaluating courses by looking at them retrospectively. A technique called 'figure of eight' evaluation has been developed which ensures that evaluation looks outwards into the results in the organisation.[11]

CONCLUSIONS AND IMPLICATIONS

If the trainer whose main responsibilities include management development intends to develop his role along this more inter-ventionist path, then the implications are manifold. First of all he needs to get the *balance* of his own activities more appropriately geared to getting it right and making it stick. This might mean developing a whole lot of new skills. Then, he will need to redefine his *boundary* from training and development, the training school and his training programmes so that it embraces the whole organisation. His *interest* must now encompass the processes, systems, relationships and goals within the organisation as well as the individual managers and their training needs. His *focus* shifts from concentrating on individual managers and their development to developing groups of managers and whole departments to meet their particular organ-isational goals. His *language* becomes the manager's language of management rather than the trainer's language: fluent in both he becomes an effective translator. Finally, he learns to deal in organisational currencies, in achievements and results of the organisation and not only with training and learning currencies and achievements within his training events.

Eventually he becomes not the trainer to whom managers go to be developed, sometimes sceptically and reluctantly, but the resource whom they invite in to help them with their organisational problems. Although that might sound like a promised land far beyond the reach of many management trainers, more and more are beginning to tread the path towards it. The taxonomy offers some signposts along that path.

REFERENCES

(1) See the series of articles in *European Training Journal*, vol. 4, no. 5, 1975; G. S. Odiorne, 'Training to be Ready for the '90s', *Training and Development Journal*, December, 1980.

(2) Bennis, W., *Organisation Development*, Addison-Wesley, 1969.

(3) French, W. L. and Bell, C. H. Jnr., *Organisation Development*, Prentice-Hall, 1973.

(4) Argyris, C., *Intervention Theory and Method*, Addison-Wesley, 1970.

(5) Binsted, D. and Stuart, R., 'Designing Reality in Management Learning Events', *Personnel Review*, vol. 8, no. 3, 1979.

(6) Huczynski, A. and Logan, D., 'Learning to Change', *Leadership and Organisation Development Journal*, vol. 1, no. 3, 1980.

(7) Zender, J., 'The Painful Turnabout in Training', *Training and Development Journal*, December, 1980.

(8) Manpower Services Commission, First Report of the Training of Trainers' Committee, 1979.

(9) Kolb, D., *Experiential Learning*, Prentice-Hall, 1984.

(10) Honey, P. and Mumford, A., *Manual of Learning Styles*, Honey, 1982.

(11) Jones, J. A. G., 'Figure of Eight Evaluation – A Fundamental Change in the Trainer's Approach', *The Training Officer*, vol. 17, no. 9, September, 1981.

22

Evaluation

Peter Bramley

The idea of the training department as a passive provider of a menu of courses appears to be giving way to the concept of training as a management function which contributes to the growth and development of the organisation. As a result, training managers' roles are changing and their skills of boundary management (for instance acquiring resources, building relationships and co-ordinating activities with other functions) are becoming even more crucial to the survival of their departments as the latter become more exposed. At some time, all institutions, whether medical, educational or political, are required to provide some evidence of their effectiveness. With training departments this evidence has usually been established by reputation – of the trainers, the training manager or by repeat business – and not by indices of changed participant behaviour or increases in organisational effectiveness. When it becomes necessary to struggle for resources, reputations do not offer strong support for arguments and more convincing evaluative information can help. The act of following up training to discover if it has met the needs identified also helps to build a better relationship between the training department and the line managers. These relationships can become crucial in survival battles. There are also obvious benefits for the trainers in that the information collected provides a more accurate appreciation of the training need as well as indicating strengths and weaknesses of various parts of the programme and any problems of transferring back to the workplace. Evaluation can thus provide a sound track record, improve boundary relationships and also increase the professionalism and thus the status of the training department. It is intended that the word 'training' should be defined broadly, as a process which assists managers to learn and improve their ability to perform management tasks, rather than narrowly, as a procedure aimed at highly specific and immediately useful skills. The choice of the word 'training', rather than 'development' does, however, imply that the emphasis is upon management learning from the organisational rather than the individual point of view.

PURPOSES OF EVALUATION

The strategy employed in an evaluation, the techniques used and the particular aspect of the learning process which is examined, all vary with the purpose for which the evaluation is intended. Five main purposes can be identified: feedback, control, research, intervention and power games.

Feedback

Feedback evaluation provides quality control over the design and delivery of training activities. In general the trainer will be most concerned with direct feedback related to learning:

What did the trainees learn?

Did that role play provide realistic interactions?

but may be interested in longer term issues:

Were the correct objectives set?

How much of the learning is being used in the workplace?

Feedback during learning will also be of interest to the participants. It is considered to be an essential part of the learning process in all three fundamental approaches to management training – behaviour shaping, information processing and experiential learning.

Control

Control evaluation relates training policy and practice to organisational goals. The training manager will often wish to evaluate how well training policy reflects organisational purposes:

Does this training help towards any of the organisation's goals? There could also be concern for value for money provided by the training function:

Is that (external) course worth the money?

Is CBL likely to be cheaper than traditional instruction, and at least as effective as conventional group training, for achieving those objectives?

Control evaluation could also answer questions like:

Will training give a better solution to the problem than re-structuring or job design?

Research

Research evaluation seeks to add to knowledge of training principles and practice in a way that will have a more general application than feedback evaluation:

What factors help people to transfer learning back to the work-place?

What do people learn from role playing?

Research evaluation can also serve to improve the techniques available for other purposes (feedback, control and intervention).

Intervention

Discussing evaluation issues with line managers can lead to a reappraisal of their responsibility for ensuring that learning is trans-ferred. Specifically, it can change the way in which the employing manager selects people for training, briefs them before the event and debriefs them afterwards. Increasing his activity in these areas must improve the effectiveness of the training. Planned intervention through evaluation can also change the way in which the training department works. Different organisations have different levels of receptivity to the idea of evaluating programmes. The differences reflect, on the one hand, opinions concerning the feasibility and desirability of evaluation and, on the other, specific policy pressures and priorities. In many training departments the intervention will be aimed at unfreezing the attitude that evaluation is a good idea in principle but too difficult to practice.

Power games

Evaluation measures can be misused to play power games. Someone decides what the conclusion ought to be and then assembles 'evaluation evidence' to support it. This is not uncommon and it poses problems for the evaluator. External consultants may realise that they are being used and may be able to avoid further manipulative use of data. Internal evaluators may, however, not be able to refuse to continue with the evaluation even when they are aware of the uses to which the data is being put.

APPROACHES TO EVALUATION

Having decided on a purpose, or set of purposes, for the evaluation, the next phase is to select a suitable approach. Most authors of papers describing evaluations appear to suggest that the approach which they are advocating is unique. In a sense this is true, no one ever exactly replicates an evaluation, but it is possible to classify approaches into five types – goal-based, systems, goal-free, professional review and quasi-legal.

Goal-based

Goal-based evaluation starts from the position that training activities are cyclic. Firstly, needs are identified and then precise, specific (and preferably behavioural) objectives are set. The cycle ends with assessments of the extent to which the objectives have been attained, of the relationship between amounts of learning and methods employed and of the extent to which the objectives achieved contribute to meeting the need identified. This approach is almost universally recommended by trainers for trainers and there have been numbers of attempts to describe various levels at which the objectives should be set. Figure 22.1 is an attempt to cross-classify the better known approaches. The framework used on the left is chronological, based on the sequence of events in learning and then trying to apply the learning in the workplace.

The most comprehensive and convincing of these frameworks is that proposed by Hamblin (1974).[1] The five levels of evaluation are linked by a cause and effect chain ie.

Areas	Components	Suchman[14] (1967)	Kirkpatrick[15] (1967)	Warr, Bird & Rackham[16] (1970)	Glossary[17] (1971)	Hamblin[1] (1974)
Within the Training	Judgements of the quality of trainee's experiences		Reactions	Reaction		Reaction
	Feedback to trainees about learning					
	Measures of gain or change	Immediate	Learning	Immediate	Internal Validation	Learning
	Feedback to trainers about methods					
At the Job after training	Relevance of the learning goals				External Validation	
	Measures of use of learning or change of behaviour	Intermediate	Behaviour	Intermediate		Job Behaviour
	Retrospective feedback to trainers					
Organisational Effectiveness	Measures of change in organisational performance	Ultimate	Results	Ultimate	Evaluation?	Organisation
	Implementation of individual action plans or projects					
Social or cultural values	Measures of social costs and benefits				Evaluation?	Ultimate
	Human resource accounting					Ultimate

Figure 22.1 Levels at which objectives can be set

	training
leads to	**reactions**
which leads to	**learning**
which leads to	**changes in behaviour**
which leads to	**changes in the organisation**
which leads to	**changes in the achievement of**
	ultimate goals

which can break between any of the levels.

Few trainers carry the logic of the goals based approach through to asking about how worthwhile the training was. When this is done a number of problems arise, as it is difficult to demonstrate clear linkages between the objectives of higher and lower levels in the organisation and hence to establish the link between training objectives and organisational goals. This is particularly true of management training where there may be no clear connection between job tasks, nominal training objectives and training content. The choice of appropriate objectives may also be complicated by the co-existence of both official goals and actual goals which govern behaviour and rewards. It is also the case that in some 'training' events the symbolic importance of attending becomes more important than the content; in this case, evaluation against objectives would be irrelevant.

There is a clear bias within this chapter towards the idea that successful training is based upon a fairly precise specification of aims and objectives. This does not imply that 'development' is not worthwhile, rather that there should be some clarity in the expectations of the parties involved in the process. For instance, some management programmes are habitually justified by managers and trainers as providing 'a broadening experience'. When pressed to explain the concept of 'broadening' most responses can be classified into two areas:

1   improving contacts across functional boundaries;
2   learning to work in teams rather than as an individual.

At this level of conceptualisation, it is possible to write objectives. What is being suggested is that trainers have to tread a path between setting aims so vague that no one can tell whether or not they have been achieved, and setting behavioural objectives so tightly drawn that no room is left for unintended outcomes and the complexity and subtlety of human behaviour.

Systems

Systems evaluation sets out to answer questions like:
    Is the programme reaching the target population?
    Is it effective?
    Is it cost effective?
These sorts of questions are posed by policymakers looking for 'hard' data and they largely exclude the opinions of those involved. The main difficulty in applying this approach (which is widely recommended for evaluating social and educational programmes) to training, is to decide on criteria of effectiveness. Effectiveness criteria which satisfy accountants are hard enough to find in technical training, they are virtually impossible to find in management training. This approach is used in some organisations and training departments must take some responsibility for it. Many of them produce statistics each year which represent the 'business' that they are doing in terms of numbers on courses. No one, within the training department, believes that the headcount has more than a tenuous relationship to learning which is of use to the organisation. Using this headcount as the sole form of evaluation is tantamount to abdicating and leaving the field to accountants.

Goal-free evaluation

Objectives or goal-based evaluation yields a measure of intent and this may not be all that has been achieved. The evaluator measures what he expects to find and tends not to recognise, or value, unanticipated learning and behaviour change. Goal-free methods of evaluation overcome this problem. They have usually been proposed as a reaction to the ubiquity of goal-based evaluations but their value to trainers is more likely to be in the ways they can complement rather than challenge that approach.

The evaluator sets out, deliberately unaware of the objectives for the programme, to talk to participants about whether some of their needs were met. It is thus possible to pick up unintended effects as well as those expected by the programme organisers. It is also possible to discuss, with the participants, alternative ways in which their needs might have been met.

Goal-free methods emphasise opinions and they have the problem of gaining consensus on the criteria by which opinions can be judged. They are worth considering when it is necessary to evaluate management learning activities where reasons for attending vary widely and where the participants go back to a variety of jobs. The strategy of goal-free methods can also complement goal-based evaluations where the participants are being followed-up in interviews. Questions about the individual's needs when attending, to what extent they were met and alternative ways of meeting them, can clearly add valuable information. It is more likely that this information will be wide ranging if these questions are asked before the participants are focused on the intended goals of the programme.

Professional review

Most courses leading to professional recognition are approved by a committee which reviews evidence of what the course will contain and whether it reaches the desired standard. This sort of approach can be used within an organisation, to consider the relevance of a syllabus to organisational requirements, and the breadth and quality of a training programme. An informal variety of this is quite common; the training manager offers a particular programme and puts it into the brochure because he/she has carried out a 'professional review' of it.

The approach should be made rather more formal if it is to carry weight. As a minimum the reviewing body should include some diversity of opinion and should agree some criteria of judgement. This might well be an economic way of evaluating a programme but there are likely to be some political problems. Trainers, like most professional people, do not like to have others investigating the way in which they work and they deeply resent public criticism.

Quasi-legal

To adopt this approach, a tribunal is set up and witnesses are called to testify and submit evidence. Great care is taken to hear a wide range of evidence (opinions, values and beliefs) from the organisers of the programme and the 'users' as well as accountants. Such an approach has been used to evaluate social programmes but not, to our knowledge, for learning activities sponsored by organisations. It might, however, be suitable for something wide ranging – for instance, a full review of the purpose, strategy and value of management training and development.

Reliability and validity

It should be obvious, from a consideration of the various strategies open, that evaluation will never produce absolute truth. The objectives and systems approaches lead to the collection of 'hard' facts which can be reliably measured but the evaluators hold values which determine which pieces of information are collected. The other approaches are subjective in their method of collecting information but attempt to get at a wider 'truth'. Qualitative techniques can be made more reliable by using experimental design considerations, for instance:

1   make sure that the sample interviewed is representative of the target population;
2   use a standardised interview schedule and record the answers verbatim;
3   use more than one interviewer and agree on what has been said;
4   interview a sample of those who have not yet attended training as a control for organisational peaks and troughs.

The evidence produced in an evaluation report should be both credible (i.e. have some reliability of measurement) and useful. It is a mistake to concentrate on reliable, objective facts if they convince no one. It is better to use more subjective methods of data collection and relate conclusions and interpretations to the data in a way that can be defended as 'fair'. The objectivity comes from a certainty that if someone else had carried out the evaluation he/she would have come to similar conclusions.

TECHNIQUES FOR EVALUATING TRAINING

Figure 22.2 (adapted from Bramley & Newby, 1984)[2] is an attempt to link elements of the training cycle with suitable evaluation techniques.

Area of Evaluation and Component Elements	Techniques
1. Within the training	
1.1. Judgements of the quality of trainees' experience.	Sessional and terminal reactions forms; Group discussion; Structured and un-structured individual comment.
1.2. Feedback to trainees concerning learning performance.	Programmed learning and CBT; Video and audio recording; Attitude questionnaires; Objective tests of knowledge, skill or attitude acquisition; Mutual observation; Repertory Grid.
1.3. Measures of learning gain or behaviour change as a result of training.	Pre/post tests of knowledge, skill or attitude changes; Gain ratios; Oral examination; Self-analysis.
1.4. Immediate feedback to trainers concerning learning methods.	Session reaction scales; Results of tests of learning (from 1.2 & 1.3); Reactions notebooks; Observation by trainers/researchers; Interview.
2. Back at the job, after the training.	
2.1. Relevance of the learning goals to the originally specified needs.	Re-examination of original identified training needs; Questionnaire; Action Planning; Performance Review.
2.2. Measures of the use of learning or change of behaviour at work tasks.	Pre-post sampling of work activities; Observation; Critical incident analysis; Interview (with manager, or other); Appraisal or Performance Review; Self-appraisal;
2.3. Retrospective/considered feedback to trainers on learning methods and training strategy.	Data from 1.4 combined with interview; Comparative analysis of cost-effectiveness.
2.4. Studies of factors affecting use of learning in the workplace.	Data from 2.2 combined with interview.
2.5. Studies of individual learning and development/ uniqueness of learning.	Participant observation; Interview; Repertory Grid; Self-analysis.
3. Organisational Effectiveness	Output goals like quantity, quality, variety, System goals like growth, productivity.
3.1. Measures of change in indices of organisational performance.	Resource acquisition/competitiveness satisfying customers Internal processes like team effectiveness, morale, boundary management.
3.2. Measures of trainee implementation of individual action plans, or projects.	Reviews (individual or group-based) of progress in implementing plans or projects; 3.2 may usefully be combined with 2.4.
3.3 Cost effectiveness of training.	Costing training; Cost-benefit analysis; Cost-effectiveness analysis; Cost-utility analysis; "Absence of Problems".

Figure 22.2 Elements of the training cycle and evaluation techniques

During or at the end of the course	3 to 6 months after the course
Knowledge acquisition	Retention of new knowledge
Increase in skills	Retention/application of skills
Attitude change	Maintenance of new attitudes
Perceived learning	Implementation of action plans
Ratings of the course	
Ratings of the tutors	
Satisfaction	
Classroom behaviour	

Figure 22.3 Evaluation criteria: Individual changes (taken from Bramley, 1985) [3]

ASSESSMENT OF INDIVIDUAL CHANGES

Criteria by which individual changes can be assessed are given in Figure 22.3.

The last four items on the left of Figure 22.3 are trainee reactions to the learning activity. They are usually measured by a 'reactionnaire' filled in during the programme. Many management training events are evaluated solely at this level and the reactionnaires tend to monitor enjoyment in the belief that what we enjoy we remember. There are, however, better criteria available. For instance, Hamblin (1974)[1] describes how to set objectives at this level which will improve the quality of the feedback. It is also the case that most learning activities are intended to change levels of knowledge or skills or attitudes and these can usually be measured.

Changes in knowledge

Many jobs can be described by the sort of knowledge required at three levels:

1 Knowing a range of simple facts, rules, lists etc.
2 Knowing a range of procedures, how to do things

3   Recognising or analysing a situation and then selecting a suitable procedure.

The function of training can be seen as identifying what knowledge is required at each of these levels for satisfactory job performance, identifying what the trainees know before training and attempting to close the gap. It is clear from this that the evaluation process should be a test of knowledge linked to the required levels and given before and after training. This procedure is quite rare in management training, probably because the initial analysis is not carried out, there is very little research on what managers actually need to know in order to do their jobs. Knowledge is usually taught in the belief that it is necessary for satisfactory job performance and the evaluation is thus not complete until the participant has been followed back into the job to discover if the new knowledge is useful.

A simple questionnaire may well be sufficient. Questions like:
How useful is knowledge of this for your job?
Have you used knowledge of this in the last six months?
Was the reference material given out adequate?
are asked for each topic discussed during the learning activity. The use of such questionnaires can be very revealing. Tutors have a tendency to show their expertise by discussing some topics in far more depth than is necessary, thus taking up time which could be more valuably used for other (more needed) topics.

Changes in attitudes and interpersonal skills

This is a very confused area in which to attempt to evaluate. It is confused because most of the trainers are actually trying to change attitudes but are calling it skills training. An attitude may be viewed as a predisposition to act, a state of readiness or a tendency to react in a certain way. Attitudes can be changed in training programmes and the changes are often assessed by some form of reactionnaire or end-of-course feedback session. A better technique is a pre/post assessment using a simple form of repertory grid (Honey, 1979,[4] provides a very detailed example of how to do this). Following up attitude changing activities to discover whether the changes are maintained in the workplace is quite difficult to do and it is doubtful whether this actually is worthwhile. The assumption is that changing the attitude actually changes behaviour. This assumption can be avoided by enlisting the employing managers' help in filling in questionnaires which rate the frequency of the desired behaviour shown by the participant before and after training. The manager's interest is usually crucial to whether any change in attitude achieved on the programme will result in change in behaviour at the workplace and if he/she cannot be persuaded to help in the evaluation it will usually imply little transfer of learning.

A skills training model is very different from a generalised attitude change design. The skill must be specific, clearly described, and isolated from critical job incidents as being important to job success. In training, the skill is demonstrated then the participants practise it and get feedback on their performance. The crucial aspect of the training is the level of fidelity of the practice and feedback. Some psychological fidelity – that the participants perceive it as being like the real situation – is necessary for motivation and thus learning. High environmental fidelity – the extent to which the learning situation duplicates the actual stimuli and gives an opportunity to respond in realistic ways – is necessary for transfer. The model is derived from operator skills training and has proved successful in supervisory and management training for such skills as: conducting a performance review; handling a discrimination complaint; correcting inadequate work quality. How the training was designed and evaluated is described in a very useful book by Goldstein and Sorcher, 1974,[5] and further evaluations were carried out by Latham and Saari, 1979.[6]

Other skills like 'appraisal interviewing' and 'chairmanship' have also been trained using the skills model. The design and evaluations are described in Rackham and Morgan (1977).[7] In both these skills approaches the feedback was given in job situations rather than in training centres. They also differ from most inter-personal skills courses, in that the behaviours trained were very specific and very carefully identified from critical incident analysis. Many inter-personal skills learning activities are very generalised and reflect the trainers' view of what is desirable, rather than actual job situations. It has proved to be very difficult to evaluate such programmes against job changes, indeed many would argue that such training cannot be expected to produce job changes.

Perceived learning and action plans

Sometimes it is not clear to the tutors which aspects of a programme will be most useful to the participants. In such situations the participants can be asked to develop an action plan during the course. At the end of each day they are asked to feed back to the group any useful things they have learned during that day and how they think they might apply them at work. By the end of the programme they will have a list of items which can then be clustered and ranked in some order of priority. Good action plans specify what the participants will do on return to the workplace, i.e. behavioural statements in some detail. The action plan produced is a useful piece of feedback to the course tutors, it is also an excellent basis for a follow-up of the programme. On return to work it should be discussed with the employing manager and he/she or the course tutors can review progress after some months.

How much of the action plan has been implemented?

Which actions are still likely?

What positive organisational benefits have arisen from your action plan?

Follow-up interviews

Interviewing is expensive and it should only be used when questionnaires will not provide the quality of information necessary. Situations where this might be the case include:

1   re-appraising previously identified training needs
2   exploring transfer of learning to the workplace
3   relating training events to organisational goals

(and some others as suggested in Figure 22.2).

The interview schedule should start with open-ended questions to allow the participant to express views or describe effects which may be unexpected (i.e. a goal-free approach). Later in the interview the topics covered on the programme can be discussed as well as the objectives that were set. Often at this stage, information can be collected by the use of simple questionnaires interspersed with more open questions.

IS EVALUATION WORTH THE INVESTMENT?

Evaluation requires the expenditure of energy and time and, if it is to be an integral part of training practice, a high level of commitment. The costs can be heavy and, if the evaluation is to be an investment rather than a loss, the importance, frequency and cost of the training programme must be examined. Importance is best judged against anticipated benefits from the learning or the consequences of not ensuring that the training has been effective (for instance in safety training). Some training events are essentially social (chances to meet people from other functions etc.) and, although valued by the organisations and by the participants, would not be important in our sense. It seems unlikely that evaluation of such events would be worth the cost. Frequency is also an obvious criterion. Evaluation of one-off programmes is often not worth the time and money. However, if the training event was designed to help solve an important problem, that criterion would outweigh frequency. Some evaluation information can be gathered relatively inexpensively but follow-up interviewing is always costly. If this is being planned, it needs to be costed and the cost compared with that of the programme and the likely uses of the evaluation report. Interviewing does however, have a great value in setting up links with employing managers and this aspect of boundary management ought not to be ignored.

The data produced in an evaluation study is likely to be a source of power. How the findings are used, indeed to whom they are delivered, can determine who will benefit and who might lose. This will certainly be the case where the primary purpose of the evaluation is that of control, for example central evaluation of decentralised training, or management commissioned evaluation. Most evaluation feedback should be useful rather than threatening but the training product can never be evaluated without some judgement being made about the trainer responsible. This could account for the widespread defensiveness among practitioners when faced with proposals for evaluation. In this chapter it has been argued that evaluation can increase the quality of the training produced and thus the effectiveness of the training department. It can also improve relationships with the functions which use the training services. Management trainers have largely avoided the challenge of evaluating their services. The consequence may be that, by default, they will be assessed only in terms of financial appraisal.

ORGANISATIONAL EFFECTIVENESS

Many would argue that management training and development cannot be evaluated against organisational effectiveness because the effort of individuals has little effect upon the overall performance to the organisation. This is understandable, but it is a mistake to consider organisational effectiveness only in terms of the achievement of high level organisational goals. Organisational effectiveness is not a unitary concept, there are many ways in which one can look at it, for instance: achieving product goals; achieving system goals; satisfying customers; acquiring the necessary or desirable share of resources; the quality of internal processes like teamwork or co-operation across functional boundaries.

The word 'organisation' can be defined as the whole organisation, the function, or the workgroup. In a survey of views on the effectiveness of training, which was carried out for a large UK industrial organisation, we found all of these levels and varieties of concept being used to explain what individuals meant by effective work practices. Over two thirds of the responses given were related to the work group or function level, and were about how the group or function was valued by others in the organisation, or how good communications were within the group or function. In that organisation other criteria of organisational effectiveness, besides high level goals, were being used and the criteria were in areas where training can have a marked effect and where its effect can be isolated from other organisational variables. Peters and Waterman (1982)[8] indicate that knowing what 'good' is, is something that has to be learned and that the learning comes from asking questions like, 'what things of superb quality happen in the . . . area?' They believe that excellence is achieved by increasing the likelihood of high quality things happening and that this is an incremental process; a thousand little things done a little better rather than solving 'the big problem'. This supports the view that management training goals defined in terms of organisational effectiveness, should be fairly precise and also modest.

Product goals

Many organisations have basic measurements of work output, for instance:

Quantity: produced, completed, processed, sold, turnover etc.

Quality: rejects, scrap, error rates etc.

Variety: diversity of products etc.

It is sometimes possible to evaluate training events against this sort of criterion (for instance Latham and Saari, 1979,[5] showed that the groups working for trained foremen were more productive than those working to 'untrained' foremen) but it is necessary to control for variations in organisational performance which have nothing to do with training. This means that the output of a comparable part of the organisation, where training has not yet been given, is monitored on the same time series of measurements as the group under examination. Often this is just not possible; if the organisation believes that the training is likely to be useful it will be reluctant not to give it to the 'control' departments/branches etc. simply to set up an experimental comparison. It is also very difficult to set up a true control group. There is usually some incidental learning involved in the process of measurement and via the organisational grapevine. This may affect levels of performance and thus obscure the effect of the 'official' learning achieved on the programme.

System goals

Most organisations have systems goals like:

growth in assets, sales, manpower or

deadline rates, percentage of quota achieved, on-time shipments or

reduction of stoppages, machine down time, overtime worked.

Provided techniques of assessing these have been developed within the organisations they can be used as criteria against which to assess management learning. Once again, however, some sort of control will be necessary to isolate the effect of the learning from the peaks and troughs of organisational performance. If the techniques of assessing system goals do not already exist it is doubtful whether the evaluator will be able to develop them within a reasonable cost, for the evaluation. One way of trying to achieve system goals (and also product goals) through learning is to adopt a problem solving or project based approach. What little is known about motivation in adults suggests that they are eager to solve what they regard as important problems. It would thus seem likely that learning experiences which enable them to tackle current problems would be well received. This may account for the growing popularity of self-development and action-learning approaches to management learning. Certainly, problem centred approaches can give good return on training investment. Woodward (1975)[9] for instance, was able to show an average return on investment of 2.9:1 on projects done as part of a NEBSS course.

Acquiring resources

Effectiveness can be assessed by the extent to which the organisation acquires needed resources, the emphasis being on inputs to increase competitiveness rather than on outputs. The criteria for evaluation are usually long-term comparisons and it is difficult to isolate the effects of learning activities. However, aspects of resource acquisition which can easily be related to training output are:

Increasing the pool of trained staff;

Increasing employment flexibility;

Developing skills and abilities for future job requirements.

Satisfying customers

Many organisations survey customer satisfaction in some way and it may be possible to relate this to learning activities. Care must be taken to control for variations in image which have nothing to do with training. For instance, at the time of writing, British Rail are training staff in customer relations and advertising on television to tell the public that this is happening. If this initiative results in fewer complaints, it will be extremely difficult to decide how much of the reduction is attributable to training.

If the 'organisation' is defined as the workgroup or department, then how well this satisfies those who contact it can be more directly related to training. Surveys of things like 'confidence in', 'loyalty to' and 'what they do which obstructs things which we want to do' can be carried out before and after training.

Ford Europe recently carried out a large scale organisational development project based upon this sort of approach. The heads of the various functions were asked to write down what the other functions did which helped them and what each did which hindered. These lists were assembled into wall displays and, for the first time, the top few managers in each function were able to see how each of the other functions valued their contribution. The training input was largely a facilitation of group problem solving so that functions could draw up plans for how to improve their 'image'.

Internal processes

Effectiveness can be defined in terms of smooth information flows, lack of internal strain, clear definitions of roles, good co-operation between functions or effective teamwork. Efforts to improve indices of these might be evaluated in terms of hard data like grievances, disciplinary actions, absenteeism, sick rates, or turnover but are more likely to be assessed by use of subjective opinions of 'how we were' or 'how we would like to be'. A whole range of survey instruments to measure attitudes in this area has been produced within the organisational development movement. A useful source of such instruments is Cook *et al.* (1981)[10]

Team development

Quite often problems in the internal process area are tackled by development of a work team, either to solve problems, improve interpersonal skills or to clarify roles. Working with a team to help it tackle what it sees as problems can give a high return on training investment. Many quality circles have achieved greater levels of productivity and quality and the average return on training investment is quoted at between 5:1 and 8:1 (Robson, 1982).[11] Working on interpersonal skills within groups (e.g. Woodcock, 1979)[12] can be shown to be effective by using pre/post surveys of opinions within the group. Groups regularly report improvements in agreeing goals, increasing co-operation and reducing conflict. There is not so much evidence that these improvements can be linked to higher levels of organisational effectiveness. Clarifying roles within groups is also a potentially fruitful strategy. Belbin (1981)[13] describes ways in which this can be done and some criteria for evaluation.

TRAINING AND ORGANISATIONAL EFFECTIVENESS

Most of the attempts at changing individual behaviour are based upon an educational model – encourage the individual to learn something which is said to be useful and then let him find uses for the learning. The model is shown in Figure 22.4.

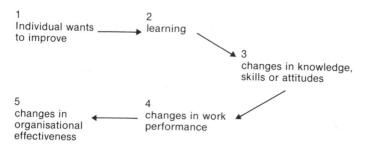

Figure 22.4

The link between 3 and 4 frequently is not made, because there is no one at the workplace to help, or the organisational climate is unsuitable. The link between 4 and 5 may not be visible because organisational effectiveness is defined at too broad a level. These are problems of transfer of training and attempts are made to overcome them by the use of action plans, precise behavioural objectives or by enlisting the help of the manager. The transfer problem is, however, inherent in, and created by the model used. Most of the methods of increasing organisational effectiveness mentioned above are actually interventions and here the model as shown in Figure 22.5 is very different.

The problem of transfer does not arise here. The learning is directly related to making progress in solving the problem identified and its effectiveness is assessed by the achievement of the incremental changes specified.

The use of this interventionist model has quite wide ranging implications for the way in which the training function operates.

1 Needs are identified by line managers and discussed with trainers. The emphasis is on problems to be solved and goal to be achieved, not on training activities.

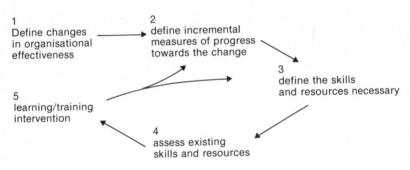

Figure 22.5

2   The trainers need more understanding of the organisation and criteria of effectiveness used by managers. They will also need to be more politically aware as they will often be operating as individuals within functions and not in a training centre with other trainers.

3   The tasking and controlling of trainers and the setting of priorities become much more difficult.

4   The methods of training are likely to be on-job facilitation of teamwork, action learning, or self development. Skills which are in rather short supply become crucial and more common skills, like polished presenting, become irrelevant.

5   Evaluation is not something done with end of course happy sheets, but is an integral part of the learning cycle. It will be carried out jointly by trainers and managers.

Training as an intervention is a trend which is gaining in strength. It is an exiting and challenging trend but it is creating a good deal of understandable anxiety. Using this model, training is evaluated as a management function which contributes to the achievement of organisational goals; it is not evaluated using cosy statistics of person/days training or number of beds filled in the training centre.

REFERENCES

(1)   Hamblin, A. C., *Evaluation and Control of Training*, McGraw-Hill, 1974.

(2)   Bramley, P. and Newby., A. C., 'Evaluation of Training',

Journal of European Industrial Training 1984, vol. 8, no. 6, 10-16.

(3) Bramley, P., *The Evaluation of Training: A Practical Guide*, BACIE, 1985.

(4) Honey, P., 'The Repertory Grid. How to use it as a pre/post test to validate courses', *Industrial and Commercial Training*, Sept. 1979, 359-369.

(5) Goldstein, A. P. and Sorcher M., *Changing Supervisor Behaviour*, Pergamon Press Inc., New York, 1974.

(6) Latham, G. P. and Saari, L. M., 'Application of Social Learning Theory to Training Supervisors through Behavioural Modeling', *Journal of Applied Psychology*, 1979, vol. 64, no. 3, pp. 239-46.

(7) Rackham, N., and Morgan, T., *Behaviour Analysis in Training*, McGraw-Hill, 1977.

(8) Peters, T. J. and Waterman, R. H., *In Search of Excellence*, Harper & Row, New York, 1982.

(9) Woodward, N., 'A cost-benefit analysis of supervisor training', *Industrial Relations Journal*, 1975, vol. 6, no. 2, pp. 41-7.

(10) Cook, J. D., Hepworth, S. J., Wall, T. D. and Warr, P. B., *The Experience of Work*, Academic Press Inc., London, 1981.

(11) Robson, M., *Quality Circles: A Practical Guide*, Gower, 1982.

(12) Woodcock, M., *Team Development Manual*, Gower, 1982.

(13) Belbin, M., *Management Teams: Why they succeed or fail*, Heinemann, London, 1981.

(14) Suchman, E. A., *Evaluative Research*, Russell Sage, 1967.

(15) Kirkpatrick, D. L., 'Evaluation of Training', in Craig R. L. and Bittel, L. R. (eds), *Training and Development Handbook*, McGraw-Hill, New York, 1967.

(16) Warr, P., Bird, M., and Rackham, N., *Evaluation of Management Training*, Gower, 1970.

(17) 'Glossary of Training Terms', HMSO, London, 1971.

23

Team building*

Bill Critchley and David Casey

TEAMBUILDING – AT WHAT PRICE AND AT WHOSE COST?

It all started during one of those midnight conversations between consultants in a residential workshop. We were running a team-building session with a top management group and something very odd began to appear. Our disturbing (but also exciting) discovery was that for most of their time this group of people had absolutely no need to work as a team; indeed the attempt to do so was causing more puzzlement and scepticism than motivation and commitment. In our midnight reflections we were honest enough to confess to each other that this wasn't the first time our team building efforts had cast doubts on the very validity of teamwork itself, within our client groups.

We admitted that we had both been working from some implicit assumptions that good teamwork is a characteristic of healthy, effectively functioning organisations. Now we started to question those assumptions. First, we flushed out what our assumptions actually were. In essence it came down to something like the following.

We had been assuming that the top group in any organisation (be it the board of directors or the local authority management committee

---

*First published in *Management Education and Development*, vol. 15, part 2, 1984.

or whatever the top group is called) should be a team and ought to work as a team. Teamwork at the top is crucial to organisational success, we assumed.

We further assumed that a properly functioning team is one in which:

1 people care for each other;
2 people are open and truthful;
3 there is a high level of trust;
4 decisions are made by consensus;
5 there is strong team commitment;
6 conflict is faced up to and worked through;
7 people really listen to ideas and to feelings;
8 feelings are expressed freely;
9 process issues (task and feelings) are dealt with.

Finally, it had always seemed logical to us, that a teambuilding catalyst could always help any team to function better – and so help any organisation perform better as an organisation. Better functioning would lead the organisation to achieve its purposes more effectively.

The harsh reality we now came up against was at odds with this cosy view of teams, teamwork and teambuilding. In truth the director of education has little need to work in harness with his fellow chief officers in a county council. He or she might need the support of the chief executive and the chair of the elected members' education committee, but the other chief officers in that local authority have neither the expertise nor the interest, nor indeed the time, to contribute to what is essentially very specialised work.

Even in industry, whilst it is clear that the marketing and production directors of a company must work closely together to ensure that the production schedule is synchronised with sales forecasts and the finance director needs to be involved – to look at the cash flow implications of varying stock levels – they do not need to involve the *whole* team. And they certainly do not need to develop high levels of trust and openness to work through those kinds of business issues.

On the other hand, most people would agree that *strategic* decisions, concerned with the future direction of the whole enterprise, should involve all those at the top. Strategy should demand an input from every member of the top group, and for strategic discussion and strategic decision making, teamwork at the top is essential. But how much time do most top management groups actually spend discussing strategy? Our experiences, in a wide variety of organisations, suggest that 10 per cent is a high figure for most organisations — often 5 per cent would be nearer the mark. This means that 90-95 per cent of decisions in organisations are essentially operational; that is decisions made within departments based usually on a fair amount of information and expertise. In those conditions, high levels of trust and openness may be nice, but are not necessary; consensus is strictly not an issue and in any case would take up far too much time. There is therefore no need for high levels of interpersonal skills.

Why then, is so much time and money invested in teambuilding, we asked ourselves. At this stage in our discussions we began to face a rather disturbing possibility. Perhaps the spread of teambuilding has more to do with teambuilders and *their* needs and values rather than a careful analysis of what is appropriate and necessary for the organisation. To test out this alarming hypothesis we each wrote down an honest and frank list of reasons why we ourselves engaged in teambuilding. We recommend this as an enlightening activity for other teambuilders — perhaps, like us, they will arrive at this kind of conclusion: teambuilders work as catalysts to help management groups function better as open teams for a variety of reasons, including the following:

1 They like it — enjoy the risks.
2 Because they are good at it.
3 It's flattering to be asked.
4 They receive rewarding personal feedback.
5 Professional kudos — not many people do teambuilding with top teams.
6 There's money in it.
7 It accords with their values: for instance democracy is preferred to autocracy.
8 They gain power. Process interventions are powerful in business settings where the client is on home ground and can bamboozle the consultant in business discussions.

All those reasons are concerned with the needs, skills and values of the *teambuilder* rather than the management group being 'helped'.

This could explain why many teambuilding exercises leave the so-called 'management team' excited and stimulated by the experience, only to find they are spending an unnecessary amount of time together discussing other people's departmental issues. Later on, because they cannot see the benefit of working together on such issues, they abandon 'teamwork' altogether. Such a management group has been accidentally led to disillusionment with the whole idea of teamwork and the value of teambuilding.

We began to see, as our discussions went on through the small hours, that there is a very *large* proportion of most managers' work where teamwork is not needed (and to attempt to inculcate teamwork is dysfunctional). There is, at the same time a very *small* proportion of their work where teamwork is absolutely vital (and to ignore teamworking skills is to invite disaster).This latter work, which demands a team approach, is typified by strategic work but not limited to strategic work. It is any work characterised by a high level of choice and by the condition of maximum uncertainty.

Most people find choice and uncertainty uncomfortable. Many senior managers attempt to deny the choice element by the employment of complex models and techniques. We do not think most people's management experience teaches them to make choices about the future for instance; it puts the main emphasis on establishing as many facts as possible and reviewing options in the light of past experience. That's why models like, for example, the Boston portfolio model and the General Electric matrix are so popular. They provide comforting analytic frameworks for looking at strategic options, but they are appealing really to our operational mentality. The hope often is that they will magic up a solution to the strategic question. But of course they cannot make choices for people and they do not throw any light on the future.

The top team of an organisation, if it is to achieve quality and commitment in its decisions about future directions, will need to pool the full extent of each individual's wisdom and experience. That means something quite different from reacting to a problem in terms of their own functional knowledge and experience. It means *exposing fully* their uncertainties, taking unaccustomed risks by airing their own subjective view of the world and struggling to build some common perceptions and possibilities. This is where that much abused word 'sharing' really comes into its own. In this context it is not merely a value-laden exhortation, it is vital to the future of the organisation. Ideas and opinions are all we have to inform our view of the future, but if we are to take a risk with a fragile idea or opinion, unsubstantiated by facts, we will only take it if the climate is right. Conversely, if we take the risk and the sheer airiness and vulnerability of the idea attracts forth a volley of ridicule and abuse, then it will die on the instant, lost forever, snuffed out like Tinkerbell.

Most functional executives, brought up in the hurly-burly of politics and inter-functional warfare, find the transition from functional to strategic mode very difficult to make. They do not always see the difference, and if they do, they are reluctant to leave their mountain top, the summit of knowledge, experience and hence power, for the equality and shared uncertainty of strategic decision making. And yet this is one area where real teamwork is not only necessary but vital.

We had now got ourselves thoroughly confused. We seemed to be forcing teambuilding on groups which had no need to be a team and missing the one area where teamwork is essential − because choice and uncertainty are at a maximum and for this very reason managers were shying away from the work − work which can *only* be done by a team. We resorted to diagrams to help clear our minds and these new diagrams form the basis of the next section of this chapter.

THEORETICAL CONSIDERATIONS CONCERNING MANAGEMENT GROUPS

We found these kinds of discussions taking us farther and farther away from teambuilding and closer and closer to an understanding of why management groups work, or do not work, in the ways they do. In the end, we developed two basic diagrams, showing the relationships between a number of variables which operate in management groups:

1 the degree of uncertainty in the management task;
2 the need for sharing in the group;
3 modes of working;
4 different kinds of internal group process;
5 different levels of interpersonal skills;
6 the role of the leader.

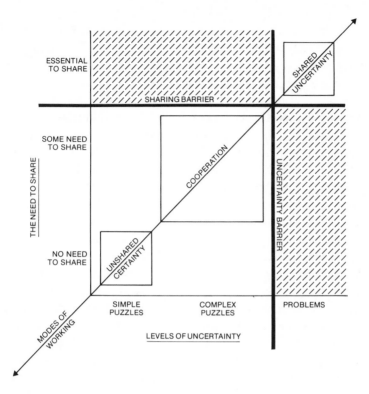

Figure 23.1 The more uncertainty in its task the more any group has to share

We would now like to present these two framework diagrams as diagnostic tools, which a dozen or so management groups have found very useful in coming to terms with how they work and why. These simple diagrams are helping groups see what kind of groups they are and when and if they want to be a team, rather than jumping to the conclusion that all groups need teambuilding.

Throughout the discussion, we will be talking about the management group − that is the leader plus those immediately responsible to him or her, perhaps five to ten people in all, at the top of their organisation or their part of the organisation.

The first diagram (Figure 23.1) shows the relationship between the level of uncertainty inherent in any group task and the need for members of that group to share with each other. Expressed simply −

'The more uncertainty – the more need to share'. Everyday examples of this truism are: children holding hands for comfort in the dark or NASA research scientists brainstorming for fresh ideas on the frontiers of man's knowledge – any uncertainty, emotional, physical or intellectual, can best be coped with by sharing.

However, the converse is also true – where there is less uncertainty, there is less need to share. The same children will feel no need to hold hands round the breakfast table where all is secure; the NASA scientists during the final launch will each get on with their own well-rehearsed part of the launch programme in relative isolation from each other. Only if something goes wrong (uncertainty floods back) will they need to share, quickly and fully. It took us a long time to realise the full significance of that in terms of the need to share in a management group.

We are dealing here only with the top group of the organisation where task is the dominant imperative. There are other situations in which other objectives demand sharing, for instance if one is dealing with the whole fabric of a complete organisation and attempting a global shift in attitudes, then culture-building may become the dominant imperative and sharing at all levels in that organisation may become necessary. But that is a different situation – we are focusing here on the top management group where task must be the dominant imperative.

In Figure 23.1 we have used Revans' powerful distinction between problems (no answer is known to exist) and puzzles (the answer exists somewhere – just find it) to describe different levels of uncertainty. To illustrate the difference between a problem and a puzzle – deciding about capital punishment is a problem for society; tracking down a murderer is a puzzle for the police.

Work groups dealing with genuine problems (of which strategy is only one example) would be well advised to share as much as possible with each other. They should share feelings to gain support, as well as ideas to penetrate the unknown. Figure 23.1 shows two shaded areas. These shaded areas must be avoided. The shaded area on the right indicates the futility of tackling real problems unless people are prepared to share. The shaded area at the top indicates that there is no point in sharing to solve mere puzzles.

Two 'barriers' appear on our model; they indicate that a positive effort must be made if a breakthrough to a new level of working is to be accomplished. For instance the uncertainty barrier represents a step into the unknown − a deliberate attempt to work in areas of ambiguity, uncertainty and ambivalence. To avoid the shaded areas and arrive in the top righthand corner, the group break through *both* barriers at the *same* time. This is the *only* way to solve genuine problems. Most management groups stay behind both barriers in Figure 23.1 and handle work which is in the nature of a puzzle − and to achieve this they co-operate, rather than share with each other. As long as they continue to limit their work to solving puzzles, they are quite right to stay within the sharing and uncertainty barriers of Figure 23.1.

As teambuilders, we now see that we must spend time identifying which modes of working any management group operates. The three modes of working come out in Figure 23.1 as the diagonal and we would like to describe each mode, by working up the diagonal of Figure 23.1 from left to right:

Mode of unshared certainty The proper mode for simple puzzles of a technical nature in everyday work where every member of the group is relatively competent within his/her field and speaks from the authority of his/her specialism. Ideal when the work issues are independent of each other − as they often are. A healthy attitude is 'I will pull my weight and see that my part is done well'. Attitudes can become unhealthy if they move towards 'my interests must come first'.

Mode of co-operation The appropriate mode for complex puzzles which impinge on the work of several members of the management group. In this mode (very common in local authorities) group members recognise the need for give-and-take, co-operation, negotiation and passing of information on a need-to-know basis. The attitude is 'I'll co-operate for the good of the whole and because other members of this group have their rights and problems too'. Sharing is restricted to what is necessary and each group member still works from the security (certainty) of his own professional base, recognising the professional bases of his colleagues.

Mode of shared uncertainty A rare mode. Partly because it is appropriate only for genuine problems (such as strategy) where nobody knows what to do, uncertainty is rife and full sharing between members is the only way out; partly because, even when it is the appropriate mode, many management groups never reach these professional heights. The attitude of members has to be 'the good of the whole outweighs any one member's interests – including mine. I carry an equal responsibility with my colleagues for the whole, and for this particular work I am not able to rely on my specialism, because my functional expertise is, for this problem we all face, irrelevant'.

Clearly this top mode of 'shared uncertainty' is extremely demanding and it is not surprising that many management groups try hard to avoid it. We know several boards of directors and even more local authority management 'teams' who have devised a brilliant trick to avoid handling genuine problems requiring genuine sharing in the top mode. Quite simply – they turn all strategic problems into operational puzzles! How? There are very many variations of this trick available:

Appoint a working party
Ask a consultant to recommend
Recruit a corporate planner
Set up a think-tank,
Etc.

To make sure the trick works, the terms of reference are 'Your recommendation must be short and must ask us to decide between option A or option B'. Choosing between A and B is an operational puzzle they *can* solve and it leaves them with the comfortable illusion that they have actually been engaging in strategic problem resolution work, whereas the truth is they have avoided uncertainty, avoided sharing their fears and ideas, avoided their real work, by converting frightening problems into manageable puzzles. And who can blame them!

We do not feel we have the right to censure top groups for not working in the top mode of shared uncertainty. We do feel we have the obligation to analyse quite rigorously how top groups actually work, before we plunge in with our teambuilding help.

In Figure 23.1 the size of the box for each mode indicates very roughly how frequently each mode might be needed by most management groups. Sadly, we see many management groups working in modes which are inappropriate to the work being done. It is not just that many top groups fail to push through to the top mode; many management groups get stuck in the bottom box quite a lot of the time, when they should be working in the middle mode. On the other hand other groups go through a pantomime of sitting round a table trying to work in the middle mode, but in truth feeling bored and uninterested because the middle mode is inappropriate and each member of the group could carry on separately with his own work, without pretending to share it with his colleagues, who do not need to know anyway. In other words their appropriate mode is unshared certainty and attempts at sharing are boring or frustrating facades.

Our diagram shows an arrow on both ends of the diagonal, to illustrate that all three modes of working are necessary at different times and effective work groups can and should slide up and down the diagonal. We do not see any management group working in one mode all the time − the really effective group is able to move from mode to mode as the *task* requires. Although it may think of itself as a management 'team', a top group will be truly functioning as a team only when it is operating in the top mode.

We use the word team here, in the sense used in the first part of this chapter, which we believe is the sense used by most teambuilders in teambuilding work. Because we now believe that working in the top mode of shared uncertainty is called for infrequently − by the nature of the work − and is actually practised even less frequently, we now doubt the value of teambuilding work with most management groups − when there is so much more urgent work to be done with these groups.

We found in Figure 23.1 that when we plot the level of uncertainty in the work, against the need to share, we discover three modes of working, on the diagonal of Figure 23.1. These three modes of working are:

1   unshared certainty
2   co-operation
3   shared uncertainty

We now want to go on to answer the question 'How does a management group work in each of these modes? What *processes* are needed, what *skills* are required, and how does the *leader* function?'

The format of Figure 23.2 is the same as Figure 23.1, only the variables are different. The vertical axis of Figure 23.2 is the diagonal lifted from Figure 23.1 (modes) and two new variables are introduced

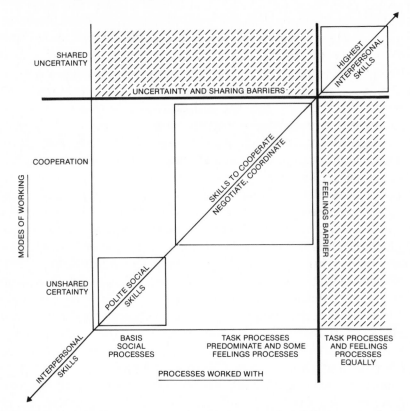

Figure 23.2 Different modes of working require different methods

—*processes* on the horizontal axis and *interpersonal skills* become the new diagonal.

Processes

To start with the horizontal axis — processes. We distinguish three levels of process in any group. At the most perfunctory there are *polite social processes*, very important to sustain the social lubrication of a healthy group but not focused on the work itself. The work is accomplished largely via *task processes* — the way work is organised, distributed, ideas generated and shared, decisions made and so forth. The third level of process concerns people's feelings (*feelings processes*) and how these are handled by themselves and by others.

Reference to Figure 23.2 will make it clear that as the mode of working becomes more difficult, ascending the vertical axis, from unshared certainty towards shared uncertainty, so the processes needed to accomplish this more difficult work, also become more difficult, as the group moves along the horizontal axis from simple basic social processes, through task processes, towards the much more difficult processes of working with people's deeper feelings.

Many groups never reach the top mode of shared uncertainty, where people's feelings are actually *part of the work* and all is uncertainty, excitement and trust.

The shaded areas are to be avoided (as in Figure 23.1). The right-hand shaded area indicates that it is absurd to indulge in work with people's feelings if the group is working only in the two lower modes of unshared certainty and cooperation – to engage in soul-searching to accomplish this kind of work is ridiculous and brings teambuilding into disrepute. The top shaded area indicates similarly that there is no need to share deeply when only the two lower levels of processes (basic social processes and task processes) are operating.

However, a management group faced with the need to tackle uncertainty can either 'funk' the whole thing, by staying safely behind the barriers (which is what most management groups appear to do) or, it can have the courage to break through both barriers simultaneously, arriving (breathlessly) in the top righthand corner where the mode of working is shared uncertainty and the necessary processes are task *and* feelings processes together. Those few management groups which accomplish this – become *teams*.

Interpersonal skills

The final variable is the diagonal of Figure 23.2 'interpersonal skills' and clearly there is an ascending order of skill from the lowest (but *not* least important) level of polite social skills to the highest possible level of interpersonal skills required in the rarified atmosphere of highest uncertainty and real teamwork. But, for the middle mode, a solid raft of straightforward interpersonal skills is needed by all managers – empathy, co-operation, communication, listening, negotiating and many more. We have come to believe that here is the greatest area of need.

The leader's role

The group leader and group leadership have not been mentioned so far, in an attempt to keep things simple. The whole question of leadership is fundamental to the operation of all management groups and we would like to make some observations now.

Leader's role in the mode of unshared certainty

The leader is hardly needed at all in the unshared certainty mode and, indeed, the social lubrication processes of a group working in this mode may well be carried out much better by an informal leader — there is nothing so embarrassing as the formal group leader bravely trying to lead the group through its Christmas lunch in the local pub!

Some local authority chief executives (so called) suffer an even worse fate — they cannot find a role at all, because the members of their management team (so called) steadfastly refuse to move out of the bottom mode of working, tacitly deciding *not* to work together and denying the chief executive any place in the organisation at all! This is not uncommon.

Leader's role in the mode of co-operation

The leader's role in the central (co-operation) mode, is well established in management convention. For example a clear role at meetings has been universally recognised to enable the leader to manage the task processes in particular. This role is of course the chairperson. Co-ordination of the task is at its core and most group leaders find this role relatively clear.

Leader's role in the mode of shared uncertainty

No such role has yet been universally recognised to deal with the processes in the highest mode, of shared uncertainty. In Britain, we have the added difficulty of our cultural resistance to working with feelings (in action learning language 'No sets please, we're British'). In this sophisticated mode of working, the word 'catalyst' seems more appropriate than the word chairperson and often a teambuilder is invited in to carry out this role. But where does this leave the group leader? All management group leaders have learned to be the chairperson, very few have yet learned to be the catalyst. And in any case, to be the catalyst and the leader at the same time, is to attempt the North face of the Eiger of interpersonal skills. It can be done, but not in carpet slippers. If on the other hand, the role of catalyst is performed by an outsider, the leadership dynamic becomes *immensely* complex and adds a significant overlay of difficulty when working in a mode which we have already shown to be extremely difficult in the first place. No wonder teambuilding often fails.

CONCLUSIONS

Many teambuilders are unaware of the shaded no-go areas and dreamily assume that any progress towards open attitudes, free expression of feelings and genuine sharing in any management group, is beneficial. This is not so – to be of benefit there needs to be a very delicate and deliberate balance between what *work* the group has decided to pursue (what level of *uncertainty*) and the degree of sharing and expression of feelings the group is prepared for, to accomplish that work. Only if the balance is right will the management group be able to aim accurately at the top righthand corner of Figures 23.1 and 2 and succeed in breaking through all the barriers at the same time, to experience real teamwork. Attempts to push through only *one* barrier (trying to handle uncertainty without sharing; sharing for the sake of sharing; being open for the sake of being open) will fail and in failing will probably make things worse for that management group.

Strategic planners are often guilty of pushing management groups towards handling uncertainty *without* the concomitant abilities to share and work with feelings. Teambuilders are often guilty of the converse sin – pushing management groups to be open and share their feelings, when the group has no intention whatever of getting into work where the level of uncertainty is high. Neither will succeed. It is no coincidence that both strategic planning and teambuilding can fall quickly into disrepute; it may be too late to save strategic planning from the management scrapheap – it is not too late to save teambuilding.

24

Choosing resources

Mike Abrahams

This chapter outlines resources available to a Management Development Specialist (MDS) and some methods which the writer has found to be practical in making a choice of suitable development suppliers. It will cover business schools, management colleges, management consultancies, management consultants, public training courses, and training packages.

The comments made in this chapter presume that a careful analysis of needs has been undertaken as described in Andrew Stewart's chapter (Chapter 4). It is inefficient and ineffective to look at resources if you have not established needs.

The decision to use outside resources to address training or development needs is usually taken with care. Serious discussions may have led inexorably to a realisation that the organisation does not have sufficient trained or qualified personnel capable of providing the knowledge and skills required for their management. The care employed in making that decision does not always extend to the choice of resources.

There are a plethora of claims contained in mail shots from individuals and from prestigious business schools; words such as new, unique, tried, tested, etc. are part and parcel of their marketing pitch. It is of little use to initiate discussions with Human Resource Development Suppliers (HRDS) in response to the number of colours used in their brochures or their geographical proximity to the client organisation. Equally, to choose to use a resource simply because the chief executive had some 'good experiences' with it in the past may be politic but it will not be a decision based on up-to-date knowledge.

There is in the human psyche a deep desire to codify, categorise and label behaviour. The work done by psychologists to encapsulate characteristics of behaviour and personality within psychometric tests and the willingness of organisations to buy the latest thinking in order to improve their selection processes are tributes to hope rather than acknowledgements of realities. Similarly if the MDS were to administer psychometric tests to a putative HRDS there is likely to be little correlation between forecast and outcome. Therefore the choice of individuals or institutions as HRDS to an organisation narrows down to the chemistry between the MDS and that supplier. Evidence, provided by the use of written material, references and observation are necessary and the following sections aim to provide guidance on how to obtain evidence and to suggest ways in which that evidence might be used to make choices.

There has been an increase in the availability of HRDS since the 1960s and also an improvement in quality. In the early part of the 1960s many individuals were setting up as consultants and with the advent of Industry Training Boards and levies on organisations for training purposes, growth was encouraged yet further. Inevitably a fall out took place during the downturn of the 1970s and now individual HRDS are more professional and less likely to be displaced marketing men or refugees from correspondence colleges whilst the institutions of management teaching are far more rigorous than in the past. Nevertheless it pays to be choosy and the first step should be to contact organisations who can give advice about HRDS.

The organisations shown below will supply information. Those marked * are not without interest in supplying HRDS themselves but they maintain a professional distance when asked for advice.

The Association of Teachers of Management,
Polytechnic of Central London,
Marylebone Road,
LONDON,
NW1.

*The British Institute of Management,
Management House,
Cottingham Road,
CORBY,
Northants.
NN17 1TT.

*Brunel University,
BIOSS,
UXBRIDGE,
Middx.
UB8 3PH.

*The Institute of Personnel Management,
IPM House,
Camp Road,
Wimbledon,
LONDON,
SW19 4UW.

The following provide data banks of material.

The National Training Index,
7 Princes Street,
LONDON,
W1R 7RB.

Brickers Executive Education Service,
425A Family Farm Road,
Woodside,
California 94026,
USA.

The experience of other management development specialists or management trainers within the public and private sectors cannot be discounted. Networks of MDS exist and their knowledge and skills in choosing HRDS can be useful to an individual in the early stages. It is a worthwhile exercise to make contact and to tap into various professional groupings possibly by joining one run by the Association of Teachers of Management. Initially, there will be a tendency to accept the judgement of others; it must be remembered, however, that one HRDS may be meat to one organisation and poison to another.

BUSINESS SCHOOLS

For a given level of management, business school programmes can look similar. The objectives are almost interchangeable and the core content which accounts for something like 70 per cent of the offering is predictable. Each institution will claim that its faculty and visiting faculty is excellent and indeed the aim of excellence in terms of genuinely wishing to provide a worthwhile educative experience is maintained throughout a wide spectrum of business schools; the problem for a MDS lies in choosing the best programme to fit the prospective participants and the objectives of their organisation. For example, a business school programme with a strong bias towards industrial marketing will not necessarily benefit an individual from a service industry such as insurance. It will be of interest and it may be filed away for future reference, but any application of technique or knowledge may never take place simply because the fields of endeavour are so diverse. The programme will need to show that a member of the faculty has had some experience in marketing services such as banking or preferably, in this instance, insurance.

Another example of a possible mismatch between participant and programme could be where a programme shows a distinct leaning towards the social sciences (behavioural science) with elements of personal exposure implicit in the objectives. Little benefit will accrue to an individual whose expectations are geared towards improving his/her financial knowledge, decision making skills or powers of business analysis. The questions to be asked by a MDS before choosing a business school programme could include the following:

1   What managers do we have that need a development activity?
2   Have we undertaken a proper analysis of their individual needs?
3   Do they require an intensive educational programme or a skills programme?
4   Is the timing this year or next?
5   How does their experience shape the type of programme to be used — are they specialists that need to know more about their specialisation or about another one?
6   Are they managers whose experience has been in a limited number of functional areas and do they therefore need exposure to a range of issues facing the organisation?

HOW TO CHOOSE THE APPROPRIATE BUSINESS SCHOOL

Having determined the specific educational requirement for an individual and decided to use a business school the MDS may find the following series of actions and questions useful. (Note: experience will enable a MDS to eliminate a number of the following points).

Collecting data by post

Brochures outlining courses are the marketing and public relations side of a business school. Their function is to sell and to give outline information; the more prestigious the school the more the emphasis there is on information and on ensuring applications are from suitably high calibre management (the exception to this is Harvard's Advanced Management Program Brochure which is 'patrician' in the information it is willing to divulge, emphasising its implicit importance in the management education field!). Medium order business schools may stress uniqueness and novelty and it is not unusual for some institutions to promote the setting of their colleges or the age of the buildings in order to establish an aura of retreat or solidity.

Objectives

The course objectives will indicate whether the level of managers targeted is correct; for example if objectives outline strategic thinking, macro-economics, international takeovers; and suggest that the course is aimed at middle management then the course is patently misdirected.

The brochure can indicate the inter-relationship between the different levels of courses offered and will therefore give clues on the thinking and house style of the school. Two European Schools are particularly good in this area. IMEDE (International Management Development Institute, Lausanne) and IMI (International Management Institute, Geneva) give clear structures and reasoning for the targeting of their courses at different management levels and make the choice of programme that much easier for a new MDS (see Figures 24.1 and 24.2).

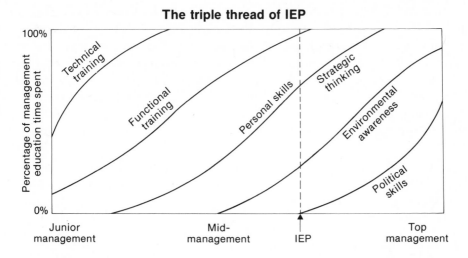

The triple thread of IEP

Figure 24.1

Courses within the Programme	WEEK I	WEEK II	WEEK III	WEEK VI	SESSIONS TAUGHT
BUSINESS LEVEL Management Information & Control	Accounting Measurements for reporting and control Making effective use of information technologies				9
Operations Management	Productivity management Quality-based strategies				6
Marketing	Product market strategies Allocation of marketing resources				9
CORPORATE LEVEL Political Analysis		Political structures and national policies			3
Strategic Management		Competitive strategies in global industries Strategic management of diversification			10
Financial Management		Financial analysis and management Capital budgeting: Financial structure			10
Economics			Economic Policy International Trade		8
Organisational Behaviour	Interpersonal communcication and leadership style			Human resources management	11

Figure 24.2

Figure 24.1 shows the position of a course – the IEP or International Executive Programme run by the International Management Institution in Geneva. It indicates how the IEP fits into other educational programmes and the level of management for whom it is designed.

Figure 24.2 shows an outline programme for the 4 week management course at Insead, in Fontainebleau. It shows course content and emphases. The content shows that the course is for senior executive level.

Faculty

A list of faculty members should form part of the information in the brochure. The list may indicate whether the faculty is full time, part time, visiting etc. and indicate the mix of nationalities. Brief study will also show the alma mater of each member of faculty and therefore whether there is a preponderance of US trained professors and lecturers or if there is a balance between New World trained and the European or Asian educated faculty. A balance is useful particularly if the school is European and the intending participant is to be a European based manager. Many American managers based in Europe bemoan the over-emphasis placed on US trained faculty in European business schools and the over-use of US case study material.

Teaching methods

The teaching methods should also be indicated in the brochure. Some schools use case study only, following the lead given by Harvard. It has been proposed that this method is designed to teach people to analyse business problems and make theoretical decisions whilst divorcing them from reality. It must be said that the method does not suit all managers as the reading work load of sometimes 2-3 cases a day for between 15 and 70 days, depending on the length of the course, is onerous and can be counter productive to learning. Equally some schools use a high number of lectures, say 3-4 per day. This method can be numbing both to mind and rear end! Some schools have accepted that teaching methods need to be varied, and use case study, lectures, simulation, role play and advanced audio visual presentation techniques to make teaching points.

Participants

A list of recent participants will enable the MDS to assess the levels and backgrounds of the managers attending programmes. It would need to be noted if a high proportion of the participants hailed from one sector of endeavour – say merchant banking. If this is obvious and the MDS is employed by a plastic containers producer then the course is likely to be less than fruitful for the production manager. Similarly if the majority of participants came from one geographical area, e.g. Scandinavia or Nigeria, then the benefit of a mixed international flavour would be diluted. The level of management attending programmes can be gauged by the job titles given, but it needs to be remembered that in American companies vice presidents abound and that there appear to be a large number of senior executives in merchant banking who are disarmingly young and inexperienced!

Contacting the MDS in a company shown to have had a manager as a participant on a course, or contacting the manager him/herself in order to discuss the individual's view of the programme, is time well spent.

Publications

It is useful to obtain a list of recent research publications and articles. This will give the MDS an idea of the research strengths of the school and whether some of the published material might be applicable to the MDS's own organisation, thus indicating the possibility of members of faculty having a closer understanding of the MDS's organisational needs.

MBA Programme

If the school has an MBA programme it will be necessary to get information on the curriculum, the number of students, the programme demands, the average age, conditions of entry, breakdown of nationalities etc. These can form the basis of discussion on a subsequent visit to the school.

The information of the type outlined above can be obtained by post. There is no substitute for visiting a school particularly when a programme of the type most interesting to the MDS is in progress.

VISITING A SCHOOL

The following is a series of questions that can be asked of directors, staff faculty and participants and some suggested areas to observe.

Management structure

Where are the decisions made?
What is the level of independence of the faculty versus their awareness and understanding of their client companies' view?
Is there an Advisory Board?
What is its function?
Who are represented?
How is it structured?

Short courses

What is the percentage of standard programmes (i.e. 'off the shelf') to 'in company' programmes?
What changes in the profile of courses has taken place over the past five years?
What is the most supported courses and as a corollary the least supported course?
What are the candidates' entry qualifications for a particular course?
How many applications does a school not accept?
What are the average numbers of people on courses against their targeted number?

The last is an important question. Some schools have in the past accepted too many people for a programme either because they did not wish to disappoint or because they wished to maintain income. Conversely some courses have too few people on them and should have been cancelled.

MBAs

What percentage leave for immediate employment?

What is the percentage of 'funded' students?

How many 'drop out' or are asked to 'drop out' during a programme?

Is there a counsellor for the students?

What is the pass rate?

Is there an alumni school of MBA's? How does it support the school?

General

Which teaching area is particularly strong?

Which research area is particularly strong?

What is the academic turnover rate?

What proportion of an academic's time is given over to consultancy?

Does any of the faculty hold directorial appointments?

Observation points

1   Sit in on a class. Observe and listen to the level of participation; if the class is being conducted in English, do any of the participants have difficulty with the language? (If so, the question to the directing staff can be 'What steps do they take to ensure that a candidate who has English as a second or third language is fluent?' (There are tests available!)

2   Are there any 'course clowns' or 'sleepers'? These will indicate either a disaffection with the subject or the teacher, or it might mean simply that the individual should not be on the programme and that the admission committee were lax.

3   Are the teaching methods appropriate to the subject? To give a lecture with no visual aids or participation on the subject of Capital Evaluation Techniques does not bear thinking about, but it happens.

4   What 'energy level' do the participants display for the subject? Talk to a cross-section of participants and get views on the course and faculty and, where possible, comparisons with other

courses that individuals may have attended earlier on in their career.

5   How many participants turn up late for class? This is often a measure of disaffection with the tutor or the programme.

6   Who does most of the talking in a case study class? If it is the tutor then the class has not done enough work on the case or has not understood it.

7   How often does the programme director appear to have contact with participants? Little is gained if the director introduces the programme, disappears for its duration and then turns up to take brickbats or plaudits at the end.

8   Is there a confusion between working hard and learning well? They are not necessarily one and the same thing.

9   Have the faculty talked to each other before the programme? It can be evident that overlaps have occurred because some tutors have failed to discuss content.

The principal

It is worthwhile meeting the Head of the School and if possible posing the question, 'What in the school's view are the critical problems facing management education and how will the school respond?' Responses can indicate whether the actions being considered are in line with the MDS's own thinking. The principal of a school can have great or little influence on the institution and it is useful to check out their record in innovation and steering by having discussions with experienced MDSs.

Business schools are usually amenable to visits from MDSs. It is significant that for all the number of organisations represented on the 'rolls of honour' as having had participants in programmes, very few MDS's from those organisations visit programmes and talk with the faculty or directing staff. An investment in time and money of up to £20,000 for a senior manager to undertake a business school programme without a specialist visiting and undertaking some of the questioning and observations shown on the checklist will not serve the interest of the nominators or indeed the business schools.

Figure 24.3 shows some results of data sharing among four large UK based organisations in reviewing some UK and European business schools.

Centres	Programme	Duration weeks	Accommodation & meals included	Company A	Company B	Company C	Company D
London Business School	Senior Executive Programme	6	Yes	Not 'international' enough. Probably best school in UK. Company has strong connections. New wing being built mainly with company money. Faculty used in internal programmes	Senior Programme run by Walter Reid is good. LBS is best school in UK Company on Management Advisory Committee	The best school in UK but not international enough. Use some faculty on internal programmes	Hardly ever use LBS. Not international enough.
	London Executive Programme	9	Yes				
				LBS have started to mount more short programmes (3 days-1 week) aimed at specific areas. This is in response to the market place which is showing scepticism about long courses. They are now willing to cut their longer programme.			
				Limited quota of overseas students-therefore courses can be narrow.			
Manchester Business School	Senior Executive Course	3	Yes	Not international. Tudor Rickards used on creativity programmes in Co.	No heavyweights around. Like Senior Course with its built-in visit to Europe	2nd best Business School in UK	Used more than London
	The Management Course		Yes				
Cranfield School of Management	Senior Managers' Programme	5	Yes	Used rarely	Cranfield are pragmatic	Use management Development Programme for Senior Production Managers going generalist	Do not use Cranfield
	Management Development Programme	9	Yes				
International Management Institute (Geneva)	International Executive Programme	4	No	Use it rarely, although many of the faculty are used in 'inco' programmes. When used it compares well with Senior international programmes in the States.	Very heavy usage-like the international aspect. Rate the faculty highly. Tibor Mende-Very good. Gerald Curzon-Very good. Prefer short sharp programmes.	Little used in last 3 years Concentrated more on United States courses for international flavour	Have moved from IMI to Insead recently-there appears to be little reason for this action
	International Advanced Management Programme	8	No				
Insead (Fontainebleau)	Advanced Management Programme	4	Some meals	Some use-faculty used on 'inco' programmes	Heavy usage. Management. Multinational Enterprises. Highly commended	1 person to 4 week programme in last 2 years.	Now beginning to use Insead as main European training centre for some management
	Executive Programme	7	Some Meals				

Figure 24.3

MANAGEMENT COLLEGES

These are mainly a UK/European phenomenon. The US is far more geared to pre-experience education (viz. 60,000 MBAs v 1000 in the UK 1983-84).

Colleges provide short courses on general management, specific discipline and management skills essentially for post experience managers. The work is usually sound but needs to be approached with caution if senior management is being considered for placement. The faculty will usually have had previous management experience or have been management consultants. The approach recommended for business schools, i.e. the questions and observation notes, apply equally to management colleges such as Ashridge or Henley.

CONSULTANTS

'People who borrow your watch to tell you what time it is and then walk off with it' (Robert Townsend, author of *Up the Organization* describing management consultants).

The type of consultants with which this section deals are not those who collate the collective wisdom of the workers in an organisation and feed it to the board in a large report and then walk away after making a number of recommendations that everyone knew they would make. Human resource development consultants do speak to people in an organisation but on the whole they stay to carry out their recommendations themselves.

Consultants can be private individuals who work on their own or occasionally with other consultants; or they can be part of a consultancy group or associates. Sometimes they are people who are encouraged to act as consultants as part of their contract at a business school, management college or in some cases from private commercial organisations.

The decision to employ an external consultant is often made because an organisation's own specialists are fully engaged or they do not have the expertise. A consultant can be an advantage because he or she will be seen as neutral and have no involvement in the internal politics of the organisation. At the same time, the external consultant is likely to have greater credibility and experience to draw upon than many internal consultants. (There may be 'a prophet is not without honour save in his own land' syndrome here!)

Before contracting to employ external consultants it is as well to check out their work either by seeing them in operation if they conduct courses, or by talking with the MDSs of those organisations where a consultant's work has been successful. The consultants will always refer an enquiring MDS to where they had successes; the secret is to tease out where success has not been achieved. No one likes to advertise their failures; but if the consultants are experienced, assured and successful they will not wish to appear omnipotent and will, if questioned, volunteer organisations where in their early days, when 'cutting their teeth', they had a number of experiences they would not wish to repeat. Check out successes and check out failures.

It would be useful if before making a choice the MDS arranged to meet a number of consultants. The MDS should use a similar format for each encounter and check out the responses and reactions of each consultant. The MDS will need to look at his/her own reaction to the consultants; after all, the MDS initially will be working closely with the consultant. A meeting would be useful, if the consultant was likeable and manifested the kind of behaviour patterns and skills that the MDS might wish members of the organisation to model themselves upon.

Another criterion for the MDS to apply is whether the consultant is someone who would be acceptable within the culture of the organisation in terms of their training style. A training consultant who uses psycho drama or bioenergenetics may not be suitable in an organisation whose managers expect training to be conducted in a more cognitive mode. The question is — what methods does the consultant favour and can they be flexible within their repertoire?

It is worth mentioning at this stage that discussions are concerned with contracts with an individual, not a consultancy. Problems often occur if the MDS has built a rapport with a consultant only to find that he or she then sub-contracts to someone who may not be acceptable to the organisation.

The final points that it will be necessary to clarify before contracting a consultant are: What will it cost? What time will the consultant be able to devote to the proposed assignment?

After initial discussion of the problem, the consultant should be asked to send a note setting out what he/she understands to be the

---

Questions to a consultant or consultancies

---

1. What experience have you had with my type of organisation or sector?

2. What experience have you had with the type of contract I have in mind, e.g. training in process or content?

3. What experience have you had working at the level of management we have in mind and with the volume we are expecting?

4. Can you give me evidence of results within other organisations?

5. Who else in the consultancy might be working on the assignment? What evidence is there of competency?

6. Are you willing to make modifications to the work as we proceed?

7. What methods of evaluation can you recommend and will you be involved with them?

8. Can you cope with the expected volume of work?

9. How much will it cost my company-broken down by consultant days and an outline of expenses charged?

Figure 24.4

issue/problem in question and outlining a course of action that he/she would propose to take. (See Figure 24.4 for suggested approaches.) If the consultant has understood the MDS, which should be evident from the clarity of the proposal, and if the outline is acceptable, with only some 'fine tuning' required, then there is a likelihood of a working arrangement being achieved.

PUBLIC COURSES

Various organisations promote public courses. Courses associated with technical expertise, computers, textile technology, engineering etc, where individuals are being technically trained or updated on the 'state of the art' are not the subject of this section. Public courses and training packages abound with 'the elixir effect' which claim to have the ultimate solution to all human resource development problems.

Figure 24.5 shows a course curriculum for one such offering. It is aimed at 'younger professional managers' and at first sight it appears comprehensive. It is. The problem lies in the duration of the course. To cover the subjects outlined properly would probably take 3-4 weeks. The course promoters believed that two days would be sufficient. No limit on the numbers attending was shown on the course brochure and the cost was equivalent to nearly a week at a good business school.

CHOOSING A COURSE

What are the course objectives? What will participants know, and more important do, that they did not know or do before the course? If this area is not clear then the likelihood is that the content will be woolly as well.

What methods are employed? In the course shown in Figure 24.5 the participants were lectured for 11 hours by one person! It might be one way of getting into the Guinness Book of Records but it is hardly training and development; the methods should recognise that learning is not entirely a listening process but a talking, doing, practising activity as well.

The objective, content and methods must be in harmony. The objectives should be limited to achievable and quantifiable behaviourial or learning targets; the content must be adequate to cover the objectives but must not be a huge list of words and phrases designed to flag the erudition of the trainer; the methods must be appropriate to the subject, i.e. behaviour modification is not achieved by lecture, and marketing strategy analysis is unlikely to be learnt using interpersonal process recall.

The quality of the course tutor is critical. There are some very charismatic seminar leaders, particularly in the marketing field where bravura performances are applauded but they are not necessarily good at facilitating learning. On this latter subject the grapevine of MDSs can be consulted as can the National Training Index. The problem is as ever, one person's evaluation of an individual can be widely different from another and there is no agreed datum.

Price is no guide. The more expensive the course means that the

Curriculum

1 KNOWING THE BUSINESS
a Company Goals
  1 The long term plan
  2 The short term plan
  3 Past track record
  4 The business environment
b Company Philosophy
  1 Style of business
  2 Attitudes
  3 Company metier
c Company Operations
  1 Departmental
  2 Product
  3 Project
  4 Staff functions
  5 Special facilities

2 KNOWING YOURSELF
a Self Awareness
  1 Value
  2 Attitudes
  3 Behaviour
  4 Strengths
  5 Weaknesses
b Self Analysis
  1 Personal goals
  2 Business aims
c Improvement Plan
  1 Building on strengths
  2 Clear communications
  3 Use of time

3 KNOWING OTHERS
a People in General
  1 Human needs
  2 Self-respect

5 MONITORING ACHIEVEMENT
a Reviewing Progress
b Measuring Results
c Correcting Shortcomings

6 DEVELOPING EFFICIENCY
a Improving Techniques
b Successful Staffing
c Training

7 COPING WITH CONFLICT
a Conflict Minimisation
b Overcoming Stress
  1 For self
  2 For subordinates

8 MANAGING YOUR UNIT
a Efficient Planning
  1 Realistic milestones
  2 Time & cost targets
  3 Scheduling techniques
  4 Operations analysis
b Effective Control
  1 Ensuring proper feedback
  2 Correct management
  3 Instrumentation
  4 Timing
  5 Action
c Proper Communication
  1 Reporting upwards
  2 Status reports
  3 Cost v. time
d Team Building
  1 Needs of the group
  2 Leader expectations

  2 Permanent or temporary
  3 Establish feasibility
  4 Time requirements
d Taking Action
  1 Co-ordinating staff
  2 Obtaining clearance
  3 New procedures
  4 Training programmes
e Creative Problem Solving Techniques
  1 Brainstorming
  2 Morphological analysis
  3 PABLA and AIDA
  4 Mind maps

12 MANAGING CHANGE
a Putting Ideas To Work
  1 Acting as a catalyst
  2 The task force
  3 Project leadership
b Resolving Conflict
  1 Understanding sources
  2 Setting the problem in perspective
  3 Playing for the benefits
c Role of the Manager
  1 Listener
  2 Clarifier
  3 Empathiser

13 MONEY ASPECTS
a Money & The Business
  1 Profit generation
  2 Cash flow
  3 Capital
  4 Revenue
  5 Management ratios

442

3 Self-esteem
4 Self-realisation
5 Self-confidence
6 Need to belong
7 Motivation
b Your Subordinates
  1 Behaviour patterns
  2 Their backgrounds
  3 Their aspirations
  4 Outside influences
c Your Peers
  1 Roles & Responsibilities
  2 Their capabilities
  3 Chain of command
  4 How not to lose
d Your Boss
  1 Need to understand
  2 Types of boss
  3 How to please
  4 How to influence

4 THE KEY ROLES
a Leadership
b Organisation
c Communications
d Problem Resolution
  1 Co-ordinating action
  2 By example
e Planning
  1 Developing objectives
  2 Organising tasks
  3 Establishing procedures
  4 Setting targets

3 Traits of a winning team
4 Barriers to team development

9 DECISION MAKING
a Types Of Decision
b Characteristics Of Decisions
c Forcing Good Decisions
d Reducing The Risk Element

10 ORGANISING CO-ORDINATION
a Meeting The Business's Needs
  1 Line v. staff
  2 Projects v. functions
b Working Groups
  1 Forming
  2 Storing (sic)
  3 Norming and performing
c Obtaining Co-ordination
  1 Meetings
  2 Teach-ins
  3 Critiques
d Changing The Organisation
  1 Power and influence
  2 Persuasion and motivation

11 PROBLEM SOLVING
a Identifying problems
  1 Classifying the problem
  2 Potential problem analysis
b Basic Procedure
  1 Gathering information
  2 Examining the facts
  3 Developing alternatives
c Solutions
  1 Short or long term

b Cost Estimates & Forecasts
  1 Go/No Go financial decisions
  2 Budgets
  3 Estimate analysis sheets
c Cost Improvement Programmes
  1 Cost control v. cost reduction
  2 Value engineering & analysis approaches
  3 Life cycle costs

14 THE EFFECTIVE MANAGER
a Appropriate Style
  1 Authoritarian
  2 Laissez-faire
a Setting Priorities
  1 Concentrating on the important
  2 Placing work carefully
  3 Minimising hindrances
c Developing Strategies For Success
  1 Improvement plan
  2 Monthly check-up
  3 Keeping it simple

Figure 24.5

course is more expensive. There are courses available mounted by polytechnics, regional management centres and university departments which are professionally tutored, well run and inexpensive. The exception to these is when a very highly qualified management Guru does a tour and knows that she or he can command high fees. Then it is worthwhile considering whether a book by the same person will give better value than an in the flesh sighting.

The final check on a public course is either to send a suitable candidate whose judgement can be trusted or for the MDS to attend the course him/herself. If the candidate or MDS is satisfied that the objectives of the programme are met, that the content is appropriate and that the course leader was able, then the course could prove worthwhile.

TRAINING PACKAGES

Training Packages which contain 'all the trainer needs to conduct effective training at every level' can be attractive to a new MDS. Indeed, they can be a useful adjunct to development activities already in operation or they can form the basis of a whole range of associated activities.

Their ease can be their failing if a MDS does not concern him/herself with the underlying theoretical framework. Recipients of such packages soon see through hollow trainers who mouth the course manual words and are not able to think on their feet, read the group and respond to it.

Some organisations who promote training packages offer to train trainers in their use. What they often do not do is to check whether the packages will be appropriate to the MDS's organisation. They claim that their training package can easily be assimilated within any current training or development activities. This needs careful analysis, for the following reasons:

1 Many packages originate in the US and changing 'sidewalk' to 'pavement' or dubbing a Home Counties voice on a video will not necessarily bridge the culture gap.
2 'Ra, Ra', training may suit the marketing department of a floor polish company but not a firm of accountants.

3   Packages which provide all materials down to flip chart workings and notepaper and which do not allow the buyer to 'personalise' or 'customise' them are inflexible and show that they are not sensitive to the needs of the purchasing organisation.

SUMMARY

The choice of human resource development suppliers is often left to chance – the whim of the chief executive, the proximity of organisation to institution or even shared varied experiences between the MDS and the HRDS. In the final analysis the question to be asked is – Does the development activity provided by the HRDS offer dividends for the organisation which the MDS represents? If the dividends are observable or quantifiable by whatever means deemed appropriate then the supplier will have been effective.

FURTHER READING

Alan Armstrong and Associates, *Management Training Directory*, Block, P., *Flawless Consulting*, University Associates, 1981.

Huczynski, A., *Encyclopedia of Management Development Methods*, Gower, 1983.

Pond, S. A., *Bricker's International Directory*, Bricker Education Service, 1986.

Index